W9-AYX-175

12TH EDITION

THE ULTIMATE KAUAI GUIDEBOOK

KAUAI REVEALED

ANDREW DOUGHTY

DIRECTOR OF PHOTOGRAPHY LEONA BOYD

Revealed
TRAVEL GUIDES

Wai'ale'ale Crater, with its 3,000-foot, waterfall-etched walls, was the spiritual center of the ancient Hawaiian universe. Normally shrouded by clouds, this photo was taken from 10,000 feet after an explosive rainstorm passed on one of only two days a year when the sun is directly overhead, leaving no shadows on the walls.

The Ultimate Kauai Guidebook
Kauai Revealed 12th Edition

Published by Wizard Publications, Inc.
Post Office Box 991
Lihu'e, Hawai'i 96766–0991

ISBN: 978-1-949678-08-6   1071
Library of Congress Control Number 2021934644
Printed in China

> **Cataloging-in-Publication Data**
>
> Doughty, Andrew
>   The Ultimate Kauai guidebook : Kauai revealed / Andrew Doughty - 12th ed.
> Lihue, HI : Wizard Publications, Inc., 2022
>   p. 272: col. illus., col. photos, col. maps ; 21 cm.
>   Includes index.
>   Summary: A complete traveler's reference to the Hawaiian island of Kauai, with
> full-color illustrations, maps, directions and candid advice by an author who resides in
> Hawaii.
>   ISBN 978-1-949678-08-6
>   LCCN 2021934644
>   1. Kaua'i (Hawaii) - Guidebooks. 2. Kaua'i (Hawaii) – Description and travel.
>   I. Title.
>
> DU 628.K3   919.69'41__dc22

Cover space imagery courtesy of Earthstar Geographics (earth-imagery.com).
Cartography by Andrew Doughty.
All artwork and illustrations by Andrew Doughty.

We welcome any comments, questions, criticisms or contributions you may have, and we have incorporated some of your suggestions into this edition. Please send to the address above or email us at **aloha@revealedtravelguides.com**.

Check out our website at **revealedtravelguides.com** for up-to-the-minute changes. Find us on **Facebook, Instagram, YouTube** and **Twitter**.

Dedicated to Sammie Dollar,
who soars on the wind with the white-tailed tropicbirds.

CONTENTS

BEACHES
98

ADVENTURES
199

ACTIVITIES
126

ISLAND DINING
220

ABOUT THE AUTHOR
265

INDEX
266

In a sense, this is not a guidebook; it's more of a love story. Having first seen the island as a tourist, I was immediately smitten. I had no idea that a place like this could exist anywhere in the world. Now as a resident, I marvel at its beauty every day.

Kaua'i is a unique place. People who visit here recognize this immediately. There are plenty of places in the world featuring sun and sea, but no other place offers the incomparable beauty, lushness and serenity of Kaua'i. Living here, we get to see first-time visitors driving around with their jaws open, shaking their heads in disbelief at what they see. Without a doubt, you will never see more smiles than during your visit to Kaua'i.

Our job is unusual, to say the least. We hike the trails, ride the boats, eat in the restaurants, explore the reefs and do the things we write about. It takes us two years, full time, to do a first edition book, and we visit places *anonymously*. We marvel at writers who can do it all in a couple of weeks staying in a hotel. Wow, they must be *really* fast. Our method, though it takes much longer, gives us the ability to tell it like it is in a way no one else can. We put in many long hours, and doing all these activities is a burdensome grind. But we do it all for you—only for you. (Feel free to gag at this point.)

We produce brand new editions of our books every year or two, but in the intervening time we constantly incorporate changes into the text nearly every time we do a new printing. We also post these changes on our website. This allows us to make some modifications throughout the life of each edition.

In this day of easy-to-access online reviews from countless sources, you can get "ratings" for nearly every company out there. What you get from our reviews is a single source, *beholden to none*, with a comprehensive exposure to all of the companies. There are two critical shortcomings to online reviews. One is that you don't know the source or agenda of the reviewer. Nearly every company that offers a service to the public *thinks* they are doing a good job. (But as you know, not everyone does.) So who can blame a company for trying to rig the system by seeding good reviews of their company at every opportunity or having friends write good reviews? Many also encourage *satisfied* customers to write favorable online reviews (obviously not encouraging *unhappy* customers to do so). But maybe their enemies or competitors retaliate with bad reviews. The point is, you never *really* *know* where those reviews come from, and it's almost impossible to reconcile terrible reviews right next to glowing ones for the same company. Which do you believe?

The other problem is a lack of a frame of reference. A visitor to Hawai'i goes on a snorkel boat and has a great time. (Hey, he snorkeled in Hawai'i, swam with a turtle—*cool!*) When he goes back home, he posts good reviews all around. That's great. But the problem is, he only went on *one* snorkel boat. We do 'em all. If only he realized that another company *he didn't even know about* did a much better job, had way better food, and a much nicer boat for the same price.

We are also blessed with hundreds of thousands of readers—from our books as well as our smartphone apps—who alert us to issues with companies and places. Every single message from our readers is received, placed in a special database that we constantly have available while we're out and about, and we personally follow up on every observation made by our readers. So when we walk into a business or restaurant, we check to see what our readers say and tips they send us, and we use them to our advantage. (Thanks for the head's up about that incredible coconut cake at so-and-so restaurant—I know what *I'll* be ordering for dessert today.) With such a resource, and after decades reviewing companies in Hawai'i full time, there ain't much that's gonna get past us.

A quick look at this book will reveal features never before used in other guidebooks. Let's start with the maps. They are more detailed than any other maps you'll find, and yet they omit extraneous information that can sometimes make map reading a chore. We know that people in unfamiliar territory sometimes have a hard time determining where they are on a map, so we include landmarks. Most notable among these are mile markers. At every mile on main roads, the government has erected numbered markers to tell you where you are. Where needed, we've drawn legal public beach access in yellow, so you'll *know* when you're legally entitled to cross someone's land. Most guidebooks have the infuriating habit of mentioning a particular place or sight but then fail to mention how to get there! You won't find that in our book. We tell you exactly how to find the hidden gems and use our own special maps to guide you.

As you read this book, you will also notice that we are very candid in assessing businesses. Unlike some other guidebooks that send out questionnaires asking a business if they are any good (gee, they *all* say they're good), we've had personal contact with the businesses listed in this book. One of the dirty little secrets about guidebook writers is that they sometimes make cozy little deals for good reviews. Well, you won't find that here. We accept no payment for our reviews, we make no deals with businesses for saying nice things, and there are no advertisements in our book. What we've seen and experienced is what you get. If we gush over a certain company, it comes from personal experience. If we rail against a business, it is for the same reason. All businesses mentioned in this book are here by *our* choosing. None has had any input into what we say, and we have not received *a single cent* from any of them for their inclusion. (In fact, there are some who would probably pay to be left out, given our comments.) We always review businesses as anonymous visitors and only later as guidebook writers if we need more information. This ensures that we are treated the same as you. (Amazingly, most travel writers *announce* themselves.) What you get is our opinion on how a business operates. Nothing more, nothing less.

Sometimes our candor gets us into trouble. More than once we've had our books pulled from shelves because our comments hit a little too close to home. That's ok, because we don't work for the people who *sell* the book; we work for the people who *read* the book. It's also true that a handful of local residents have become upset because we've told readers about places that they'd rather keep for themselves. Ironically, it's usually not people born and raised here who have this selfish attitude, but rather the newcomers who have read about these places *in our book* (of all things), then adopted the *I'm here now—close the door mentality.*

This book is intended to bring you independence in exploring Kaua'i. We don't want to waste any of your precious time by giving you bad advice or bad directions. We want you to experience the best that the island has to offer. Our objective in writing this book is to give you the tools and information necessary to have the greatest Hawaiian experience possible.

We hope we succeed.

Andrew Doughty
Kapa'a, Hawai'i

The walls of Wai'ale'ale Crater, from which the island of Kaua'i burst forth in a fiery cataclysm, are now home to innumerable waterfalls. This part of the crater is called the Weeping Wall.

As with people, volcanic islands have a life cycle. They emerge from their sea floor womb to be greeted by the warmth of the sun. They grow and mature and eventually die before sinking forever beneath the sea.

HOW IT BEGAN

The Hawaiian Islands were born of fire thousands of feet below the surface in the icy cold waters on the Pacific Ocean floor. A rupture in the earth's crust caused a vent to spew hot magma that built upon itself as it reached upward. When it began, no one knows exactly, but the first of the still-existing islands to boil to the surface was Kure. Nothing remains of that island today but its fringing coral reef, called an atoll.

As the Pacific plate shifted over the opening of the vent like steel over a cutting torch, more islands were created. Midway, French Frigate Shoal, Necker, Nihoa—all of these once-great islands were born and then mostly consumed by the angry ocean. What we call Hawai'i is just the last in a series of islands created by this vent. Someday these, too, will be nothing more than atolls, footnotes in the geologic history of the earth. But this vent isn't finished yet. The Big Island of Hawai'i is still expanding as lava from its active volcano continues even now to create additional real estate on that island. As we sit here, the future island of Loʻihi is being created 20 miles southeast of the Big Island. Although still 3,100 feet below the surface of the ocean, in but a geologic moment, the Hawaiian volcano goddess Pele will add yet another piece of paradise to her impressive domain.

These virgin islands were barren at birth. The first life forms to appreciate these new islands of volcanic rock were marine creatures. Fish, mammals and microscopic animals discovered this new underwater haven and made homes for themselves. Coral polyps attached themselves to the lava rock, and succeeding generations built upon these, creating what would become a coral reef.

Meanwhile, on land, seeds carried by the winds were struggling to colonize the rocky land, eking out a living and breaking down the lava rock. Storms brought the occasional bird, hopelessly blown off course. The lucky ones found the islands. The even luckier ones arrived with mates or had fertilized eggs when they got here. Other animals, stranded on a piece of floating debris, washed ashore against all odds and went on to colonize the islands. These introductions of new species were rare events. It took an extraordinary set of circumstances for a new species to actually make it to the islands. Single specimens were destined to live out their lives in lonely solitude. On average, a new species was successfully deposited here only once every 20,000 years.

As the plants and animals lived out their lives, they broke up the rock, forming soil and organic debris. The ocean, meanwhile, was busily working to reclaim the horizon from these interruptions of land. Waves battered unmercifully against the fragile lava rock. In this battle between titans, there can be but one winner. While the creation of land eventually ceases on an individual island, the ocean never gives up. Wave after wave eventually takes its toll.

In addition to the ocean, rain carves up the islands. As the islands thrust themselves upward into the moisture-laden trade winds, their challenge to the rain clouds is accepted. As the air encounters the slopes of these tall islands, it rises and cools, causing the air to release its humidity in the form of rain. This rain forms channels that easily carve valleys in the soft lava rock.

Each successive wave is like a sculptor's hand, slowly shaping the island. Large storms can generate powerful waves, such as this one, which, over the eons, patiently return the island to the sea.

Ancient Hawaiian petroglyphs, such as this one near the banks of the Wailua River, can still be found tucked away in the jungle.

So what is the result of all this destruction? Paradise. Absolute paradise. There are few things more beautiful than Mother Nature reclaiming that which she gave birth to. The older the island, the more beautiful the landscape. A Hawaiian island is never more lovely than in its middle age, when the scars of constant environmental battles are carved into its face. Lush landscaped valleys, razorback ridges, long, sandy beaches—those things we cherish so much are the result of this destructive battle.

Kaua'i consists of 553 square miles of beach, rainforest, desert, mountains and plains. The island's landscape is as varied as its people. At Wai'ale'ale in the island's center, it rains nearly every day, making it one of the wettest places on earth. Just a few miles to the west, rain is rare, creating dry, almost arid conditions. The north shore is as lush as any place on the planet. The south shore is a sunny playground. The island's first inhabitants surely must have felt blessed at the discovery of this diversity.

THE FIRST SETTLERS

Sometime around the fourth or fifth century AD, a large, double-hulled voyaging canoe, held together with flexible sennit lashings and propelled by sails made of woven pandanus, slid onto the sand on the Big Island of Hawai'i. These first intrepid adventurers encountered an island chain of unimaginable beauty.

They had left their home in the Marquesas Islands, 2,500 miles away, for reasons we will never know. Though some say it was because of war, overpopulation or drought, it was more likely part of a purposeful exploration from a culture that had mastered the art of making their way through the featureless seas using celestial navigation and reading subtle signs in the ocean. Their navigational abilities far exceeded all of the other "advanced" societies of the time. Whatever their reasons, these initial settlers took a big chance and surely must have been highly motivated. They could not have known that there were islands in these waters since Hawai'i is the most isolated island chain in the world.

Those who did arrive brought with them food staples from home: taro, breadfruit, pigs, dogs and several types of fowl. This was a pivotal decision. These first settlers found a land that contained almost no edible plants. With no land mammals other than the Hawaiian bat, the first settlers subsisted on fish until their crops could mature. From then on, they lived largely on fish and taro. Although we associate throw-net fishing with Hawai'i, this practice was introduced by Japanese immigrants much later. The ancient Hawaiians used fishhooks and spears for the most part or drove fish into a net already placed into the water. They also had domesticated animals that were used as ritual foods or reserved for chiefs.

As the culture evolved and flourished, it developed into a hierarchical system of order. The society was governed by chiefs, called *ali'i*, who established a long list of taboos called *kapu*. These kapu were designed to keep order, and the penalty for breaking one was usually death by strangulation, club or fire. If the violation was serious enough, the guilty party's family might also be killed. It was kapu, for instance, for your shadow to fall across the shadow of the ali'i. It was kapu to interrupt the chief if he was speaking. It was kapu to prepare men's food in the same container used for women's food. It was kapu for women to eat pork or bananas. It was kapu for men and women to eat together. It was kapu not to observe the days designated to the gods. Certain areas were kapu for fishing if they became depleted. This allowed the area to replenish itself.

While harsh by our standards today, this system kept order. Most ali'i were sensitive to the disturbance their presence caused and often ventured outside only at night, or a scout was sent ahead to warn people that an ali'i was on his way. All commoners were required to pay taxes to the ali'i in the form of food, labor and in other ways.

Who Were the Menehune?

Although the legend of Menehune exists throughout the Hawaiian Islands, the folklore is strongest on Kaua'i. Hawaiian legend speaks of a mythical race of people living in the islands before the Polynesians. Called the Menehune, these people were always thought of as being small in stature. The legend initially referred to their social stature, but it evolved to mean that they were physically short and lived in the jungle away from the Hawaiians. (The ancient Hawaiians avoided living in the jungle, fearing that it held evil spirits, and instead settled on the coastal plains.) The Menehune were purported to build fabulous structures, always in one night. Their numbers were said to be vast, as many as 500,000. Today, archeologists speculate that a second wave of colonists, probably from Tahiti, may have subdued these initial inhabitants, forcing them to live in the woods. It is interesting to note that in a census taken of Kaua'i around 1800, 65 people from the upper region of the Wainiha Valley identified themselves as Menehune.

Today, Menehune are jokingly blamed for anything that goes wrong. If you lost your wallet, Menehune took it. If your car won't start, Menehune have been tinkering with it. Kaua'i residents greatly cherish their legends of the Menehune.

OUTSIDE WORLD DISCOVERS HAWAI'I

In January 1778 an event occurred that would forever change Hawai'i. Captain James Cook, who usually had a genius for predicting where to find islands, stumbled upon Hawai'i. He had not expected islands to be there. He was on his way to Alaska to search for the Northwest Passage linking the Atlantic and Pacific oceans.

As Cook approached the shores of Waimea, Kaua'i, on January 19, 1778, the island's inhabitants thought they were being visited by gods. Rushing aboard to greet their visitors, the Kauaians were fascinated by what they saw: pointy-headed beings (the British wore tricornered hats) breathing fire (smoking pipes) and possessing a death-dealing instrument identified as a water squirter (guns). The amount of iron on the ship was incredible. (Hawaiians had only seen iron in the form of nails on driftwood but never knew the source.) Cook left Kaua'i and briefly explored Ni'ihau before heading north for his mission on February 2, 1778.

When Cook returned to the Big Island of Hawai'i after failing to find the Northwest Passage, he was killed in a petty skirmish over a stolen rowboat. The Hawaiians were horrified that they had killed a man they had earlier presumed to be a god.

KAMEHAMEHA THE GREAT

Just after this, Kamehameha the Great of the Big Island began consolidating his power by conquering the other islands in the chain. Kaua'i, however, presented a unique problem. Cut off from the rest of the chain by the treacherous Kaua'i Channel, Kaua'i's King Kaumuali'i had no intention of submitting himself to Kamehameha. In the spring of 1796 Kamehameha tried to invade Kaua'i. He and his fleet of 1,200 canoes carrying 10,000 soldiers left O'ahu at midnight hoping to

Ancient Hawaiians lived off the sea. With reefs teeming with life, island waters have always been generous to the people of Hawai'i.

The earliest Hawaiians built elaborate terraces to grow taro, used to make poi. This terrace, in Limahuli Garden, is estimated to be 700 years old.

reach Wailua, Kaua'i, by daybreak. They were in the middle of the Kaua'i Channel when the wind and seas picked up. Many of the canoes were swamped. Reluctantly, Kamehameha ordered a retreat, but too late to stop some of his advance troops who were slaughtered after they arrived at the south shore beach of Maha'ulepu.

In 1804 Kamehameha tried again. He gathered 7,000 men, all heavily armed, and prepared to set sail for Kaua'i. Just before they were to leave, typhoid struck, decimating his troops and advisers. Kamehameha himself contracted the disease but managed to pull through. Kaua'i's king must have seen the writing on the wall and agreed to give his kingdom of Kaua'i over to Kamehameha. When Kamehameha died, his son, in order to solidify his power on Kaua'i, arranged to kidnap Kaua'i's King Kaumuali'i and forced him to marry his stepmother, the powerful widow of Kamehameha. Kaua'i's last king would never return and was eventually buried on Maui.

MODERN HAWAI'I

During the 19th century, Hawai'i's character changed dramatically. Businessmen from all over the world came here to exploit Hawai'i's sandalwood, whales, land and people. Hawai'i's leaders, for their part, actively participated in these ventures and took a piece of the action for themselves. Workers were brought in from many parts of the world, changing the racial makeup of the islands. Government corruption became the order of the day, and everyone seemed to be profiting except the Hawaiian commoner. By the time Queen Lili'uokalani lost her throne to a group of American businessmen in 1893, Hawai'i had become directionless. It barely resembled the Hawai'i Captain Cook had encountered in the previous century. The kapu system had been abolished by the Hawaiians shortly after the death of Kamehameha the Great. The *Great Mahele*, begun in 1848, had changed the relationship Hawaiians had with the land. Large tracts of land were sold by the Hawaiian gov-

INTRODUCTION

What's it Like in the Wettest Spot on Earth?

The center of the island is called Mount Wai'ale'ale, meaning "rippling waters." It is here that you will find one of the rainiest spots on the planet with an average of 432 inches. Rain around the rest of the island is a fraction of this (see chart on page 27). The ancient Hawaiians recognized the importance of this spot and built a temple on the summit, its remains visible to this day. Unless you're up for an extremely adventurous hike (see page 209), the only way you will get to see Wai'ale'ale up close and personal is by air.

The top of Mount Wai'ale'ale is somewhat barren. While this might sound strange given its moniker as the wettest spot on Earth, remember that few plants in this world are genetically programmed to deal with that much rain at that altitude. Plus the ever-present rain clouds prevent sunshine from enriching the plants. The bogs on top of the mountain make for a less-than-well-defined soil base, and fungi and lichen flourish in the constant moisture. The result is few trees. Those trees that do survive are stunted by nature's over-generous gift of water.

The summit of Wai'ale'ale feeds the Wailua River 3,000 feet below the sheer cliffs.

Just below the summit—3,000 feet straight down, to be precise—exists the unimaginable lushness one would expect from abundant rain. As the clouds are forced up the walls of Wai'ale'ale Crater, they shed a portion of their moisture. With the majority of the rain falling on the summit, the crater floor is left with just the perfect amount. With volcanically rich soil left over from the fiery eruptions, the crater floor has become a haven for anything green. Ferns rule the crater. The ground shakes beneath your feet as your footsteps echo through generations of water-saturated fallen ferns, which have created a soft underbelly on what was once a savage, lava-spewing giant.

There is a surprising lack of insect presence. And most that do live there are endemic, appearing nowhere else on earth. Aside from mosquitoes in the stream beds, we've encountered almost no insects in the dense fern growth of the crater. The only exception was a single flightless grasshopper. We have found some 'o'opu fish inhabiting streams between towering waterfalls. They live in these isolated pools and use their pelvic fins to actually climb the falls.

Everywhere one looks, plants have taken root. Every rock has moss, every fallen tree has other plants growing on it, every crevice has growth. Surely no other place on earth is as lush as Wai'ale'ale Crater.

ernment to royalty, government officials, commoners and foreigners, effectively stripping many Hawaiians of land they had lived on for generations.

The United States recognized the Republic of Hawai'i in 1894 with Sanford Dole as its president. It was later annexed and then became a territory in 1900. During the 19th and 20th centuries, sugar established itself as king. Pineapple was also heavily grown in the islands, and the entire island of Lana'i was purchased for the purpose of growing pineapple. As the 20th century rolled on, Hawaiian sugar and pineapple workers found themselves in a lofty position—they became the highest paid workers for these crops in the world. As land prices rose and competition from other parts of the world increased, sugar and pineapple became less and less profitable. Today, these crops no longer hold the position they once had. In the 1990s the "Pineapple Island" of Lana'i completely shifted away from pineapple and started luring tourists. And where dozens of sugar companies once dotted the islands, the last one, on Maui, shut down for good in 2016. Former sugar workers have moved into other vocations, usually tourist-related or farming.

The story of Hawai'i is not a story of good versus evil. Nearly everyone shares in the blame for what happened to the Hawaiian people and their culture. Nevertheless, today Hawai'i is struggling to redefine its identity. The islands are looking back to the past for guidance. During your stay you will be exposed to a place that is attempting to recapture its cultural roots. There is more interest in Hawaiian culture and language than ever before. Sometimes the process is clumsy, sometimes awkward. There is no common agreement regarding how to do it, but in the end, a reinvigoration of the Hawaiian spirit will no doubt be enjoyed by all.

NI'IHAU

No man is an island, or so they say. But in Hawai'i, one family can own one. The island of Ni'ihau is a dry, somewhat barren island of 46,000 acres located 17 miles to

On Kaua'i, the first settlers found an Eden more beautiful than any place they'd ever known.

The private island of Ni'ihau has mile after mile of beautiful, untouched beaches. Unfortunately, the only way you'll see this scene is to take a pricey tour with Ni'ihau Helicopters.

the west of Kaua'i. When Scottish-born Eliza Sinclair was sailing in the islands with her family in 1863, they were looking for land on which to settle. Having turned down offers of several tracts on O'ahu (including Waikiki, which they dismissed as showing no promise), they were about to leave for California when King Kamehameha V offered to sell them Ni'ihau. When Eliza's sons went to look at it, they found a green, wet island with abundant grass—perfect for raising cattle. What they were unaware of at the time was that Ni'ihau had experienced a *rare* rainy period and was flourishing as a result. The Sinclairs offered $6,000, the king countered with $10,000, and they took it.

This was 1864 and, unfortunately for the Sinclairs, the residents of Ni'ihau did not respect their ownership and resisted them. They had a further setback when an old Hawaiian showed them a deed indicating ownership to a crucial 50-acre sliver of Ni'ihau deeded to the old man by King Kamehameha III. The Sinclairs were in a bind and solicited the aid of

Valdemar Knudsen to negotiate the purchase of the remaining 50 acres. He spoke fluent Hawaiian and was well known and respected by the islanders. Knudsen went to Ni'ihau and offered $1,000 to the old man by slowly stacking the silver coins on a table while he explained how much better off the old man would be if he sold his land and lived in comfort on Kaua'i. After repeated refusals from the man, Knudsen went to take the money away when the old Hawaiian's wife grabbed the money, and the deal was consummated on the spot.

When the Sinclairs discovered that the land was actually dry and barren, unsuitable for a cattle ranch at that time, they arranged to buy 21,000 acres of West Kaua'i. (They would continue to buy land on Kaua'i, eventually acquiring 51,000 acres of the island, which they own to this day.) If you take a helicopter ride, you may see their fabulous estate nestled high in the mountains near Olokele.

Today, about 130 Hawaiians live on Ni'ihau. Most use bicycles for short trips on the unpaved roads, horses for trips more than a few miles and trucks for longer journeys. No telephones, except for a wireless two-way to Kaua'i, no broadcast TV and no internet, by order of the Robinsons—the descendants of Eliza Sinclair. Intermittent power is supplied by generator and solar.

Ni'ihau's one school hosts around 20 students K–12. The sense of family on the island is strong, and only Hawaiian is spoken in most homes. (Classes, however, are taught in English.) Ni'ihau residents are a deeply religious people, and crime against one another is almost unknown. They are intensely proud of their community and feel strongly that their people, their heritage and their way of life are special and are protected by God. They are quick to smile and laugh.

They live in one village called Pu'uwai (located in the only part of Ni'ihau where you can't see Kaua'i) and receive their mail once a week—the Post Office only delivers as far as Makaweli on Kaua'i. They shop for clothes and other durable items on Kaua'i, where most have family.

Time is fluid there. If someone says they'll see you on Wednesday, it could be any time of the day. There's no such thing as being late on Ni'ihau.

With a warehouse for staples and gardens for their fruits and vegetables, Ni'ihau islanders are reasonably self-sufficient. Travel to and from the island is via old military transport boats (like the kind that stormed the beaches of Normandy in WWII), and the rough, bumpy ride takes around three hours each way (during which many get seasick).

Life on Ni'ihau is certainly not without problems. No drugs or alcohol are allowed on the island, and families have been banished forever from the island for growing pakalolo (marijuana). Their mortality rate is high. Virtually everyone receives welfare and/or food stamps. With no permanent streams on the island, water is scarce, so they live off catchment. Although the largest lake in the state is on Ni'ihau, it is usually only a few feet deep, muddy and generally unpleasant.

The Robinson's land is valued at well over a *billion* dollars, but crushing tax burdens and losses (from Kaua'i operations) leave them relatively cash poor. Though the land has been in the family for over a century and a half, every time a land-owning relative dies, the government takes a huge bite out of the family in massive inheritance taxes. They claim that they can only afford to go out to dinner a few times a year. (You can dry your eyes now after that one.) They warmed to the idea of using some of their Kaua'i land for tourism for a few years, then backed away. They almost allowed the federal government to install (for a fee) rocket launchers on Ni'ihau as part of an expansion of the Pacific Missile Range Facility on Kaua'i's west side. The deal fell through when the government insisted on an ethnographic survey, which the secretive Robinsons feared would be used to create precedents that would allow native Hawaiians *from Kaua'i* to visit the island (for constitutionally allowed ritual or gathering purposes). Instead, they now lease much of their Kaua'i land to large, mainland seed growers cultivating genetically modified plants. They are also increasing their cattle operations, built a slaughterhouse here, raising eland (a large, African antelope), distributing venison from Maui and Moloka'i, and bring about 50 sheep a week over from Ni'ihau and market them to restaurants, calling it "forbidden lamb chops."

The Robinsons claim that their unique deed to the island gives them ownership of Ni'ihau's beaches—directly in conflict with state law that proclaims that *all* beaches in Hawai'i are public beaches. To date nobody has challenged them in court. If you land on a beach on Ni'ihau, you will be asked to leave. If you refuse, a truly *gargantuan* Hawaiian gentleman will be summoned, and he will ask you a bit more firmly. This request is usually sufficient to persuade all but the most determined individuals to leave.

Whether it's exotic and imported, such as this night blooming orchid, or native to Hawai'i, flowers abound on the Garden Island.

GETTING HERE

In order to get to the islands, you've got to fly here. While this may sound painfully obvious, many people contemplate cruises to the islands. Here's a tip—there isn't a single speck of land between the west coast and Hawai'i. And 2,500 miles of open water is a pretty monotonous stretch to cover.

When planning your trip, a travel agent can be helpful, though that method is becoming less and less common. The Internet has sites such as Orbitz, Expedia, Cheaptickets, Cheapair, Pandaonline, Priceline, Travelocity, Kayak, etc. If you don't want to or can't go through these sources, there are large wholesalers that can get you airfare, hotel and a rental car, often cheaper than you can get airfare on your own. **Pleasant Holidays** (800-742-9244) provides complete package tours.

Another option is to consult our smartphone app, *Hawaii Revealed,* which has reviews of every resort as well as powerful filters that help you find the place you want to stay with all the features that are important to you. You can get our app from the Apple App or Google Play stores. The *Where to Stay* section is free. Simply select "free preview" when prompted.

The prices listed in the *Where to Stay* section reflect the *rack* rates, meaning the published rates before any discounts. Rates can be significantly lower if you go through a travel company or book online.

When you pick your travel source, shop around—the differences can be dramatic. A diligent effort can make the difference between affording a *one-week* vacation and a *two-week* vacation.

Though most visitors fly into Honolulu before arriving, there are some direct flights to Kaua'i. Not having to cool your heels while changing planes on O'ahu is a *big* plus since interisland flights aren't quite as convenient—or cheap—as they used to be. If you fly to Kaua'i from Honolulu, the best views are usually on the left side (seats with an "A"). When flying to Honolulu from the mainland, sit on the left side coming in, the right going home. Interisland flights are done by **Hawaiian** (800-367-5320) and **Southwest** (800-435-9792). We like Southwest's two free checked bags policy. Flight attendants zip up and down the aisle hurling juice at you for the short, interisland flights.

WHAT TO BRING

This list will be helpful in planning what to bring. Obviously, you won't bring everything on the list, but it might help you think of things you may otherwise overlook:

- Water-resistant, reef-safe sunscreen (SPF 30 or higher, with the ingredients zinc oxide and/or titanium dioxide)
- Two bathing suits
- Shoes—flip-flops, trashable sneakers, water shoes, hiking or trail shoes
- Mask, snorkel and fins
- Camera with lots of memory
- Waterproof case for phone
- Hiking sticks (carbide-tipped ones are good for boulder-hopping hikes)
- Shorts and other cool cotton clothing
- Hat or cap for sun protection
- Mosquito repellent for some hikes (Lotions with at least 10 percent DEET seem to work best

- Light windbreaker jacket (for trip to Kalalau Lookout or helicopter trip)
- Cheap, simple backpack—you don't need to go backpacking to use one; a 10-minute trek to a secluded beach is much easier if you bring a simple pack.
- Long, lightweight pants for hiking if you are going through jungle country.
- Wool socks for walking on hot Polihale sand. (If you've been there before, you *know* what it's like.)

GETTING AROUND
Rental Cars

The rental car prices in Hawai'i have *traditionally* been cheaper than almost anywhere else in the country, and the competition is ferocious. (The pandemic, though, created havoc with rental car fleet sizes that sometimes results in scarcity and huge price spikes.) Nearly every visitor to Kaua'i gets around in a rental car, and for good reason. The island's towns are separated by distances sufficient to discourage walking. Many of Kaua'i's best sights can only be reached if you have independent transportation.

At Lihu'e Airport, rental cars can easily be obtained from the booths across the street from the main terminal. It's usually a good idea to reserve your car in advance since companies can run out of cars during peak times. Don't forget to check **Turo.com** for car sharing.

This seems like a good place to mention that **Uber** and **Lyft** both have a presence on the island, though they *may* be hard to get from time to time.

The Big Guys
Alamo—**(877) 222-9075**
   Locally: (808) 246-0645
Avis—**(800) 321-3712**
   Locally: (808) 245-3512

Budget—**(800) 527-0700**
  Locally: (808) 245-9031
Discount Hawaii Car Rental
  (800) 292-1930
  Locally: (808) 292-1930
Dollar—(800) 800-4000
Hertz—(800) 654-3131
  Locally: (808) 245-3356
National—(877) 222-9058
  Locally: (808) 245-5638
Thrifty—(800) 367-5238

The Little Guys

Island Cars—(808) 246-6000
Kaua'i Rent A Car—(808) 634-8855
Rent A Car Kauai—(808) 822-9272
Rent-A-Wreck Kauai—(808) 245-7177

Rental Car Tips

Island Cars (808-246-6000) upgraded their fleet and have been a good local source for rentals. If you're 21–24 years old, most of the companies will rent to you, but you'll pay about $25 extra *per day* for the crime of being young and reckless. (**Rent-A-Wreck** at 808-245-7177 and **Kaua'i Rent A Car** at 808-634-8855 don't charge extra.) If you're under 21—rent a bike or moped or take the bus. Below are a few tips to keep in mind when you rent your car on Kaua'i.

Many **Collision Damage Waivers** will not cover vehicles on unpaved roads or beaches. Consider this when driving on dirt roads or at Polihale. Also note that some deals aren't as great as they might seem online. Discount car rental companies only allow a collision damage waiver if your personal auto insurance will cover you in Hawai'i and will *call your insurance company* before they let you drive off their lot. Many policies do not offer the kind of coverage they require, and so you are forced to buy their insurance (starting at $16/day).

Car break-ins can be a problem anywhere. They seem to be more frequent in the summer due to school vacations. The places usually hit are those that require you to leave your car in a secluded place for an extended period of time. Contrary to popular belief, locals are targeted nearly as often as tourists. To protect yourself, don't leave anything valuable in the car. (Well…maybe the seats can stay.) At secluded spots that have recently been robbed, savvy locals will often leave their doors unlocked and the windows partially open to prevent having their windows smashed, but doing so *might* negate your rental car insurance. If you park in a secluded spot and notice several piles of glass on the ground, it's evidence that some juvenile has a new hobby. Don't kid yourself into believing that trunks are safe—they are often easier to open than doors. One place thieves rarely look is under the hood. But don't put something there after you arrive at your destination since someone might be watching. We once drove up to the parking area at Secret Beach, and there was a suspicious looking guy there. Mr. Slick acted busy by spending considerable time checking the oil in his car—*but the rusted hulk had no wheels all the way around.* Be alert and you should be OK.

All of this is not meant to convey the impression that car break-ins are rampant. In fact, the opposite is true. You could probably spend your entire life here and never experience one. (We haven't.) But if you lose your brand new $1,000 auto-everything digital SLR camera to some juvenile dipstick because you were one of the few…well, won't *you* feel sick?

4-Wheel Drive

With its many rugged roads, one of the best ways to see Kaua'i is by four-wheel

Hey, I Recognize That Place...

When Hollywood wants to convey the impression of beauty, lushness and the exotic, it's no contest what location they choose. Kaua'i has long been the location of choice for movie directors looking for something special.

As you drive around the island, keep an eye out for the locations of scenes from some of these movies: Jungle Cruise, Hobbs and Shaw, Pirates of the Caribbean 4, The Descendants, Just Go With It, Soul Surfer, first three Jurassic Park movies, Tropic Thunder, Dragonfly, To End All Wars, Six Days/Seven Nights,

Mighty Joe Young, George of the Jungle, Outbreak, North, Honeymoon in Vegas, Hook, Lord of the Flies, Flight of the Intruder, Throw Momma From the Train, The Thorn Birds, Uncommon Valor, Body Heat, Raiders of the Lost Ark, Fantasy Island, King Kong, Acapulco Gold, Islands in the Stream, The Hawaiians, Lost Flight, Hawai'i, Paradise Hawaiian Style, Girls! Girls! Girls!, Donovan's Reef, Blue Hawai'i, South Pacific, Miss Sadie Thompson *and many more. Hollywood discovered Kaua'i years ago.*

Harrison Ford rehearsing at Maha'ulepu for the movie, Six Days/Seven Nights.

We had no idea when we stumbled upon this "resort" in the middle of nowhere during a flight that it was where Dwayne "The Rock" Johnson was filming Disney's Jungle Cruise.

drive. These can be difficult to come by at times. Ask the rental car company if they have disabled the 4WD mechanism. If you use a gold credit card for the automatic insurance, check with the card carrier to see if you are covered when you're on unpaved roads. Another tip is to avoid deep, soft sand. Even 4WD vehicles can get stuck in sand if they have the wrong tires. If you must drive on sand, let much of the air out of the tires to get more sand traction. (We'll leave it up to you how to get the air back in.) If you already *are* stuck in sand, try pulling the carpet from the trunk and driving on it to get out. (Oh, the car companies will love us for *that* one.) Rental car companies are always changing the vehicles to keep them new. At press time, all the *big* companies we list

Relics of a bygone era, the sugar industry is dead on Kaua'i. Whether you love 'em or hate 'em, GMO crop research is the industry that is trying to replace it.

had SUVs or other 4WD vehicles. Expect to pay up to double or triple than a standard car per day for the privilege of cheating the road builders.

Buses

Kaua'i has a bus system called the **Kauai Bus** (clever, eh?). It goes from Kekaha to Hanalei, and fares are $2 or a $5 all day pass. A monthly pass is $65, and most have bike racks, but once full they won't take anymore. There are stops all along the main highway, but they aren't always marked as well as they should be. For a bus schedule or more information, call 808-246-8110.

Less Than 4 Wheels

If you really want to ham it up, try renting a **HOG**. (*Note:* The Supreme Court recently ruled that publishers cannot be held liable for bad puns.) **Kaua'i Harley-Davidson** on the highway in Puhi (808-241-7020) rents HOGs. Good selection.

Rates are $230 for 24-hours for HOGs. Expensive? You bet! But nothing else feels like a genuine Harley. (Except perhaps an Indian Motorcycle—which I prefer—but you can't rent one on Kaua'i.) A cheaper way if you own a bike is **riders-share.com**, a ride share site.

Scooters/mopeds are also available. We've seen some pretty close calls and consider them too unstable to recommend. Be *real* careful on hills, and stay off the highway between Lihu'e and Kapa'a.

Taxis

If you want to tour the island by taxi… you have entirely too much money to burn. For those who need an occasional taxi service, you will find these available: **North Shore Cab** (808-639-7829), **Akiko's** (808-822-7588) on the east shore, or **City Cab** (808-245-3227) on the south shore. Both **Uber** and **Lyft** are also active here, though rates are pretty similar to taxis.

Camper Vans

Want to take your accommodations with you? **Kaua'i Camper Rental** (808-346-0957) rents 1985–1990 Volkswagen Vanagon Westfalia Campers. That's right—see the tropics from a VW bus just like the hippies of yore. In all seriousness, Kaua'i lends itself to being explored by camper van, especially the north and west shores. Having the versatility to just replant yourself at each camping location means getting to see a lot more of the island. Though not exactly cheap ($155–$165/day or $1,050/week), the vans come loaded with everything you'll need (except refrigeration).

Wheelchair Accessible Vans

These are available from **Wheelers of Hawaii** (877-735-6365). Rates are $135 per day if you rent for a week, plus $200 for pickup at airport. Don't forget to bring your placard. Also, if you're looking to rent a wheelchair, **Gammie HomeCare** (808-632-2333) in Lihu'e has beach wheelchairs, but reserve them well in advance.

Get Around Kaua'i

If you'd prefer booking a ride instead of driving, the county has created a fairly useful system that helps connect travelers with more environmentally friendly options that aren't rental vehicles. The website is called **GetAroundKauai.com** and offers information on shuttle services, public transit, taxis and rideshare companies, and it even has a map that shows you Kaua'i bus routes. If you're planning on avoiding cars altogether, there's also a tab that focuses on alternative options, including bike and e-bike rentals, as well as motorcycle and moped rentals. They don't allow you to book directly from their website, but the information is useful and well-organized, so it's a good resource if you're shopping for rental cars and wondering what else is out there.

GETTING MARRIED ON KAUA'I

The beauty of Kaua'i has provided the backdrop for many engagements, weddings and vow renewals. And why not? It's in the air here. People are genuinely happy on Kaua'i, and the aroma of joy can make your life together even sweeter. Whether you choose a natural or manmade waterfall, a sunset on a beach, an elegant chapel, beautiful garden or an ancient Hawaiian temple, Kaua'i can create nuptial memories that will last a lifetime.

Thanks to email and the internet, you can arrange your own wedding, no matter how far away you are. All of the legal requirements, as well as possible wedding locations, are just a click away. Everything—from helicopter flights landing at private waterfalls to just the two of you on a beach at sunset with a minister—is available.

Some of the more popular wedding locations are at the **Royal Sonesta Kaua'i Resort, Koloa Landing Resort, Grand Hyatt, Sheraton** and the **Waimea Plantation Cottages**. Many resorts have wedding coordinators and private wedding sites on property. You might also want to consider renting a private home for you and your guests. Don't let the *rack* rates and wedding package prices scare you off. Nothing's carved in stone.

The number of details in planning a wedding is dizzying, and many couples prefer the assistance of an independent wedding coordinator. They can be tremendously helpful in navigating the complicated waters of your marriage. (Well, the ceremony, at least. After that, you're on your own.) Don't let yourself get herded into activities (for which they get a commission), and be on the lookout for add-ons that can ratchet up the price. Be especially selective of your photographer and videographer. This is a one-time event that can't be duplicated.

Some of the more reputable companies are listed below. Unlike most activities, we can't review each in depth. It's not possible to get married a dozen times and critique the way each coordinator did their job. We have, however, anonymously contacted virtually all of the coordinators on the island (in the guise of planning a wedding) and these stood out:

Ali'i Kaua'i Weddings
(808) 854-1003
Aloha Ever After
(877) 711-3003
Coconut Coast Weddings
(808) 212-7332
Island Weddings & Blessings
(808) 828-1548

Obtaining a Marriage License

Contact the **State Department of Health** (808-586-4545) on Kaua'i (or visit their website) to obtain an application or to get the names of license agents on Kaua'i. Both parties must be at least 18. No residency or blood tests are required. The fee is $60 *in cash*, and the license is good for 30 days. Both parties must be present with photo IDs at the time of the appointment with the marriage license agent.

WEATHER

Kaua'i doesn't have the best weather in the state, but the best weather in the state is on Kaua'i. What do we mean by that? Well, when it's good here, it's as good as weather can get—brilliant sunshine, crystal clear air, and gentle but constant breezes. That's when it's good.

Yeah, but I've heard it always rains on Kaua'i. We heard this many times before we came here for the first time. The reality of Kaua'i is that it gets more rain than the other Hawaiian islands. In fact, one of the rainiest spots on earth is smack dab in the middle of the island. Mount Wai'ale'ale is an undisputed *year-round* rain magnet, receiving around 400 inches per year, which is a staggering 33 *feet* annually. (Though they've measured rainfall there for over a century, stating an average is more of an art than a science since there were times in the past they went up to read that gauge, perhaps after a year, only to find it overflowing—so they guessed. Also, it varies a lot. In 2018 it got 519 inches!)

The mountain is shaped like a funnel pointing directly into the moisture-laden trade winds, which are forced to drop their precious cargo during their march up the slopes. The summit of Wai'ale'ale is other-worldly, with plants stunted and dwarfed by the constant inundation of rain. Moss, fungi and lichen flourish in the swamp just west of the actual peak. Alaka'i Swamp contains flora and fauna found nowhere else in the world. On the opposite side of the mountain, the spent clouds can do no more than drift by, making the west side of the island rather arid. What rain it does get comes from the sporadic Kona winds. (Throughout the islands, Kona winds refer to winds that come from the southwest and are often associated with inclement weather.)

All that said, the odds are overwhelming that rain will *not* ruin your Kaua'i vacation. The coast gets *far* less rain than the waterlogged central interior, and throughout Kaua'i the lion's share of rain falls at night. When it does rain during the day, it is usually quite short-lived, often lasting a matter of a few minutes. One of the things that takes a little getting used to is the fleeting nature of the weather here. In many parts of the country, rain or sunshine are words used *by themselves* to describe the day's weather. On Kaua'i, a warm, passing shower is to be expected and

rarely signifies that a long period of rain is to follow. If you call the local telephone number for the **National Weather Service** (808-245-6001), you will probably hear something like this. "Today—mostly sunny, with a few passing windward and *mauka* (mountain) showers. Tonight—mostly fair with a few passing windward and *mauka* showers. Tomorrow—mostly sunny, with a few passing windward and *mauka* showers." So don't get bummed if it suddenly looks ominous in the sky. It'll probably pass within a few minutes, leaving happy plants in its wake.

If you want to know whether to take the top down on the convertible, look into the wind, and you'll be able to see the weather coming. Dark clouds drop rain— the darker the cloud, the harder the rain. It's as simple as that, and you will often see locals looking windward if they feel a drop on their heads. If you're inland, you will often be able to *hear* the rain approaching. When you hear the sound of a rushing river but there isn't one around,

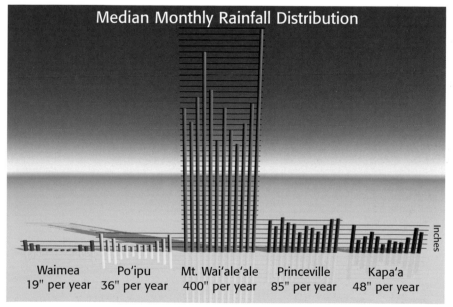

Median Monthly Rainfall Distribution

Inches

Waimea	Po'ipu	Mt. Wai'ale'ale	Princeville	Kapa'a
19" per year	36" per year	400" per year	85" per year	48" per year

take cover until it passes. (Mango trees are ideal for this purpose and have ancillary benefits, as well.)

In planning your daily activities, a good rule of thumb is that if it is going to be a rainy day, the south shore will probably be sunny, and the west shore will almost certainly be sunny. The exception is during Kona winds when weather is the opposite of normal.

Storm systems do discover the state from time to time. Sometimes they're here for days. If one happens to hang around during your trip, don't despair. I first met Kaua'i during one of the wettest times in decades. There was even lightning, which is rare. And it was during that stay that I fell in love with the island and vowed to make it my home. Kaua'i in the rain is still Kaua'i.

As far as hurricanes are concerned, don't waste your time worrying about them. It's true, we had a real 'okole kicker back in 1992. Hurricane 'Iniki was a category 4 storm that stripped the island bare, ironically striking on September 11th of that year. But after this pruning, the island recovered and became greener than ever.

Hurricanes are few and far between here. The only previous hurricanes to hit the island last century were 'Iwa in 1982 and Dot in 1959. When Isabella Bird traveled here in 1873, where she penned her excellent book, *Six Months in the Sandwich Isles,* she reported that "hurricanes are unknown in the islands," which means that there hadn't been one in living memory. (Of course, if one *does* strike during your stay, kindly disregard this last statement.)

As far as **temperatures** are concerned, Kaua'i is incredibly temperate. The average *high* during January is 78 °F, whereas our hottest time, late August/early September, has an average *high* of 85 °F. With humidity percentages usually in the 60s and low 70s, Kaua'i is almost always pleasant. The exception is the extreme west side, which is about 3 degrees hotter. (That might not sound like much, but you sure do notice it.)

Kaua'i's surface **water temperatures** range from a low of 73.4 °F in February to a high of 80 °F in October. Most people find this to be an ideal water temperature range. (Ocean water near a river mouth, such as Lydgate Beach Park,

Thunderstorms are relatively uncommon on Kaua'i. But when we get 'em, they can be dramatic.

can get colder—we've seen the ocean get as low as 70 °F there during unusually cold Februarys.)

To get current weather or ocean information, call the **National Weather Service Weather Forecast** (808-245-6001).

WHERE SHOULD I STAY?

If your decision about when to visit and where to stay takes rainfall amounts into account (look at the graph on page 27), winter is our rainiest season. (But that's also when you will see the waterfalls at their best.) The north shore is a more popular place to stay in the summer, and the south shore is more popular in the winter due to rainfall distribution and surf.

What part of the island you want to stay on will dictate, to a degree, what kind of vacation you have. Although Kaua'i is small enough to do a driving tour in one day, where you stay will dominate certain activities.

The **north shore** is probably the prettiest part of the island and is dominated by one large hotel and lots of condos and vacation rentals. The weather is usually great in the summer and can be quite a bit wetter in the winter. Though the scenery is incomparable, the down side is the remoteness you'll feel when you want to venture to other parts of the island.

The **east shore** is the most geographically convenient. Trips to the north or south shore don't feel as daunting. There are plenty of hotels and condos and the most dining and shopping options. The down side is traffic in Kapa'a (especially heading south on Hwy 56), and the scenery and beaches aren't as good as the north shore.

The **south shore** has better weather year round and some great beaches. Several big hotels and lots of condos dominate. But the backdrop isn't as nice as the north or even east shores, and there aren't as many dining or shopping choices as the east shore. Also, construction of new condos will be ever-present.

Finally there's the **west shore**. It's nearly always sunny, it's the hottest and driest part of the island and has only one resort plus a few vacation rentals to choose from. If you plan to spend all your time hiking in Koke'e and Waimea Canyon, it's convenient. Otherwise, it's isolated and remote.

Detailed Resort & Condo Reviews

Kaua'i has it all, accommodations-wise, and as you consider where you want to stay—hotel or condo, by the beach or with a mountain view—you might find it intimidating to wade through the vast number of choices.

So here's what we did. We have *personally reviewed* every resort on the island. We have *exhaustively* cataloged all the amenities, formed opinions on what different properties have to offer and created comprehensive reviews. Sure, you can go online and look at reviews by people who have been to one or maybe two resorts. But none of those sources knows them all and can compare one to the other.

Because this information is so exhaustive, there isn't enough room in our book to include it all. So we have put all of our reviews in our smartphone app, *Hawaii Revealed*, and made that portion available for free. There you can sort and sift through the resorts in a matter of minutes using our special filters. We also include our own aerial photos, so you'll know if oceanfront really means oceanfront.

For instance, you might say, *I want a hotel on the south shore, on a sandy beach, that's good for families, has an outdoor lanai, a children's pool, room service, children's program, does weddings on site... oh, and takes service*

Hey...what are you looking at?

around most of the coastal areas. Its rainfall is more varied than any place in the world. The northern and eastern parts of the island (called the windward side) receive the majority of the rain, with the southern and western sections (leeward side) considerably drier. (See rain graph on page 27.)

Looking at the inside back cover map, you will notice that a highway stretches *almost* all the way around the island. This means that Ke'e is as far as you can go by car on the north shore, and Polihale or the top of Waimea Canyon Drive is as far as you can go on the west side. An attempt to link the two a few years back ended with almost comic results. (See page 97.)

animals. With the filters in our app, you can cut through all 75 or so resorts and get to exactly what you want by reading our in-depth, brutally honest review. How's that for cutting through the noise?

The maps in our book are unique in that they show the roadside mile markers. These correspond to the little green signs you will see along the main roads of Kaua'i. This will give you a perspective regarding distances beyond the map scales. Another feature of our maps is that north *usually* points up. We have found that many people get confused when they try to use a map where south is pointing to where east should be, etc. The only exceptions we made were a couple trail maps that benefited from using a specific elevated perspective.

GEOGRAPHY

Kaua'i is located in the tropics at 22 degrees latitude, meaning that it receives direct overhead sunlight twice each year three weeks before and after the summer solstice. (No part of the mainland United States ever receives direct overhead sunshine due to its more northern location.) The island is 553 square miles, with 50 of its 113 miles of shoreline composed of sand beaches. Compared to the other Hawaiian Islands, Kaua'i and O'ahu have by far the highest proportion of sand beach shorelines. You might read in brochures about "white sand beaches." Actually, they are *golden* sand beaches, unlike the truly white sand beaches found in other parts of the world. Kaua'i is too old to have any volcanic black sand beaches since the creation of *volcanic* black sand ends when the lava flow stops. (Waimea's black sand beach is from lava flecks chipped from riverbeds and from dirt.)

Kaua'i's interior is mountainous, with deeply eroded valleys and large plains

In getting around, distances are usually measured in time, rather than miles. See inside back cover map for **driving times between towns.**

HAZARDS
The Sun

Excluding our food prices, the hazard that affects by far the most people is the sun. Kaua'i's latitude means we receive sunlight that's more directly overhead than anywhere on the mainland. (The more overhead the sunlight is, the less atmosphere it is filtered through, and it's also more concentrated than it is farther north.)

If you want to enjoy your *entire* vacation, make sure that you wear a strong sunscreen. We recommend a water-resistant, reef-safe sunscreen with *at least* an SPF of 30. Apply 30 minutes before exposure for the most effectiveness. *Physical* sunblocks (those containing zinc oxide or titanium dioxide) are said to be more reef-safe than *chemical* sunblocks, which are more common. **Gels** work best in the ocean, **lotions** are best if you're staying dry, and lotions meant for infants and kids work best on your face and head. (Less painful if it gets in your eyes.) Try to avoid the sun between 11 a.m. and 2 p.m. since the sun's rays are particularly strong during this time. If you are fair-skinned or unaccustomed to the sun and want to lay out, 15–20 minutes per side is all you should consider the first day. You can increase it a bit each day. *Beware of the fact that Kaua'i's ever-constant trade winds will hide the symptoms of a burn until it's too late.* You

may find that trying to get your tan as golden as possible isn't worth it; tropical suntans are notoriously short-lived, whereas you are sure to remember a bad burn far longer.

Water Hazards

The most serious water hazard is the surf. During the winter, many beaches are not swimmable. Eastern and northern beaches are especially dangerous, and the sad fact is that more people drown in Hawai'i each year than anywhere else in the country. This isn't said to keep you from enjoying the ocean, but rather to instill in you a healthy respect for Hawaiian waters. See *Beach Safety* on page 98 for more information on this.

Ocean Critters

Hawaiian marine life, for the most part, is quite friendly. There are, however, a few notable exceptions. Below is a list of those that you should be aware of. This is

Watch where you choose to take a nap.

not mentioned to frighten you out of the water. The odds are overwhelming that you won't have any trouble with any of the beasties listed below. But should you encounter one, this information should be of some help.

Sharks—Kaua'i does have sharks. They are mostly white-tipped reef sharks with an occasional hammerhead or tiger shark. Contrary to what most people think, sharks are in every ocean and don't pose the level of danger people attribute to them. In the past 25 years, there have been so few documented shark attacks off Kaua'i—less than one per year—that they haven't been able to create a statistical average. (But the state as a whole had an unusually large number in 2013–14 in all.) When one *does* occur, it's usually tigers attacking surfers. Considering the number of people who swam in our waters during that time, you are more likely to choke to death on a bone at a lu'au than be attacked by a shark. If you do happen to come upon a shark, however, swim away slowly. This kind of movement doesn't interest them. *Don't* splash about rapidly. By doing this you are imitating a fish in distress, and you don't want to do that. The one kind of ocean water you want to avoid is murky water, typically found near river mouths. These are not interesting to swim in anyway. Most shark attacks occur in murky water at dawn or dusk since sharks are basically cowards who like to sneak up on their prey. In general, don't go around worrying about sharks. *Any* animal can be threatening, not just Jaws.

Sea Urchins—These are like living pin cushions. If you step on one or accidentally grab one, remove as much of the spine as possible with tweezers. See a physician if necessary.

Cone Shells—People tend to forget that shells are created by organisms to serve as housing. Most of these creatures are capable of protecting themselves by the use of a long stinger called a proboscis, which injects venom. You might hear that it's safer to pick up a shell by the large end. You should be aware that many shells have stingers that can reach any part of the shell and can penetrate gloves. Therefore, it is recommended that you do not pick up live shells. If you do find yourself stung, immediately apply hot water, as it breaks down the protein venom.

Portuguese Man-of-War—These are related to jellyfish but are unable to swim.

They are instead propelled by a small sail and are at the mercy of the wind. Though small, they are capable of inflicting a painful sting. This occurs when the long, trailing tentacles are touched, triggering hundreds of thousands of spring-loaded stingers, called nematocysts, which inject venom. The resulting burning sensation is usually very unpleasant but not fatal. Fortunately, the Portuguese Man-of-War is not a common visitor to Kaua'i. When they *do* come ashore, usually during the summer and fall on the east shore, they might do so in great numbers, jostled by a strong storm offshore. If you see them on the beach, don't go in the water. If you do get stung, immediately remove the tentacles with a gloved hand, stick or whatever is handy and rinse thoroughly with vinegar. Then apply ice for pain control. If the condition worsens, see a doctor. The folk cure is urine, and for some of us it comes in a handy applicator, but you might look pretty silly applying it.

Coral—Coral skeletons are very sharp and, since the skeleton is overlaid by millions of living coral polyps, a scrape can leave proteinaceous matter in the wound, causing infection. This is why coral cuts are frustratingly slow to heal. Immediate cleansing and disinfecting of coral cuts should speed up healing time. We don't have fire coral around Kaua'i.

Sea Anemones—Related to the jellyfish, these also have stingers and are usually found attached to rocks or coral. It's best not to touch them with your bare hands. Treatment for a sting is similar to that of a Portuguese Man-of-War.

Bugs

Though devoid of the myriad of hideous buggies found in other parts of the world, there are a few evil critters brought here from elsewhere that you should know about.

The worst are **centipedes**. They can get to be six or more inches long and are aggressive predators. If you do happen to get stung, you won't die (but you might wish you had). You'll probably never see one, but if you get stung, even by a baby, the pain can range from a bad bee sting to a mild gunshot blast. Some local doctors say the only cure is to stay drunk for three days. (*Gotta* love a doctor who will prescribe rum.) Others say to use meat tenderizer or green papaya. Pain relievers like ibuprofen and ice are going to be your best bet.

Cane spiders are big, dark and look horrifying, but they're not poisonous. (But they seem to *think* they are. I've had *them* chase *me* across the room when *I* had the broom in my hand.) We *don't* have no-see-ums, those irritating sand fleas common in the South Pacific and Caribbean.

Mosquitoes were unknown in the islands until the first stowaways arrived on Maui on the *Wellington* in 1826. Since then they have thrived. A good mosquito repellent containing deet will come in handy, especially if you plan to go hiking. *Lotions* (not thin liquids) with DEET seem to work and stick best. Forget the guidebooks that tell you to take vitamin B_{12} to keep mosquitoes away; it just gives the little critters a healthier diet. If you find one dive bombing you at night in your room, turn on your overhead fan to help keep them away.

Bees are more common on the drier west side of the island. Usually, the only way you'll get stung is if you run into one. If you rent a scooter, beware: I received my first bee sting while singing *Come Sail Away* on a motorcycle. A bee sting in the mouth can definitely ruin one of your precious vacation days. Watch for them rolling around and disoriented at the beach.

Regarding **cockroaches**, there's good news and bad news. The bad news is that here, some are bigger than your thumb and can fly. The good news is that you probably won't see one. One of their predators is the **gecko**. This small, lizard-like creature makes a surprisingly loud chirp at night. They are cute and considered good luck in the islands (probably because they eat mosquitoes and roaches).

Snakes

One thing nearly all visitors have heard is there are no snakes in Hawai'i (aside from a rare, tiny, worm-like, blind burrowing snake said to be found here on occasion). There is concern that the brown tree snake *might* make its way onto the islands from Guam. Although mostly harmless to humans, these snakes can spell extinction to native birds. Guam has lost nearly all of its birds due to this egg-eating curse. Once they are fertilized, the snakes can reproduce for life from a single specimen. If there are any on Kaua'i (none are known to be on the island at this time), it would be a major disaster. Government officials aren't allowed to tell you this, but we will: If you ever see one anywhere in Hawai'i, please *kill it* and contact the **Pest Hotline** (808-643-7378). At the very least, call them immediately. The entire bird population of Hawai'i will be grateful.

Pigs

We're not referring to your dining choice. We mean the wild ones you may encounter on a hiking trail. Generally, pigs will avoid you before you ever see them. If you happen to come upon any piglets and accidentally get between them and their mother, immediately bark like a big dog. Wild pigs are conditioned to run from local dogs (and their hunter masters), and Momma will leave her kids faster than you can say, "Pass the bacon."

Road Hazards

There are a couple things you should know about driving around Kaua'i. The speed limits here are probably slower than what you are used to, and Kaua'i police do have a few places where they regularly catch people. (That's code for speed traps.) We mention some in the tours. Also be aware that we have something on Kaua'i called **contra flow**. During commute hours, orange cones are placed on the lane divisions, forcing you to drive on the wrong side of the road. The area between Lihu'e and Wailua is an example of contra flow, and it can be a bit unnerving for the uninitiated.

Seat belt and **child restraint** use are required by law, and the police will pull you over for this alone. It's also illegal for drivers to use a **cell phone** without a head-

set. You should know that the Kaua'i Police Department regularly receives funds to enhance their seat belt violation enforcement, speeding enforcement and their sobriety checkpoints. So don't even think about violating these laws, or you'll likely get stung.

Lastly, even in paradise we have our **traffic.** Don't overlook the Kapa'a Bypass on the east shore, the Koloa-Po'ipu Bypass on the south shore and the Puhi Bypass near Lihu'e. In fact, driving *south* through Kapa'a can be a pain almost *any time* of day. If you don't take the bypass, consider taking the scenic route up 581 (at the ABC Store) to 580. Might not save any time, but it's prettier than someone else's bumper.

Dirt

Dirt? Yes, dirt. Kaua'i's infamous red dirt has ruined many new pairs of Nikes. If you are driving on a cane road on the west side and have your window rolled down, you will eat a lot of it. It's always best to bring some trashable sneakers if you plan to do any hiking. And leave your silk argyle socks at home. If you want to know how staining it can be, just ask the makers of *Red Dirt Shirts.* They use one bucket of Kaua'i mud to dye *five hundred* shirts.

Dehydration

Bring and drink lots of water when you are out and about, especially when you are hiking. Dehydration sneaks up on people. By the time you are thirsty, you're already dehydrated. It's a good idea to take an insulated water jug with you in the car or one of those 1.5 liter bottles of water. Our weather is almost certainly different than what you left behind, and you will probably find yourself thirstier than usual. Just fill it before you leave in the morning and *suck 'em up* (as we say here) all day.

If "carefree" had an address, it would be here.

Swimming in Streams

Kaua'i offers lots of opportunities to swim in streams and sometimes under waterfalls. It's a fulfillment of a fantasy for many people. But there are several hazards you need to know about.

Leptospirosis is bacteria found in some of Hawai'i's fresh water. It is transmitted from animal (usually pig and cattle) urine and can enter the body through open cuts, eyes and by drinking. Around 100 people a year in Hawai'i are diagnosed with the bacteria, which is treated with antibiotics if caught relatively early. You should avoid swimming in streams if you have open cuts, and treat all water found in nature before drinking. (Some filters are ineffective for lepto—we've had good luck with Sawyer filters.)

Also, while swimming in freshwater streams, try to use your arms as much as possible. Kicking an unseen rock is easier than you think. Consider wearing water shoes or, better yet, tabis, while in streams. (Tabis are sort of a fuzzy mitten for your feet that grab slippery rocks quite effectively.) You can get them at Walmart in Lihu'e, or the Longs Drugs in Kapa'a.

Another bacteria to be aware of is **Enterococcus**, which can be found in rivers or the ocean in high concentrations after heavy rains. If the ocean water is looking brown, don't go swimming. The **Surfrider Foundation's** Kaua'i chapter regularly tests water from 25 spots around the island and posts the latest findings on their website. Under normal conditions, if you don't have open cuts or swallow much water, your body will not be adversely affected by the bad stuff.

Though rare, **flash floods** can occur in any freshwater stream anywhere in the world, even paradise. Be alert for them.

Lastly, remember while lingering under waterfalls that not everything that comes over the top of the falls will be as soft as water. Rocks coming down from above could definitely ruin the moment.

Grocery Stores

Definitely a hazard. Restaurants may be expensive, but don't think you'll get off cheap in grocery stores. Though you'll certainly save money cooking your own food, a trip to the store here can be startling. Phrases like *they charge how much for milk?* echo throughout the stores. One tip: **Foodland** and **Safeway** both offer discount cards (called Maika'i Cards and Safeway Club Cards, respectively) that can bring pretty big savings off their otherwise confiscatory rates. Kapaʻa's stores are easily seen along the highway; north shore has Foodland at Princeville Shopping Center and **Big Save** in Hanalei. The south shore has Big Save in Koloa on Koloa Road. If you're a **Costco** member, we have one near Kukui Grove in Lihuʻe. If you're not a member and will be here awhile, consider joining as they have the best prices. If you just don't want to shop, **Kauaʻi Island Shopping Service** (808-822-5477) will shop and deliver for a fee plus cost of food—certain areas only.

Roosters

OK, so you don't normally think of roosters as hazards. And normally they're not. These guys are wild in many parts of the island and can be charming. But our roosters have proliferated since Hurricane ʻIniki freed so many back in 1992, and they are particularly stupid here. They don't seem to know when they're supposed to crow, so they do it *all day long* just to cover themselves. (Probably for liability purposes.) If any of these two-legged alarm clocks are near where you're staying, you may find yourself waking up *real* early.

TRAVELING WITH CHILDREN (KEIKI)

Perhaps we should have put this section under *Hazards*. Kauaʻi (and Hawaiʻi in general) is very kid friendly if you know the best places to go, have the right gear, and enjoy the great outdoors. Your kid's age and your comfort level are the biggest factors to consider when planning your trip. **Sun protection** is a must (keiki-sized UV blocking rashguards and hats) as is having plenty of water. Personal hydration packs (such as CamelBak) are great for hiking and going to the beach. They even come in kids' sizes (which is nice since you'll be carrying most everything else). If your crumb crunchers are 5 or younger and you want to do some hiking, a baby-frame backpack (like those made by Kelty) is essential. Not only do they keep your keiki out of harm's way, but most of these packs also have a surprising amount of room for hauling other gear. Sure, you might look and feel like a pack mule, but sharing the outdoor experience with your little ones is sure to make for lifelong memories. (Plus your kid is already well-positioned for taking selfies with you.) These packs can be checked *for free* with most airlines

Baby Beach in Lawaʻi lands another satisfied customer.

since they count as child transport (as do car seats and strollers).

Hiking trails here are plentiful, but many are too strenuous for kids. If you have a baby frame pack, then your options increase, but you don't want to be clambering up and down cliffs either. Listed here are trails that can easily be done with kids aged 5–10. We assume that kids older than this can handle some of the more varied terrain of other, more difficult hikes. In general, we think anything more than 3 miles would be pushing it for kids (gotta include rest stops), but only you can make the judgment call on what is appropriate. Trails don't have guardrails or fencing to keep you from drop-offs, and often the surrounding vegetation hides some steep hillsides. Keep your kids close and don't let them wander.

Koke'e Trails—Kaluapuhi Trail, Water Tank Trail and Berry Flat (see map on page 154).

North Shore—Historic Kilauea Stone Dam Hike.

East Shore—Sleeping Giant, Kuilau Ridge Trail and Ho'opi'i Falls.

South Shore—Po'ipu Shoreline Sandstone Hikes. (You'll definitely need sun protection and water; be sure to take breaks whenever you find shade.)

If you need a crib, stroller, car seat, baby pack and things you never even thought you needed (especially if you're staying at a condo) **Babylicious** (808-652-4273) or **Kauai Baby Rentals** (808-651-9269) have it all.

As far as swimming in the ocean with your little one, **Lydgate Beach Park** in Wailua has a boulder-enclosed keiki (kid) pond that is wildly popular. It also has two playgrounds (Kamalani), the best free one on the island. Overall, it's a nice place for keiki. Also check out **Salt Pond Beach Park** in Hanapepe and **Baby Beach. Po'ipu**

Beach Park in Po'ipu is popular with local parents, as well as visitors. These are considered the best places for children, except during periods of high surf. Obviously, surf and keiki don't go well together.

During calm summer surf, **Kalihiwai Beach** can be a pleasant place to bring kids. While not as protected as Lydgate or Salt Pond, it's picturesque, and your kids will make many new local friends.

Train lovers might want to check out **Kaua'i Plantation Railway** (808-245-7245). They cruise through 2.5 miles of the Kilohana Plantation in Lihu'e. You'll stop and feed pigs along the way, which the kids go crazy over.

Kaua'i Mini Golf (808-828-2118) is a pretty good putt-putt. Grounds are lush and there are lots of water hazards here. (You're going in the water at some point, so deal with it.) A good selection of sandwiches, snacks and ice cream for sale, and the price is $19 for adults (who will enjoy it), $15 for young'uns 4–12, and free for keiki ages 3 and under. Easy to recommend. Only complaint is the closeness to the highway there in Kilauea. They also have a small, well-marked botanical garden.

If going to the **movies** is your thing, Kaua'i is more limited than any other island. We don't get all the movies you find on the mainland since the pandemic killed our only large theater. The only theater is on the west side. The historic, one-screen **Waimea Theater** (808-338-0282) was built in the 1930s. They've done a nice job restoring it, and it has a lot of charm, but they can be a bit behind on new releases.

If you are looking for **babysitters**, nearly every hotel on the island has lists of professional services, as well as employees who babysit. Some hotels, such as the Hyatt and the Royal Sonesta Kaua'i Resort, offer rather elaborate services that can be a rug-rat's dream. If you are staying at a place that has no front desk, contact your rental agent for an up-to-date list of sitters.

Traveling With Children Best Bets

Best Kid-friendly Beaches— 'Anini on right side or Kahili (Rock Quarry) in summer on North Shore. Boulder Ponds at Lydgate on East Shore. Po'ipu Beach Park, left side on South Shore. Salt Pond Beach Park, far left side on West Shore.

Best Playground—Kamalani Playground at Lydgate Beach Park

Best Library—Princeville Library

Best Big Resort Pool—Grand Hyatt Kauai in Po'ipu

Best Resort Pool That Won't Drown Your Wallet—Waipouli Beach Resort in Kapa'a

Best Lu'au to Keep Your Kid's Attention—Lu'au Kalamaku at Kilohana

Best Shops to Find a Unique Toy— Beachrail Lines in Nawiliwili or Magic Dragon Toy & Art Supply in Princeville

Best Place to Have a Locally Made Root Beer—Kaua'i Beer Company

Best Weekly Event for Kids & Adults— Hanapepe Art Night

Best Place for Family Camping—Koke'e State Park

THE PEOPLE

The people of Kaua'i are the friendliest people in the entire country. "Oh, come on!" you might say. But this is not the admittedly biased opinion of someone who lives here. This conclusion was reached by the participants in the *Condé Nast Readers' Choice Awards*. This is a sophisticated and savvy lot. *Condé Nast* is the magazine of choice for world travelers. When asked in their yearly poll, readers rate Kaua'i at or near the top of the list in friendliness nearly every year.

What does this mean? Well, you will notice that people smile here more than other places. Drivers wave at complete strangers (without any particular fingers leading the way). If you try to analyze the reason, it probably comes down to a matter of happiness. People are happy here, and happy people are friendly people. It's just that simple. Some people compare a trip to Kaua'i with a trip back in time, when smiles weren't rare, and politeness and courtesy were the order of the day.

Ethnic Breakdown

Kaua'i has an ethnic mix that is as diversified as any you will find. Here, *everyone* is a minority; there is no majority. The current census estimate revealed the ethnic makeup below.

White	.33%
Asian	.31%
Hawaiian or other Pacific Islander	.9.1%
Hispanic	.11.4%
Black or African American	.0.7%
Native American or Alaska Native	.0.5%
Mixed or didn't respond	.25.7%
Total population	72,293

SOME TERMS

If you are confused regarding terms in Hawai'i, this should help. A person of Hawaiian blood is **Hawaiian**. That is a racial term, not a geographic one, so only people of the Hawaiian race are called Hawaiian. They are also called **Kanaka Maoli**, but only another Hawaiian can use this term. Anybody who was born here, regardless of race (except whites), is called a **local**. If you were born elsewhere but have lived here a while, you are called a **kama'aina**. If you are white, you are a **haole**. It doesn't matter if you have been

A beautiful sunset can mean only one thing—time for a mai tai.

here a day or your family has been here for over a century, you will always be a **haole**. The term comes from the time when westerners first encountered these islands. Its precise meaning has been lost, but it is thought to refer to people with no background (since westerners could not chant the kanaenae of their ancestors).

The continental United States is called the **mainland**. If you are returning home, you are not "going back to the states" (we *are* a state). When somebody leaves the island, they are **off-island**.

HAWAIIAN TIME

One aspect of Hawaiian culture you may have heard of is Hawaiian Time. The stereotype is that everyone in Hawai'i moves just a little bit more slowly than on the mainland. We are supposed to be more laid back and don't let things get to us as easily as people on the mainland. This is the stereotype…OK, it's *not* a stereotype. It's real. During your visit, if you get in the rhythm, you'll notice that this feeling infects *you* as well. You might find yourself letting another driver cut in front of you in circumstances that would incur your wrath back home. You might find yourself willing to wait for a red light without feeling like you're going to explode. The whole reason for coming to Hawai'i is to experience beauty and a sense of peace, so let it happen. If someone else is moving a bit slower than you would like, just go with it.

THE HAWAIIAN LANGUAGE

The Hawaiian language is a beautiful, gentle and melodious language that flows smoothly off the tongue. Just the sounds of the words conjure up trees gently swaying in the breeze and the sound of the surf. Most Polynesian languages share the same roots, and many have common words. Today, Hawaiian is spoken *as an everyday language* only on the privately owned island of Ni'ihau, 17 miles off the coast of Kaua'i. Visitors are often intimidated by Hawaiian. With a few ground rules you'll come to realize that pronunciation is not as tough as you might think.

When missionaries discovered that the Hawaiians had no written language, they sat down and created an alphabet. This Hawaiian alphabet has only 12 letters. Five vowels; **a, e, i, o** and **u**, as well as seven consonants; **h, k, l, m, n, p** and **w**.

The consonants are pronounced just as they are in English with the exception of **W**. It is often pronounced as a V if it is in the middle of a word and comes after an E or I. Vowels are pronounced as follows:

A—pronounced as in *Ah* if stressed, or *above* if not stressed.

E—pronounced as in *say* if stressed, or *dent* if not stressed.

I—pronounced as in *bee*.

O—pronounced as in *no*.

U—pronounced as in *boo*.

One thing you will notice in this book are glottal stops. These are represented by an upside-down apostrophe ' and are meant to convey a hard stop in the pronunciation. So if we are talking about the type of lava called **ʻaʻa**, it is pronounced as two separate As (AH-AH).

Another feature you will encounter are **diphthongs**, where two letters glide together. They are **ae, ai, ao, au, ei, eu, oi,** and **ou**. Unlike many English diphthongs, the second vowel is always pronounced. One word you will read in this book, referring to Hawaiian temples, is *heiau* (HEY-YOW). The **e** and **i** flow together as a single sound, then the **a** and **u** flow together as a single sound. The **Y** sound binds the two sounds, making the whole word flow together.

Let's take a word that might seem impossible to pronounce. When you see how easy this word is, the rest will seem like a snap. The Hawaiʻi state fish is the **humuhumunukunukuapuaʻa**. At first glance it seems like a nightmare. But if you read the word slowly, it is pronounced just like it looks and isn't nearly as horrifying as it appears. Try it. **Humu** (hoo-moo) is pronounced twice. **Nuku** (noo-koo) is pronounced twice. A (ah) is pronounced once. **Pu** (poo) is pronounced once. Aʻa (ah-ah) is the ah sound pronounced twice, the

glottal stop indicating a hard stop between sounds. Now you should try it again. **Humuhumunukunukuapuaʻa.** Now, wasn't that easy? OK, so it's not easy, but it's not impossible either.

Below are some words that you might hear during your visit:

ʻAina (EYE-na)—Land.

Akamai (AH-ka-MY)—Wise or shrewd.

Aliʻi (ah-LEE-ee)—A Hawaiian chief; a member of the chiefly class.

Aloha (ah-LO-ha)—Hello, goodbye, or a feeling or the spirit of love, affection or kindness.

Hala (HA-la)—Pandanus tree.

Hale (HA-leh)—House or building.

Hana (HA-na)—Work.

Hana hou (HA-na-HO)—To do again.

Haole (HOW-leh)—Originally foreigner, now means Caucasian.

Heiau (HEY-YOW)—Hawaiian temple.

Hula (HOO-la)—The storytelling dance of Hawaiʻi.

Imu (EE-moo)—An underground oven.

ʻIniki (ee-NEE-key)—Sharp and piercing wind (as in Hurricane ʻIniki).

Kahuna (ka-HOO-na)—A priest or minister; someone who is an expert in a profession.

Kai (kigh)—The sea.

Kalua (KA-LOO-ah)—Cooking food underground.

Kamaʻaina (KA-ma-EYE-na)—Long-time Hawaiʻi resident.

Kane (KA-neh)—Boy or man.

Kapu (KA-poo)—Forbidden, taboo; keep out.

Keiki (KAY-key)—Child or children.

Kokua (KO-KOO-ah)—Help.

Kona (KO-na)—Leeward side of the island; wind blowing from the south, southwest direction.

Kuleana (KOO-leh-AH-na)—Concern, responsibility or jurisdiction.

Lanai (LA-NIGH)—Porch, veranda, patio.

Lani (LA-nee)—Sky or heaven.

Lei (lay)—Necklace of flowers, shells or feathers.

Liliko'i (LEE-lee-KO-ee)—Passion fruit.

Limu (LEE-moo)—Edible seaweed.

Lomi (LOW-me)—To rub or massage; lomi salmon is raw salmon rubbed with salt and spices.

Lu'au (LOO-OW)—Hawaiian feast; literally means taro leaves.

Mahalo (ma-HA-low)—Thank you.

Makai (ma-KIGH)—Toward the sea.

Malihini (MA-lee-HEE-nee)—A newcomer, visitor or guest.

Mauka (MOW-ka)—Toward the mountain.

Moana (mo-AH-na)—Ocean.

Mo'o (MO-oh)—Lizard.

Nani (NA-nee)—Beautiful, pretty.

Nui (NEW-ee)—Big, important, great.

'Ohana (oh-HA-na)—Family.

'Okole (OH-KO-leh)—Derrière.

'Ono (OH-no)—Delicious, the best.

Pakalolo (pa-ka-LO-LO)—Marijuana.

Pali (PA-lee)—A cliff.

Paniolo (PA-nee-OH-lo)—Hawaiian cowboy.

Pau (pow)—Finish, end; pau hana means quitting time from work.

Poi (poy)—Pounded kalo (taro) root that forms a paste.

Pono (PO-no)—Goodness, excellence, correct, proper.

Pua (POO-ah)—Flower.

Puka (POO-ka)—Hole.

Pupu (POO-POO)—Appetizer, snacks or finger food.

Wahine (vah-HEE-neh)—Woman.

Wai (why)—Fresh water.

Wikiwiki (WEE-kee-WEE-kee)—To hurry up, very quick.

Quick Pidgin Lesson

Hawaiian pidgin is fun to listen to. It's like ear candy. It is colorful, rhythmic and sways in the wind. Below is a list of some of the words and phrases you might hear on your visit. It's tempting to read some of these and try to use them. If you do, the odds are you will simply look foolish. These words and phrases are used in certain ways and with certain inflections. People who have spent years living in the islands still feel uncomfortable using them. Thick pidgin can be incomprehensible to the untrained ear (that's the idea). If you are someplace and hear two people engaged in a discussion in pidgin, stop and eavesdrop for a bit. You won't forget it.

Waterfalls and wild chickens—It doesn't get more Kaua'i than this.

Ainokea— I no care/I don't care. Try saying it slowly to hear it.

All bus—Drunk.

An' den—And then? So?

Any kine—Anything; any kind.

Ass right—That's right.

Ass why—That's why.

Beef—A problem one has with another.

Brah—Bruddah; friend; brother.

Broke da mout—Delicious.

Buggah—That's the one; it is difficult.

Bus laugh—To laugh out loud.

Chicken skin kine—Something that gives you goosebumps.

Choke—Plenty; a lot.

Cockaroach—Steal; rip off.

Da kine—A noun or verb used in place of whatever the speaker wishes. Heard constantly.

Das how—That's right.

Fo days—plenty; "He get hair fo days."

Geevum—Go for it! Give 'em hell!

Grind—To eat.

Grinds—Food.

Hold ass—A close call when driving your new car.

How you figga?—How do you figure that? It makes no sense.

Howzit?—How is it going? How are you? Also, Howzit o wot?

I owe you money or wat?—What to say when someone is staring at you.

Lolo—Crazy, stupid.

Lose money— What you say when something bad happens, like if you drop your shave ice.

Mek ass—Make a fool of yourself.

Mek house—Make yourself at home.

Mo' bettah—This is better.

Moke—A large, tough local male. (Don't say it unless you *like scrap*.)

No can—Cannot; I cannot do it.

No mek lidat—Stop doing that.

No, yeah?—No, or is "no" correct?

'Okole squeezer—Something that suddenly frightens you ('okole meaning derrière).

Pau hana—Quit work. (A time of daily, intense celebration in the islands.) Also another name for Happy Hour.

Poi dog—A mutt.

Shahkbait—Shark bait, meaning pale, untanned people or a beach newbie.

Shaka—Great! All right!

Shoots, den—Affirmative/Okay, then. As in "We're meeting for lunch at noon." *Shoots, den.*

Shredding—Riding a gnarly wave.

Slippahs—Flip-flops, thongs, zoris.

Stink eye—Dirty looks; facial expression denoting displeasure.

Suck rocks—Buzz off, or pound sand.

Talk stink—Speak bad about somebody.

Talk story—Shooting the breeze; to rap.

Tanks ah?—Thank you.

Tita—A female moke. Same *scrap* results.

Training brah—A haole trying (unsuccessfully) to speak pidgin.

Yeah?—Used at the end of sentences.

BOOKS

There is an astonishing variety of books available about Hawai'i and Kaua'i. Everything from history, legends, geology, children's stories and just plain ol' novels. In Hanapepe, **Talk Story Bookstore** (808-335-6469) has a very nice selection, as well as hard-to-find used books. And don't forget the **Kaua'i Museum** (808-245-6931) in Lihu'e. They, too, have interesting and hard-to-find books.

MUSIC

Hawaiian music is far more diverse than most people think. Many often picture Hawaiian music as someone twanging away on an 'ukulele (pronounced OO-KOO-LAY-LAY, not YOU-KA-LAY-LEE) with his voice slipping and sliding all over the

*If you came to Hawai'i to get lei'd,
this is one place that lovers lay them.*

place, as though he has an ice cube down his back. In reality, the music here can be outstanding. There is the melodic sound of the more traditional music. There are young local bands putting out modern music with a Hawaiian beat. There is even Hawaiian reggae and hip hop. If you get a chance, check out your favorite music app or tune into some local radio stations while you are here.

THE HULA

The hula evolved as a means of worship, later becoming a forum for telling a story with chants (called **mele**), hands and body movement. It can be fascinating to watch. When most people think of the hula, they picture a woman in a grass skirt swinging her hips to the strumming of an 'ukulele. But in reality there are two types of hula. The modern hula, or **hula 'auana**, uses musical instruments and vocals to augment the dancer. It came about after westerners first encountered the islands. Missionaries found the hula distasteful, and the old style was driven underground. The modern type came about as a form of entertainment

and was practiced in places where missionaries had no influence. Ancient Hawaiians didn't even use grass skirts. They were brought in later by Gilbert Islanders.

The old style of hula is called **hula kahiko** (also called 'olapa). It consists of chants and is accompanied only by percussion and takes years of training. It can be exciting to watch as performers work together in synchronous harmony. Both men and women participate, with women's hula somewhat softer (though no less disciplined) and men's hula more active. This type of hula is physically demanding and requires strong concentration. Keiki (children's) hula can be charming to watch as well.

Kaua'i was the home of the most prestigious hula school in all the islands. People came from every part of the island chain to learn the hula at the Ka-ulu-Paoa. Great discipline was required, and the teachers could be very strict. The remains of this school are still evident on a plateau above Ke'e Beach.

The lu'au around the island usually have entertaining hula shows, though not as "authentic" as some of the festival demonstrations seen on occasion. Some resorts and shopping centers also have hula shows on occasion.

FARMERS MARKETS

Called **Sunshine Markets** locally, you'll find them every day of the week, great places to pick up locally grown fruits and produce. Get there before they open, because things go fast.

Monday—In Kapa'a at Kealia Farm across from Kealia Beach at 3 p.m. and in Lihu'e at the Kukui Grove Center at 3 p.m.

Tuesday—In Kapa'a at Coconut Marketplace at 9 a.m. and at the Waipa Park N Ride parking lot in Hanalei before mile marker 4 at 3 p.m.

Wednesday—In Kapa'a at Kapa'a Beach Park at 3 p.m. In Po'ipu at Shops at Kukui'ula at 3:30 p.m.

Thursday—In Hanapepe at Hanapepe Park at 3 p.m., and in Waimea, at Hale Puna, 9567 Huakai Road at 3:30 p.m., and in Kapa'a at Coconut Marketplace at 9 a.m.

Friday—In Kapa'a at Kealia Farm across from Kealia Beach at 3 p.m.

Saturday—In Kilauea off Hwy at Anaina Hou near mini golf at 9 a.m. In Puhi at the Kaua'i Community College parking lot at 9:30 a.m.

Sunday—In Hanalei, mauka side of highway just past town at noon.

A NOTE ON PERSONAL RESPONSIBILITY

In past editions we've had the sad task of removing places that you can no longer visit. The reason, universally cited, is *liability*. Although Hawai'i has a statute indemnifying landowners, the mere threat is often enough to get something closed. Because we, more than any other publication, have exposed heretofore un-

known attractions, we feel the need to pass this along.

You need to assess what kind of traveler you are. We've been accused of leaning a bit toward the adventurous side, so you should take that into account when deciding if something's right for you. To paraphrase from the movie *Top Gun*, "Don't let your ego write checks your body can't cash."

You will probably be more physical during your trip, so *train* for it. Doctors and officials strongly believe that the biggest cause of injury and death of visitors stems from people who aren't active at home, coming here and blowing a gasket from all the recreating they've dreamed of doing here. If you plan on doing any hiking, snorkeling or other activities, spend the month before coming here exercising as much as you can. Your body will reward you, we promise.

Please remember that this isn't Disneyland—it's nature. Mother Nature is hard, slippery, sharp and unpredictable. If you go exploring and get into trouble, whether it's your ego that's bruised or something more tangible, please remember that neither the state, the private landowner nor this publication *told* you to go. You *chose* to explore, which is what life, and this book, are all about. And if you complain to or threaten someone controlling land, they'll rarely fix the problem you identified. They'll simply close it… and it will be gone for good.

Sometimes even good intentions can lead to disaster. At one adventure, a trailhead led hikers to the base of a wonderful waterfall. There was only *one* trail, to the left at the parking lot, that a person could take. Neither we, other guides nor websites ever said, "Stay on the trail to the left," because at the time there was only one trail to take. The state (in their zeal to protect themselves from liability at an unmaintained trail) came along and put up a "Danger Keep Out" sign at the trailhead. Travelers encountering the sign assumed they were on the wrong trail and started to beat a path to the right instead. But that direction started sloping downward and ended abruptly at a 150-foot-high cliff. Hikers retreated and in a short time a previously non-existent trail to the right became as prominent as the correct (and heretofore *only*) path to the left. Not long after the state's well-intentioned sign went up, an unwitting pair of hikers took the new, incorrect trail to the right and fell to their deaths. They died because they had been dissuaded from taking the correct trail by a state sign theoretically erected to keep people safe. The result? You'll now see more warning signs than ever in Hawai'i.

Our point is that nothing is static and nothing can take the place of your own observations and good judgment. If you're doing one of the activities you read about in our book or someplace else and your instinct tells you something is wrong, *trust your judgment* and go do another activity. There are lots of wonderful things to do on the island, and we want you safe and happy.

And also remember to always leave the island the same way you found it.

A NOTE ABOUT ACCESS

If a lawful landowner posts a "No Trespassing" sign on their land, you need to respect their wishes. That seems simple enough. But here's where it gets tricky.

It's common in Hawai'i for someone who doesn't own or control land to erect "No Trespassing", "Keep Out" and "Road Closed" signs. Picture a shoreline fisherman who doesn't want anyone else near his cherished spot, putting up a store-bought sign to protect his solitude. Or a neighbor on a dirt road who hates the dust from cars driving by, so he puts up a sign that he knows locals will ignore, but it might dissuade unwary visitors.

In the past we did our best to try to ferret out when No Trespassing signs were valid and when they were not, and we took *a lot* of heat from residents who mistakenly thought we were encouraging trespassing when we weren't. But the current environment doesn't permit us to do that anymore. So if you're heading to one of the places we describe and you encounter a No Trespassing sign, even if you think it's not authorized by the landowner (and even if it's on *public* land), we have to advise you to turn around and heed the sign. All descriptions in our book come with the explicit assumption that you have obtained the permission of the legal landowner, and unfortunately, it'll usually be up to you to determine who that is and how to get it. But please, under no circumstances are we suggesting that you trespass. Plain and clear. Don't trespass… ever…for any reason…period.

MISCELLANEOUS INFORMATION

Kaua'i has no distinct visitor season. People come here year round to enjoy the island's blessings. However, certain times of the year are more popular than others. Christmas is always a particularly busy time, and you may have trouble getting a room if you are determined to stay at a particular resort. The island never feels crowded the way other destinations can feel. This might sound surprising, given poll results. When pollsters ask people where they would like to go, Kaua'i is always in the top 10.

The **area code** for the entire state is 808. **Daylight saving time** isn't observed in Hawai'i.

A mai tai that's too pretty to drink...
well, almost.

Plastic bags are banned on the island, and rather than springing for paper bags, many stores will simply hand you your purchases, no matter how numerous. Consider bringing your own reusable bag.

If you are planning to see either the National Tropical Botanical Garden or the Grove Farm Sugar Plantation Museum, make your reservations before you get here to assure admittance.

Campers should also obtain their permits before they arrive, especially for the Na Pali Coast. See Camping in the *Activities* chapter.

If you have an **early checkout** (or a **late flight**) and need a place to freshen up before your flight, consider the bathrooms at Lydgate State Park, several miles north of the airport, which have showers. Upon entering the road to Lydgate, the showers to the right on Nehe Street are a bit more private.

If you wear **sunglasses**, *polarized* lenses are highly recommended. Not only are colors more brilliant here, but the lower latitudes of Hawai'i make polarized lenses particularly effective.

It is customary on Kaua'i for *everyone* to remove their shoes upon entering someone's house (sometimes their office). Kaua'i's **red dirt** can be particularly pernicious, and nobody wants to spend their day cleaning floors.

If you are going to spend any time at the beach (and you really should), woven bamboo **beach mats** can be found all over the island for about $4. Some roll up, some can be folded. The sand comes off these more easily than it comes off towels.

If you want to arrange a **flower lei** for you or your honey as you arrive at the airport on a direct flight (no interisland flights), call **LeiGreeting.com** (800) 665-7959 before you arrive. You can get a nice lei on Kaua'i for around $29. (I know where you're going with that—stop it!)

Finally, if you're staying on the south shore and you have a medical issue, **Po'ipu Mobile MD** (808-652-7021) makes house (hotel/condo) calls 8 a.m. to 5 p.m. for non-emergency care. Fees range from $100 for a phone consultation to $600 for a house call. It may sound pricey, but I'd rather be in my hotel room sipping a mai tai than sitting in the ER with a sprained ankle.

VOLUNTEERING ON VACATION

There are many opportunities to give back while you are visiting from building homes to beach cleanups. One of our favorites is the **Kaua'i Humane Society** (808-632-0610) Shelter Dog Field Trip program. Basically, you spend the day with an unloved dog by picking one up in the morning (as early as 10 or 11 a.m.) and returning one hour before closing in the afternoon. They provide all the supplies you need, and you supply a $200 credit card deposit. This has led to many adoptions, and they'll help with that, too.

SMARTPHONE APPS

We love books, which are naturally and instinctively approachable. They convey information in a way that is timeless. But at the same time, new technology allows us to do things with smartphones that can't occur in books. Our app, *Hawaii Revealed*, is unlike *any* travel app you've ever seen. All the information from the books is there, but the app costs a little extra because we have also harnessed and *invented* features that will blow you away.

For instance, you want to go to Tunnels Beach to snorkel today? You can flip to the page in the book and read all about it. But with our app, you tap to the entry and you can read all about it and find out that today isn't a good day to get into the water due to high surf. Want to do a hike on the North Shore? Well, the author woke up this morning, saw that the weather was going to be bad on the on that side, circled a part of the map that he thought might be affected and for how long, and every entry in that area that is weather-sensitive will be updated to reflect the bad weather.

Want to find a restaurant that matches perfectly to your vision? *I want to dine at a place in Poʻipu, that has a romantic atmosphere, an ocean view, is vegetarian-friendly, full bar, easy parking, outdoor seating, not part of a national chain… oh, and has gluten-free options?* With the filters in our app you can cut through all of the restaurants and get to *exactly* what you want, read our in-depth and brutally honest review and get direc-tions. How's that for cutting through the noise? There's more—*a lot* more.

GPS Driving Tour App

When friends and relatives from the mainland come to visit, I often end up tagging along with them in the car showing them the island and expanding on things that I didn't have room for here. I always wished I could do that for all my readers, and now through the magic of smartphone technology, *I can.*

Our *Kauai Revealed Drive Tour* app is just like having me in the backseat showing you the island. (It's actually better, because you don't have to buy me a mai tai at the end of the day.) I have personally narrated all the places we will drive and include lots of additional information, stories and legends along with the occasional personal story associated with a particular place. Your phone's GPS triggers the narrations as you drive over specific points in specific directions and doesn't require a cell signal, so don't worry about being out of range. I absolutely love creating this book app you are holding, but creating these audio tours has been one of the most fulfilling things I've ever done. I hope you enjoy using them as much as I did creating them.

You'll find both apps in the Apple or Google Play stores.

A WORD ABOUT COVID-19

Hawaiʻi shut its doors to all travelers when the pandemic broke in the spring of 2020 and stayed that way for most of the year. When it opened to tourism again, it was a constantly shifting situation until things stabilized. During that time we stayed on top of all the changes through our app, *Hawaii Revealed* and on our website's blog at revealedtravel-guides.com/blogs/.

Raining in the mountains and sunny at the beach. The North Shore is lovely no matter what the weather is doing.

Kaua'i's north shore…where lushness takes on a whole new meaning. Every shade of green imaginable is represented in its myriad plant life. Its beaches are exquisite and its mountains unmatched in their sheer majesty. After a heavy rain, you will literally be unable to count the number of waterfalls etched into the sides of the north shore mountains.

For the sake of clarity, we will identify the north shore as everything north of Kapa'a. While this description includes Anahola (which some may consider east shore), it is easier to remember it this way, and anyone driving north of Kapa'a is usually going to the north shore anyway. The main highway, which stretches around the island, occasionally changing its name, has mile markers every mile. These little green signs can be a big help in knowing where you are at any given time. Therefore, we have placed them on the maps represented as a number inside a small box. We will often describe a certain feature or unmarked road as being "0.4 miles past mile marker 16." We hope this helps.

Everything is either on the *mauka* side of the highway (toward the mountains) or *makai* (toward the ocean). Since people get these confused, we'll refer to them as *mauka side* and *ocean side*.

All beaches we mention are described in detail in the chapter on *Beaches*.

Driving north of Kapa'a, you'll see **Kealia Beach** on your right, just past mile marker 10. This is a popular boogie boarding beach. At this beach you can often see water spitting into the air from the collision of an incoming and outgoing wave, called *clapotis* for the trivia-minded. (Doesn't that sound more like something a sailor might pick up while on shore leave?)

ANAHOLA

Next, comes the town of Anahola. This area is designated Hawaiian Homelands, meaning it is available to persons of Hawaiian descent. The spike-shaped mountain you see on the *mauka* side is **Kalalea Mountain**, also called **King Kong's Profile**. As you drive north of Anahola, look back, and you will see the striking resemblance to King Kong.

To the right of the profile is a small hole in the mountain called (this is clever) **Hole-in-the-Mountain**. It used to be bigger, but a landslide in the early 1980s closed off most of it. You can see it best between mile markers 15 and 16.

One legend says that a supernatural bird named Hulu pecked the hole in order to see Anahola on the other side. Geologists say that there was once a long lava tube stretching from Wai'ale'ale to the sea. The mountain mass on either side of the ridge has been removed by ceaseless erosion, leaving only the ridge and its ghost of a lava tube.

There are several secluded beaches north of Anahola that require walks of various lengths, including **Waiakalua Beach** and **Larsen's Beach**. (See *Beaches* and map on page 51.) In 2014 the founder of a fairly successful website reportedly paid *$200 million* for the land fronting Larsen's so he could build a vacation home. We have it labeled on the map as Zuckerland.

Near mile marker 17 is the **Moloa'a Sunrise Juice Bar** (808-822-1441). A good place for smoothies and juices, but the food is somewhat underwhelming. The selection of fresh fruit can be hit or miss and overpriced—you can find better options at a farmer's market.

Perched on a bluff overlooking the vast Pacific Ocean, the Kilauea Lighthouse stands as a silent sentry.

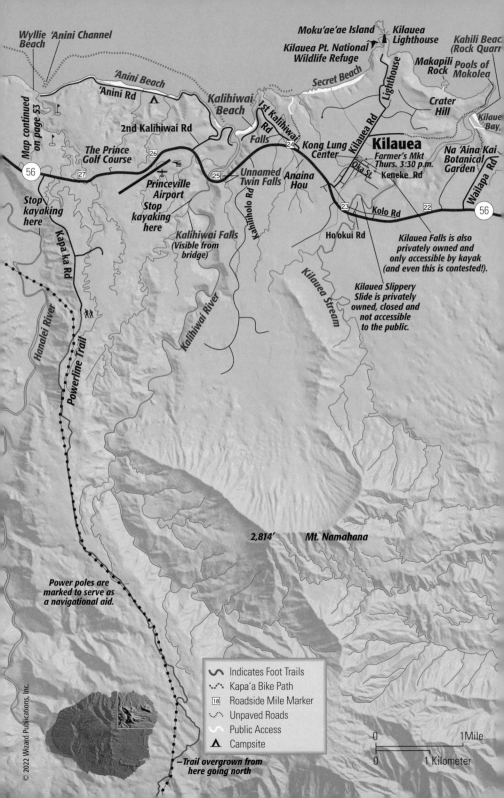

Wyllie
'Anini Channel
Beach

Moku'ae'ae Island
Kilauea Pt. National
Wildlife Refuge

Kilauea
Lighthouse

Kahili Beac
(Rock Quarr

'Anini Beach

'Anini Rd

Secret Beach

Lighthouse

Makapili
Rock

Pools of
Mokolea

Kalihiwai
Beach

Crater
Hill

2nd Kalihiwai Rd

1st Kalihiwai Rd

Kilauea Rd

Kilauea
Bay.

Kalihiwai
Falls

Kong Lung
Center

Kilauea

Na 'Aina Kai
Botanical
Garden

The Prince
Golf Course

26

24

Farmer's Mkt
Thurs. 3:30 p.m.

Oka St

Keneke Rd

27

56

25

Unnamed
Twin Falls

Anaina
Hou

23

Kolo Rd

22

56

Princeville
Airport

Kahiliholo Rd

Stop
kayaking
here

Ho'okui Rd

Map continued on page 53

Stop
kayaking
here

Kalihiwai Falls
(Visible from
bridge)

Kilauea Falls is also
privately owned and
only accessible by kayak
(and even this is contested!).

Kalihiwai River

Kilauea Stream

Kilauea Slippery
Slide is privately
owned, closed and
not accessible
to the public.

Kapa ka Rd

Hanalei River

Powerline Trail

2,814'   Mt. Namahana

Power poles are
marked to serve as
a navigational aid.

Symbol	Legend
∿	Indicates Foot Trails
⋰⋰	Kapa'a Bike Path
18	Roadside Mile Marker
⋰⋰	Unpaved Roads
∿	Public Access
⛺	Campsite

0   1 Mile
0   1 Kilometer

—Trail overgrown from
here going north

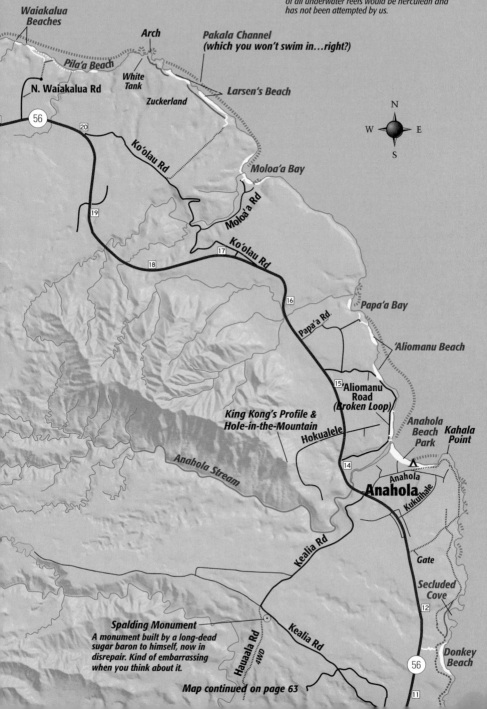

The reef edges are denoted by ··························· and come directly from government topographic maps. The task of verifying the precise location of all underwater reefs would be herculean and has not been attempted by us.

Waiakalua Beaches

Pila'a Beach

Arch

Pakala Channel (which you won't swim in…right?)

White Tank

N. Waiakalua Rd

Zuckerland

Larsen's Beach

56

20

N
W E
S

Ko'olau Rd

Moloa'a Bay

19

Moloa'a Rd

Ko'olau Rd

18

17

16

Papa'a Bay

Papa'a Rd

'Aliomanu Beach

15

Aliomanu Road (Broken Loop)

King Kong's Profile & Hole-in-the-Mountain

Anahola Beach Park

Kahala Point

Hokualele

14

Anahola Stream

Anahola

Anahola

Kukuihale

Kealia Rd

Gate

Secluded Cove

12

Spalding Monument
A monument built by a long-dead sugar baron to himself, now in disrepair. Kind of embarrassing when you think about it.

Hauaala Rd 4WD

Kealia Rd

56

Donkey Beach

11

Map continued on page 63

At the end of Wailapa Road (on the ocean side of the highway between mile markers 21 and 22) is the Na 'Aina Kai Botanical Garden (808-828-0525). This is what happens when you have someone with obvious big bucks (in this case the first wife of the late *Peanuts* creator Charles Schulz) with a dream and vision to create 240 acres of tropical gardens, sculptures, a teak wood plantation, a desert garden, secluded beach and stream, all scrupulously maintained. Guided tours are expensive— $40 for the recommended 1.5-hour tour— but it's such an exceptionally beautiful area that it's worth it. Arrange in advance. Other guided tours of different lengths also available. Check out what we say about it in *Activities* on page 178.

KILAUEA

The former plantation town of Kilauea is just past mile marker 23 and is accessible off Kolo Road. It is known for the Kilauea Lighthouse (808-828-1413). This is a post-card-perfect landmark perched on a bluff and represents the northernmost point of the main Hawaiian Islands. When it was built in 1913, it had the largest clamshell lens in existence and was used until the mid '70s when it was replaced by a beacon.

Directly offshore is Moku'ae'ae Island, a bird sanctuary. Self-guided tours of the lighthouse area are available, though you can't go upstairs and visit the light itself. The view from the bluff is smashing and worth your time. Open 10 a.m. to 4 p.m., it's $10 per person to get in (kids are free). Open Thursday through Saturday. They may be closed other days too, and you might have to make a reservation to get past the overlook by booking online at Recreation.gov. Take Kilauea Road.

Kilauea has also become a high-priced refuge for the super rich. Many exotic compounds are sprinkled about the area, just beyond sight.

Princeville to Na Pali

© 2022 Wizard Publications, Inc.

Princeville

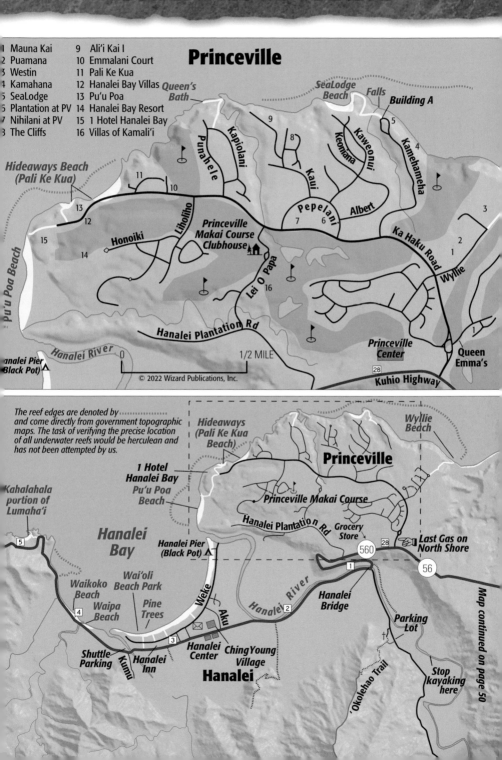

Queen's Bath

SeaLodge Beach

Falls

Building A

Hideaways Beach (Pali Ke Kua)

Punahele

Kapiolani

Keoniana

Kaweonui

Kamehameha

Kaui

Pepelani

Albert

Honoiki

Liholiho

Princeville Makai Course Clubhouse

Lei O Papa

Ka Haku Road

Wyllie

Pu'u Poa Beach

Hanalei Plantation Rd

Princeville Center

Queen Emma's

Hanalei River

Hanalei Pier (Black Pot)

0   1/2 MILE

© 2022 Wizard Publications, Inc.

Kuhio Highway

28

The reef edges are denoted by .... and come directly from government topographic maps. The task of verifying the precise location of all underwater reefs would be herculean and has not been attempted by us.

Hideaways (Pali Ke Kua Beach)

Wyllie Beach

Princeville

1 Hotel Hanalei Bay

Pu'u Poa Beach

Princeville Makai Course

Kahalahala portion of Lumaha'i

Hanalei Bay

Grocery Store

Hanalei Plantation Rd

Last Gas on North Shore

560   28

56

Hanalei Pier (Black Pot)

Waikoko Beach

Wai'oli Beach Park

Waipa Beach

Pine Trees

Wete

Aku

Hanalei River

1

Hanalei Bridge

2

Parking Lot

Shuttle Parking

Kumu

Hanalei Inn

Hanalei Center

ChingYoung Village

Hanalei

Stop kayaking here

Okolehao Trail

Map continued on page 50

Just north of Kilauea, on the *mauka* side, is **Banana Joe's Fruit Stand** (808- 828- 1092). Historically this has been a good place for fresh fruits, smoothies and frosties, but on recent visits we haven't found bananas, fresh fruit… or even Joe. It's now run by a chocolate company.

Nearby is **Kaua'i Mini Golf & Botanical Gardens** (808-828-2118). See page 37 if you're in a putting mood. It's a pretty nice putt putt.

KALIHIWAI

After Kilauea you will notice two Kalihiwai Roads on the map. It used to be a loop connected at the bottom via a bridge. The bridge was erased by a tsunami in 1957, and the state hasn't replaced it yet. (Give 'em time; they're still debating whether smart phones are just another passing fad.) The first Kalihiwai Road leads to a beautiful little bay, Kalihiwai Bay. (Keep an eye out for a small, pretty hidden falls on your right after a bridge.) Kalihiwai is a good place to stretch your legs and enjoy the scenery.

Back on the highway, there's a road 0.5 miles past mile marker 24 called Kahiliholo Road. It's the only place you can park to walk to an **unnamed falls** 0.5 miles farther up the road on the left. (The falls are sometimes used by people to rinse off saltwater after they've been to **Secret Beach**.) The stream flows under the road and falls again into the valley. The long bridge past the falls has a narrow walkway.

Visible on the *mauka* side is **Kalihiwai Falls**, a gorgeous, two-tiered falls. The cars on this bridge *seem* to go by at 110 mph, so be careful. Sometimes they let the brush over-grow along the side of the road and it becomes hazardous to walk there. (You might have a tough time seeing the falls unless you walk out onto the bridge.) You might see the remains of a vehicle turnout right at the bridge. The state closed it because of our old buddy, *liability*.

As you continue, take the second Kalihiwai Road to 'Anini Road, which leads to **'Anini Beach Park**, where many of the

Driving through a tropic wonderland.

rich and famous choose to build their homes. This is one of the safest places on the north shore to swim and is protected by a long, fringing reef.

PRINCEVILLE

Continuing on Highway 56, the resort area of Princeville beckons. It was named after Prince Albert, the visiting 2-year-old son of King Kamehameha IV. Although the young lad died two years later, the name stuck. The resort is renowned for its ocean bluff condominiums.

Princeville's cliffs lead many to think that it has no beaches to offer. *Au contraire*. Beaches don't get much better than **Hideaways**, a very pleasant little pocket of coarse sand. The catch is that you need to hike down about 5–10 minutes to it. The other catch is, the trail *might* be closed—see *Beaches* on page 105.

Another gem (in the summer) is **Queen's Bath**. This is a natural pool located on a lava bench. See *Beaches* on page 106.

If you are staying in Princeville, you may choke over the prices at Foodland or Big Save in Hanalei. Consider stocking up on food in Kapaʻa where it's *somewhat* cheaper.

As you leave Princeville, note that the highway changes names again and the mile markers start at 0. The gas station here is the last place to get gas on the north shore (and they have the prices to prove it!). Across the street is the **Hanalei Lookout**. Many postcards have been sold featuring this view, though they sometimes let vegetation block the scene. This valley is where most of the taro in Hawaiʻi is grown. Taro corm (the root portion) is pounded to make poi. This is the stuff everyone told you not to eat when you came to Hawaiʻi. If you go to a luʻau, try it anyway. Then you can badmouth it with authority.

HANALEI

Going down the road, you come to the old-style **Hanalei Bridge**. Its wood planks are slippery when wet. This is a good time to tell you about Kauaʻi's one-lane bridge etiquette. All vehicles (up to seven or eight) on one side proceed, so if the car directly in front of you goes, you go. Otherwise, stop and wait for cars on the other side to go first. Most bridges from here on have one lane. Hanalei Bridge has a 15-ton weight limit, so you won't see big tour buses past this point. One bridge, called the Waipa Bridge, was built in 1912 for $4,000. It's so sturdy that it has *never* needed a major repair. The state found this intolerable and planned to replace it with a $5 million bridge that would hopefully require *lots* of maintenance. Local residents banded together in the late '90s and successfully fought 'em off. It was eventually replaced after the flooding of 2018.

The area around **Hanalei Bay** (meaning wreath-shaped or crescent-shaped) is a pretty little community. The surfing here is famous throughout the islands for its challenging nature during the winter. The entire bay is ringed by beach. A wide assortment of people live in Hanalei, including longtime locals, itinerant surfers, new age types, celebrities and every other type of individual you can imagine. You're as likely to see locals driving a Mercedes or a Tesla as you are a car held together with bungee cords and duct tape.

After Hanalei, you ascend the road to a turnout overlooking **Lumahaʻi Beach** (if the vegetation next to the turnout is not overgrown). This is a fantastic-looking beach made famous when Mitzi Gaynor washed that man right out of her hair in the classic Kauaʻi-made movie *South Pacific* in 1957. (If you haven't seen the movie, that last statement must sound awfully stupid.) The eastern portion is the best

Sunset from Hanalei Pier.

but requires a hike down. Otherwise, you can walk right onto it just before the **Lumaha'i Stream**.

Notice how lush everything looks from here on? This part of the island gets the perfect amount of rain and sunshine, making anything green very happy.

HA'ENA

Wainiha Beach Park, past mile marker 6, is often a great place to beachcomb, but the swimming is not good. Check out our review on page 103.

One of the best **snorkel** and shore SCU-BA spots on the island, **Tunnels Beach**, is past mile marker 8. (See *Beaches* on page 102.) This is the same spot that the world renowned surfer, Bethany Hamilton, lost her arm to a tiger shark in 2003. Her story got the Hollywood treatment in the film *Soul Surfer*. Don't let this deter you from seeing this amazing beach. See *Hazards* on page 32 for reassurance.

Before you get to mile marker 9, the road dips at **Manoa Stream**. The stream flows over the road and is always creating potholes. It often creates a hole big and deep enough to pop your tire, so look for it as you cross.

You are now at **Ha'ena Beach Park**. The beach is lovely year round (but the *swimming* isn't always lovely; see our record in *Beaches* on page 102).

Across the street from Ha'ena Beach Park is the **Manini-holo Dry Cave**. Manini-holo was said to be the chief fisherman for the Menehune. He and other Menehune dug the cave looking for supernatural beasts called akua who had been stealing their fish, but they didn't find *da buggah*.

Below mile marker 9 is a pile of rocks, all that remains of a heiau that was destroyed when they built the road. Called **Hale Pohaku**, it was where they raised small white dogs that served two purposes. One was food for the chiefs. The other was for chiefesses who gave birth. Often times children born to important chiefesses were removed and raised by others. So the small dogs would have their teeth pulled so they could nurse from the chiefesses to relieve the pressure in their breasts from the milk. If you look around, you'll find that one of the rocks has a petroglyph of a dog still on it.

Past mile marker 9 you will come to **Limahuli Stream**. Many people (including us) use this stream to rinse off the saltwater after their day at Ke'e Beach, which is still ahead, or use it to rinse SCUBA gear after a dive at Tunnels.

Above Limahuli Stream is the Limahuli Garden (808-826-1053). It is part of the National Tropical Botanical Garden. They have guided tours (by reservation only) of the gardens for $40, self-guided tours for $25 Tuesdays through Saturdays. The va-riety of endangered plants is refreshing. A real treat is the ancient terrace system, crafted by some of the earliest Hawaiians, estimated to be 700 years old and in fantastic condition.

Just past the Limahuli Stream you come to a parking lot. The last .3 miles of highway is closed to vehicles. In order to park here you need to reserve it pretty far in advance,

The Day of the Deluge

In a place where rainfall can sometimes be heavy, nobody could imagine a rain event of such unprecedented magnitude that life on the north shore would be altered for an entire year.

In Hawai'i, most of the heavy rains occur in the mountains, because as the trade winds encounter the rising slopes, the air cools, condenses and sheds moisture in the form of rain. It's called orographic—or mountain-caused—rain, and it's why we have so many pretty waterfalls. But in April 2018, a perfect combination of conditions conspired to unleash rains that have never been recorded anywhere in the United States since records have been kept.

Rains had been heavy the day before, but starting at midnight on April 15, 2018, under nearly continuous lightning, rainfall of biblical proportions fell for the next 24 hours on the north shore. Not just in the mountains, but also at the shoreline, with one of the rain gauges recording just a hair shy of 50 inches in a single day.

The results were devastating. Homes were destroyed, and landslides covered (and even removed) the highway in several sections. Past Hanalei, all residents were cut off from the rest of the island. The only way in and out was by boat. It took weeks just to clear enough road for vehicles to get through, but the damage was so severe that it would take over a year to fix the highway. One of the issues was that part of the mountain had replumbed itself after the flooding, and now after even modest rains, short-lived waterfalls that never occurred before drop water onto stretches of highway that were not engineered to divert the water. So during the repairs, outside traffic was not allowed in, and local residents were not allowed to drive unescorted. And so began the convoys.

Imagine you lived past Hanalei. And imagine that for a year the only way to get to and from your home was to line up with all the other cars at certain times and ride in a government-led convoy. Locals became a slave to the convey schedule, and tensions flared between residents and local authorities. But the bright side for them was that they had the north shore all to themselves. No visitors, not even residents from other parts of Kaua'i, were allowed in. When the convoys weren't running, the streets, beaches and parks were empty. We spoke to north shore residents who said they hoped the road would never open again. But all emergencies come to an end, and the end of the road was built for all to enjoy, not just residents.

usually *at least* a month. The reason is that the end of the road at **Ke'e Beach**, called **Ha'ena State Park** and **Na Pali Coast State Park** (ahead) was being loved to death by more visitors than the park could handle. So the state decided to start limiting the number of visitors. In order to visit Ke'e now you need to get permits online at go-haena.com. It's $5 per person. If parking permits are available, it costs $10 until 12:30 p.m. and another $10 for parking from 12:30 p.m. until 5:30 p.m. (though your parking fee does cover entry for you and your passengers). If parking permits are *not* available, you can catch the shuttle (gohaena.com) from Hanalei at the **Waipa Park & Ride** (between mile markers 3 and 4). But it's a pricey $35 *per person* to use the shuttle to visit the park. If you're doing any overnight camping along the **Kalalau Trail** (see *Adventures* on page 203) and have the appropriate permits, you are not subject to the reservation system or the visitor limit (they already counted you). Hawai'i residents are not subject to these reservation requirements.

From the parking you might see a trail across the street (and it may be closed) that leads to one of the two **Wet Caves**, called **Waikapala'e Cave** and **Waikanaloa Cave**. The upper Waikapala'e Cave contains a clean, freshwater pool. Until some years ago the back portion of the cave (reachable only by swimming in the cold water) hid a phenomenon called the **Blue Room** (a chamber where the light turned everything blue). But the water level is now too low, and too much light has erased the blue from the blue room. The wet and dry caves are former sea caves, gouged by waves when the sea level was higher than it is today. We were silly enough to SCUBA dive the upper cave and can report that there is not much to see, but it was kind of fun anyway (and spooky when we swam past where you could see the light entering the cave). Hawaiian legend has it that these caves were dug by the fire goddess Pele. She dug them for her lover but left them when they became filled with water. The lower cave, right off the closed part of the highway, can be visited when you return from Ke'e Beach.

From the parking lot a boardwalk meanders 0.3 miles to **Ke'e Beach** at the end of the road. Ke'e is marked by a fabulous lagoon that offers great swimming and snorkeling when it's calm. The well-known

A REAL GEM

Walk the shoreline trail past Ke'e Beach for a great view of Na Pali.

Kalalau Trail begins here. Eleven miles of hills and switchbacks culminate in a glorious beach setting, complete with a waterfall. The first leg of the hike leads to **Hanakapiʻai Beach** with a side trip to **Hanakapiʻai Falls**. You sure ain't gonna do this trail on a whim, so for more on the Kalalau Trail, see what we say in the *Adventures* on page 203.

Keʻe is where **Na Pali Coast** begins. You can see its edges from here. Numerous movie scenes have been filmed at this location. If you walk past Keʻe Beach on the shoreline trail beside the rocks (when seas aren't raging), you'll get an enticing look at the rugged **Na Pali coastline**. Look up toward the mountains, and you'll see **Bali Hai** (Hawaiian name **Makana Peak**). Clever photography turned the peak into the mystical island of Bali Hai in the movie *South Pacific*. As you stare at this peak with its incredibly steep sides, picture the following scene that took place in ancient times.

Men would climb the 1,600-foot peak carrying special spears made of hau and papala. The trail was so difficult in spots that they had to cling to the side of the mountain for dear life. When it got dark, they would light the spears and hurl them as hard as they could toward the ocean below. The spears were designed to leave a fire trail behind and were light enough to get caught in the updrafts. The light show was immensely popular.

From the end of Keʻe Beach, a trail cuts through the jungle up to the **Ka-ulu-Paoa Heiau**, still visible by the pavement of stones outlining its foundations next to a lava cliff. All the land here is state or county, even the rundown house in the jungle (despite an oddly out-of-place "Private Property" sign on land deeded to the county *decades* ago). But nearby residents—and sometimes bull-horn-equipped lifeguards—not legally authorized by the state to control access, often dissuade people from walking on this public land to the heiau due to its sacred nature. Whether they have the authority or not, if you are dissuaded, you should respect their wishes. For over 1,000 years this heiau served as the most important and prestigious school for hula in the islands. Would-be students came from around the island chain to learn from the *kumu hula,* or hula master. Please don't disturb any rocks lying about. Just past the heiau a short trail leads to a small waterfall (which is merely a trickle during dry times). *Fifty* generations of hot, thirsty students came to this tiny waterfall, sat on these very rocks and talked about their lives, hopes, fears and dreams. It's humbling to share these rocks with their spirits. It's as if you can still hear the echo of their lives in the sound of the gurgling water.

Just east of Ke'e is where the infamous Taylor Camp used to be. This is where Howard Taylor, brother of the late Elizabeth Taylor, owned a piece of land in the 1960s and encouraged other "hippies" to come and live off the land. The camp swelled to more than 100 people who mostly ended up living off residents or the government. Before the state condemned the property in 1977, camp residents began what would become the national *puka shell* craze when one of the residents fashioned a necklace of shells and gave it to Howard, who in turn gave it to his famous sister Liz.

NORTH SHORE BEST BETS

Best Beach—Ke'e or Hideaways
Best Snorkeling—Tunnels, Hideaways or Ke'e
Best Treat—Apple Cobbler at Village Snack & Bakery
Best Lava Swimming Pool—in the Queen's Bath
Best Secluded Beach—Waiakalua
Best Swimming When Calm—Ke'e
Best Shore Scuba Dive—Tunnels Beach
Best Beachcombing—Wainiha Beach
Best View—Sunset from Ke'e Overlooking Na Pali, or from Hanalei Pier
Best Parking Spot—One of the Few Available at Tunnels
Best Place to Gas Up *Only When Desperate*—76 Station in Princeville
Best Place to be Glad You're Wearing Comfortable Shoes—The End of the 11-Mile Long Kalalau Trail

Shave Ice: An Island Delicacy

One local treat everyone should try is shave ice. Lest you be confused, shave ice is not a snow cone. Snow cones are made from crushed ice with a little fruit syrup sprinkled on. True shave ice (that's shave, *not* shaved*) uses a sharp blade to literally "shave" a large block of ice, creating an infinitely fine powder. (Keeping the blade sharp is vital.) Add to this copious amounts of exotic fruit flavors, put it all on top of a big scoop of ice cream, and you have an island delight that is truly* broke da mout.

In our constant quest to provide as thorough a review as possible, we have unselfishly tried nearly every combination of shave ice. The result: We recommend the rainbow shave ice with macadamia nut ice cream. But by all means, engage in research of your own to see if you can come up with a better combination. The best shave ice on the island is at Hee Fat General Store *in Kapa'a,* JoJo's Shave Ice *in Waimea and* Wishing Well Shave Ice *in Hanalei. See full reviews in the* Island Dining *chapter.*

Wailua is known as the Coconut Coast.

Kaua'i's east shore is where the majority of the population resides. The kings of yesteryear chose the Wailua River area to live, making it forever royal ground. All members of Kaua'i royalty were born in this area. Kuamo'o Road, designated as 580 on the maps, is also called the King's Highway. In ancient times only the king could walk along the spine of this ridge. (Kuamo'o means the lizard's spine.)

Today, the east shore is often referred to as the **Coconut Coast**. One drive through Wailua and it's obvious why: thousands of coconut trees planted over a century ago by an idealistic young German immigrant who dreamed of overseeing a giant copra (dried coconut) empire. Unfortunately, nobody told him how long coconut trees took to mature, and the plantation was not economically successful, but his legacy lives on in the form of a gigantic coconut grove. These trees have already lived longer than their expected lifespan, so the grove is starting to thin out a bit. The resort across from Wailua Beach ensconced in all those coconut trees was called **Coco Palms**. It got whacked by a hurricane on September 11, 1992, and has been closed ever since. Even with its rich Hawaiian history (and even though Elvis Presley filmed *Blue Hawai'i* there), none of its subsequent owners has been able to figure out a way to reopen it, though the current owner has ambitious plans.

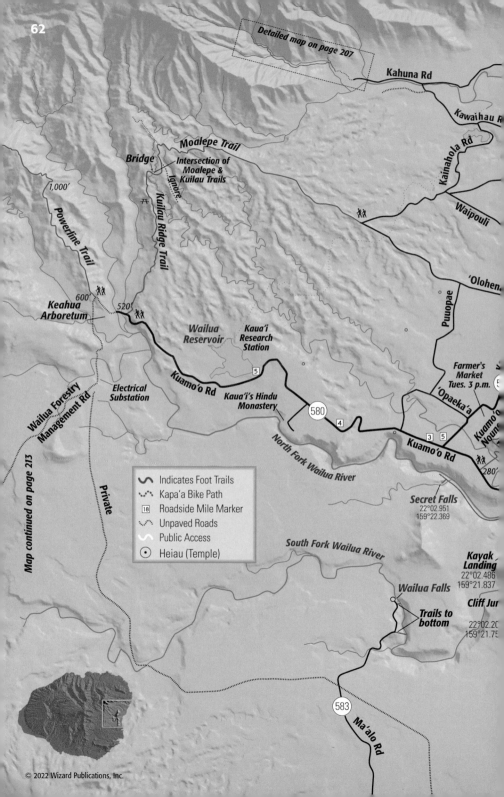

Detailed map on page 207

Kahuna Rd

Kawaihau Rd

Kainahola Rd

Waipouli

Moalepe Trail

Bridge

Intersection of
Moalepe &
Kuilau Trails

Ignore.

'Olohena

1,000'

Powerline Trail

Kuilau Ridge Trail

Puuopae

600'

Keahua
Arboretum

520'

Wailua
Reservoir

Kaua'i
Research
Station

Farmer's
Market
Tues. 3 p.m.

Wailua Forestry
Management Rd

Electrical
Substation

Kuamo'o Rd

5

Kaua'i's Hindu
Monastery

580

4

'Opaeka'a

3 5

Kuamo'o
Ngun

Kuamo'o Rd

280'

Map continued on page 213

Private

North Fork Wailua River

Secret Falls
22°02.951
159°22.369

Indicates Foot Trails
Kapa'a Bike Path
18 Roadside Mile Marker
Unpaved Roads
Public Access
Heiau (Temple)

South Fork Wailua River

Kayak
Landing
22°02.486
159°21.837

Wailua Falls

Cliff Jur

Trails to
bottom

22°02.20
159°21.75

583

Ma'alo Rd

© 2022 Wizard Publications, Inc.

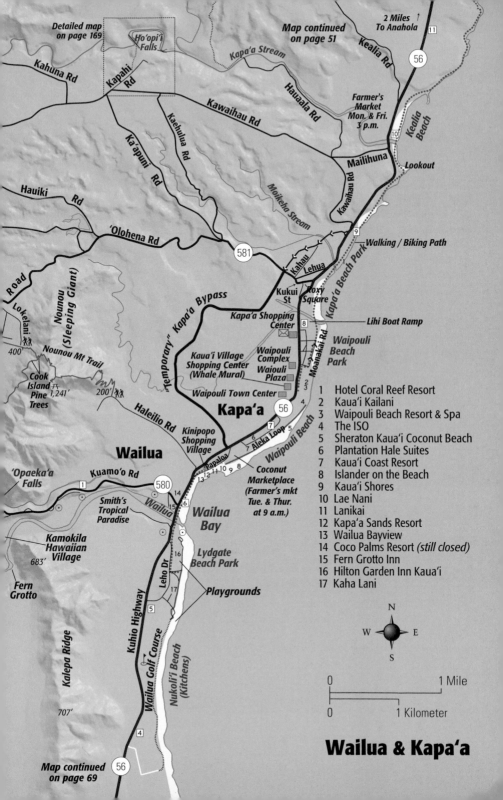

Map continued on page 51

2 Miles ↑ To Anahola

Detailed map on page 169

Ho'opi'i Falls

Kapahi Rd

Kahuna Rd

Kealia Rd

56

Kapa'a Stream

Kawaihau Rd

Hauaala Rd

Kealia Beach

Farmer's Market Mon. & Fri. 3 p.m.

Kaehulua Rd

10

Ka'apuni Rd

Mailihuna

Lookout

Hauiki Rd

Moikeha Stream

Kawaihau Rd

'Olohena Rd

581

9

Walking / Biking Path

Kahau

Lehua

Road

Nounou (Sleeping Giant)

Lokelani

"Temporary" Kapa'a Bypass

Kukui St

Roxy Square

400'

Nounou Mt Trail

Kapa'a Shopping Center

8

Lihi Boat Ramp

Cook Island Pine Trees 1,241'

200'

Kaua'i Village Shopping Center (Whale Mural)

Waipouli Complex

Moanakai Rd

Waipouli Beach Park

Waiouli Plaza

Haleilio Rd

Waipouli Town Center

Kapa'a

56

1   Hotel Coral Reef Resort
2   Kaua'i Kailani
3   Waipouli Beach Resort & Spa
4   The ISO
5   Sheraton Kaua'i Coconut Beach
6   Plantation Hale Suites
7   Kaua'i Coast Resort
8   Islander on the Beach
9   Kaua'i Shores
10 Lae Nani
11 Lanikai
12 Kapa'a Sands Resort
13 Wailua Bayview
14 Coco Palms Resort (still closed)
15 Fern Grotto Inn
16 Hilton Garden Inn Kaua'i
17 Kaha Lani

Waipouli Beach

Kinipopo Shopping Village

Wailua

'Opaeka'a Falls

Kuamo'o Rd

1

580

Papaloa

Aleka Loop

Smith's Tropical Paradise

Wailua

13 12 11 10 9   8

14

15

Coconut Marketplace (Farmer's mkt Tue. & Thur. at 9 a.m.)

Kamokila Hawaiian Village

683'

Wailua Bay

6

16

Lydgate Beach Park

Leho Dr

Fern Grotto

17

Playgrounds

Kuhio Highway

5

Kalepa Ridge

Nukoli'i Beach (Kitchens)

Wailua Golf Course

N
W   E
S

0 ——————— 1 Mile
0 ——————— 1 Kilometer

707'

4

Map continued on page 69

56

Wailua & Kapa'a

For our description, the east shore means the Wailua/Kapa'a area to Lihu'e. (Take a look at the inside back cover map to orient yourself.) Both areas are heavily populated. (This is a relative term; together they have about 25,000 residents.)

The same descriptive ground rules that we discussed at the beginning of *North Shore Sights* apply here.

Unlike other areas of the island where a single road dominates your tour, this area has many significant sights located off the main road. Therefore, we will describe them in a more scattershot manner and generally work our way from north to south.

WAILUA/KAPA'A

In the extreme northern part of Kapa'a is a delightful waterfall called **Ho'opi'i Falls**, which you can hike to. See *Hiking* on page 169.

While we are up the road off the main highway, there are several hikes in this area that provide excellent views. The **Nounou Mountain Trail** (also called the **Sleeping Giant**), the **Kuilau Ridge Trail**, the **Jungle Hike** and the **Secret Tunnel to the North Shore** are all located inland and all are worthy of consideration. (See *Hiking* in *Activities* for more.)

One aspect of ancient Hawaiian culture that can be seen to this day is the heiau, a structure carefully built from lava rocks and used for religious purposes. There are seven heiau stretching from the mouth of the **Wailua River** to the top of **Mount Wai'ale'ale**. The mouth of the Wailua River was well known, not only throughout the Hawaiian Islands, but also in parts of central Polynesia as well. Ancient Polynesians are thought to have come all the way from Tahiti to visit it.

Wailua is also known for ghosts and spirits. It was thought that during a certain phase of the moon, spirits of those who had recently died would paddle down the river in large numbers and work their way around the island to a cliff at Polihale (described on page 93) where they would leap to the next life. Known as **night marchers**, these ghosts are still believed by many Hawaiians to exist, and sightings are most prevalent along the highway between Wailua and Lihu'e. Interestingly, this stretch of road has also been responsible for many bad car accidents. Of course, police blame the wrecks on another type of spirit—the kind that comes in a bottle.

The first heiau, near the mouth of the Wailua River on the southern side, is called **Hauola, City of Refuge**. It is part of what was a larger structure called **Hikina-akala**, meaning the rising of the sun. If a person committed an offense worthy of execution (such as allowing his shadow to touch the shadow of a chief or interrupting an important person), he would attempt to elude his executioners by coming here. By staying at the site and performing certain rites prescribed by the priest, he would earn the right to leave without harm.

The second temple is on the *mauka* side of the highway between the north end of Leho Road and the road to **Smith's Tropical Paradise**. This is called **Malae** and at 273 by 324 feet, it is the largest heiau on Kaua'i. Legend states that it was built by Menehune. There is not a lot to see. If you decide to visit it, be wary of your footing.

The third heiau is just up Kuamo'o Road (580) on the left side. This area had several names and several functions. The first portion that you see is called **Holoholoku**. Some archeologists say that this area was used for human sacrifice. Most of the time those sacrificed were prisoners of war. If none could be found, however, the kahuna would select a com-

Kealia Beach is so easy to access, local residents even drive onto the sand at the south end.

moner and have the executioner strangle him secretly at night. Some archaeologists find this interpretation of Hawaiian history in spiritual bad taste, given its very close proximity to the Birthstones, described below, and assume that the area was used for animal sacrifices. The heiau was later purposely desecrated and used as a pigpen by the wife of the last king of Kaua'i, who did so as a signal that the ancient religious ways should be abandoned in favor of Christianity.

Just a few dozen feet up the road from **Holoholoku** are the **Birthstones**. It was essential that all kings of Kaua'i be born here, even if they were not of chiefly origin. One of the two stones supported the back of the mother-to-be while the other was where she placed her legs while giving birth. The outline of stones near here indicates where a grass shack once stood, where the pregnant mother stayed until it was time to give birth. The flat slab of sandstone that you see on the ground covered the remains of a sacrificed dog, indicating that the place was kapu,

or forbidden to commoners. The giant crack in the rock wall was where the umbilical cord of the newborn was placed. If a rat came and took the cord, it was a sign that the child would grow up to be a thief (or worse, a tax collector); otherwise, all was well.

Continuing up 580, a short way past mile marker 1, there's a dirt road angling back toward the ocean. (You're allowed to walk around the yellow gate.) Located at the end of the road are two large boulders probably surrounded by weeds. Though few residents are aware of it, the rocks' position is no accident and dates back over 1,000 years.

The ancient Hawaiians didn't live in a world of well-defined seasons. They didn't even measure their own lives in years, but rather stages of life. But they did need to keep track of the passage of the sun for planting and religious reasons. These two multi-ton rounded and shaped **Solstice Rocks** are perfectly offset so that if you align yourself with them so they appear to touch with the right one closer to you,

Lacy 'Opaeka'a Falls is a Wailua landmark. At press time you could only see half due to invasive species trees blocking it. If the state cuts them down, it will look like the photo inset.

the sun will rise from the intersection on the summer solstice. (Winter solstice involves aligning the right side of the left boulder with the thumb-like hill on Sleeping Giant behind you.) Imagine the importance they must have attributed to this task by considering the difficulty of hauling these boulders up from the Wailua River, perhaps one boulder from each fork for symmetry. (Hawaiians *loved* symmetry.)

Past those boulders, if you walk down the path about 100 feet past the guardrail, there are several large stones. One of them was known as the **Bellstone** and, if thwacked properly, can produce a metallic clank (not the gong we have come to expect from metal bells). This sound supposedly carried throughout the entire Wailua Valley. The stone was struck in ancient times to signal the birth of what

would be a new chief. Unfortunately, the state has allowed vegetation to swallow up the giant solstice rocks, and the Bellstone is so overgrown you'd need to buy a machete and hire a Menehune guide to find it.

Still on 580 just before you get to the 'Opaeka'a Falls turnout is the last heiau you will see. Called **Poli'ahu**, this is a rather mysterious heiau and the one that is most worth your time. Legend states that it was built by Menehune, the legendary people of small stature, and was devoted to the interests and activities of the gods, demigods and high ali'i. There is also a nice **Wailua River Lookout** here.

The actual final heiau in this chain rests atop the rain-soaked plateau of **Wai'ale'ale**. The remnants of this most sacred heiau are still visible today. Called **Ka'awako**, the altar itself stood 2 feet high, 5 feet wide and 7 feet long. Toward the rear, standing on one end was a phallic stone. It is located on one of the wettest spots in the entire world. According to the USGS, this spot receives 432 inches of rain per year. (You read a lot of numbers about the annual rainfall on Wai'ale'ale—this number comes straight from the people who read the rain gauges. The original gauge is in the Kaua'i Museum.)

The ancient Hawaiians were bothered that the small, sacred pool on top of Wai'ale'ale didn't feed their most sacred river, the Wailua. Not to worry. In a project that would make the Army Corps of Engineers proud, they cut a trench at the top of the mountain from the small pool to the edge of the cliff so the water would add to the waterfalls that feed the Wailua River. Then they could say the most sacred pool fed the most sacred river.

While on Kuamo'o Road (*a well-known speed trap*), stop by the 'Opaeka'a Falls Lookout. These lacy 151-foot **NOT TO BE** falls flow year round. Late morning light is best, around 10:30 a.m. There is another **MISSED!** Wailua River Lookout across from the 'Opaeka'a Lookout.

Kamokila Hawaiian Village (808-823-0559) is across the street from 'Opaeka'a Falls. It's 4.5 acres of private land with numerous huts scattered about. Some might find it interesting; others might get antsy, but it's only $5 per person to get in and wander around. It'll probably take 40 minutes or less to see it, and it's certainly *not* indispensable. If you are guided, it will be *very* slow paced, but delivered

from the heart. You can also rent a canoe, stand-up paddleboard or kayak (all for $35) for a trip to Secret Falls from here. (See *Kayaking* on page 175.)

Further up Kuamo'o Road, past some hairpin turns, is a road on the left called Kaholalele. At the end is **Kaua'i's Hindu Monastery** (888-735-1619). This is an *incredible* place, but they only give free 90-minute tours by reservation once a week. (It varies depending on the Hindu calendar—call for dates, and you may want to call again the day before to confirm you will actually get to see the temple up close. They sometimes close it without warning depending on the type of work they are doing.) It's set in an absolutely idyllic environment next to the Wailua River. This temple is built entirely of hand-carved stones from India. Some stones take as long as seven years to carve, and there are 4,000 of them. And their special Roman-inspired fly ash concrete foundation is designed to be crack-free for a thousand years. (When we had our driveway paved, they guaranteed it *would* crack within a month—

These petroglyphs are usually submerged in the mouth of the Wailua River, but they can appear after heavy rains.

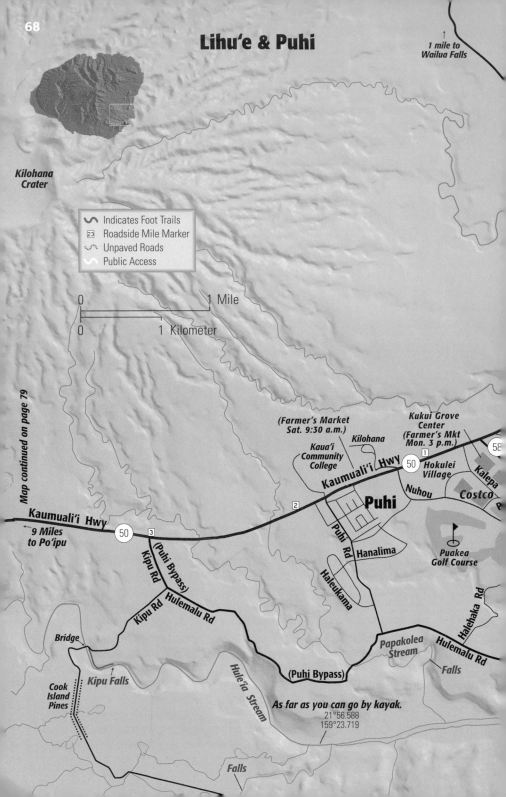

Lihu'e & Puhi

1 mile to
Wailua Falls

*Kilohana
Crater*

Indicates Foot Trails
23 Roadside Mile Marker
Unpaved Roads
Public Access

0   1 Mile

0   1 Kilometer

Map continued on page 79

(Farmer's Market
Sat. 9:30 a.m.)

Kukui Grove
Center
(Farmer's Mkt
Mon. 3 p.m.)

Kaua'i
Community
College

Kilohana

58

1

50 Hokulei
Village

Kalepa

Kaumuali'i Hwy

Nuhou

Puhi

Costco

2

Kaumuali'i Hwy

50

← 9 Miles
to Po'ipu

50

3

Puhi Rd

Hanalima

Puakea
Golf Course

(Puhi Bypass)

Kipu Rd

Haleukama

Halehaka Rd

Kipu Rd Hulemalu Rd

Bridge

Papakolea
Stream

Hulemalu Rd

Kipu Falls

Falls

(Puhi Bypass)

Huleʻia Stream

*Cook
Island
Pines*

As far as you can go by kayak.
21°56.588
159°23.719

Falls

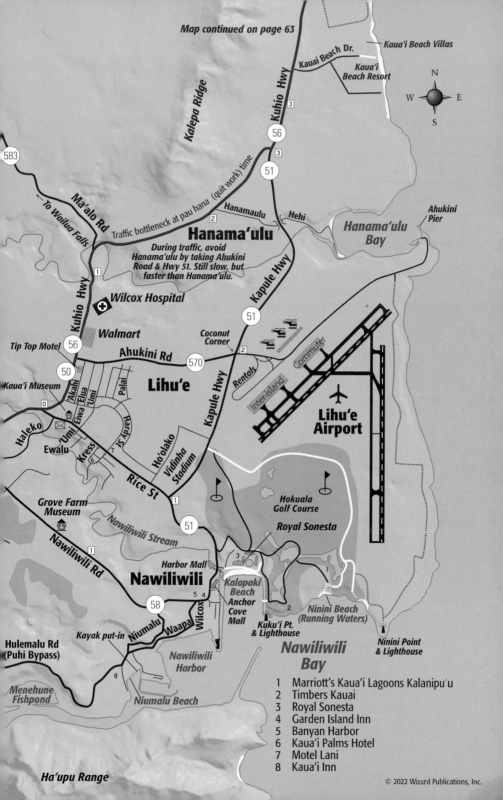

Map continued on page 63

Kaua'i Beach Villas

Kauai Beach Dr.

Kaua'i Beach Resort

Kuhio Hwy

N
W E
S

583

Kalepa Ridge

56

3

51

3

Ma'alo Rd

To Wailua Falls

Traffic bottleneck at pau hana (quit work) time

Hanamaulu

Hehi

Ahukini Pier

Hanama'ulu

2

Hanama'ulu Bay

During traffic, avoid Hanama'ulu by taking Ahukini Road & Hwy 51. Still slow, but faster than Hanama'ulu.

Kuhio Hwy

1

Wilcox Hospital

Kapule Hwy

51

Tip Top Motel

56

Walmart

Coconut Corner

Rentals

Commuter

50

Ahukini Rd

570

2

Inter-Island

Kaua'i Museum

'Akahi

Palai

Lihu'e

Kapule Hwy

Lihu'e Airport

0

'Umi

'Elua

'Umi

Hardy St

Haleko

Ewalu

'Umi

Ewa

Kress

6

7

Ho'olako

Vidinha Stadium

Rice St

1

Grove Farm Museum

Nawiliwili Stream

Hokuala Golf Course

51

Royal Sonesta

Nawiliwili Rd

1

Harbor Mall

3

1

58

Nawiliwili

5

4

Kalapaki Beach

Anchor Cove Mall

Ninini Beach (Running Waters)

Kayak put-in

Niumalu

Waapa

Wilcox

Kuku'i Pt. & Lighthouse

2

Ninini Point & Lighthouse

Hulemalu Rd (Puhi Bypass)

Nawiliwili Harbor

Nawiliwili Bay

Menehune Fishpond

8

Niumalu Beach

1 Marriott's Kaua'i Lagoons Kalanipu'u
2 Timbers Kauai
3 Royal Sonesta
4 Garden Island Inn
5 Banyan Harbor
6 Kaua'i Palms Hotel
7 Motel Lani
8 Kaua'i Inn

Ha'upu Range

© 2022 Wizard Publications, Inc.

A construction site like no other at Kaua'i's Hindu Monastery. Begun in 1990, every stone is hand carved in India, they still aren't finished, and yes—that's real gold.

and it did.) They say it's the only pure stone temple being built anywhere in the world and should be complete sometime during this decade, but their narrative, details and completion date seem to change with every visit. They have a strict dress code, so wear long pants and shirts with short or long sleeves or use one of their free sarongs. Hindu worshipers can visit at 9 a.m., other visitors between 10:30 a.m and noon. If you get a chance, a tour is highly recommended, though we've noticed that when groups get too large, the quality suffers. They also have self-guided tours that'll only take 10 minutes or so. You won't see the temple, though you'll get to check out their incredible sprawling banyan tree. An interesting gift shop featuring all things Hindu. Bring mosquito repellent.

Continuing several miles up Kuamo'o Road, the road eventually crosses a bridge and becomes unpaved. The second crossing is literally *in* the stream, and it occasionally flows too heavily over the road to cross in your car. See the detailed map on page 213. A 4WD is often a necessity beyond the stream crossing while regular cars are at the mercy of the maintenance cycle of the road and the weather. (Sometimes the wimpiest Neon can make it; other times pre-maintenance ruts become too much for some 4WDs.) Large puddles are usually lined with small rocks, not mud. Several trailheads are in this region. A pretty one, before the road becomes unpaved, is the **Kuilau Ridge Trail**. The **Keahua Arboretum** is located near here, but it's been rather unkempt for years, so don't knock yourself out to see it.

The unpaved section of this road is **Wailua Forest Management Road**. The area feels like a giant oxygen factory. Take a big whiff, and you'll almost get a buzz from the purity of the air. The **Jungle Hike** on page 168 and the **Secret Tunnel to the North Shore** on page 213 are back here, as well as stunning forests. This area is excellent for mountain biking.

Back on the main highway, you'll find that traffic in downtown Kapa'a (on the highway) can get congested at times, *espe-*

cially going south. The county opened up a "temporary" bypass road across from **Coconut Marketplace** on the south end, and up mauka from the ABC store at the north end. (See map on page 62.) The "permanent" bypass road is scheduled to be completed sometime during the next ice age. All the land around the bypass area was for sale some years back. Kaua'i residents were worried that someone would buy the 1,400 acres and develop it, connecting Kapa'a to Wailua and creating a big-city feel. Entertainer Bette Midler (a part-time resident) bought it instead and promised never to put anything other than trees on it.

One of Kapa'a's notable views is the **Sleeping Giant**. The best angle is from the small turnout kitty-corner from the Texaco station (on the main highway). Look *mauka* and you will see the outline of a giant. (This is your *ink blot* test for the day.) According to legend, the giant you see (you *do* see it, don't you?) was a friendly sort who flattened areas where

he sat. Local villagers liked this and also planted bananas in his footsteps. One day the chief ordered a heiau to be built. Villagers were too busy, so the giant volunteered. It took two weeks and he did a great job. Villagers threw a party to celebrate, and the giant ate a bit too much. (If you've been to a lu'au, you can relate.) He fell asleep and has not been roused since, but is expected to wake up any time (maybe during your visit).

Local folklore says that if Kaua'i's people learned of an attempt to invade their island, they would light fires behind the Sleeping Giant in order to illuminate his profile at night. This would frighten invading warriors into thinking that Kaua'i had some really big dudes and that intruders should rethink their invasion plans.

While you are in Wailua, riverboat trips up the **Wailua River** can take you to the **Fern Grotto** for $30 per person. This is a natural amphitheater filled with ferns and is a popular place for weddings. See *River Trips* in the *Activities* chapter. The Wailua

At Kapa'a's Baby Beach, they sing,
"Mamas, don't let your babies grow up…without sunscreen."

River is usually called the only navigable river in all Hawai'i, but that depends on your definition of navigable. The mouth of the river has several stones with ancient **petroglyphs** carved in them. After heavy rains, the river sometimes washes away large amounts of sand, revealing these stones for a short period of time. The mouth itself is always changing, and watching it wash over its banks after a heavy rain can be wild. The river mouth can go from not flowing at all to carving up the mouth in a matter of hours.

There is a paved **beachside walking path** behind the Courtyard Kauai Resort at Coconut Beach, and a longer path from Kapa'a Beach Park north to Donkey Beach. They are great for a stroll or to ride a bike. A good place to take a *sandy* beach walk is from Lydgate Beach Park south as far as the Kauai Beach Resort. The sand is continuous almost the whole way.

Lydgate Beach Park is one of the safest places to swim on the island. It has a boulder-enclosed pond that allows water and fish in but keeps out the ocean's force. See *Beaches* on page 116. There is even a keiki (kid) pond, which is shallower. Add to this showers, restrooms and two playgrounds, and you have a nice little park for a day at the beach for those who don't want to expose themselves to the open ocean.

On the southern side of the Wailua River is **Smith's Tropical Paradise** (808-821-6895). Here you will find a nice garden (not in the same league as other nicer island gardens) in which to stroll, filled with tropical plants and wailing peacocks (which sound like cats being tortured). Entrance is $10 per person ($5 for children 3–12). They also hold a pretty good lu'au here. See page 262.

As you pass the **Wailua Municipal Golf Course** going south toward Lihu'e, realize that the entire coast fronting course is a sandy beach. Called **Nukoli'i Beach**, there are rarely more than a few people on it.

LIHU'E

Coming from Kapa'a and just before you enter Lihu'e from Highway 56, you see Ma'alo Road (583) on the *mauka* side. This leads to **Wailua Falls**. The state is so proud of this popular attraction they have devoted a whopping *four* parking spaces for cars and festooned the area with no parking signs, which seem to be universally ignored from what we've seen. In ancient times (and as recently as 2016, which you can see on YouTube), men would jump off the top of the falls to prove their manhood (which was often left on the rocks below). This test can be fatal. Government maps list the falls' height at 80 feet.

NOT TO BE MISSED!

That always bothered us because it sure *looks* taller. So, a while back we dropped a fishing line and sinker to the bottom from the lip of the falls (boy, did *we* look stupid) and measured it. To our amazement, it was 173 feet of solid drop. (We measured it *twice* to be sure.) That's actually taller than Niagara Falls, though the latter has a tad more water flowing.

You might see people splashing about in the pool below the falls. It's a wonderful scene and lots of fun. Those people got down there by hopping the stone wall (at the far end of the lookout, away from the falls) and then walking behind the chain link fence about 100 feet to a steep trail with exposed tree roots for handholds. That, or they took the less steep trail 0.3 mile back down the road from the end of the turn-around. (See map on page 63.) The latter is easier but requires a much longer walk and includes awkward river walking. Neither are profes-

Wailua Falls is one of the easiest falls on the island to access—just drive up and gawk.

sionally maintained, and both can be slippery when wet. The state, in their paranoia about liability, has erected signs telling you not to take the trails to the bottom. They even cut the ropes (but users keep replacing them) that get strung to make it safer and easier. (Making it *less* safe apparently makes some bureaucrats *feel* safer.) Those people below ignored the signs—and might be local residents who have played at the bottom of the falls for generations—but state bureaucrats don't want you down there, so you should stay on top.

The falls plunge into a pool that's 33 feet deep. Why so exact? Because in one of those *just because* moods (before the state put up the signs), we hiked down with some friends, hauling scuba gear (gee, those ropes sure did help), and SCUBA-dived the pool. (We also brought a kayak—what were we *thinking?*) There we found 14-inch long small-mouthed bass and some Tahitian prawns with bodies over 8 inches long, plus arms. Lingering beneath the falls, the scene is like an upside-down battlefield with explosions of white that will cause percussive waves to sweep through your entire body, your air-filled chest shuddering from the blasts. We also found rental car keys (perhaps tossed by an irate but shortsighted spouse), bolt cutters, a cane knife, and other odds and ends.

Back on the highway, if we're just trying to get *through* Lihu'e during traffic, we usually take 51 to 570 (Ahukini Road) to Hwy 56. (See map on page 69 for this to make sense.) It bypasses Hanama'ulu and much of Lihu'e.

In Lihu'e, one place worth stopping for if you have a strong love of culture and history is the **Kaua'i Museum** (808-245-6931) on Rice Street. This isn't exactly the Smithsonian, but they have a mildly interesting display of Hawaiian artifacts and a permanent display called *The Story of Kaua'i* as well as other rotating displays. Their gift shop is well stocked with books, maps and assorted items. If you are looking for topographic maps of the various areas (serious hikers prefer these as traveling companions) or just an obscure book on Kaua'i or Hawai'i, this is a good place to stop. Admission is $15 per person unless you are going to the gift shop, which is free.

If museums ain't your cup of tea, maybe a pint of beer is. One of Hawai'i's best breweries is a little farther down Rice Street just past Kress Street. The **Kaua'i Beer Company** brews several tasty adult beverages as well as their own root beer. See *Island Dining* for more info.

Taking Rice Street east leads you to **Nawiliwili Harbor**. There are two shopping centers here called **Harbor Mall** and **Anchor Cove Shopping Center**. **Kalapaki Beach**, behind Anchor Cove, is a good place to watch sailboats, outrigger canoes and cruise ships, in addition to the beach's other attributes.

On Rice Street, you will pass the main entrance to the **Royal Sonesta Kaua'i Resort**. Its other entrance is off Kapule Highway (51) and leads through **Hokuala Kaua'i** to either **Ninini Beach/Running Waters Beach** or the **Ninini Lighthouse**. The lighthouse uses a 4.7 million candlepower light. We remember how that sounded like *a lot* the first time we heard it, until we realized you can go to the store and buy *15 million* candlepower flashlights for $30. To get to the lighthouse, you pass a golf course.

Rice Street loops around and becomes Nawiliwili Road. It is here that you will find **Grove Farm Sugar Plantation** (808-245-3202). This was the private home of George N. Wilcox and his nieces. It was turned into a museum by Mabel Wilcox shortly before her death in 1978. With 80 acres and several buildings to browse through, it is quite popular. (And they make an awesome sugar cookie here.) Groups of about six are escorted around the grounds and house for 2 hours for $20 per person. Even if this isn't normally your cup of tea, you will probably find it interesting. It's the story of an incredible family's rise to prominence in the old, sugar-dominated Kaua'i. Reservations are required. Tours on Mondays, Wednesdays and Thursdays.

Off Nawiliwili Road is Wa'apa Road. Take this road to Hulemalu Road, and you will come to a scenic overlook for the **Menehune (Alekoko) Fishpond**. This is a large, impressive fishpond adjacent to the **Hule'ia Stream**. According to legend, it was built in one night by the Menehune as a gift for a princess and her brother. Estimates of its age range as high as 1,000 years. Today, it is privately owned and has fallen into disrepair as a fishpond. Nonetheless, it is a remarkable landmark that is worth a look.

Back on the main highway (which has changed its name to Hwy 50, the Kaumuali'i Hwy), you'll find yourself heading south. Before mile marker 1 is **Kukui Grove Shopping Center**, the biggest shopping center on the island. It's more geared toward locals but might have something to offer you. Past it is our island **Costco**.

Past mile marker 1 you will see **Kilohana** (808-245-5608) on your right. This was the home of Gaylord and Ethel Wilcox and has been lovingly restored to its former glory. Gaylord Wilcox was

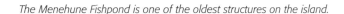

The Menehune Fishpond is one of the oldest structures on the island.

manager of the Grove Farm Plantation. Walk through the door of this 16,000-square-foot mansion, and you get a sense of Kaua'i in days past. The furniture, fittings and motif all harken back to a simpler day when sugar was king. Inside is a good restaurant called **The Plantation House by Gaylords**, as well as several shops, galleries, a lu'au and the tasting room for **Koloa Rum**, distilled here on the island. Their spiced rum is the best we've ever tried. They also have a train ride for $20 that kids ($14) might enjoy. See page 37 for more on that.

Across from mile marker 3 on the main highway is Kipu Road, which also acts as a bypass road. Located off this road is a glorious little waterfall called **Kipu Falls**. Though people have been swinging off a rope swing and jumping into the pool here for over a century, and though you may read about it elsewhere, the current landowner does *not* allow access. There is now a fence to keep you out and trust me—they *don't* want you here due to safety and liability concerns. In 2011 these falls became notorious in the islands when a bill passed through the state house that would have effectively *ended all travel writing of any kind* about Hawai'i because of controversy (in part) over access to these falls. So do everyone a favor: Keep the peace, and stay away from Kipu Falls.

If you were to continue on Kipu Road, you would quickly come to a magnificent strand of Cook Island pines. These trees were highly valued as ship's masts in the Age of Discovery. This entire area is called **Kipu** and is currently leased to the Rice family and the Waterhouse Trust. William Hyde Rice was a cattle rancher, and a monument to him was erected here by his Japanese workers. Behind Ha'upu mountain is the fabulous beach called

Kipu Kai. This long crescent of sand is a beachgoer's dream. Unfortunately, the only way to reach it is by boat or over the private road owned by Kipu Ranch and the Waterhouse Trust. This road is closed to the public, though you can get a glimpse of Kipu Kai from the ATV tour. John Waterhouse ordered that the 1,096 acres of leased state land revert to the state at the time of death of the last of his nieces (all in their 70s). We've tried walking to Kipu Kai from Ha'ula Beach. The horse path up and over the tall mountain is riddled with evil plants with thorns that turned our exposed legs to hamburger.

EAST SHORE BEST BETS

Best Beach Walk—Lydgate Beach Park to Kauai Beach Resort

Best View—From the Top of Sleeping Giant for Hikers; Sunrise over Lydgate for Non-Hikers

Best Place to Let Little Ones Swim in the Ocean—Baby Beach

Best Treat to Share with 10 Friends—One Slice of Hula Pie at Duke's Kaua'i

Best Hidden Gem—Ho'opi'i Falls

Best Uncrowded Beach—In Front of Wailua Golf Course

Best Playground—Kamalani Playground at Lydgate Park

Best Boogie Boarding—Kealia Beach

Best Evening Stroll—Paved Beach Path between Kapa'a Beach Park and Kealia

Best Lu'au—Smith's Tropical Paradise or Kalamaku at Kilohana

Best Way to Spend Seven Years—Carving One Stone for the Kaua'i Hindu Monastery

Best Place to Grab a Drink and Head to the Beach—Poolside Bar at Islander on the Beach

Best Place to Make Your Pupils Big—Mile-Long Secret Tunnel to the North Shore

The Tree Tunnel is your entrance to the South Shore. You can thank a wealthy resident who had all these trees left over from his gardening project.

The sunny south shore... where rainfall is less frequent, and sunshine is abundant. Many people prefer the sunnier quality of the south shore to the lushness of the north shore. Fortunately, you can have it all.

For the sake of this discussion, we will consider the south shore as everything past Puhi to Kalaheo. (Look at the inside back cover map.) Past Kalaheo, the character of the island changes again, and we will cover that in the *West Shore Sights* chapter.

The same descriptive ground rules that we discussed at the beginning of *North Shore Sights* applies to this chapter.

All beaches we mention are described in detail in the *Beaches* chapter.

Driving to Po'ipu from Lihu'e along the main highway, you will pass through the **Knudsen Gap** between mile markers 6 and 8. A century ago this was the scariest part of the island. The small gap between the mountains was the only route you could take to the south shore and was a perfect place for an ambush. Even the local sheriff always dreaded going through the Knudsen Gap.

Past mile marker 6 you will come to Hwy 520, or Maluhia Road. This road to Koloa and Po'ipu is called the **Tree Tunnel**. When Walter Duncan McBryde was landscaping his home in the early 1900s, he found that he had over 500 eucalyptus trees *left over*. He donated these trees,

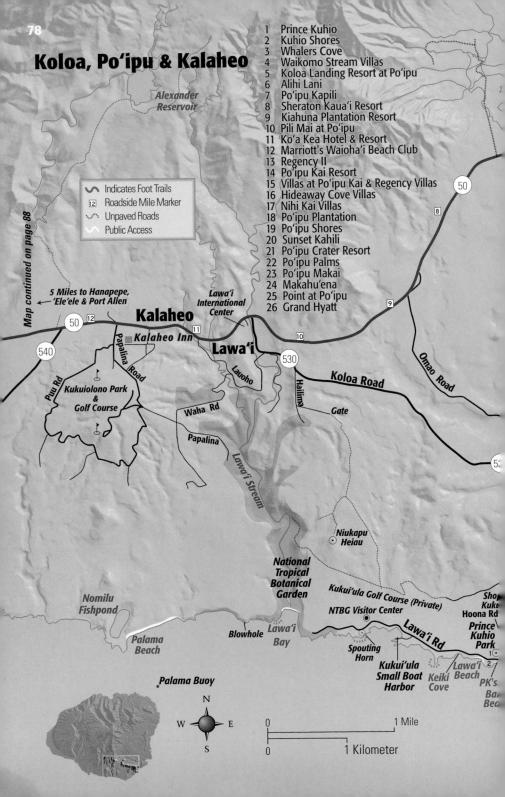

Koloa, Po'ipu & Kalaheo

1 Prince Kuhio
2 Kuhio Shores
3 Whalers Cove
4 Waikomo Stream Villas
5 Koloa Landing Resort at Po'ipu
6 Alihi Lani
7 Po'ipu Kapili
8 Sheraton Kaua'i Resort
9 Kiahuna Plantation Resort
10 Pili Mai at Po'ipu
11 Ko'a Kea Hotel & Resort
12 Marriott's Waioha'i Beach Club
13 Regency II
14 Po'ipu Kai Resort
15 Villas at Po'ipu Kai & Regency Villas
16 Hideaway Cove Villas
17 Nihi Kai Villas
18 Po'ipu Plantation
19 Po'ipu Shores
20 Sunset Kahili
21 Po'ipu Crater Resort
22 Po'ipu Palms
23 Po'ipu Makai
24 Makahu'ena
25 Point at Po'ipu
26 Grand Hyatt

Alexander Reservoir

⌇ Indicates Foot Trails
12 Roadside Mile Marker
⋯ Unpaved Roads
⌇ Public Access

Map continued on page 88

5 Miles to Hanapepe, 'Ele'ele & Port Allen

Lawa'i International Center

50 12

Kalaheo

■ Kalaheo Inn

11

540

Papalina Road

Puu Rd

Kukuiolono Park & Golf Course

Waha Rd

Papalina

Lawa'i

530

Lauoho

Hailima

Koloa Road

Gate

Omao Road

50

8

9

10

Lawa'i Stream

Niukapu Heiau

National Tropical Botanical Garden

Kukui'ula Golf Course (Private)

NTBG Visitor Center

Sho Kuk
Hoona Rd

Prince Kuhio Park

Nomilu Fishpond

Palama Beach

Blowhole

Lawa'i Bay

Spouting Horn

Kukui'ula Small Boat Harbor

Keiki Cove

Lawa'i Beach

Lawa'i Rd

PK's
Ba
Bea

1

2

• Palama Buoy

N
W   E
S

0 ———————— 1 Mile

0 ———————— 1 Kilometer

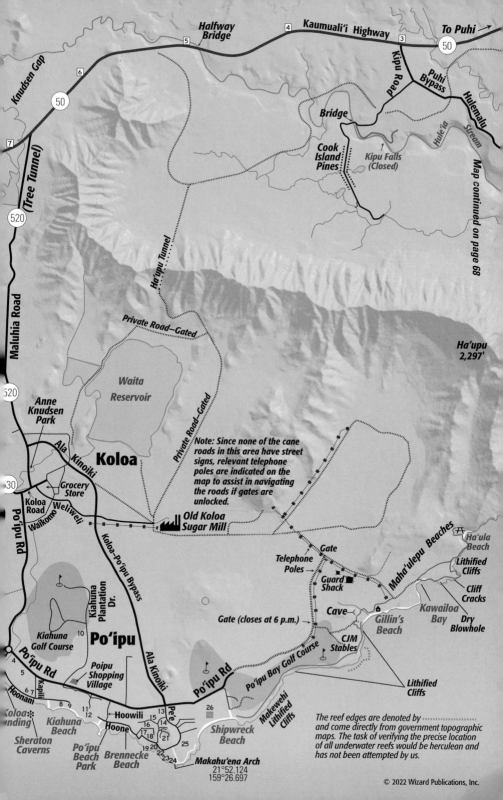

Halfway Bridge

Kaumuali'i Highway

To Puhi

50

Knudsen Gap

50

Puhi Bypass

Kipu Road

Hulemalu

Bridge

Cook Island Pines

Kipu Falls (Closed)

Hule'ia Stream

Map continued on page 68

(Tree Tunnel)

520

Ha'upu Tunnel

Private Road–Gated

Ha'upu 2,297'

Maluhia Road

Waita Reservoir

520

Anne Knudsen Park

Private Road–Gated

Koloa

Note: Since none of the cane roads in this area have street signs, relevant telephone poles are indicated on the map to assist in navigating the roads if gates are unlocked.

Ala Kinoiki

30

Grocery Store

Koloa Road

Weliweli

Waikomo

Old Koloa Sugar Mill

Gate

Telephone Poles

Guard Shack

Maha'ulepu Beaches

Ha'ula Beach

Lithified Cliffs

Cliff Cracks

Po'ipu Rd

Koloa-Po'ipu Bypass

Kiahuna Plantation Dr.

Gate (closes at 6 p.m.)

Cave

Gillin's Beach

Kawailoa Bay

Dry Blowhole

Kiahuna Golf Course

10

Po'ipu

Ala Kinoiki

CJM Stables

Lithified Cliffs

Po'ipu Rd

4

Poipu Shopping Village

Po'ipu Rd

Po'ipu Bay Golf Course

Kapili

5

Hoonani

6 7

Koloa Landing

8 9

11 12

Hoowili

Pe'e

Makewehi Lithified Cliffs

Lithified Cliffs

Kiahuna Beach

Hoone

13

15 16 17 18

19 14 21

20 22 23 24

26

Shipwreck Beach

The reef edges are denoted by ···········
and come directly from government topographic maps. The task of verifying the precise location of all underwater reefs would be herculean and has not been attempted by us.

Sheraton Caverns

Po'ipu Beach Park

Brennecke Beach

25

Makahu'ena Arch
21°52.124
159°26.697

© 2022 Wizard Publications, Inc.

The south shore is all about beaches and resorts and snorkeling and... well, that about covers it.

called swamp mahogany, to the county. Many residents showed up to help plant the trees. The result is the **Tree Tunnel**. (Part of it was torn down in the '50s when they rerouted the highway.) The beginning part is the most beautiful; farther south the branches don't intertwine at the top the way they did before either Hurricane 'Iwa in 1982 or 'Iniki on September 11, 1992.

KOLOA

Driving down Hwy 520 you come to the town of Koloa, sometimes called Old Koloa Town. This was the first sugar plantation town in all the islands when Kamehameha III leased the land to Ladd and Company in 1835. The town has much charm and is worth a stop. Perusing the historic plaques and taking in the sights can be done in an hour. Next to the **Crazy Shirts** store there is a marvelous **monkeypod tree** whose branches seem to meander forever.

Across the street (kitty-corner) from the shops are the remnants of an **old sugar mill** built over 170 years ago. There you will also find a plaque dedicated to the sugar plantation workers and a good (if somewhat dated) synopsis of sugar history on the island.

Looking at the map on page 79, you will see a road leading to **Waita Reservoir** and **Ha'upu Range Tunnel**. They are gated and not available to visit unless you book an ATV or 4WD van tour. We used to think these gates were a relatively modern annoyance until we stumbled across an old local newspaper from 1934. In a letter to the editor the writer warned people not to accept an invitation from a well-known plantation manager when he said he "wanted to show you something interesting." Apparently the crafty manager did this whenever he had a long way to drive and wanted to have somebody along to open and close all the gates.

PO'IPU

Continuing to Po'ipu on Hwy 520 and doglegging onto Po'ipu Road, watch your speed. This is a notorious **speed trap** and sobriety checkpoint area, and the limit is 25 mph, slowing to 15 mph near the school. (The Koloa-Po'ipu Bypass shown on the map on page 79 is an even more effective speed trap because you are easily lulled into going over 40 mph.)

Past mile marker 4 as you approach Po'ipu, the offshoot on the far side of the traffic circle instead takes you onto Lawai Road where you'll come to **Prince Kuhio Park**. (Enter the park from the left side of the wall.) There you will find a monument to Prince Kuhio, the last royally designated heir to the Hawaiian throne. He went on to become a delegate to Congress until the early 1920s. In this park you will also find the Ho'ai Heiau, impressive in its perfection and almost chiseled appearance. The entrance is toward the rear on the left side.

The palm trees between here and Baby Beach often fill dramatically at sunset with vast numbers of non-native parakeets, who leave just as suddenly at sunrise. They will spend the night clinging to the bottom of the fronds in even the strongest of winds.

Continuing along Lawa'i Road, you will come to **Spouting Horn Beach Park**. **NOT TO BE MISSED!** This wonderful delight is a small lava shelf where water from waves is thrust through an opening, causing water and air to squirt out a blowhole.

This particular site distinguishes itself from other blowholes around Hawai'i in that it has an additional hole that blows only air, causing a loud moaning and gasping sound. Legend has it that the entire coastline in this area was once guarded by a giant female lizard called a mo'o. She would eat anyone who tried to swim or fish in the area. One day a man named Liko went fishing. The mo'o went to attack Liko, who threw a spear into the mo'o's mouth. The angry mo'o chased Liko into the lava tube. Liko escaped, but the mo'o became trapped in what we now call Spouting Horn, where its cries of hunger and pain can be heard to this day.

The Spouting Horn was formerly dwarfed by an adjacent blowhole called

Spouting Horn is often more dramatic at high tide.

the Kukui'ula Seaplume. That seaplume would shoot much higher—as high as 200 feet into the air. But on an early Sunday morning back in the 1920s a sugar company manager ordered one of his workers to drop blasting powder into the hole to widen it so the plume wouldn't shoot into the air. The reason? The salt spray from the geyser was stunting the growth of 10 acres of cane (among the company's many thousands of acres), and the manager would not stand for that. Looking down on the lava shelf you can see its remains in the form of a large rectangular aperture to the left of the current blowhole opening.

The view from the lookout can be quite dramatic during large, summer swells. (Watching the spout from Kukui'ula Small Boat Harbor across the bay can be more picturesque, especially at sunset.) At one time you could walk down onto the lava bench, but there have been incidents where people have been swept to their deaths into the Horn. Now you can be fined for going past the guardrail.

If you ever happen upon another blowhole in Hawai'i where there are no signs forbidding you to get close, *never* stand between the hole and the ocean. A very large wave would have no difficulty dragging you in. Some years ago two visitors from San Francisco were knocked in while they stood between the Spouting Horn and the ocean. One was *on crutches* at the time. They were lucky—rather than being crushed inside the hole, they were immediately sucked out of the blowhole and into the open ocean where they were rescued by some phone workers on their break.

Just before Spouting Horn is the entrance to the National Tropical Botanical Garden. This incredibly beautiful garden consists of 252 acres called the McBryde Garden and 80 acres called the Allerton Garden (808-742-2623). Even if you normally wouldn't visit a garden, you'll probably like this one. See *Land Tours* in the *Activities* chapter.

Going back the way you came, just before the fork is a road leading to Koloa Landing. This is a popular SCUBA shore dive. Until the 1900s this was Kaua'i's main port. Whaling ships used to winter here, and all goods brought to Kaua'i came through either Koloa Landing or Waimea.

Going back to the traffic circle, take the branch toward Po'ipu, which is turtle country. Look out at the water for any reasonable length of time, and you'll see green sea turtles swimming nearby. This area was developed in the '70s and '80s and has become a much sought-after visitor destination. Swanky hotels and condominium resorts line the road. The beaches in this area are fantastic, with the

best of the best located past the resorts at a place called Maha'ulepu. This beach (see *Beaches* on page 117) sports lots of places to walk and some incredible sandstone cliffs. The dirt roads around here can be good places to ride mountain bikes. Horseback riding, snorkeling, fishing and more are all available in this area. The lithified cliffs from Maha'ulepu to Shipwreck Beach offer delicious shoreline hikes. See *Hiking* on page 171.

One thing that totally escaped our attention until an alert reader pointed it out to us was the presence of a cool-looking lava arch at the shoreline between the Point at Poipu Resort and Makahu'ena at the southern tip of the island. Park at Pe'e and Oluolu Streets and walk toward the shoreline. If that fenceline boundary of Makahu'ena condos were to continue, it would lead to the arch. Don't let the ocean smack you around here.

These lithified sand dunes of Maha'ulepu are a stunning testament to the power of the ocean.

There's lots of cactus along this part of the island. It was imported in the 1800s because it made a perfect natural cattle fence—and you don't even need to repair it.

KALAHEO

After Lawa'i comes Kalaheo. There are a handful of good restaurants and shopping opportunities here (including some pretty good pizza—see *Island Dining*). One of Kalaheo's lesser known gems is the Kukuilono Park & Golf Course (see *Golfing* in the *Activities* chapter). This is the private course and garden donated by Walter McBryde to the people of Kaua'i. If you want to try your hand at golf, this is the place to learn. The price is $15 *per day* (cash only). The small Japanese garden located on the course was Mr. McBryde's pride and joy. This is

where he chose to be buried, near the 8th tee.

Although it was sugar that drove the economy along here for over a century, it was phased out in the 1990s to grow coffee, on the assumption it would be more profitable. It struggled for years, and the company was sold in 2011 to the same Italian coffee conglomerate that owns Hills Bros. The Kaua'i Coffee Company has 3,100 acres under cultivation. To be honest, it's not very good coffee. Most of the trees are an unimpressive breed called *yellow catuai*. Don't confuse it with the *far* superior coffee grown on the Kona coast of the Big Island where the coffee-growing environment is ideal. Also, most Kaua'i coffee is machine-picked, so beans slightly under and over their peak get picked in the process. Kaua'i Coffee has smaller

Semi-protected Po'ipu Beach Park is one of the many beaches that blesses the south shore.

Watch your step around these ficus roots at the Allerton Garden in Lawa'i. This beast of a tree was planted from a sapling in 1952. Now you know why they call this the Garden Island.

fields of *blue mountain,* and *red catuai,* which is better, but it's expensive, and we've only found this coffee at their visitor center located on Hwy 540 just past mile marker 12 on Hwy 50. That 4-mile-long road, sometimes called the Coffee Highway, cuts through much of the coffee plantation. The visitor center is popular with tour buses but is only marginally interesting, and their museum is particularly scant. Only for hard-core coffee groupies.

Incidentally, any fixed-wing pilot on the island will tell you they *love* coffee trees. Their leaves are dark and dense, which capture the sun and heat the air around them. This makes them exceptional gen-

erators of thermal currents, providing free lift when the heated air rises.

Just after mile marker 14 you will come to the Hanapepe Valley Lookout. As you gaze over the peaceful vista, it's hard to believe that this was the scene of the bloodiest and most savage battle known to have taken place on Kaua'i. The embittered son of Kaua'i's last king started a revolt against government rule. Remember that Kaua'i had never been conquered by Kamehameha the Great. Both of his invasion attempts had been costly in terms of men, and neither had even reached Kaua'i in large numbers. Even though Kaua'i's last king voluntarily accepted Kamehameha's rule, it forever stuck in the royal craw that Kaua'i had not been *forced* into submission. So when this revolt occurred, it was a perfect excuse to send Hawai'i troops over to show those Kauaians who was boss. Government troops sent to put down the revolt were unimaginably brutal, and their methods were reviled even among their supporters. Men, women and children were needlessly slaughtered, and the wanton killing continued for 10 days.

Everything past here is covered in the *West Shore Sights* chapter.

SOUTH SHORE BEST BETS

Best Strolling Beach—Maha'ulepu
Best Short Cliff Stroll—To the Left of Shipwreck Beach near Hyatt
Best Snorkeling—Around the sandy point at Po'ipu Beach Park
Best Sunset View—At Spouting Horn

Best Hot Dog—Puka Dog
Best Treat—Chocolate Gelato at Lappert's
Best Place To Watch Fools Jump Off A Cliff—Shipwreck Beach in Front of the Hyatt Po'ipu
Best Secluded Beach—Ha'ula Beach
Best Swimming—Po'ipu Beach Park
Best Pizza—Brick Oven Pizza
Best Beachcombing—Kawailoa Bay
Best Golf—Po'ipu Bay Golf Course
Best Hotel Grounds—Grand Hyatt
Best Chance of Seeing a Beached Monk Seal—Po'ipu Beach Park
Best Massive Burrito to Go—Da Crack
Best Romantic Restaurant—Tidepools at Grand Hyatt or Beach House at Sunset
Best Place for a Sunset Cocktail—The Sheraton Kauai Resort

Ni'ihau Shell Lei

The women of Ni'ihau carry on a tradition dating back centuries. With indescribable patience, they collect tiny Ni'ihau shells, then clean, drill, string and pack them with fiber, creating fabulous leis. This is no easy task. An entire day's labor often reaps only four or five useable shells. And it requires thousands of shells to make a lei. Some women only search for shells at night, believing that the sunlight dulls the shell's luster. While costing from several hundred to several thousand dollars each, this is a relative bargain given the amount of labor that goes into one. It can take several years to complete the more ornate leis. The result is a perfect, handcrafted and tightly packed lei representing one of the last truly Hawaiian art forms. There are fewer and fewer people on Ni'ihau who are willing to participate in this process, and many consider it a matter of time before this art form will be lost.

If you purchase one, the best selection on the island is at the **Hawaiian Trading Post** *(808-332-7404) on the corner of Highways 50 and 530 (Koloa Road) in Lawa'i. Make sure it was actually made on Ni'ihau, and not a copycat made on Kaua'i.*

One last caveat: If you buy one, do it for yourself. It would be crushing to spend all that money only to show your lei to someone and have 'em say, "Oh, yeah, I got one for free at Hilo Hattie's." While Ni'ihau shell leis are infinitely more beautiful, some might not appreciate the difference.

Polihale is where the Na Pali coastline gives way to 12-plus miles of uninterrupted sand beach.

If the south shore is called the sunny south shore, western Kaua'i should be called the *very* sunny west shore. That's because rain is very scant indeed, and the temperature is 3 to 4 degrees hotter than most of the rest of the island. The first two things visitors notice on this side of the island are the relative aridity of the land and the red color of the soil. Trade winds coming from the northeast lose the bulk of their rain on Mount Wai'ale'ale, creating a rain shadow on the west side. Unless there are Kona winds (meaning from the south or west), you can pretty much be assured that it will be dry and sunny on the west side. The red dirt is especially vibrant because of the high iron content of our volcanic soil. This combined with lots of

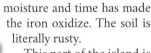

moisture and time has made the iron oxidize. The soil is literally rusty.

This part of the island is dominated by two attractions: the 12.5-mile-long sand beach stretching from Waimea to Polihale and the incredible Waimea Canyon in the interior.

HANAPEPE

As you drive along the main highway leaving Kalaheo, you will come to the **Hanapepe Valley Lookout**, described in the *South Shore Sights* chapter. After you go through 'Ele'ele (where many of the boat tours depart), you come to Hanapepe. Called Kaua'i's "Biggest Little Town," Hanapepe is but a shadow of its former self. It was founded by Chinese rice farmers in the mid- to late 1800s. They were

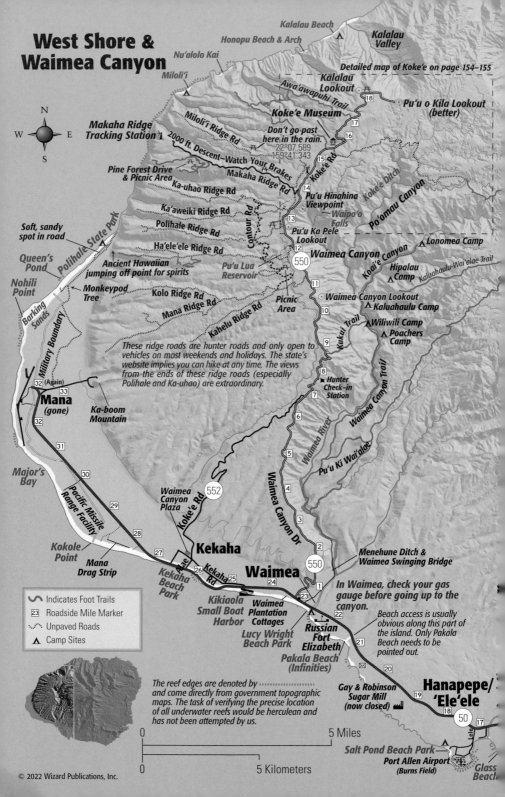

West Shore & Waimea Canyon

Kalalau Beach

Honopu Beach & Arch

Kalalau Valley

Nu'alolo Kai

Miloli'i

Kalalau Lookout

Awa'awapuhi Trail

Detailed map of Koke'e on page 154–155

Pu'u o Kila Lookout (better)

Koke'e Museum

Makaha Ridge Tracking Station

Miloli'i Ridge Rd

18

Don't go past here in the rain.

17

22°07.589 159°41.343

16

2000 ft. Descent—Watch Your Brakes

Koke'e Rd

Pine Forest Drive & Picnic Area

Makaha Ridge Rd

15

Ka-uhao Ridge Rd

14

Pu'u Hinahina Viewpoint

Ka'aweiki Ridge Rd

Contour Rd

Waipo'o Falls

Koke'e Ditch

Po'omau Canyon

Polihale Ridge Rd

13

Pu'u Ka Pele Lookout

Soft, sandy spot in road

Ha'ele'ele Ridge Rd

12

Waimea Canyon

550

Koai'e Canyon

Lonomea Camp

Queen's Pond

Ancient Hawaiian jumping off point for spirits

Pu'u Lua Reservoir

Hipalau Camp

Kaluahaulu-Wai'alae Trail

Nohili Point

Monkeypod Tree

Kolo Ridge Rd

11

Waimea Canyon Lookout

Kaluahaulu Camp

Polihale State Park

Picnic Area

10

Wiliwili Camp

Poachers Camp

Mana Ridge Rd

Kahelu Ridge Rd

Kukui Trail

9

These ridge roads are hunter roads and only open to vehicles on most weekends and holidays. The state's website implies you can hike at any time. The views from the ends of these ridge roads (especially Polihale and Ka-uhao) are extraordinary.

8

Hunter Check-in Station

7

32 (Again)

33

Mana (gone)

Ka-boom Mountain

6

Waimea River

Waimea Canyon Trail

32

5

Major's Bay

31

Pu'u Ki Wai'alae

30

4

Waimea Canyon Plaza

552

Koke'e Rd

29

3

28

Waimea Canyon Dr

Kokole Point

27

Mana Drag Strip

Kekaha

2

Menehune Ditch & Waimea Swinging Bridge

26

Kekaha Rd

25

Waimea

550

24

In Waimea, check your gas gauge before going up to the canyon.

Kekaha Beach Park

1

23

22

Beach access is usually obvious along this part of the island. Only Pakala Beach needs to be pointed out.

Kikiaola Small Boat Harbor

Waimea Plantation Cottages

Lucy Wright Beach Park

Russian Fort Elizabeth

21

Pakala Beach (Infinities)

20

Hanapepe/ 'Ele'ele

Gay & Robinson Sugar Mill (now closed)

19

50

18

17

Legend

〰	Indicates Foot Trails
23	Roadside Mile Marker
⋰	Unpaved Roads
⋀	Camp Sites

The reef edges are denoted by ••••••••• and come directly from government topographic maps. The task of verifying the precise location of all underwater reefs would be herculean and has not been attempted by us.

Salt Pond Beach Park

Port Allen Airport (Burns Field)

Glass Beach

0 ——— 5 Miles

0 ——— 5 Kilometers

© 2022 Wizard Publications, Inc.

opium-smoking bachelors, and underground opium shops could be found there as recently as the 1930s. Hanapepe was the only non-plantation town on the island, and it gained a reputation as Kaua'i's wildest spot. A 1924 riot killed 16 Filipino workers and four police officers in town. Despite the violence, this was also a flamboyant place that had as many bars as churches. It began to decline in the late '70s, and the 1982 opening of Kukui Grove Shopping Center in Lihu'e marked the end of an era for Hanapepe's business community.

A good analogy for Hanapepe today is that of an old chair. While some people look at an aged stick of furniture and see a priceless antique, others see a decrepit, used item to be replaced by a newer one. Depending on your outlook, you will either find downtown Hanapepe charming or see it as a quasi-ghost town. Although Hanapepe is rising out of the ashes with some nice rehabilitation work, during most of the week we probably agree with the ghost town description. If you have a few minutes to spare, you might want to blow through downtown to decide for yourself. There are several shops and galleries you might want to explore, including the **Talk Story Bookstore**, which lays claim to the title of "the westernmost bookstore of the United States" with a good collection of Hawaiiana. Friday night is **Art Night**, and it's when the town really wakes up with live music, good food options, craft vendors and a changing roster of other activities. There's a **swinging bridge**

over the **Hanapepe River** that replaced the old bridge that swung off during the 1992 hurricane.

This area is where most of Kauai's power is generated. People assume that, living on a tropical island, we must have some exotic way of making our electricity. Sorry to burst your bubble, but we burn oil for about 60% of it—it's just that simple—and we have the electricity bills to prove it! The rest comes from burning wood chips, solar and a bit of hydro.

If you take Lele Road (Hwy 543), you come to **Salt Pond Beach Park** where folks continue the time-honored craft of making salt out of seawater (see *Beaches* on page 122). This park usually offers very safe swimming as well as **restrooms**. (Hard to find in this area.)

Before you get to Waimea, you will see a road to **Fort Elizabeth** just past mile marker 22. (The sign has been misspelled for years.) Here are the vague re-

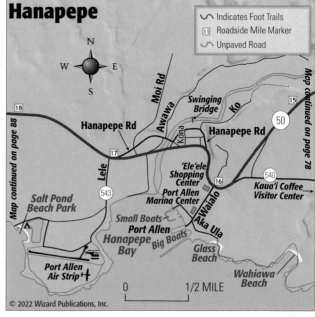

Hanapepe

Indicates Foot Trails
11 Roadside Mile Marker
Unpaved Road

Map continued on page 88

Map continued on page 78

Moi Rd
Awawa
Kona
Swinging Bridge
Ko
18
Hanapepe Rd
Hanapepe Rd
50
17
15
'Ele'ele Shopping Center
Lele
Port Allen Marina Center
16
540
Salt Pond Beach Park
543
Small Boats
Waialo
Kaua'i Coffee Visitor Center
Port Allen
Big Boats
Aka Ula
Hanapepe Bay
Glass Beach
Port Allen Air Strip
Wahiawa Beach
0   1/2 MILE

© 2022 Wizard Publications, Inc.

mains of a **Russian fort** built in 1816 by George Scheffer.

Scheffer was a German-born doctor working for a Russian company. A difficult, quarrelsome and conceited man, he had a habit of eventually alienating most people he met. (Know the type?) He did make a good *first* impression, however, and managed to sufficiently impress a Russian official, who sent Scheffer to Hawai'i to ingratiate himself with King Kamehameha and recover a lost ship's cargo. When Kamehameha eventually became suspicious of Scheffer, the German moved on to Kaua'i. There he found a receptive King Kaumuali'i who, although he had officially given his kingdom to Kamehameha, still resisted offshore rule. Kaua'i's king-in-name-only saw a chance to get the Russians involved and perhaps restore his power. The two men realized how much they could help each other and soon hatched plans to conquer the other islands using Russian ships. By this time Scheffer had become intoxicated by his status on Kaua'i and lost sight of the fact that he could not deliver on any of the promises he was making to Kaua'i's king. He built a second fort where Princeville is today and even renamed Hanalei Valley, calling it Schefferthal, with the king's blessing.

As Scheffer began building the Russian Fort in honor of Elizabeth, a Russian consort, his sponsors back in Russia were beginning to get a hint of Scheffer's tactics. They sent a ship to Hawai'i to tell Scheffer that he was to pack and leave the island. Scheffer ignored the message and continued building the fort. By this time Kaua'i's king was becoming suspicious, and a group of American businessmen saw an opportunity to rid the island of Scheffer and Russia. They started the rumor that Russia and America were at war. Kaua'i's king abandoned Scheffer, who fled the island in a leaky old ship and set sail for O'ahu. Once there, Scheffer was told he would be taken prisoner. He fled to Brazil where he changed his name to Count von Frankenthal and tried to lure colonists to his estate of the same name.

The dark sand at the mouth of the Waimea River beautifully contrasts with the ocean foam slithering into the river.

Why are we telling you all this? Because the story's more interesting than the actual site—little more than a perimeter of rocks from the foundation. (By the way, there are lots of bees here.)

If you drive through Fort Elizabeth and take the dirt road, you'll come to the **mouth of the Waimea River**. This can be a beautiful area to linger and watch the interaction of the ocean with the river, especially when the river flow is low. The dark, rich sand separating the ocean from the river is saturated with water from the river. White waves sometimes gently lap up and down the sand without sinking in, creating a delicate show of contrasts. You'll notice an olive green tint to the sand here. This is from a semi-precious gem called olivine, which the Waimea River tirelessly mines from its lava bed along with black flecks of lava, making the floor of the Waimea Canyon lower and lower in the process.

WAIMEA

Back on the main highway you come to the town of Waimea. This part of the island usually looks best (and greenest) in the winter. Off to your right you will see the **Captain Cook Monument**. It was in Waimea that the great explorer first set foot in Hawai'i in January 1778. (He was later killed on the Big Island in a petty dispute over a stolen rowboat.)

Travel 1.3 miles up Menehune Road on the *mauka* side of the highway to see the **Menehune Ditch**, a smooth, rock-lined irrigation ditch designed to bring water from the Waimea River to the taro fields. Only the top of a tiny section is now visible because previous road-builders literally *paved* right up to this ancient structure. It's mostly buried and not visually striking. But it's impressive to think that the rocks used for its con-

struction are said to have come from a quarry more than 6 miles away. This is one of the few Hawaiian relics that almost certainly wasn't created by the current race of Hawaiians who came from Tahiti around 1,000 ad. *That* group didn't cut and dress stones—as is the case at Menehune Ditch—they simply stacked them. This irrigation ditch is much older and was probably built by the initial inhabitants—the original "native Hawaiians"—who came from the Marquesas Islands around 500 ad. These first settlers lived a peaceful though less structured life until the Tahitian invaders displaced them and their culture 500 years later, establishing the Hawaiian culture we know today.

Across from the ditch is the **Waimea Swinging Bridge**. Like the one in Hanapepe, it, too, is a replacement for the old one blown away in 1992. *Sometimes* seedy characters hang out here making visitors feel unwelcome.

The **Waimea** (meaning red water) **River** is full of sediment that dyes the water red. All the beaches in the vicinity of the river are murky due to river runoff, and the swimming is correspondingly poor. According to legend, there was a beautiful chief's daughter named Komali'u who was sought after by many men in the village. One day a man named Mano asked her to marry him. When she refused, he killed her at a waterfall where her blood ran into the river. The chief named the village, canyon and river Waimea in memory of his daughter.

To help cool down while in Waimea you have a few frosty options. **JoJo's Shave Ice** (across from mile marker 23) is the go-to shave ice shop in town. If you're wanting a heartier and healthy option, **G's Juicebar** next to the **Waimea Theater** has some killer juices and smoothies.

KEKAHA

From Waimea, most people go up the road to the Waimea Canyon, but we will get to that later. Assuming you are continuing along the coast, you arrive in Kekaha. This is the last town on this side of the island. Past mile marker 25 the highway hugs the beach for 2 miles. It's a nice place to stop and enjoy views of Ni'ihau past mile marker 26, and beach access here is accomplished by simply falling out of your car onto the sand.

Waimea Canyon Plaza is the last area with food along here. The **Menehune Food Mart** has sandwiches and hot dogs. Things aren't as hideously expensive there as you'd expect, given the remoteness of the location.

While driving along the west side past Waimea, take note of the cliffs to your right. Those are former sea cliffs cut off from the sea. The land you are driving on is different than most other land in the island chain. It's not technically volcanic. When the massive **Waimea Canyon** (described later) was formed, the river carried the rock and soil out of the canyon where the ocean's current drove it along the shore to the northwest (as it still does today). Some of it washed up on shore. There it joined a gigantic amount of sand that was actually made by sea creatures *on the north shore* and transported down the Na Pali coast by the ocean. The result is one kickin' place to grow sugar—just ask the Robinsons, who grew thousands of acres of it here until 2009. In that year they shut down the island's last sugar mill, though some of the remaining sugar cane under cultivation is used by the **Koloa Rum Company** to make Kaua'i rum. The Robinsons, along with the state of Hawai'i, now lease 12,000 acres to several mainland seed companies that take advantage of the perfect year-round growing conditions to grow mostly GMO (genetically modified) seed corn and soybeans in the former sugar cane fields. They also raise shrimp on the makai side of mile marker 29, using a 500-foot deep well that taps into clean ocean water. **Kaua'i Shrimp** is available at some restaurants and from an outlet in downtown Hanapepe and is probably the tastiest shrimp we've found.

Many maps list a town farther north called Mana. It was once a thriving little community until the mid-1900s. This area was formerly marshy and famous for its mirages. Now the town of **Mana** is a mirage, nothing more than two mango trees and a mule. Some of its homes were moved and are now part of Waimea Plantation Cottages Resort. You can tell a former Mana cottage because it always had a door facing north and one facing south so passing spirits wouldn't get stuck inside.

From here on, the coastline is pure sand from the same north shore source described above. There's a great opportunity to have a huge stretch of sand to yourself along here. See **Kokole Point** in *Beaches* on page 124.

You will pass the **Pacific Missile Range Facility**. About every two months they do a Star Wars missile test. (When they fire missiles, rather than move the rockets, they literally move the building out of the way.) Offshore, submarine hunting exercises take place almost continuously. This is a repository for some of the most sophisticated sensing equipment in the world, and they are capable of detecting a bottle bobbing up and down in the choppy water. (But for some reason, when a fishing boat is missing in the area, they seem incapable of finding it.) Fronting part of the base is **Barking Sands Beach**. The sand grains at this beach have a thin coating of silica and are supposed to make a barking sound if you walk on them when conditions are

right. Access is a problem, though. See *Beaches* on page 124 for more.

A well-known surf site here is **Major's Bay**, so called because it's off the old commanding officer's quarters. *Hey, wait a minute. This is a Navy base. Isn't major an Army rank?* True, but it *used* to be an Army base, and the name stuck.

POLIHALE

Looking at the map on page 88, you'll notice that the highway ends after the first mile marker 32. Follow the map, and the first dirt road will take you to Polihale. (It's a public access, misleading signs notwithstanding.) On the very rare occasions that it rains heavily here, the road to Polihale can get pretty sloppy. (It also gets potholed at times, and officials at State Parks like to close it once in a while as they wait to rescrape it.) From the extreme northern end of the beach, the magnificent cliffs of **Na Pali** beckon you with their sheer majesty. The **dunes of Polihale** are up to 100 feet high. The *Beaches* chapter provides more information on **Polihale**.

As soon as you leave Hwy 50 on your way to Polihale, look at the mountain in front of you. It's a **military restricted area**.

Beware of large, low-flying birds at the south end of Salt Pond Beach.

They've bored caves into the mountain where they store ammunition, such as bombs and bullets. With so much explosives, you're about as welcome there as a pack of matches.

If it's summer, you might see kayaks coming (or rolling) in for a surf landing. From here you could walk to the left for 12.5 miles in the sand. (Maybe another day, huh?) Winds are usually calm here. There are facilities, including showers, restrooms and drinking water.

The Hawaiians believed that the cliffs at the end of **Polihale Beach**, called **Ha'ele'ele**, were the jumping off point for spirits or 'uhane leaving this world. There they would leave this life and join their ancestors forever. If there was no 'aumakua, or family of spirits, to receive them, they would wander around the area, attaching themselves to rocks and generally causing mischief. That's why it's considered unwise to take anything, such as stones, from this area. You may bring back a wayward spirit itching to get back home.

Splendid Waimea Canyon provides yet another facet of Kaua'i's personality.

WAIMEA CANYON & KOKE'E

Waimea Canyon is a spectacular gorge that defies description. Island legend states that when Mark Twain was here, he dubbed it "the Grand Canyon of the Pacific." (Unfortunately, when you read his biography, you find that when he visited Hawai'i, he never set foot on Kaua'i. Oops, there goes another urban legend.) Regardless, the layers evident on the sides of the canyon are reminiscent of the grander canyon in Arizona. Each layer represents a different eruption and subsequent lava flow. The canyon is 10 miles long, 1 mile wide and more than 3,600 feet deep.

To get to the canyon, take **Waimea Canyon Drive** from Waimea. They *want* you to go up from Koke'e Road in Kekaha because they hope you'll buy something there, but the views are better going up from Waimea. On your return from the canyon, you can take **Koke'e Road** (between mile markers 6 and 7) down for a different view of the coast.

Before you go up the road, check your gas gauge. There are no stations up there (but restrooms are available at the major lookouts), and you've got a 40-mile round trip ahead of you with a 4,000-foot elevation rise. The temperature is 10–15 degrees cooler up there, and a sweater or light jacket might be wise, depending on conditions. There are more good hiking trails in this area than anywhere in Hawai'i. For more hiking information in the Waimea/Koke'e area, see *Hiking* on page 151.

To reach the canyon, turn *mauka* onto Waimea Canyon Drive just past mile marker 23 near a church. The road twists and turns its way up the canyon's side. On the way, keep an eye out to the west for **Ni'ihau**. There are some great views of that private island from up here. (Even on cloudless days there's almost always a cloud over Ni'ihau. Its land mass causes them.) Past mile marker 10 is the **Waimea Canyon Lookout**. It costs $10 per vehicle to park plus a $5 per person entrance fee to enter the parks (the fees are good for both Waimea Canyon and Koke'e State Parks). This is one of several vantage points and definitely worth a stop. From here on, you will probably see lots of wild chickens about. They thrive in this environment.

NOT TO BE MISSED!

The canyon lookout is an awesome vista. At one time three rivers, fed from the island's center by the **Alaka'i Swamp** on Mt. Wai'ale'ale, all ran down the gently sloping shield volcano, emptying into the ocean at separate points like the spokes of a wheel. That's what created the now-dry valleys you see on your way out to Polihale. When a fault caused the collapse of part of the volcano's flank, the three rivers were forced to combine as they ran down into the fault. This new, opportunistic river carved a place for itself in the splintered and fractured lava flows. The results are extraordinary.

As you drive upward, there are numerous areas along the road from which to view the canyon. From the **Pu'u Ka Pele Lookout**, the **Waipo'o Falls** are visible after a heavy rain, especially in the winter. The hike there (see *Hiking* on page 157) is fabulous. The **Pu'u Hinahina Lookout**, located past mile marker 13, has a **Ni'ihau Viewpoint** in addition to its canyon look-out. If it's clear (and if the park staff haven't let the vegetation cover the viewpoint, which is common), the view of **Ni'ihau** is great.

Shortly after this lookout, there is a paved road on your left leading to the **Makaha Ridge Tracking Station** run by the military in conjunction with the **Pacific Missile Range Facility**. The road drops 2,000 feet over a relatively short distance and can be a real brake burner. Not far before the gate at the station you will see several dirt roads leading into a pleasant forested area with picnic tables.

Looking at the map on page 88, you'll see that there are dirt hunter-roads all along this part of the coast. The views from the edge of the ridges are mind-boggling, but they are only open certain weekends and are *supposed* to be used by hunters. The only one that's always open and available is Miloli'i Ridge Road. See *Adventures* on page 205.

A Koke'e stream deep into Mohihi-Camp 10 Road is only accessible if you have 4WD.

Past mile marker 15 is the **Koke'e Museum** (808-335-9975). This is a good place to stretch your legs, and the parking lot is usually loaded with wild chickens. The small, museum won't take up much time but has several interesting displays, and its three-dimensional map of the canyon really gives you a sense of what you are seeing. A donation of $1 is suggested.

The **Koke'e Lodge** (808-335-6061) next door is the *best place in Koke'e* to get lunch. (It wins first place in a contest of one.)

As you ascend the road, note how different the vegetation is up here. Remember how dry it was down at the bottom near Waimea? Here it is always cool, and there is more rainfall than on the plain below.

Just past the lodge (on the opposite side of the road), driving Waineke Road to Mohihi Road makes a wonderful diversion if you happen to have a 4WD vehicle. You can drive 6 miles into the interior of Koke'e, visiting beautiful sights along the way.

At mile marker 18 is the **Kalalau Lookout** where most people stop. We suggest that you drive right past it and go to the *far* superior, but less used, **Pu'u o Kila Lookout**. You are not about to see another canyon lookout. You are about to be treated to one of the greatest views in the Pacific.

The **Kalalau Valley** is the largest valley on **Na Pali**. It was inhabited until 1919, and its beach is only reachable by an 11-mile hike or by kayak (see the *Adventures* chapter). For now, just revel in the view. Clouds are always moving in and out of the valley, so if it's cloudy, wait a while before you give up. It's well worth it. The earlier you go, the fewer clouds there tend to be. You can usually see clouds coming from the interior of the island. When they encounter the valley, they sink. Sinking air warms, and warmer air can hold more moisture. So if conditions are right, during normal trade winds, the clouds disappear into humidity in less than a minute right

The Kalalau Valley is best viewed not from the Kalalau Lookout, but from the Pu'u o Kila Lookout.

before your eyes. If the winds are coming from the ocean (not the norm), clouds back up in the valley, and it won't clear up.

According to historians, there used to be a *steep* trail into the valley from here leading down across a ridge called *ka-pea*, a Hawaiian word for scrotum. It was so-named because the trail was so steep that it made your…well, *you* figure it out.

Hawaiian geese, called **nene**, tend to hang out at the lookouts. These are endemic to Hawai'i (found nowhere else) and are what you get when you take wayward Canada geese and isolate them in the tropics for a million years. They've adapted to higher altitudes, lost most of the webbing on their feet and have no fear of cars or people, so be careful driving around at the lookout. They also try to make their living begging food from visitors. Please try to resist.

This is the end of the road. As the crow flies, Ha'ena on the north shore is less than 7 miles away, but you ain't no crow. They tried to build a road from here to Ha'ena in the '50s. Anybody who has ever hiked the **Alaka'i Swamp Trail** before they installed a boardwalk could tell you that a road in these parts is next to impossible. The results of this boondoggle are monuments in the form of heavy earthmoving equipment still stuck in the swamp where the prison work crews left them. A stroll from here down part of the **Pihea Trail** can be a pleasant diversion. This is where the road to Ha'ena was supposed to start.

In 1870, Queen Emma made a famous trek through the **Alaka'i Swamp** to the **Kilohana Lookout**. (As an aside, Alaka'i means "to lead," because it's impossible to get around in there without a guide.) She had a hundred people accompany her and stopped at awkward times to insist on hula demonstrations. Her guide vowed never to go into Alaka'i again,

The nene of Koke'e are accomplished beggars. This one flew off in a huff when we said no.

and the trip became legendary throughout the islands.

By not having a road completely encircling the island, Kaua'i has been able to escape the fate that has befallen O'ahu. As long as the dots aren't connected, there will always be parts of Kaua'i that are remote.

WEST SHORE BEST BETS

Best Sunset View—A Couple Miles Up Waimea Canyon Drive

Best Treat—Shave Ice at JoJo's Shave Ice in Waimea

Best Hearty Food—Chili and Cornbread at the Koke'e Lodge

Best Place for Quiet Contemplation—To the Right of the Viewing Platform at Pu'u o Kila Lookout

Best Swimming—Salt Pond Beach Park or Queen's Pond at Polihale (if calm)

Best Place to Get Away From it All and Write the Great American Novel—Waimea Plantation Cottages

Best Place to Have Good Brakes—Makaha Ridge Road

Best Thing to Wear While Walking on Hot Sand—Wool Socks, No Shoes

*Ke'e Beach and its reef lagoon offer some of the best swimming on the north shore.
This is how it looks from the Kalalau Trail.*

Because Kaua'i is older than the other major Hawaiian islands, it is blessed with having more sand beaches per mile of shoreline than any other. No part of the island is without sandy beaches. Many are accessible by merely driving up and falling into the sand. Others are deliciously secluded, requiring walks of various lengths. Some are local secrets; others are unknown even to most locals. In this chapter we will describe virtually all of Kaua'i's beaches starting from the north shore and working our way around the island clockwise. All of these beaches are located on the maps of the various areas. A few beaches are in the *Adventures* chapter because that's the only way you'll see 'em.

BEACH SAFETY

The beaches of Kaua'i, and Hawai'i in general, are beautiful, warm and, unfortunately, can be dangerous. The waves, currents and popularity of beachgoing have caused Hawai'i to become the drowning capital of the United States. If you're going to swim in the ocean, you need to bear several things in mind. We are not trying to be killjoys here, but there are several reasons why Hawai'i's beaches can be particularly dangerous. The waves are stronger here in the open ocean than in most other places. Rip currents can form, cease and form again with no warning. Large "rogue" waves can come ashore with no warning. These usually occur when two or more waves fuse at sea, becoming a larger wave. Even calm seas are no guarantee of safety. Many people have been caught unaware by large waves during ostensibly "calm seas." We swam and snorkeled most of the beaches we describe in this book on at least two occasions (usually more than two). But beaches change. The underwater topography changes throughout the year. Storms can take a very safe beach and re-arrange the sand, turning it into a dangerous beach. Just because we describe a beach as being in a certain condition does not mean it will be in that same condition when *you* visit it.

Consequently, you should consider the beach descriptions as a snapshot in calm times. If seas aren't calm, you probably shouldn't go in the water. If you observe a rip current, you probably shouldn't go in the water. If you get caught in a strong rip current that pulls you away from the shoreline, *don't* panic and *don't* try to fight your way back in. Swim parallel to shore and try to signal for help. If you're at a re-mote beach, consider asking a local person about conditions. Most will be helpful. If you aren't a comfortable swimmer, you should probably never go in the water,

except at those beaches that have lifeguards and protected pools, such as Lydgate Beach Park. But during abnormally high seas, even these are potentially hazardous. Kaua'i averages nine drownings per year—most of these are visitors. We don't want you to become part of that statistic. There is no way we can tell you that a certain beach will be swimmable on a certain day, and we claim no such prescience. There is no substitution for your own observations and judgment. And though it might sound obvious, one of the biggest con-tributors to drownings is alcohol. Hey, we're not lecturing. Go ahead, *suck 'em up* if you like. But stay on dry land and off the roads when you do.

Sprinkled among remote island beaches are yellow rescue tubes. If you see someone in distress and you're a good swimmer with fins, you can grab one and take it out and possibly save a life.

In general, the north shore beaches are calmest during the summer months (mean-ing April–September). The south shore is calmest during the winter months (meaning October–May). North shore high surf is stronger than south shore high surf since our location in the northern hemisphere

Walking on the rocks next to the ocean may seem safe, but both photos are of Queen's Bath. Don't put yourself into a position where you're relying on Mother Nature smiling. She can be moody.

Where people were in photo.

The Hawaiian Monk Seal

The endangered Hawaiian monk seal occasionally comes ashore after a heavy meal or to avoid a predator. Many people assume the seals are sick or injured and attempt to coax them back into the water. If you are lucky enough to encounter one, please leave it alone. Beaching is perfectly normal. The fines for disturbing one can range as high as $25,000. The seals dive as deep as 1,500 feet to feed and are considered the most primitive seals in the world with ancient social behavior. Unlike other seals, they don't come ashore in large numbers.

makes us closer to northern winter storms than southern hemisphere storms. But drownings have occurred all too frequently even on the south shore.

A few of the standard safety tips apply. Never turn your back on the ocean. Never swim alone. Never swim in the mouth of a river. Never swim in murky water. Never swim when the seas are not calm. Don't walk too close to the shore break; a large wave can come and knock you over and pull you in. Observe ocean conditions carefully. Don't let small children play in the water unsupervised. (In fact, it's best to keep them at the protected ponds such as Lydgate.) Fins give you *far* more power and speed and are a much underappreciated safety device (besides being more fun). If you are comfortable in a mask and snorkel, they provide considerable peace of mind, in addition to opening up the underwater world. Lastly, don't let Kaua'i's idyllic environment cloud your judgment. Recognize the ocean for what it is: a powerful force that needs to be respected.

To get **ocean safety information**, visit: hawaiibeachsafety.com/kauai.

Remember to only use water-resistant, **reef-safe sunscreen** with an SPF 30 or higher and the ingredients zinc oxide and/or titanium dioxide. Reapply as needed.

When frolicking at a beach, especially a rocky one, **water shoes** are invaluable for protecting your feet from cuts. They can turn a marginal beach into a fun beach.

People tend to get fatigued while walking in sand. The trick to making it easier is to walk with a very gentle, relaxed stride while lightly striking the sand almost flat-footed.

Beach conditions are usually best in the first half of the day. And remember that weekends—like weekends every-where—are more popular with local beach-goers, so it's best to plan your beach ac-tivities for weekdays, if possible.

The Hawai'i Supreme Court ruled in 2006 that *all* beaches are public to "the upper reaches of the wash of the waves… at high tide during the season of the year in which the highest wash of the waves occurs." This means that you can park yourself on any stretch of shoreline sand you like. The trick, sometimes, can be access. You might have to cross private land to get to a public beach. We've pointed out a legal way to every beach on the island, and some maps have access routes in yellow to show you the way. This, along with descriptions and directions, will assist you in finding the beach of your choice. But public access is an involved and often murky subject. We did our best to get it right, but there *may* be some that are marked where *somebody* may object. (E.g., "This *used* to be public access, but the county easement wasn't filed properly when the moon was full, and my attorney talked to their attorney, and together they drafted this 85-page document describing the protocols necessary when accessing every fourth Tuesday…") You get the idea. Use your best judgment.

The beaches that are *supposed* to have lifeguards are highlighted with this ⊕ symbol. They are Ke'e, Ha'ena Beach Park, Pine Trees, Hanalei Pavilion, Anahola, Kealia, Lydgate, Po'ipu Beach Park, Salt Pond and Kekaha.

When we mention that a beach has fa-cilities, it usually includes restrooms, show-ers, picnic tables and drinking water. Fa-cilities are sometimes less than pristine.

A WORD ABOUT SHELLS

A walk along Hawaiian beaches reveals that seashells are relatively rare here com-pared to other parts of the world. This is due, in part, to rough seas and the obstacles between where the shell making creatures live and the shore. As a result, it's especially rare to find a whole shell without some kind of damage. So please do your part by resisting the desire to bring one back as a souvenir. Once we were snorkeling at Larsen's when a visitor asked us, "How come I don't see any such and such type of shells anymore? We were here five years ago and saw *lots* of them. I have a whole bag of 'em back home in my garage." We told him, "Maybe we don't have 'em anymore because they're all in that bag of yours in the garage."

NORTH SHORE BEACHES

⊕ Ke'e Beach

This is as far as you can go on the north shore. The beach here is called Ke'e (also called Ha'ena *State* Park), and it's a swimming, snorkeling and sunbathing favorite that can get crowded. The sand volume here varies tremendously. Some summers the sand fills the lagoon, creat-ing a knee-deep sand swimming pool. During these times *on flat calm days* the snorkeling just *outside* the reef is unreal. Tons of fish, clear water and so many tur-tles you'll lose count as you cruise out the reef opening on the left side and head right. But calm seas are the *only* time you should consider *leaving* the lagoon. During winter months and at other times, large waves may wash over the reef, creating an excess of lagoon water. During these times the beach usually closed to swimming. Since Ke'e has the only reef opening, this water has only one place to go to equalize the volume—out the reef opening on the left side. That's why it's important to observe ocean conditions carefully. Big waves mean big currents in the reef openings and big problems for you unless you stay away from the reef opening.

This is the nicest state park that you might not be able to visit. The state wanted to prevent overcrowding here and requires you to get permits far in advance. See page 58 to find out how to get access to this beach park.

The highway's end is also where the **Kalalau Trail** begins. It leads to **Hanakapi'ai Beach** and **Kalalau Beach**, which are described in *Adventures*.

✪ Ha'ena Beach Park

This very pretty beach has complete facilities and lifeguard. It is located across from the **Dry Cave**. Get there early, as the parking lot fills up quickly. Sand is very coarse (and therefore, comes off very easily). Although you might see people swimming here, the shore is totally exposed, lacking any reef protection. The smallest of waves has a surprising amount of force. Lifeguards often close the beach to swimming in the winter months. A popular surf spot off to the left of the beach is called **Cannons**. Since the beach is very steep, a small wave could knock you over and the backwash could pull you in; therefore, swimming is hazardous except during very calm seas.

❖ Tunnels Beach / Makua Beach

One of Kaua'i's snorkeling nirvanas. This superb beach has a wide-fringing reef that is so large it can be seen from space. There is often a lateral rip current, but it's *normally* quite weak, making Tunnels a good snorkeling spot most of the time. The beach is quite popular, and you will often see SCUBA divers here, as well as surfers and windsurfers. All this makes it sound crowded, but a lack of street parking keeps the numbers relatively low. The kaleidoscope of underwater life is usually profuse and definitely worth your time to explore. See page 190 for some useful snorkeling tips. Also see *SCUBA* on page 180. Public access is by either of two short dirt roads past mile marker 8 on Hwy 560. The first (and best if you're snorkeling) one is 0.4 miles past mile marker 8. It is actually privately owned (by the seven surrounding landowners), and they don't want you parking on it. Fortunately, one of the nearby landowners wrote to us pointing out that the deed to the road says, "There is an easement in favor of the county of Kauai." Perhaps this is why the county has listed it as a public access. The second one is almost 0.6 miles past mile marker 8 and has shorter access to the sand. Get there early to assure a parking spot. If they're full, park at Ha'ena Beach Park and walk to the right. You could also take Alealea Street before mile marker 8, park near the sand, and walk to the left along the beach. (It's a half-mile walk in sand that way, but it's pretty.) You should know that if you park on the highway itself, they *do* give tickets.

❖ Kepuhi Beach

The snorkeling is good here but not nearly as good as Tunnels. You'll rarely find many people on this beach, so if you're in the area and want easy access but no crowds, this is the beach for you. This long strip of sand is fronted by an even longer coral reef. The makeup of this reef causes a slightly stronger current. Check out conditions before you snorkel. Because most of it is not located directly off the main highway, it tends to be forgotten, even by locals. It is, however, still used on occasion by

Ahh, Tunnels Beach…

throw-net fishermen. Access is at the eastern end of Alamoo Road. See map on page 52. Limited parking.

❖ Wainiha Beach Park

Hazardous surf and its location at the mouth of the Wainiha River make it murky and unsuitable for anything other than shoreline fishing and beachcombing.

❖ Lumaha'i Beach

This is the long, wide, golden, glorious beach you see just after you've passed Hanalei Bay. Pictured on countless post-cards and posters, this beach was first made famous as a location for the movie *South Pacific*, where Mitzi Gaynor spent considerable time washing that man right out of her hair. If you're looking for a huge, picture-perfect stretch of sand on the north shore, Lumaha'i shouldn't be missed. If you're looking for safe swim-ming, Lumaha'i shouldn't be touched. This beach and Hanakapi'ai on the Na Pali Coast are the two most dangerous beaches on Kaua'i. Exposed to open ocean, the waves here, even small ones, are frighteningly powerful. We've come to this beach after seeing it absolutely flat at Ha'ena Beach Park, a few miles away, only to be utterly assaulted by Lumaha'i's waves. Put simply, most of Lumaha'i is almost never safe to swim. The waves, currents and backwash are not to be underestimated. Lumaha'i Stream on the left side is sometimes crossable during calm seas and low stream flow. It serves as an estuary for 'o'opu during the summer when the shifting sands tend to cut off the river from the ocean. During this time, the closed river mouth is sometimes safe to swim. But absent these conditions, swimming in Lumaha'i Stream has caused numerous individuals to be swept out to sea. Surfers and boogie boarders often use the left side of the beach near the rocks, but unless you're an expert on Hawaiian surf, this should not be attempted.

Separated by lava rock to the right (east) of Lumaha'i is **Kahalahala Beach** (technically part of Lumaha'i, but who's quibbling?). Swimming here is a different story. You access it from a marvelous 3–4 minute walk down through lush jungle to the beach 100 feet below. During calm summer days the water here can be like a crystal-clear swimming pool. There's a tidepool for keiki to splash about, a fair amount of shade, and a tall rock that some people love jumping off. (Our general rule is to never jump off anything you haven't checked out first.) When seas are calm here, this area is utter paradise. Big surf, however, which is not uncommon in the winter, makes this part of the beach nearly as dangerous as the rest of Lumaha'i.

Access to these beaches can be obtained either via a trail from the top of the lookout at the eastern edge of the beach *before* mile marker 5 on Hwy 560 (this gets you to the eastern part, which is the best part), or from the parking area just before you get to the Lumaha'i Stream. See map on page 52.

❖ Hanalei Bay

Four beaches are part of Hanalei Bay: Waikoko, Wai'oli, Hanalei Pavilion and Black Pot. With its single long crescent of sand, the bay is beautiful to look at but not great to swim in. Pounding shore break, backwash and rip currents, especially during the winter months, make Hanalei Bay less than ideal as a swimming beach.

Lumaha'i is the widest beach on the north shore. But the better swimming is at the far, narrower end.

But that doesn't make it any less pretty. Large surfing waves make Hanalei Bay very popular with surfers, who come from other islands to experience the extremely long-lasting waves.

❖ Waikoko Beach

Easy access and good reef protection at this one portion of Hanalei Bay make this a popular beach during moderate surf periods, but the water is shallow, which makes for marginal swimming conditions. The snorkeling is better than the swimming if stream flow isn't high. Located between mile markers 4 and 5 as the road begins to ascend. Access is near the 25 mph sign. See map on page 53.

⊕ Wai'oli Beach Park

Located at the end of either He'e or 'Ama'ama Roads in Hanalei and often referred to as **Pine Trees** (though there are no pine trees there—only ironwood trees). The underwater topography focuses more of the ocean's force here, making the swimming hazardous except during very calm seas. Swimming is much better at nearby Hanalei Pavilion Beach Park. Access is from Weke Road in Hanalei. A reader pointed out (and we verified) that this

beach has particularly good sand for building **sand castles**. The stuff sticks together like cement.

✪ Hanalei Pavilion Beach Park

Also located on Weke Road in Hanalei, it includes facilities and a lifeguard. Popular with boogie boarders and surfers, the shore break and backwash make for less-than-ideal swimming conditions most of the time, but it's better than Wai'oli Beach Park.

❖ Black Pot

Located near the mouth of the **Hanalei River**, swimming conditions are marginal. (We've had several readers tell us that this is a favorite for swimming, but they probably aren't taking into account the high bacteria levels from the river.) During calm summer surf, boogie boarding is possible near the pier area. Black Pot refers to a large black cooking pot residents used to keep at the beach. This is the area where kayakers put in to paddle up the Hanalei River. The picturesque pier here makes a good sunset photo. Facilities available at beach. Camping with county permit. Super busy on weekends.

❖ Pu'u Poa Beach

Located next to the site of the 1 Hotel Hanalei Bay, the beach has a fringing reef and offers good snorkeling possibilities during calm seas. During the winter, the waters off the outer edge of the reef offer some of the best and most challenging surfing in the state (for experts only). Access is through a cement path starting just to the left of the gate house at the Princeville Resort. Free valet parking for going to the public beach, except for the tip, though. Getting to the beach necessitates negotiating 632 steps. (Yes, we counted…it was a slow day.) From here you can

walk all the way to the mouth of the Hanalei River. Another access is from Black Pot Beach and requires wading to come across the usually shallow water at the mouth of the Hanalei River. The final access is from the end of Hanalei Plantation Road (see map on page 53). It's an easy walk but a half mile (described on page 162), so pack light.

❖ Pali Ke Kua / Hideaways

A REAL GEM

Fifty feet before the end of Ka Haku Road there is a gate house and a corridor off to the right (next to the Pu'u Poa tennis courts). This path leads *down* (120 feet below) to Pali Ke Kua Beach, also called Hideaways. Parking is pretty limited. The first half of the descent consists of stairs and a railing. The remainder is trail. All told, it takes 5–10 minutes to get there. There are actually two beaches here, with the second one off to the right separated by a rocky point. Both offer excellent snorkeling during calm seas. The salient underwater features are good relief and a diverse fish community punctuated by the occasional turtle. With marvelous coarse sand, large false kamani trees for shade and good snorkeling when calm, this beach is a wonderful place to spend the day. You won't usually find too many people here since parking near the trailhead corridor is limited.

While the beach can be a nice place to bring the kids, some may have trouble negotiating their way down the path. (In fact, *you* might have trouble, too, if it has been raining and the path below the steps is muddy. Ropes might be there to help, if that's the case.) When seas aren't calm, rip currents can form. Check ocean conditions carefully. Unusually high surf has been known to generate waves that can sweep across the entire beach. The *other* part of

If you can negotiate the steps and path coming down to the sand, Hideaways delivers the right ingredients that make a great beach. And in the summer it's twice as long as this.

Pali Ke Kua beach can be reached by swimming to the right from Hideaways or by walking a paved trail leading down from the Pali Ke Kua condominiums. That *other* path is a private trail available only to guests at Pali Ke Kua.

Hopefully, the path will be open for your visit. In 2021 the trail to the beach was closed to all because a visitor from the mainland named Trevor Wright injured his hand on the trail and sued the county and the landowner, according to the local newspaper. The county sought to make the trail an official, protected public access. Bottom line? Please don't sue anybody if you get hurt recreating; it only messes it up for the rest of us.

❖ **Queen's Bath**

A REAL GEM

DURING SUMMER

Queen's Bath is actually a large pool the size of several swimming pools carved by nature into a lava shelf with an inlet from the ocean for fresh seawater to flow. If the surf is too high, you would never recognize this place as anything special. But *during calm seas*, Queen's Bath is a marvelous pool to swim in. Fish get in through the inlet, making it all the more charming. (Bring your mask and water shoes; no fins needed.) It's a great place to take your underwater camera. During mid-summer, if the ocean is *too* calm, the water is not refreshed as much as it should be. During high surf, it's extremely dangerous as the water flows in and out of the pond. Queen's Bath has claimed numerous lives because people got nailed by large waves during times that they should not have gone. During winter months (generally October–April), high surf assaults the area, and you should always stay away. Even when the ocean appears calm, it's always possible for a rogue wave to snap at this part of the shoreline, knocking people around, maybe even dragging them back into the open ocean. Some people think we shouldn't even mention this attraction. But this is the information age—you're *gonna* hear about it—and we'd rather you know about the safety issues than leave you with no information at all. And it *is* a gem—just one to experience only during calm seas. To get there, follow the trail off Kapiolani Road near Punahele Road in Princeville. See map on page 53. The trail (slippery when wet—hiking shoes recommended) passes a marvelous seasonal waterfall on your right after a few minutes. (Good for rinsing off the salt when you're done.) After dropping 120 feet, the trail encounters the ocean at the lava shoreline where a small waterfall drops directly into the ocean. Go to the *left* along the lava for 260 yards following the dire warning signs. (It'll seem like more.) Queen's Bath is recessed in the rock and is part of a horseshoe-shaped lava cut. If you can't find it, the ocean probably isn't cooperating.

The community association erected a fence and gate and is tasked with deciding when access to the shoreline should be restricted for safety purposes during higher surf. It's *supposed* to be closed during high surf season (around October to April) and open during low surf season. But we've seen it locked even when surf is tiny so it's hard to predict what you will find unless you go there.

❖ SeaLodge Beach

This wonderful pocket of sand is set in an indentation in the cliff. With plenty of shade courtesy of false kamani trees and heavenly coarse sand (the kind that won't stick to you with the tenacity of a barnacle), SeaLodge Beach is a real find. This beach is sometimes empty of people because most don't know it's there. During the summer in particular, it's an ideal secluded beach. Access is found in SeaLodge Resort at the end of Kamehameha Road in Princeville. Parking is an issue here. The resort has dedicated seven stalls marked "Trail". Don't park in any of the other stalls because they belong to residents or on the road because you will get a ticket or towed. The trail is next to the stalls. Where the trail encounters the ocean, it veers to the left. Look for turtles in the water here. The snorkeling can be outstanding during very calm seas, but entry and currents need to be respected. Depending on the weather, the trail can be slippery and a bit tricky in areas. (See map on page 53.) During periods of unusually high surf, waves have been known to travel all the way to the base of the cliff. Don't come here if this is the case. Once at the trailhead, the entire picturesque hike should take between 10 and 15 minutes and is well worth it. (If you had taken

The 2-mile long fringing reef at 'Anini usually gives this beach the calmest water on the north shore.

a right at the ocean instead, a short hike along the coastline would bring you to small, pretty waterfall.)

❖ 'Anini Beach Park

Protected by a *long* fringing reef, 'Anini Beach has become a popular place for the rich and famous to build homes. The water can be very shallow, and the snorkeling *can* be good in many areas when visibility cooperates, though it seems to have been over fished. The swimming is among the safest you'll find on the north shore if you stay near the shoreline. Better snorkeling is near the outer reef edge, but it's not as safe there. The channel at the western end of the beach is where the water flows out, so stay away from this part. (See the left side of map on page 50.) There are numerous areas along this stretch of sand to swim, snorkel or just frolic. There is a polo field across from the beach; check it out if you're there during summer. 'Anini Beach is a good place to learn windsurfing. Camping is allowed with county permit, facilities at the pavilion. The name used to be *Wanini Beach,* but the "W" was blasted away with a shotgun by an irate resident who felt it had been misspelled. Other residents assumed the gun-toting spell-checker must have corrected a mistake and the "new" name stuck. (*That's* typical Hawai'i.) Take the northern Kalihiwai Road (between mile markers 25 and 26) and stay to the left on 'Anini Road.

The far (west) end of the beach, on the other side of the channel, is known as **Wyllie Beach**. Residents of Princeville access it by taking a 0.25 mile-long trail from the end of Wyllie Road, which drops 20 stories. The easier way is to park near the channel on 'Anini Road (if you see a Private Road sign, you've gone too far) and wade across the stream. Wyllie Beach is a thin ribbon of sand with lots of shade from false kamani trees (whose fallen leaves turn yellow, red, orange and brown). It makes a very nice stroll as the ocean gently laps at your feet (though the sand can disappear during high tide and surf). There is a touch more sand in nearshore waters (though still plenty of rocks) than at other parts of 'Anini. Be aware that

Local children often play in the shallow stream at Kalihiwai Bay.

when the surf is breaking over the reef offshore, a rip current can form leading to the channel.

❖ Kalihiwai Beach

Located at the mouth of **Kalihiwai Stream**, you drive down from either Kalihiwai Road. (It used to be a loop, but the bridge was knocked out by a tsunami in 1957, and they haven't rebuilt it.) At the bottom of the road, you encounter a picturesque bay with a wide sand beach lined with ironwood trees to park under. There are houses on the other side of the road. The beach is popular with boogie boarders in the summer and is a good place to see local keiki learning to ride waves. It's also a good place to just enjoy the water during the summer. During the winter, surfers ride the large waves under the cliff area. The eastern (first) Kalihiwai Road is the best road to take to the beach. The only ding is that local dogs occasionally roam free, leaving—well, *you* know what they leave behind.

❖ Secret Beach

A REAL GEM

Also known as **Kauapea Beach** and known to most locals by the more enticing name of Secret Beach, this is a stunningly beautiful beach only accessible via a more-tiring-than-you'd-think 10–15 minute hike. This fact, along with its former anonymity, caused it to become Kaua'i's premier nude beach. For the record, public nudity is illegal in Hawai'i, and police issue tickets there, so it's not as prevalent as it once was. This long, golden sand beach is narrower and not swimmable during the winter, but on calm summer days it can be a delight for swimming and offers good snorkeling. It's worth the trip year-round just to see its exceptional scenic beauty. There is usually a small waterfall to rinse off your gear and a few places where water squirts from the side of the cliff. The island off to your right is **Moku'ae'ae Island**, a bird sanctuary. To get to Secret Beach, turn right off the first (eastern) Kalihiwai Road, then right on the first dirt road you encounter. (See map on page 50.) Take the trail to the bottom. (It's real slippery when it's raining.) Make a mental note of where it encounters the beach for your return. If you go to the *left* at the bottom of the trail, the shoreline leads to the **Secret Lava Pools**, pretty tidepools that are visitable on calm summer days. But a rash of deaths from people being swept out to sea during high winter seas (conditions that we *specifically* advised people to avoid) has left us thinking that these tidepools should probably be avoided.

❖ Kahili Quarry Beach

Where **Kilauea Stream** encounters the ocean is a beach sometimes called **Rock Quarry Beach**. There is good swimming on the left (western) side and good snorkeling on the right side during calm seas. Since this is a river mouth, the water can get murky at times. (Sharks, which like murky water, have been sighted here during periods of heavy stream flow.) This is a popular boogie boarding and surfing site. The river mouth can cause rip currents. Easiest access is from a dirt road off N. Wailapa Road. Avoid Rock Quarry Road from the north side as it was impassable, even with 4WD, at press time. A good hike in the area is described on page 163.

❖ Waiakalua Beach

A marvelous and undiscovered north shore beach. Although from your car it requires a steep, 5–10 minute walk to the beach 160 feet below, Waiakalua is an undisturbed, serene place to spend the afternoon.

Building some shade at Kahili Quarry Beach.

Medium coarse sand, a long, fringing reef, numerous pockets of shade and a fresh-water spring at the far end add to the charm. Observe the reef from up on the bluff. Calm summer snorkeling can be interesting but shallow; watch out for rip currents. During other times, swimming can be hazardous. To the north is a rocky point separating the two halves of the beach. The snorkeling around this point is exciting, featuring clear water teeming with big life. However, the rips, surges and surf make this area tricky—only advanced snorkelers need apply. Otherwise, just enjoy the beach. The cool spring at the far end offers sweet, fresh water. Bring an empty container and some way to filter the water—all fresh water obtained anywhere in nature should be treated to prevent bacterial disease. (It barely trickles during dry months.) To get to Waiakalua, turn onto North Waiakalua Road and take the dirt road on the left side just before the end of the road. Park when you can't

drive any more, and take the trail off to the left. The beach on your left at the bottom is **Waiakalua Beach**. The path off to your right leads to **Pila'a Beach**, which has lots of coral and good snorkeling. It can take 10–30 minutes to reach Pila'a Beach, depending on your boulder-hopping prowess. Otherwise, just stay at Waiakalua Beach. You'll probably have either one all to yourself. See map on page 51.

❖ Larsen's Beach / Lepe'uli Beach

This has crystal-clear water, lots of beachcombing and seclusion. The beach is named after a former manager at Kilauea Plantation named L. David Larsen (the rascal who introduced the hated blackberries to Koke'e). This beach is splendidly isolated but can be accessed by walking down a county access trail. Off to the right is a bunch of lava rocks that make for good snorkeling if conditions are right. To the left is a long crescent of sand broken by occasional outcroppings of rock and reef. Underwater topography creates good conditions for beachcombing. **Pakala Point**

is on the left side where the first beach ends and lava rock protrudes out into the ocean. Just before these rocks is **Pakala Channel**. (Shown on the map on page 51.) Most of the water you see breaking over the reef drains through this channel; therefore, *don't swim in or near the channel*. The water leading just up to the channel moves so swiftly at times that it seems more like rapids than a rip current. If the ocean is calm and you stay away from the channel, if the tide is right and you have some experience snorkeling, this place can be a snorkeler's paradise. Lots of coral and fish in shallow, crystal-clear water greet the eye. Relatively few beachgoers use this beach during the week. This beach is *not* a swimming beach, just for snorkeling, due to the sharp reefs and shallow water.

One thing that can be *very cool*—if you're careful—is to get in the water at the southeast end (where the trailhead is) and let the current take you toward (but not into!) the Pakala Channel. Then get out and walk back.

The end of summer is when water at reef-fringed beaches like Larsen's has the poorest visibility because it has usually been many months since it has had a good flushing by the high surf.

During periods of high surf, waves *tower* above the reef, breaking on the edge, which can be quite a spectacle.

On the opposite side of Pakala Point are two pockets of sand that are even more secluded and offer good snorkeling and a chance of spotting a monk seal. Avoid the path on the rocks if the surf is up. Larsen's is about 20 minutes north of Kapa'a; take the *north* end of Ko'olau Road (the second Ko'olau if you're coming from Kapa'a) just before mile marker 20. 1.2 miles from the north end of Ko'olau Road, take the left Beach Access road all the way until it ends—it looks like a driveway at the beginning. (See map on page 51.) Follow the

Mark Zuckerberg paid a reported $200 million for the land behind Larsen's Beach. All you gotta do is hike down the trail to it.

The south side of Moloaʻa Bay on a calm, sunny day is paradise found.

steeper trail to the bottom, which is 140 feet below you. (The easier path to the left is private property.) The beach is a 5–10 minute walk down the hill. Note where the trail hits the beach for your return. We've noticed that the far end of the beach often attracts nudists.

Lastly, consider posting a selfie of yourself here on your Facebook page. The landowner behind the beach—*Mr.* Zuckerberg to you and me—reportedly paid *$200 million* for land and will probably get a kick out of it. Or maybe not…

❖ Moloaʻa Beach

A wonderful beach on calm days. The right (southeast) side is much nicer than the northwest side. Very pretty, but not great for swimming when seas aren't calm. It's off the main highway and not as well known as other beaches. Take the first (southeastern) Koʻolau Road (before mile marker 17). Hang a right on easy-to-miss Moloaʻa Road, next to a large fruit stand.

The public access is near the end of Moloaʻa Road. Parking is *very* limited. There are a few stalls toward the end of the road; otherwise, park where there are *no* no parking signs to dissuade you. You might have to walk a ways to the beach, but it's worth it. To get to the southeast side, you'll have to walk 100 yards along the beach. There you'll find the wading, swimming and boogie boarding the best, and shade is plentiful. See map on page 51.

❖ Papaʻa Bay

Very picturesque. The beach access involves a 5-minute trail through the brush down to some rocks below. After that you'll have to boulder-hop about a hundred yards. You need to use the access to **North ʻAliomanu Beach** (see map on page 51) and look for a beach access when the road turns to the right. In addition, it is one of the few beaches on Kauaʻi where you may detect a fishy smell. When the producer of the movie *Six Days/Seven Nights* was here to film the plane crash scene, he apparently liked the location so much, he purchased all *174 acres* around the bay and built quite a compound, which sold in 2009 for $28 million. Although the land and house around the bay are private, the *beach* is public.

❖ ʻAliomanu Beach

This is really two beaches with different access points. The long, fringing reef offshore of the south beach is used heavily by locals for throw-net fishing, octopus hunting, pole fishing, torch fishing and limu harvesting. This beach, along with Pilaʻa and Larsen's, attracts families who have been limu (an edible seaweed) harvesting on the outer parts of the reef for generations. They pick the top part of the plant, leaving the roots to regenerate.

The northern (and better) beach is accessed from a parking lot 80 feet above the beach, requiring a 5-minute walk. (See map on page 51.) Although the nearshore waters are rocky, the beach is sandy and very pretty.

✛ Anahola Beach Park

The area around Anahola is designated Hawaiian Homelands, and most of the beach users are Hawaiian. Visitors aren't common but are welcome. Swimming is safest where it is protected on the right (eastern) side of the bay to just before Kahala Point. Watch for rip currents near the remains of a pier. Also nice is the northern end, which is lightly used and can be accessed from the first Aliomanu Road.

EAST SHORE BEACHES

❖ Donkey Beach / Paliku Beach

So named by drifters in the '60s who observed burros and mules being used by the sugar company to haul seed cane to the fields nearby. Donkey Beach was

You won't find any donkeys at Donkey Beach. In fact, you might not even find any people either.

once a popular nudist beach on Kaua'i due to its location, but the land's current owners have done much to end this practice. (After purchasing the land from a defunct sugar company and selling house lots for $2 million plus, they're not too thrilled with the idea of naked beachgoers.) This long stretch of sand is also popular with surfers. Interestingly, surfing in ancient times was usually done nude. (I wonder if that's where the term *hang loose* came from…)

Access is 0.5 miles north of mile marker 11 north of Kapa'a. Look for a hiking sign guiding you to the parking lot with facilities. The uncrowded beach is very attractive, with a convenient tree in the middle for shade. The foreshore at the beach is steep, creating a pounding shore break and strong backwash. Swimming is often hazardous. It's about a 10-minute (550 yard) walk on the paved path to the beach. As you near the shoreline, veer to the right for the beach. To the left (north) past the stream and over the small hill is a secluded cove (cleverly labeled "secluded cove" on our map on page 51) where the snorkeling can be very good at times. You will probably have that cove all to yourself. During rainy times, there might be a small waterfall and swimming hole behind the cove. There is yet another cool cove if you keep hiking north, but we're embarrassed to point it out because all too often it seems to be used as a dumping ground for abandoned vehicles and other litter by people who don't believe in taking care of the land the way past generations did.

➕ Kealia Beach

Drive north of Kapa'a and you will often see lots of boogie boarders and surfers in the water here. (See map on page 63.) The powerful waves are fantastic but can be treacherous. The currents and backwash are sometimes ferocious. The northern end of the beach is more protected by a breakwater and can be good for wading and occasionally snorkeling on a calm day. If you have never ridden waves, be very careful here or you might get drilled into the ground. If the surf is high, definitely leave it for the big boys. If you choose to try boogie boarding here, water shoes or short fins are a must. Lifeguard and facilities.

❖ Kapa'a Beach Park

Located in the heart of Kapa'a, this is heavily used by locals. Like any beach located close to a population center, Kapa'a Beach Park is not as pristine as other beaches you will find. That said, the northern section (the part just before the lookout as you leave Kapa'a going north) offers interesting but shallow snorkeling. Check for currents. The rest of the park is not as memorable. It is, however, a good place for a beach stroll or to watch the sunrise. There are a few large sand pockets along the beach that are swimmable when the surf isn't high. Regular facilities here plus a swimming pool. The best thing about Kapa'a Beach Park is watching the kite surfers on a windy day.

❖ Waipouli Beach

Pretty, but not a good swimming beach. There are a few small pockets along the southern portion of the beach that are relatively safe for swimming during calm periods, but be cautious. The area seaward of the beachrock fronting the beach is subject to strong currents year-round. This is normally considered a dangerous beach. There is a paved shoreline trail along much of this beach, which is perfect for jogging or a leisurely stroll.

❖ Waipouli Beach Park

Just north of Waipouli Beach is Waipouli Beach Park, also called **Fuji Beach** and sometimes **Baby Beach**. Conditions there are different. This can be a nice place to let keiki splash around in the ocean. Part of it (on Moanakai Street between Pahihi and Makana) is often protected by a long, natural sandstone breakwater. Only when the tide or surf are high does water flow over the sandstone and form a current to the left. If the tide is especially high or there's a large eastern swell, keep small children away as the current can get surprisingly strong. The most protected spot is the right (south) end of the beach near the sea wall. Most of the time, however, it's flat calm. The sand is coarse, so you'll sink a bit more into it. Check to make sure the ocean isn't making a liar out of us and that it's clean enough. Since it's located in the middle of town, it sometimes gets a little dirty.

❖ Wailua Beach

Across from the closed Coco Palms Resort, from the mouth of the Wailua River to a rocky point to the north, this is an easily accessible beach. Just drive right up. It is

The boulder-enclosed ponds at Lydgate are designed to protect you when the ocean is in a pushy mood.

popular with surfers and boogie boarders who appreciate the unprotected waves. Winter swells sometimes keep even these users out of the water. Swimmers should be aware of rip currents in several areas along the beach and pounding shore break during high seas. (Frank Sinatra learned this the hard way. During some down time while filming *None but the Brave* in 1964, Old Blue Eyes was swept 200 yards out and had to be saved by local surfers.) The river itself, which is crossable only during periods of *low flow*, can cause tricky water conditions, so caution is advised. The ocean and the river are constantly battling for supremacy, and the struggle can be dramatic. The ocean builds up a sandbar, and the river attempts to erode it. Sometimes the river is completely stopped up. When it finally breaks through the sandbar, it can be fascinating. The sandbar can erode in a matter of an hour or two, taking large amounts of sand with it. For a short time thereafter, ancient

Hawaiian petroglyphs are exposed on rocks in the river mouth.

⊕ Lydgate Beach Park

A REAL GEM

Located just south of the **Wailua River**, Lydgate is composed of a picnic area, a large patch of grass, restrooms, two nice playgrounds, showers, lifeguard and two marvelous, boulder-enclosed ponds. These ponds are nearly always safe to swim, with the smaller one meant for keiki (kids), but after a heavy rain should be avoided due to debris and water quality. These ponds were created to allow fresh seawater and fish into the pond, while protecting you from the ocean's force. And they worked well until the county dredged the ponds in 2011 to deepen them. When they dug, they tapped into goo below the sand, and the wound to the sea floor has never really healed, meaning the visibility and fish count are much lower than before the county "fixed" the pond. Nevertheless, the park facilities along with usually safe swimming make it a good place to get into the ocean. Access is just off Leho Drive in Wailua. (See map on page 63.) Camping is allowed. Note that if **Portuguese man-o-wars** happen to be present, they're usually near the rocks at the far right end. Smoking is prohibited here.

❖ Nukoli'i Beach Park

From Lydgate to the far end of the Kaua'i Beach Resort is a long sand beach called Nukoli'i Beach, known locally as *Kitchens*. This beach includes the area fronting the Wailua Golf Course. This entire stretch of sand, more than 2 miles long, is never crowded, often deserted. This is surprising given its proximity to Kapa'a, but good for you. There is a road fronting much of the golf course, until it erodes at the very end. If you just want to easily claim a large spot of beach for yourself, this is as good a place as any. The swimming conditions vary along the beach but are usually marginal. Currents and surf are the usual villains. The area in front of the golf course is the only part worth considering for swimming purposes. The snorkeling can be good when it's calm, and it's fun to hunt for golf balls in the water. You might even find a club hurled by someone having an off day. Access? Just drive right up from the dirt road between the golf course and the resort entrance (not far from mile marker 4). Or take the Kaua'i Beach Resort entrance to access the southern portion of the beach. Facilities near the resort. One caveat: Natural currents often bring to this beach flotsam, such as netting and ropes from passing ships.

❖ Hanama'ulu Beach Park

Water is usually murky (and sometimes so are its beachgoers) due to the **Hanama'ulu Stream**. Sharks are often seen in the area. The waters around Ahukini Pier can offer interesting snorkeling when it's very calm. In general, a mediocre beach with fairly good park facilities that tends to attract a marginal crowd. You probably won't want to hang here.

❖ Ninini Beach / Running Waters

Located below the golf course near the Royal Sonesta Kaua'i Resort, there's good snorkeling off to the left in front of the rocks on a calm day. However, even then it can be surgy and a bit tricky. Access via a walk along a golf cart path, then a right turn before the beach turning into a steeper dirt trail to the water. See map on page 69.

❖ Kalapaki Beach

With a gently sloping sand bottom and partial protection from the open ocean,

Kalapaki is popular with visitors and locals alike. Swimming, bodysurfing, stand-up paddleboarding (no kite surfing because of the nearby airport), beginner surfing and boogie boarding conditions are usually good except during periods of high surf. Adjacent Nawiliwili Park behind the Anchor Cove Shopping Center is a popular picnic spot. Canoes and twin-hulled sailing catamarans often come ashore here. Facilities near Anchor Cove Shopping Center. Access is by a road behind the shopping center or through the Royal Sonesta Kaua'i Resort. See map on page 69. This is a good place to be when a cruise ship goes by. Because it's at Nawiliwili Bay (where the Hule'ia and Nawiliwili streams empty), the water won't be as clear as other water around the island. When calm (which is most of the time), it's a good place to teach your little one how to ride a boogie board.

❖ Niumalu Beach Park

Good place to launch kayaks for trips up the **Hule'ia Stream** (where the opening scenes from *Raiders of the Lost Ark* were filmed). Camping by county permit, but you wouldn't want to. Other water activities are lousy due to its location so far up the river and general ickiness to the water.

SOUTH SHORE BEACHES

❖ Maha'ulepu Beaches

This marvelous coastline is wild and undeveloped, actually consisting of three separate areas known as **Gillin's Beach**, **Kawailoa Bay** and **Ha'ula Beach**.

The whole of Maha'ulepu makes for fantastic exploring and beach walking, hence the gem. The swimming can be hazardous, and seas here are often choppy. Winter is best. Ocean entry is difficult in many places. The land is privately owned and the company *has been* good about allowing access (but not always, and the gate

Kawailoa Bay at Maha'ulepu is a great place to spend a beach day.

might be locked), so locals bend over backward not to give 'em a reason to shut it off. If the gate is open, they close off access between sunset and sunrise. (They will fine your *da kines* off if you have to call them to open the gate after closing.) Please take everything out that you bring in.

Maha'ulepu is located past the Hyatt on Po'ipu Road after the road becomes dirt. Turn right when the road ends and drive past an old guard shack. See map on page 79. There can be long stretches between road maintenance past the horse stable, and it might be difficult to navigate in a regular car. Those with 4WD (and those who drive a rental car like it's stolen) will have no problem.

To get to **Gillin's Beach**, park at the lot where the road otherwise continues to the left. A short trail from the right side of the lot takes you to the beach. (See map on page 79.) This beach is named after the late Elbert Gillin whose rebuilt house (now a pricey vacation rental) is on the beach just off to your right. If you walk past it, you'll see a stream that may or may not reach the ocean. Take the trail *before* the stream and look for an offshoot to the left that has a bridge. (Generously provided by the makers of *Pirates of the Caribbean 4*.) Upstream you'll see a small, triangle-shaped opening off to your left. This is an ancient, open-roofed sandstone sinkhole called **Makauwahi Cave** with some cool features. Seven thousand years of protected sediment in one corner of the cave acts as a time machine and hides the bones of extinct birds, now-vanished palm tree species and evidence of a large pre-contact tsunami.

Local paleoecologists have been doing some studies here and sometimes have it gated off. This area is identified as a cave on the map rather than as an amphitheater because we didn't want the casual map reader to think that rock concerts were held there. If the cave is locked, there's a trail to the left that overlooks the amphitheater from above. Look for reintroduced endangered plant species up on top, salvaged from this former shallow lake.

To get to **Kawailoa Bay**, continue on the dirt road until it is directly next to the beach. Kitesurfing is popular from here to **Gillin's Beach**. They ride the waves faster than the wind, and it is a real treat to watch.

The trail to **Ha'ula Beach** (see map on page 79) used to require a walk along an elevated field of lithified sand. The constant assault from sea spray has caused the sandstone to erode into short but fantastically sharp and strangely shaped pinnacles. This is a great place to observe the power of the ocean as it smashes into the cliff. Local fishermen drop their lines into the water from here since they can see their prey before they cast. But the landowner is no longer granting access along the cliffside trail and we don't want you to trespass, so the only way to reach it is to launch a kayak at one of the other Maha'ulepu Beaches and land at the Ha'ula Beach (which is public). The beach is rarely visited except by occasional horseback tours from CJM Stables. The swimming isn't very good; in fact, it can be quite hazardous, depending on conditions. But the beach is a beautiful place to enjoy your solitude. Over the ridge to the northeast is **Kipu Kai Beach**. Totally isolated, the only way to get to it is by sea or over that ridge. And the horse trails over the ridge are generously sprinkled with evil, spiked stickers. Bring your Kevlar pants.

The area between **Ha'ula Beach** and **Kawailoa Bay** contains other lithified sand dunes as well. Fishing from the top (labeled

Cliff Cracks on the map on page 79) is incredible, but be careful—the dunes can be brittle, so don't fall in. The beach area just north of these lithified dunes often provides lots of goodies for the beachcomber. Check out the dry, sometimes gasping blowhole near the shoreline at the eastern edge of Kawailoa Bay.

Maha'ulepu was the scene of a terrific slaughter in the spring of 1796. When King Kamehameha launched the first of two invasion attempts, he and his fleet of 1,200 canoes carrying 10,000 soldiers left O'ahu at midnight, hoping to reach Wailua on Kaua'i by daybreak. They were in the middle of the treacherous **Kaua'i Channel** when the wind and seas picked up. Many of his canoes were swamped. Reluctantly, Kamehameha ordered a retreat, but too late to stop some of his advance canoes. When they landed at Maha'ulepu, they were exhausted. They awoke to the sound of enemy troops who proceeded to kill all but a few escapees. The last thing these escapees wanted to do was go back to O'ahu and tell their boss what happened. So they bolted all the way to the Big Island and kept their mouths shut.

The water is nice, but entry can be a bit awkward from this spot. Shipwreck Beach can be a good place to sit and watch frustrated fishermen cast off (literally).

❖ Shipwreck Beach

This beach was named for an old, unidentified wooden shipwreck now long gone. Also called **Keoniloa Beach**, it fronts the Hyatt. The public access road is between the Hyatt and the Po'ipu Bay Resort Golf Course. The beach is used mostly by surfers, boogie boarders, body surfers and people staying at the Hyatt. High surf can create very unfavorable conditions. Even during calm seas, swimming is sometimes difficult. The Hyatt erects colored flags to signal ocean conditions—green meaning safe. (Though we've *never* seen a green flag. Their lawyer probably confiscated it.) The cliff off to your left is called **Makawehi Point** and is a popular place for pole fishermen. You will often see foolhardy young men jumping off the cliff into the waters below. In 2013 Justin Bieber took a flying leap, then one of his bodyguards reportedly roughed up a photographer who caught the scene. The cliffs are a fascinating place to hike and are described on page 171. The Hyatt has some outdoor showers near the beach area to rinse off, but they are technically only for the guests.

❖ Brennecke Beach

Great boogie boarding and lots of turtles. Since it is so small, surfboards are not allowed near the shore. The waves are usually great and tend to break both far away and close to shore—perfect for both beginners and advanced. You can rent boogie boards across the street at **Nukumoi Surf Co**. Observe conditions carefully before you go in. Since this beach is more susceptible to change than most island beaches, you'll have to evaluate its boogie viability. Be careful bodysurfing here. The

local ER nickname is Break Neck Beach since body surfers sometimes get drilled into the sand.

➕ Po'ipu Beach Park

This is the major center of beach activity on the south shore. The swimming is nearly always safe just to the left of the tombolo/sandbar, which disappears for stretches after major storms and during those times can bring a rip current. To the left is an area semi-protected by a breakwater along with some shade. It's very popular with children. Park facilities and lifeguard are present. This park is a nice place to enjoy the ocean, though it can get very crowded. The far right side isn't as protected but features excellent snorkeling with lots of fish and good swimming if the surf isn't high. Smoking is prohibited here.

Pulverized bits of glass, rounded by the ocean, color the sand at Glass Beach.

❖ Kiahuna Beach / Sheraton Beach / Po'ipu Beach

Take your pick with regard to the name. This beach fronts the Sheraton Hotel and Kiahuna Resort. It is postcard pretty and often safe to swim, thanks to an offshore reef. Surfers ride waves outside the reef, but you should stay inside unless you really know your stuff. Boogie boarding and snorkeling help make this one of the most user-friendly beaches around. Access from the end of Hoonani Road. See map on page 79.

❖ Koloa Landing Boat Ramp

An old boat launch used as a SCUBA spot. See page 186 for more.

❖ Baby Beach / Kaheka Beach

This stretch of sand is partially protected from surf by a natural breakwater of lava boulders forming a quasi-protected pool. The sand only extends a little way into the water, giving way to a lining of lava stones, so you'll be grateful for those cheap water shoes you brought with you. These same shallow stones also capture some of the sun's heat, making the water a little warmer here. A Real Gem for people terrified of the ocean, as well as little crumb-crunchers, hence the name. Check conditions first. On Hoona (loop) Road off Lawa'i Road. Parking is pretty limited. See map on page 78.

❖ PK's

Named after the Prince Kuhio monument across the street on Lawa'i Road in **Ho'ai Bay**. Almost no sand and entry can be awkward, but snorkeling is good at times. Also used for SNUBA and SCUBA.

❖ Lawa'i Beach / Beach House

This tiny pocket of sand next to the Beach House Restaurant nearly disappears at high tide. The snorkeling in front of the restaurant is great, but the water is subject to currents during periods of high surf and needs to be respected. At other times it can be calm and a good place for the less-experienced snorkeler. SNUBA (not SCUBA) is also done here. Just stay near the shore around the restaurant.

❖ Keiki Cove

A minuscule pocket of sand just past Lawa'i Beach where the road almost clips the ocean. (A break in the low stone wall between two houses hides stairs.) It's usually protected and an excellent place to let rug-rats experience the ocean, but check it yourself first.

❖ Kukui'ula Harbor

Probably the most forgotten beach on the South Shore. When tiny little Lawa'i Beach is jammed with people, this protected harbor with a very pretty mountain backdrop, a great view of Spouting Horn, is lightly used during the week and there's plenty of parking. (Weekends are more crowded with locals launching their boats.) There's plenty of sand, a huge lawn and facilities. Snorkeling isn't great, but swimming is often protected by the boat jetty.

❖ Lawa'i Bay

Access is the problem here. There's no way to get here by land without crossing private property. But you can kayak here from Kukui'ula Harbor, which is only a mile to the east. The beach is in a particularly lovely setting, backed by the **National Tropical Botanical Garden**. If you visit the beach, you're not allowed to venture into the private garden. Garden personnel say that this is one of the rare places on the island where green sea turtles nest. (Most of Hawai'i's green sea turtles are born in French Frigate Shoals, 500 miles away.)

❖ **Palama Beach**

The only way to get to this beach is to take Kaua'i Coffee's dirt road past their visitor center in Kalaheo off Hwy 540. You'll have to fill out a waiver, take it to the nearby main office and pay $25, then wait several weeks for it to be processed. And permits are not available during coffee harvesting. If you're still with me, the beach is quiet and nearly always deserted, often visited by a monk seal or two.

WEST SHORE BEACHES

There aren't a lot of listings under *West Shore Beaches*. That's because it's almost *all beach.*

❖ **Glass Beach**

If someone told you that you gotta check out the beach near an old dump, would you believe 'em? Then if they said the reason to check it out was because stuff from the dump washes ashore, would you go? Well…you should. Glass Beach makes a rotten first impression. It's in the industrial part of 'Ele'ele backed by huge, ugly tanks full of gasoline. Add to that millions of pieces of broken glass, washed in from broken bottles and auto glass. The result? A colorful tapestry of sand and multicolored glass. (Come to think of it, doesn't glass *come* from sand?) This isn't a beach to frolic at or swim in. It's a good strolling beach, especially if you want to tie in a visit here with a hike along the Swiss cheese-type of lava farther east until a sign dissuades you further. The amount of glass varies with tides and surf—sometimes there's almost none here or ultra-fine; sometimes it's everywhere. Please don't take any of the glass

litter. (Now *there's* a bizarre statement if taken out of context.) To get to Glass Beach, drive toward Hanapepe, turn left on Waialo Road going toward Port Allen. Before the ocean, go left on Aka Ula until it's dirt. (You may want to park there.) Then take a right on the dirt to the beach. A 20-minute or so walk further east leads to **Wahiawa Beach**, a dark sand beach where tour boats sometimes moor for lunch and kayaks visit in the winter. See map on page 89.

❍ **Salt Pond Beach Park**

This area is distinguished in that it has the only natural salt ponds in Hawai'i still used to make salt. Seawater is pumped into containers and allowed to evaporate. More water is added, and then it is transferred to shallower pans. The process is repeated until the water is loaded with salt. This is allowed to evaporate completely, leaving crystallized salt behind. (Excellent in kalua pig.) During the summer you'll likely see people practicing this process. The nearby park and its facilities are a popular place for locals to bring their families. The beach is separated by two rocky points. A natural ridge of rock runs between the two points, creating an area of relative calm inside. Swimming is usually safe, and children play in the semi-protected ocean water. The exception is during periods of high surf, which can make it unsafe. In Hanapepe past mile marker 17 off Lele Road. Usually windy, especially in the afternoon. Camping with county permit. Full facilities and lots of wild cats. The parking lot and restroom area may turn you off, but the beach is very nice.

❖ **Pakala Beach**

Those cars you might see parked on the side of the road shortly after mile marker

21 belong to surfers carrying their boards to a very famous surfing site also known as **Infinities**, so named because the ride seems to last forever. The water is murky and only used for expert surfing.

❖ Lucy Wright Beach Park

Lucy Wright was a prominent member of the Waimea community when she died in 1931. It is a testament to how the townsfolk felt about her that the beach was named in her honor, especially in light of the more historic event that happened here. For it was at this spot that Captain James Cook first set foot in the Hawaiian Islands in January 1778. The beach itself is not a particularly good beach. The **Waimea River** mouth is nearby, and the silty water is less enticing than clear waters elsewhere. Some guidebooks label this a black sand beach, like the black sand beaches on the Big Island or Maui. That's not quite accurate. Though there *is* lots of black sand here—flecks of lava along with a green stone called olivine chipped from the riverbed by the Waimea River—much of the "black sand" is simply fine sediment carried by the same river. The best part of the beach is watching

the interplay of the ocean and river mouth, described on page 91. Full facilities. The river mouth is also a popular place for beginner stand-up paddleboarding.

❖ Polihale Beaches

A REAL GEM This area consists of more than 12.5 *miles* of uninterrupted sand beach. (It used to be 17 miles, but the beachwall near the highway east of Kekaha Beach Park is too sporadically sandy to consider it a beach.) There are three regions, called **Kekaha Beach Park**, **Pacific Missile Range Facility** and **Polihale State Park**. Except for a few small areas, the entire stretch is unprotected, which means it is exposed to the ocean's force. During periods of high surf, waves can travel up the beach and pull you in, so be wary. When the seas are calm, you might enjoy the water. The sand can get pretty hot out on this side—hot enough to fry your feet—so watch it. Take water with you. It's available only at Kekaha Beach Park and at the other end at Polihale State Park.

➕ **Kekaha** is the first region you encounter. High surf generates a particularly powerful rip current, and waves can be unbelievably strong; stay out or ask the lifeguard unless the water is real calm.

Past Kekaha is one of the least appreciated (and used) stretches of beach on the island. **Kokole Point** marks the beginning of PMRF. The dirt road 0.7 miles past mile marker 27 leads to the shoreline. 4WD drivers should read the part about driving on sand in the Polihale description if you want to drive on the beach. At the beach here you can often walk for a mile (especially to the west) and not find a soul. Ni'ihau seems so close from here. There's no shade, and the same swimming warnings apply as Kekaha Beach Park. But it's a great place to enjoy a wide, sandy beach and awesome for a late afternoon BBQ.

Pacific Missile Range Facility (PMRF) is operated by the U.S. Navy. Access *through the facilities* these days for visitors is pretty hard to get. It's a long and arduous process. But you are allowed to *walk along the beach* from Polihale, past the great sand dunes described below until a turnaround point. Just make sure you stay within 20 feet or so from the shoreline so you don't venture onto base property, and expect to be turned around if a rocket launch is imminent. The beach on the northern part (adjacent to Polihale State Park) is **Barking Sands Beach**. If conditions are right, the sand dune (which has numerous kiawe trees) is supposed to make a barking sound with your every step. The likely cause is a combination of uniform grain size coupled with a thin coating of silica that sticks when dry. Don't feel bad if it doesn't happen. We've jumped up and down like idiots on that sand until we were blue in the face, and we haven't even gotten it to whine. The sand needs to be *real* dry. Local legend has it that the barking sound comes from nine dogs buried in the sand.

They belonged to their master, a fisherman, in the days when dogs didn't bark. (Sometimes I wish those were *still* the days.) One day, they started acting antsy after the master tied them up before he went fishing. While he was out, a storm broke and forced him off course. A god gave the dogs the power to bark so they could guide their master home. Unfortunately, the dogs were so fearful waiting for their master that they ran around the stakes they were tied to. Around and around and around they ran until they buried themselves in the sand. The fisherman was depressed when he returned and couldn't find his dogs. He would go down to the shore every day looking for them, but he never found them. The dogs remain there to this day, barking for their master, hoping he will find them. (My neighbor's dog seems to bark for the same reason.)

Polihale State Park is the end of the line. You can't go any farther north on this part of the island without a boat. This is where the Na Pali Coast starts. (Sunsets can be dramatic here—the cliffs light up red as the sun gets close to the horizon.) Rain is rare in these parts. On the few occasions that it does rain hard, the road can get pretty sloppy. Other times potholes might slow you down, but regular cars can almost always make it. The sand can get *real* hot in the summer. Hot sand can slip into your shoes and burn you. A smart beachgoer will wear only wool socks (no shoes, despite how goofy it looks) to keep the blisters away. The four facility areas here tend to be poorly maintained but include showers, restrooms, picnic tables and drinking water (which you'll need).

The **dunes of Polihale** are famous throughout the islands. The beach averages 300 feet wide, and the dunes can get up to 100 feet high. Walking down a dune like that can be fun; walking up is a monster. Better to walk around unless you are training for the Ironman Triathlon. Locals drive their 4WD vehicles right onto the beach. If you try it, be aware that you are a *long* way from Lihu'e. The first thing a tow truck driver will probably ask you is, "Do you own your own home?" It's probably cheaper to buy a new car. And AAA won't tow a *stuck* car, only one that won't start, so yank an important-looking wire before you call them. Remember the 4WD drive trick to driving on sand is to have low air pressure in your tires (15 psi is what we use), be gentle on the gas, and *don't stop* in soft sand; let your momentum carry you. A cheap air pump from Walmart that plugs into the cigarette lighter can refill the air. Even with all that, it's still possible to get stuck. Consider taking the carpet out of the trunk and driving on it if you're stuck.

To get there, take Hwy 50 till it ends, veering right at the fork. (See map on page 88.) The first dirt road leads 3.2 miles to a large monkeypod tree. To the left is **Queen's Pond**. This is the one part of Polihale that often offers safe swimming. It is partially protected by a small fringing reef, and the swimming inside the reef is good except during periods of high surf.

If you go to the right at the monkeypod tree, there's a soft sandy spot in the road 4.5 miles from where you left the pavement. If you drive past it (*don't stop in the sand*), look for the large parking lot on your left with three small pavilions and restrooms. You'll be able to fall out of your car onto the sand.

Beaches along **Na Pali** are not reachable unless you're up for an adventure. That's why they are described *Adventures*.

Two lovers live their sunset dream at a west side beach.

Wet, warm and happy. Life is good…

If you want more from your Kaua'i vacation than a suntan, Kaua'i offers a multitude of activities that will keep you happy and busy. Among the more popular activities are helicopter tours, ocean tours of Na Pali, golfing, hiking, SCUBA diving and kayaking. You will find lots more to do here as well.

We've listed the activities here in alphabetical order. Beware of false claims on brochures. We've seen many fake scenes in some brochure racks. Computers have allowed photo manipulation to imply realities that don't exist (which *we* don't do).

Activities can be booked directly with the companies themselves. Ask them if they have any coupons floating around in the free publications or if there is a discount for booking direct. You can also book through **activity brokers** and **booths**, which are numerous and usually have signs such as free maps or island information. Allow me to translate: The word *free* usually means *I want to sell you something.*

What we're about to tell you has gotten this book pulled from some shops and badmouthed in some circles, but the truth's the truth. Their objective, as is the case with many concierges, is to sell you activities for a commission. *Occasionally,* you can get better deals through activity booths or your concierge, but not often, because 25–30 percent of what you're paying is their commission (which they call a "deposit") for making the phone call. That's why calling direct can sometimes save money. Companies are so happy they don't have to give away one-quarter to one-third of their fee to activity booths, they'll sometimes give you a discount.

Many of the activity booths strewn about the island are actually forums for selling timeshares. We are not taking a shot at timeshares. It's just that you need to know the real purpose of some of these booths. They can be very aggressive, especially with so many timeshares on the market. (To use a wilderness analogy— they are the hunters; you are the hunted. Don't let them see the fear in your eyes.)

Selling activities is a *big* business on Kaua'i, and it's important to know *why* they're pitching a certain company. If an activity booth or desk steers you to xyz helicopter company and assures you that it's the best, that's fine, but consider the source. That's usually the company that the booth gets the *biggest commission* from. We frequently check up on these booths. Some are reputable and honest, and some are outrageous liars. Few activity sellers have ever done any of the activities unless they got it *free* and the company *knew* who they were. On the other hand, we *pay* for everything we do and review activities *anonymously*. We have no stake in *any* activity company we recommend, and we receive *no* commission. We just want to steer you in the best direction we can. If you know who you want to go with (because you read our reviews and decided for yourself), call them direct first.

A warning: Many of the companies listed have a 24-hour cancellation policy. Even if the weather causes you (not them) to cancel the morning of your activity, *you will be charged.* Some credit card companies will back you in a dispute if the 24-hour policy is posted, some won't. Fair? Maybe not. But that's the way it is.

Lastly, consider booking online before you come. Good companies can fill up

in advance, and the Internet can pave the way for your activities. Our app and website (**revealedtravelguides.com**) have links to *every* company listed here that has a site, even the ones we recommend *against*.

And speaking of our smartphone app, we've GPSed all the companies in this and every other section. Not necessarily their home office (which Google might take you to) but the actual location where you are expected to check in, as well as all of our trails, all the roads, etc. You can even see where you are on our maps at all times. Can't do that in a book or eBook. But our ***Hawaii Revealed*** smartphone app does just that, even when you're out of cell phone range. It does a bunch of other cool stuff, too.

AIR TOURS

HELICOPTERS

If ever there was a place made for helicopter exploration, it's Kaua'i. Much of the island can be seen only by air, and helicopters, with their giant windows and their ability to hover, are by far the preferred method for most. Going to Kaua'i without taking a helicopter flight is like going to see the Sistine Chapel and not looking up. You will see the ruggedly beautiful Na Pali Coast and marvel at the sheerness of some of its cliffs. This is an area where razor-thin, almost two-dimensional mountains rise parallel to each other, leaving impossibly tall and narrow valleys between them. You will see vertical spires and shake your head in disbelief at the sight of a goat perched on top. The awe-inspiring Waimea Canyon unfolds beneath you. A good pilot will come up over a ridge, suddenly exposing the glorious canyon, often timed to coincide with a

Welcome to dreamland…

crescendo in the music you hear in your headphones. You will see the incredible Olokele Valley with its jagged twists and turns and stair-step waterfalls. It is impossible to keep track of all the waterfalls you will see on your flight. You will get a different view of Kaua'i's fabulous north shore beaches and reefs. You might see whales, depending on the time of year. And best of all, you will be treated to the almost spiritual splendor of Wai'ale'ale Crater. You have never seen anything like the crater—a three-sided wall of waterfalls 3,000 feet high, greens of every imaginable shade and a lushness that is beyond comprehension. Many people find themselves weeping when they enter the crater. Others find that they stop breathing—it happened to me the first time. If it has been dry lately, it's simply great; if it's been *pumping* rain in the interior, the waterfalls are spectacular.

When you are finished with the flight, you will either be speechless or babble like a fool—it happens to everyone.

Bear in mind that we're not rabidly pro-helicopter statewide. In *Maui Revealed*, we were lukewarm on flights there (fearing a bang-for-your-buck deficit). O'ahu, too, doesn't lend itself well to air tours. But on Kaua'i it's absolutely worth it.

One concern you may have is safety, and that's a valid point. As far as the industry safety record is concerned, there have been crashes and "incidents," when a craft has had to make an unscheduled landing. You can ask the companies directly about safety, but you should be aware that over the years when we've tried it, we were often misled or directly lied to. Not every time, but many times.

When we checked with the FAA, we discovered that, like many things, safety evaluations aren't that simple. A company might be cited for maintenance violations—*that* sounds ominous. Then you find out that the maintenance was carried out properly, but a log was dated incorrectly, or the company didn't fill out a particular form. Should we steer you away from them for this reason?

In the end it comes down to a matter of judgment. Below is a list of companies that we feel are qualified. Not all have spotless safety records. Things happen— a warning light comes on, and they have to land immediately. Even if it was a false alarm, it is still considered an "incident." These companies struck us as honest and forthright in their concerns about safety.

One issue that all the companies have to deal with is weather. As a pilot myself, I appreciate a company that will *cancel* due to marginal weather. Setting aside the safety factor, if cloud base is super low and it's dumping rain, how much will you get to see? When we don't like the weather, we call the companies to see which ones are canceling. The companies that seem most willing to fly when we wish they *wouldn't* are **Safari** and **Island**. Safari, especially, has really disappointed us by flying during what we consider very ugly conditions.

As far as seating is concerned, the front seat is the best. To console you, some companies might tell you otherwise when they direct you to a back seat. From the front, the island rushes at you with incredible drama. The problem is that seating arrangements are *supposed* to be made on the basis of weight. (They will discreetly weigh you at check-in.) Lighter people are generally seated up front. If you are seated in the back, the **right seat** is the best since much of the action will be on the right side. (By common agreement, companies fly clockwise around the island, making Na Pali and other areas best from the right side, though good pilots will rotate the chopper often to accommodate left seat passengers.) Although companies won't guarantee you the *front* seat, ask them if they'll at least keep you on the *right side* of the craft and let them know you'll consider them weasels if they don't comply. Most will accommodate. If they don't, consider going elsewhere.

Helicopter Types

There are many different types of helicopters. **A-Stars** seat two passengers up front and four in the back, leaving two people in the middle. Helicopter companies like these crafts since they can fly six passengers at a time. There are usually no windows to open, so glare may be a factor with your pictures. **Eco-Stars** are a roomier and more luxurious version of A-Stars. They have lots of window space, are quieter and cost more (over $3 million a pop), so tours are more expensive. **Blue Hawaiian, Maverick** and **Sunshine** use Eco-Stars. At press time nobody was using **Bell Jet Rangers** on Kaua'i, but it's a popular tour helicopter nationwide and one we try to avoid due to poor seating. **MD 500** aircraft (aka Hughes 500) seat two passengers in the front and two in the back, a great arrangement. The MD 500 has the pilot sit on the left side, out of the way. (*Some* A-Stars like Jack Harter's do, as well.) MD 500s have large, removable windows.

While the back is a bit cramped and doesn't allow the forward view that other back seats do, their side views are better. Currently, only one company, **Jack Harter** use these because the MDs cost more per person to operate per passenger than A-Stars. They'll fly with the doors off. Windy and cold in back but an awesome experience. Lastly, **Mauna Loa** flies **Robinson R-44s**. These are piston-driven (as opposed to much more reliable turbine-driven) helicopters with one-third the horsepower. Though these birds are much cheaper to buy and operate, it's not reflected in their tour prices.

All helicopters on Kaua'i are allowed to fly 500 feet over most scenic areas. (Companies that claim *only* they can fly that low…are full of beans.)

This is a hard section to write. You're going to spend a lot of money, and we *really* want to point you in the right direction. Most of the companies do a pretty good job, but they're very different. (Of course, like another activity that comes to mind—*wink, wink*—even when a helicopter ride over Kaua'i is bad…it's still good.) The difference between helicopter companies is the difference between a very pleasant flight and really experiencing the island. It's the difference between coming off the craft with a pleasant smile and leaving with a stupid grin on your face

Company	Phone	Helicopter Type	2-Way *	Departs
Blue Hawaiian Helicopters	(808) 245-5800	Eco-Star	Yes	Lihu'e, Princeville
Jack Harter Helicopters	(808) 245-3774	A-Star, MD 500	Yes	Lihu'e
Maverick Helicopters	(800) 978-0266	Eco-Star	Yes	Port Allen
Safari Helicopters	(808) 246-0136	A-Star	Yes	Lihu'e
Island Helicopters	(808) 245-8588	A-Star	Yes	Lihu'e
Mauna Loa Helicopters	(808) 245-7500	Robinson R44	Yes	Lihu'e
Sunshine Helicopters	(808) 270-3999	FX/A-Star, Eco-Star	Yes	Lihu'e
Ni'ihau Helicopters	(808) 335-3500	Agusta	Yes	Hanapepe

* Indicates whether craft contains a microphone for you to talk to the pilot.

Scale on Na Pali is hard to convey. The arch on the right side of the photo is big enough to fly an airplane through.

that won't leave you all day—between having a tale to tell and experiencing something so moving that it will stay with you for a lifetime. All this said and done, our favorites are **Blue Hawaiian** and **Jack Harter**.

Prices

The prices we list are the "out-the-door" prices (including taxes, fees and fuel surcharges), but remember that companies adjust them all the time. Flight times are the guaranteed minimum amount of time in the air. You can almost always get a discount by calling the company and asking, or booking directly on their website. Charter rates for the whole bird are between $700 and $3,000 per hour. If you weigh over 250 pounds, you may be charged extra.

Most Recommended Companies

Blue Hawaiian Helicopters (808-245-5800)—This is the company to go to if you want the cushiest flight and a great location at the airport instead of a van ride from off-site. Their Eco-Stars are the most comfortable choppers on the island and the roomiest. Giant windows (with gobs of glare, too, if you're into photos) provide a great viewing area. $339 per person for a 50-minute tour from Lihu'e. For an extra $60 you can get a recording of your flight made from four on-board cameras.

Jack Harter Helicopters (808-245-3774)—Named after the guy who started it all on Kaua'i in the early '60s, his company's tours are still in demand, so book in advance. Harter has 60-minute flights for $289 and an excellent comprehensive 90-minute flight for $434. They're the only one with such a flight, and the experience is relaxed and unhurried. Pilots come and go at all helicopter companies, so the quality of the pilot's narration can come down to training. For what it's

Vantage points like this are things mere mortals will never achieve—unless they spring for a pricey but highly memorable helicopter ride.

worth, the accuracy of Jack Harter's narrations seems pretty high. If you want a sportier trip (we think it's more fun), they also have a four-passenger MD 500 that flies with the doors off for $309. *Very* cool and great for photographers. Unlike their A-Star flights, the MD 500 has no background music. For this there's a 250-pound weight limit, 400 pounds *per couple*. By the way, despite incorrect media stories, doors-off flights are still allowed as long as restraints that can be removed quickly are used, which they are here.

Maverick Helicopters (800-978-0266) leaves from Port Allen Airport in Hanapepe, which is good and bad. Good because their route doesn't have any dead spots—you see everything people on Lihu'e flights see (except Wailua Falls), and the action is non-stop. It's bad because unless you're staying in Po'ipu, it's a long drive. Maverick

uses Eco-Stars and does a fairly good job for a large mainland company. The departure airport is quiet and chill. There's not even a tower. Avoid the $169 25-minute flight that doesn't even fly over Na Pali in favor of the $269 50-minute flight that lets you see nearly all you want to see.

Other Qualified Companies

Safari Helicopters (808-246-0136)— We're not a big fan of their tours. ($239 for 55 minutes.) They record your entire trip from multiple on-board cameras. (It's $40 extra.) The quality may be pretty bad (we get hypnotized by watching the dirt on the camera lens moving back and forth), and frankly, we think you'd be *much* happier with a professionally made video, rather than one taken on the fly (so to speak). But at least you'll get to hear your voice if you ask the pilot questions. Readers have told us that they are the most accommodating to larger passengers. They also have a trip that lands at a remote canyon where you get out and listen to a lecture about the Robinson Family history and their plans. Overpriced at $314, but Safari often has exceptional discounts on their website.

Island Helicopters (808-245-8588) has 50-minute tours in their A-Stars for $297. For $398 (check for discounts—all their prices are outrageous, but they offer deep discounts for booking online) they'll land at the waterfall seen in *Jurassic Park* called Manawaiopuna Falls (they should offer half off if you can pronounce *that* one properly) and let you get out for photos and some area info. No swimming, and people over 250 pounds (couples over 420 pounds) may have to purchase an additional ticket.

Mauna Loa Helicopters (808-245-7500) out of Lihu'e Airport promotes private tours for two or three passengers, and they do a pretty good job. It's $325 per person for the 60-minute island tour. (Currently flying only with the doors off.) Photographers may want to try their pricey photo tour for $350 per person for one hour, with a max of three people. Plan on spending at least $700 though—single riders are required to buy two tickets (probably to make up for the cost of operating the bird). You get to choose the locations. 275-pound per person weight limit.

Sunshine Helicopters (808-270-3999)—Our least favorite company. Sunshine uses FX-Stars (A-Stars) and Eco-Stars (which they call Whisper-Stars) from Lihu'e (the 50-minute tour is $269 for the FX-Star and $309 for the Whisper Star). Although helicopter companies always claim that weight distribution decides who sits up front, if you pay an extra $50, they'll distribute your butt up front. They call them "first class seats." The $60 recording of your flight is pricier than elsewhere.

Be wary of some of the information imparted during some of these flights, especially from bigger companies that may have pilots from the mainland with little knowledge of Kaua'i. They mean well, but often their "facts" are way off.

HELICOPTER TIPS
- Never take a flight of less than 50 minutes; you will only get your appetite whetted. It's too rushed.
- With a still camera, zoom lenses work best since the size of the field changes rapidly.
- Use a fast ISO speed of 400 or higher.
- Beware of the glare from the inside of the windows, and don't let your camera touch a vibrating window while shooting. Circular polarizers (which you'll have to adjust constantly) are *vital* for reducing glare. Wearing dark clothing helps, too. Polarized sunglasses help in the glare department.
- Don't get so caught up taking pictures that you lose the moment. It's hard to soak up the magic of your flight through a camera viewfinder.
- If you're in a craft that has two-way communication, don't be afraid to ask the pilot to turn so you can take a shot of something. Most will.
- If you're prone to motion sickness, take something *before* you fly.
- Remove any earrings before putting on the headphones.
- If you can't hear the pilot over the music, ask him to adjust the sound.
- If there are four or more of you, consider chartering an A-Star helicopter. It might actually be

No buffalo roam here, but the deer and the antelope play on the Forbidden Island. And the only way to see 'em is with Ni'ihau Helicopters.

cheaper and will allow you to call many of the shots during the flight: "Pilot, please hover here for a few minutes, and turn a little more to the right." If only your group is on the flight, you are effectively chartering the flight whether you realize it or not, so take advantage of it.

- Morning is usually the best time for flights (though Na Pali looks best in the afternoon). Rainy weather brings more waterfalls.
- If you take a helicopter trip, do it early in your stay. It'll help orient you to the island.
- When you see people getting off a helicopter after their tour, try not to be downwind from them. They are often foaming at the mouth from their experience and might drool on you.

FLY TO NI'IHAU

For an off-island helicopter experience, **Ni'ihau Helicopters** (808-335-3500), owned by the powerful Robinson family, flies groups to their privately owned island of Ni'ihau. For $465 you fly for 1-hour, circumnavigating Ni'ihau from a thrillingly low altitude, and land at one of its beaches for snorkeling, beachcombing and a picnic. Bring your own snorkel gear and towel. This is an awesome trip, and if you've already seen Kaua'i by air, it's highly recommended. Ni'ihau's beaches are achingly beautiful, especially when they land on the northern tip of the island. Nowhere will you find cleaner water or better beachcombing, and you can keep whatever you find. The problem you encounter with them is that they require at least five people on a flight and don't usually have enough customers to ensure a flight for you. Even if they do, their twin-engine Agusta is often being chartered for commercial work (such as the military, which uses it for electronic warfare exercises). If you are determined to take the flight, contact them as much in advance as possible to maximize the chance that they can organize a flight, but don't be surprised if it doesn't work out. Less than a thousand people a year get to visit this place. Count yourself special if you're one of them. Tours depart from Port Allen Airport on Kaua'i's west side.

AIRPLANES

If you don't like helicopters and still want to see Kaua'i by air, **Wings Over Kaua'i** (808-635-0815) has a four-seat Cessna 172 and a six-passenger Airvan with circle island tours for $150 or $160 (cheaper online). Visibility is better with the Airvan, but it scoots along pretty fast. Airplanes can't go into the narrow valleys the way helicopters can. It's nowhere *near* as thrilling as a helicopter tour, and if your objective is to see the sights, go with helicopters. But if you just want a plane ride over Kaua'i, here's your chance, and they're friendly folks. Weight limits are higher (285 pounds in the Cessna, 320 in the Airvan). You can charter the whole plane for $600. Try to sit on the right side because they fly clockwise around the island.

Air Ventures Hawai'i (808-651-0679) also does tours in their six-seat Airvan for $135 for the hour, as well as private tours in their Cessna for $199 per person (but you have to book at least two people for the flight). They also have a YMF-5 Super biplane that would make Snoopy drool. They call their pilot the "Red Baron" (who, in real life, actually flew a *triplane*.) At $473 per couple for an hour-long flight, it's similarly priced to helicopters, but they only take two passengers at a time, so tours are more personalized. Unfortunately, biplanes have fairly rotten views. The wings dominate everything you see, so your aerial photos will be rotten. (But you'll *look* cooler in your selfies decked out in their cloth helmets and goggles.)

ATVs, also called quads, can be a fun way of seeing the backcountry. They are like Tonka Toys on steroids with knobby tires. The companies here offer *very* different experiences. Unfortunately, none currently offers single-person ATVs.

Kipu Ranch Adventures (808-246-9288) is our favorite. The scenery is the nicest, the vehicles (Kawasaki Teryx 4s and KRX 1000s, as well as Mulepro FXTs) are top quality and the most comfortable of the three companies, plus their guides are the most customer-oriented.

Their most popular tour is of the beautiful Kipu Ranch. During the 3-hour tour ($187 per person for the Teryx 4, or $474 for two people in the Teryx KRX 1000) you're treated to the lump-in-your-throat backdrop of Ha'upu Range along the pastures. They'll descend into woodsier areas, along the stream where *Raiders of the Lost Ark* was filmed (bring a swimsuit and water shoes in case you "fall" in), and they usually end up at a viewpoint almost no one on Kaua'i ever gets to see—the hidden valley and beach of Kipu Kai from the road that drapes across the mountain. (Because it's private and closed, we *never* thought we'd get to see this sight.) They also offer a waterfall tour ($187 per person for the Teryx 4s or Mulepros, or $474 for two seats on a KRX 1000), which takes you along their three trails and eventually to a private waterfall where they'll let you swim for a bit. You pay for two seats whether you have a second person or not. If you prefer not to drive, you gotta pay the full price anyway, but you'll ride with a guide.

Their machines are ridiculously stable (you'll get a demonstration), and they run their tours well. Their training is excellent if you're new to ATVs. You won't be allowed to totally cut loose on your bike, but your overall moving speed is similar to Kaua'i ATV. It's a tour, and you *will* get dusty or muddy. But it's a fun way to see exceptional scenery. Minimum age for riders (*drivers* must be 18) is 9 years old for all tours.

On the other hand, **Kaua'i ATV** (808-742-2734) in Koloa is the exact opposite in almost every way. They lack the good views of Kipu Ranch and lush surroundings of Princeville Ranch. Instead of mostly trail riding here, you usually stick to dirt roads. The average moving speed is 15 mph, and you may reach 25 mph at times; it depends on the guide. If it's been raining, you're encouraged to crash through every puddle. During dry times, it's super dusty. Either way you'll get dirty. They almost never cancel due to weather. Like Kipu Ranch, they have up to 12 vehicles per group on this 3.5-hour tour. Service is pretty blank at the check-in. Their playground consists of mostly old sugar cane roads plus two stops at small waterfalls and a cool trip through a half mile-long tunnel. Two-, three- and four-person mud buggies make up the fleet (try to get one of the newer-looking ones), and they allow qualified drivers to take turns. Narrations are minimal, which is good, because when they do talk, the information is often inaccurate. Our safety concerns stem from personal observations, including seeing another customer complain that his brakes were not working. (He was told to simply

"keep his distance" instead of replacing the brakeless ATV.)

The waterfall tour is $342. It's the same price for the 4-hour Makauwahi Cave Tour, which requires a bit of hiking to get to. This is more of an amphitheater than a cave—there are walls, yet no roof—but it's still a cool sight, and having a guide explain what you're looking at makes for a nice tour. Maximum weight per person is 320 pounds. Drivers must be 18 years of age or older with a valid driver's license. Guests under the age of 18 must be accompanied by a parent or guardian 25 years of age or older. They also have the **ZipBike** tour (see page 198), which we are less enthusiastic about.

Bike lanes or shoulders of some kind line the main highway from Princeville all the way around to Mana on the west side (though some are narrow in spots, and some bridges force you into the traffic). Past Princeville, forget it. And for what it's worth, we find that Kaua'i drivers are more likely to crowd bikes off to the side than other islands. Don't know why, but it's true.

BIKING HOTSPOTS

For **mountain biking**, the dirt roads in **Po'ipu**, especially near **Maha'ulepu,** can be fun, though a bit dusty. Another good place is the cane road between Kealia Beach and Anahola. (Start at Kealia Beach and pedal north; give way to ATV riders.) And the 2.5-mile paved road from **Kealia Beach** up to **Spalding Monument** is really scenic and sparsely driven. You'll gain 400 feet of elevation in the process. The **Kuilau** and **Moalepe Trails** (see page 167) can be exciting. The roads

Beachside biking along the east shore.

past the end of Kuamo'o Road in Kapa'a leading toward Wai'ale'ale and the *Jungle Hike* (see page 168) are excellent for mountain bikes.

If you don't mind a long drive, the roads of Koke'e (see maps on page 154 and 88) offer good choices. Pay attention to **Mohihi-Camp 10 Road** (see map on page 155). The **contour road** in Koke'e is always fun. You can even travel down the spine of some of the ridges, such as Kauhao and Ka'aweiki, if you have the stones to pedal back up.

Kapa'a Bike Path

Kaua'i is in the process of spending 50 million federal dollars to construct a shoreline walking/biking path from Nawiliwili to Anahola, scheduled to be completed about the time that Lady Gaga draws her first Social Security check. Currently the only completed section is the 6-mile section from **Waipouli Beach Resort** in Kapa'a to just north of **Donkey Beach** and a 2-mile chunk from **Lydgate** to **Coconut Market-**

place. The northern section is the prettiest, and the smooth concrete path is easy to ride on beach cruisers.

BIKE RENTALS

Pedal 'n Paddle (826-9069) in Hanalei has beach cruisers and hybrids only. You'll pay $30–$60 per day.

Coconut Coasters (808-822-7368) is near the north end of Kapa'a and has a great selection of cruisers, hybrids, a range of kids' bikes, and tandems.

We really like **Hele On Kaua'i** (808-822-4628) near Pono Market. They make the rental process very simple (reserve in advance is suggested), and it's the best bang for your buck. You can get a bike for 2 hours for $15 or $35 for a tandem—enough time to do the whole paved portion. They only carry cruisers and child trailers, but anything more for the bike path is overkill.

If you want to do less work, try an eBike from **Eco eBikes Kaua'i** (808-800-0810) in Lihu'e, it will run about $80 per day. They will deliver to some areas if you book for multiple days and in advance.

Boat Tours

When Hollywood needs a beautiful, remote coastline studded with majestic cliffs and glorious valleys to film movies, they often choose Kaua'i's Na Pali Coast. *Pirates of the Caribbean 4, Six Days/ Seven Nights, King Kong* and others have all used a Na Pali backdrop to convey an idyllic paradise. From the sea, this area of the island takes on a magical quality. Many people dream of seeing the Hawaiian Islands by sea. The Na Pali region is surely the most popular area to cruise, but there are others as well. This can be a fantasy trip. Rough seas are rarely part of the fantasy, but they can be part of reality, depending on conditions.

Seeing Na Pali by boat is an incredible thrill that we highly recommend. Soaking up this coastline and being on a boat are exquisitely relaxing. You can see it by leaving from the west side or the north shore. They are two very different experiences.

If you leave from the **west side**, you'll only see half of Na Pali (and not the best half), and three-quarters of the trip isn't even along Na Pali. The boats that leave from Port Allen travel 23 miles along the relatively uninteresting (by sea) Mana Plain, then head up the dry side of Na Pali before turning around at Kalalau. (Boats that leave from Kikiaola Harbor shave 9 miles off the duller part—see

These passengers know what Hollywood knows… Na Pali is mesmerizing.

map on page 88.) If boats would cruise past Kalalau to Hanakapi'ai, we'd be much happier, because that short stretch has some beautiful sights. But most turn back at Kalalau. On the pro side, the seas tend to be calmer from the west side, especially on the return trip. Also, spinner dolphins are prevalent along the coast here—you're almost guaranteed to spot them.

A few companies, however, have permits to leave the **north shore**. Those boats that leave from Hanalei or 'Anini on the north shore have a *far* better and more exciting route, though the return trip is usually into head seas (meaning into the swells) and headwinds, so it can be bumpy.

Some west shore companies switch to south shore tours in October and return to Na Pali in April; others can do Na Pali year-round. Some combine it with a trip to Ni'ihau. If you do Na Pali in winter, expect bigger seas.

There are two main snorkeling spots: **Nu'alolo** (which is pretty good) and a spot near Polihale that the bigger boats often use called **Makole** (which is pretty bad). If you're at Makole, the best snorkeling is away from shore, not toward it. If you want to *land* at Nu'alolo and walk around and see some archeological remains, only **Captain Andy's**, **Kaua'i Sea Tours**, and **Na Pali Explorer** have the permits to come ashore.

Some of these boating companies give you discounts for booking online.

WHAT & WHO

We've spent a lot of time anonymously reviewing these boats, and here's the deal. If it's May through September and you really want to see Na Pali, you want to do this from the north shore—*period*. That means you want **Na Pali Catamaran**, **Na Pali Coast Hanalei**, **HoloHolo Charters**

or **Napali Sea Breeze**, or if you want no frills, **North Shore Charters**. As mentioned before, *nothing* a west side company can do can compete with the route these guys take. They could probably *flog* you on this trip, and they'd still be better than any boat leaving from Port Allen. If you can't book these or it's not these summer months (April and October are borderline), we recommend **HoloHolo** and **Liko Kaua'i**.

North Shore Companies

Our favorite is probably **Na Pali Catamaran** (808-826-6853). Their 35-foot power cat (no sailing) takes up to 22 people, has a slender enough profile to go into most of the sea caves, and plenty of shade. (That overhead protection comes in handy when the captain pilots the boat under a waterfall, but if you're feeling adventurous, they will let you sit on the bow.) $300 for a 4-hour tour, which includes snorkeling at Tunnels. The crew seems to genuinely care about making sure guests have a good time. They encourage passengers to get up and move around the boat to take pictures, and offer drinks (soda and juice) throughout the trip. If conditions are good, they often let you stay in the water for more than an hour, even though you are only guaranteed 45 minutes of snorkeling.

Na Pali Coast Tours (808-826-6114) also has a good product and a fun crew. Their 32-foot power cat (called UFO II) is small enough to poke into nearly all of the sea caves, and the crew does a good job. Morning tours are best with around 4 hours to sightsee, snorkel at Nu'alolo and eat a deli lunch for $285, while the 2-hour sightseeing tour does *not* include snorkeling and comes with soft drinks (or BYOB—no glass containers) and water only for $185. Up to 18 passengers; minimal shade. Wear waterproof (or none at all) shoes to wade out to the boat at the

Hanalei River. Grab a seat on the left (OK, OK, *port*) side going out for the best views. April through October is their season from the north shore. They also launch the same boat from the west side (Kekaha) in the winter season only for a similar snorkel tour but for $185.

Next on our list would be **HoloHolo Charters** (808-335-0815) summertime (April–October) RIB boats, holding up to 25 passengers. Things start off rocky with their agonizingly long process of getting everybody from the Tahiti Nui Restaurant (meeting spot) to being under way. But the fast (though loud) boat gets closer to the shore, and they'll stop in a couple of caves on the way back. Deli lunch and cookies, with snorkeling at the less-preferred Makole for $299. Shade available to deploy upon request. Good crew.

North Shore Charters (808-828-1379) leaves out of 'Anini Beach *in the summer* with 18 passengers in their 32-foot catamaran. No frills, some shade, deli sandwiches, and you'll snorkel at Nu'alolo for $225 (tax included).

Napali Sea Breeze (808-828-1285) uses a 34-foot power cat and gets *Flakiest of the North Shore Operators* award. (Multiple failed attempts to book were blamed on bad weather when other operators went out—we suspected that too few people were booked.) They carry 16 people at most (which can still feel crowded), and they snorkel at Nu'alolo. $225, which includes a deli lunch. Their narration is fairly spot on, but you need to be right next to the captain's tower to hear it. They depart from 'Anini (you'll have to wade to the boat), it takes 10 more minutes to get to Na Pali than the Hanalei guys, but you get to see some of the hidden beaches below Princeville. It would be easier to like them if the owner wasn't so tough on the employees in front of the guests.

West Shore Companies

HoloHolo Charters (808-335-0815) has a large, 65-foot power catamaran. They can feel a bit like a processing machine, but do a pretty consistent job on all their tours. Their trips are distinguished in that they go to the "forbidden" island of Ni'ihau. For $269, the 7-hour trip leaves in the morning from Port Allen and makes a beeline to Kalalau Beach on Na Pali. In light seas they're close to shore; heavier swells call for greater distance. Then they tour part of Na Pali before heading to Ni'ihau where they snorkel. (Clean, clear water and lots of fish, but currents can sometimes make snorkeling there more work.) Continental breakfast and a good deli lunch included. After the snorkeling, the open bar serves beer and wine, but they refuse to serve cookies until they're 5 minutes from port. (Maybe they're afraid you'll toss them otherwise.)

There are two large trampolines at the bow for sunning, but they and the entire bow section are off limits most of the time while motoring. Easy steps into and out of the water from the boat. HoloHolo is a good outfit and is easy to recommend. The boat is good, pretty stable, there's plenty of shade available, and the crew is very professional. They have a freshwater shower hose and adequate snorkel gear but no wetsuits available. Our only complaint is that the boat design makes it feel crowded on nice days. Most of the seating is inside, but when it's reasonably calm and sunny, most people want to be outside, which is somewhat spartan and lacking in seating, so people tend to crowd around the railings.

Their sunset tour is $159 for a buffet, beer, wine, mai tais and champagne.

They also have a smaller cat called the Leila, but we don't recommend it as much.

Liko Kaua'i Cruises (808-338-9980) offers a relaxing 5-hour tour of Na Pali on a 49-foot power catamaran with 32 people. (By the way, a lot of companies claim to be the largest boat able to enter sea caves. Liko actually is, beating the competition by 1 foot in length.) You'll leave from Kikiaola Small Boat Harbor near Kekaha and cruise north up the coast, often going as far as Ke'e Beach if the weather's good. (That's farther than any other west shore power cat goes, which pleases us greatly.) On the way back you stop and snorkel at Nu'alolo Kai or sometimes lousy Makole. Liko, a native Hawaiian, narrates with legends and stories. $169 for adults, $139 for keiki (kids 3–12), it includes water, sodas and sandwiches. One of the better priced ocean tours if you have small children. They do a great

job of following the mood of their guests and seem to genuinely enjoy having kids aboard. Afternoon/sunset tours also available in the summer.

Liko's sister company, **Makana Charters** (808-338-9980) uses a 32-foot power cat that holds 12 people and a 34-foot single hull that holds 10–12. The cost is $189, and the experience is just as relaxed and a little more personable—the Liko tours can lose some of their personal touch when their boat is packed.

Catamaran Kahanu (808-645-6176) is a small boat (18 max, which would be pretty tight) run by a gruff but likable Hawaiian captain. This is a small outfit, and what they lack in cushion (literally) is made up with their family feel. And just like family, the stories and anecdotes you'll be treated to are either endearing or pa-

Snorkeling here at Nu'alolo usually surpasses the other popular snorkel spot on Na Pali.

tronizing, depending on your outlook. Overall, a pretty good trip, with a tasty lunch. Morning 5-hour trips from Port Allen are $205 (cheaper online).

Na Pali Experience (808-635-1131) is a small outfit that takes only six passengers on their 24-foot power cats. They venture almost all the way to Ke'e Beach unless the ocean is too rough. Then they turn around at Kalalau and snorkel at Nu'alolo (they keep good, updated snorkel gear). Being in a boat this small means you're able to get into all the sea caves (seas permitting), and it also means you'll get to know your captain fairly well. They keep things more lighthearted than other operators and do a pretty good job of reading their passengers' humor and tastes. Speaking of tastes, the only ding we feel is that the small size of the boat means less room for food. A 5-hour tour on the water with snorkeling works up an appetite—all they provide are snacks (like chips) and fruit. If you want something more substantial, you'll need to bring it and endure the resentment of your fellow passengers. Otherwise, it's a good product. We like the fact that they leave from Kikiaola—it's way better than Port Allen. They offer three tours throughout the day in summer and one in the winter, $189 and each 5 hours.

Other Big Boats

Captain Andy's Sailing Adventures (808-335-6833) is the biggest operator on the island, leaving from Port Allen, and they tend to run pretty tight ships. They have three types of boats—their luxury catamaran (Southern Star), regular catamarans and their rigid hull rafts. The Southern Star is large (65 feet), plush and comfortable, and their 5.5-hour snorkel tour has a good BBQ lunch and free beer

A sea cave—with a hole in the ceiling— and a waterfall. Even Hollywood couldn't make this stuff up.

and wine for $205. If they take their full load of 49 people, it's *a bit* tight. But otherwise, it's an easy trip to recommend. Their 5.5-hour Na Pali trips in the smaller catamarans are $185. Snorkeling when conditions permit, but at lousy Makole. Deli lunch with free beer and wine. It would be a better product if they didn't pack up to *49* people on their nice 55-foot catamarans (and it *feels* crowded). You're best off if there are *more* than 49 people, because then they'll split the group onto two boats. These are sleek sailing cats, but they only sail a short time, and when they *do* raise the sail, it seems to activate the cookie-tossing instinct in some people, especially if they're using the indoor shade. (The crew is helpful and discreet with those who are nauseated.) But they are pretty capable sailboats, which will excite sailing enthusiasts. They also have a couple Zodiac tours—including one that *lands* at Nu'alolo Kai for $225, as well as a summer month sea cave tour for $159. Their excellent dinner cruise is described in *Lunch & Dinner Cruises* on page 264. With so many boats, they have *way* too many options to describe here.

Kaua'i Sea Tours (808-335-5309) leaves from Port Allen for Na Pali trips for $195. They have a 60-foot power/sailing cat called the Lucky Lady, which rides well. Think of this as a power cat, because at best they'll probably only raise the sails *while motoring* downwind. (The sails are more for decoration since this type of vessel sails like a pig.) They also have a water slide that keiki love—just watch out for back-flop entries. Continental breakfast plus a deli lunch. They also use a 24-foot rigid-hull inflatable (RIB) that lands at Nu'alolo (in the summer) for $195, but it's not in the same league as Na Pali Explorer's nicer inflatable. This 6-hour tour also includes a deli lunch. They have a dinner cruise described in *Lunch & Dinner Cruises* on page 264.

Blue Dolphin Charters (808-335-5553) has two catamarans called Blue Dolphin I and II, similar to the Lucky Lady above with similarly ineffective sailing prowess. Up to 49 people, continental breakfast (good cinnamon rolls) and deli lunch, good beer, wine and mai tais. They have a slide into the water to thrill the kids. $190 for Na Pali trips. You can SCUBA for an extra $53, which is quite reasonable. They also have intro to SCUBA where first timers can see what it's like under the sea for $97. We don't recommend going with Blue Dolphin if you've never dived before—stick with actual dive companies for that. The product feels tacked on rather than an emphasis on introduction. If you do dive, be sure to get a wetsuit—a warm, comfortable diver usually has more bottom time. Some days they also offer a Ni'ihau trip similar to HoloHolo's for $245. The crews are pretty good and their narrations fair. Plenty of shade, but avoid the inside seats at the front of the cabin. You never sail; at best they'll motor sail downwind. Po'ipu sunset tours (winter only) are $165.

East Shore Companies

Kaua'i Sail Charters (808-821-0222) has a 41-foot Beneteau Oceanis sailboat named Iwa leaves out of Nawiliwili Harbor in Lihu'e and can carry up to six passengers. You can charter the boat and start barking out orders and saying piraty things for $995 for three hours or do a shared charter (if available) for $200 per person. (Six hours cost $1,895.) If conditions allow, they'll sail around the corner and allow you to swim ashore to the otherwise inaccessible Kipu Kai Beach. They allow alcohol aboard, and you can bring your own food.

Rigid-hull Inflatable Boats (RIBs)

Blue Ocean Adventure Tours (800-451-6133) leaves from Kikiaola Harbor on the west side and heads north in their 24-foot RIB boat (no shade), shaving 9 miles of uneventful shoreline compared to boats that leave from Port Allen. $169 for the morning 4.5-hour Na Pali snorkel trip. They also have a tour that *lands* at Nuʻalolo Kai for $199. These trips include a light, deli-style lunch. No restroom on board. They also have a 48-foot power cat with *lots* of shade for $175 for 4.5 hours. If seas cooperate it's a pretty quick boat with a *thousand* horses pushing it along, but their snorkeling spot is the more unfortunate Makole instead of Nuʻalolo. Drinks and light snacks provided.

Na Pali Riders (808-742-6331) has a 4-hour trip out of Kikiaola Harbor on their 30-foot Zodiac, but it's a decidedly mixed bag. They have less of the frills and more of the thrills. On the pro side, during the summer season they go all the way to Keʻe on the north shore, so you'll see all of Na Pali. (Winter is whale watching heading south.) When they encounter dolphins, they get amazingly close. Also, inflatables can be fun on calm seas. But if seas aren't reasonably smooth, it's a rough ride because you'll feel every bump. On the con side there's no shade or restroom, if the boat is full it can feel crowded, and they only serve drinks and snacks. Price is $169. We recommend the morning tour. An afternoon trip with snottier seas in a Zodiac ain't fun.

BOATING TIPS

Many companies offer morning and afternoon trips. Morning trips usually have snorkeling and better food on board. Morning is also when you're more likely to encounter smoother seas and better weather, so that's what we recommend.

Be wary of the information given during narrations. Many boat companies, like their helicopter brethren, are particularly prone to repeating inaccurate nonsense in their attempt to "educate" you, and we've seen some who literally made it up as they went along.

Seasickness can strike anyone. If you're concerned that it will be a problem, strongly consider taking Dramamine or Bonine at least an hour *before* you leave. (The night before and morning of are best. It's useless to take it once you're on the boat.) Also, avoid any alcohol the night before. (A *big* no-no.) No greasy foods before or during the trip. And some think that citrus juices are a cause of seasickness. Ginger is a very good preventative/ treatment. Below deck or in anything enclosed is a bad place to be if you're worried about getting seasick. Without a reference point, you're much more likely to let 'er rip. Scopolamine patches work but have side effects, including (occasionally) blurred vision that can last a week. (Been there, done that, on a 10-day boat trip.) If you're feeling sick, put something cold on the back of your neck. As far as the Niʻihau trips are concerned, we've had people tell us they were prone to seasickness and ask where they should sit. The answer is...on land. The boats can be mighty rockin' in that channel between the islands, and if you have a history of easy-queasy, that trip might not be for you. Coming back from Niʻihau is almost always rough.

From the west shore, the best views are off the right (starboard) side going out to Na Pali and off the left (port) side coming back. It's the opposite when you leave from the north shore. Also remember that most boats are a lot smoother in the back than the front, but you may inhale diesel fumes back there. Just slightly ahead of the back seats is our preferred position.

People come off these trips *toasted*, especially in the summer. Make sure you slather on the reef-safe sunscreen early and often and consider having a wide-brimmed hat and light shirt to cover up with when not in the water, or you'll be sorry for the rest of your trip.

Since most trips involve driving early in the morning, consider doing the trip early in your vacation—when your body clock is still on mainland time, and it's easier to rise early.

Most companies make you remove your shoes. Also, agendas are not carved in stone. Weather, seas and opportunities along the way can alter the best laid plans. So be flexible.

There are a number of smaller boat companies with smaller boats that are crowded and have no shade, and we don't recommend them for these waters.

Boogie Boarding

Boogie boarding (riders are derisively referred to as *spongers* by surfers) is where you ride a wave on what is essentially a sawed-off surfboard. It can be a real blast. You need short, stubby fins to catch bigger waves (which break in deeper water), but you can snare small waves by simply standing in shallow water and lurching forward as the wave is breaking. If you've never done it before, stay away from big waves; they can drill you. Smooth-bottom (hard shell) boards work best. If you're not going to boogie

board with boogie fins (which some consider difficult to learn), you should do it with water shoes or some other kind of water footwear. This allows you to scramble around in the water without fear of tearing your feet up on a rock or urchin. Shirts are *very* important, especially for men. (Women already have this aspect covered.) Sand and the board itself can rub you so raw your *da kines* will glow in the dark.

RENTING BOOGIE BOARDS

Your hotel activity desk may have boards. It should cost you $6–$8 per day, $22–$30 per week. Other places include:

North Shore—Hanalei Surf Company (808-826-9000) or **Pedal 'n Paddle** (808-826-9069).

East Shore—Boss Frog (808-822-4334).

South Shore—Po'ipu Surf (808-742-8797) in The Shops at Kukui'ula or **Nukumoi Beach & Surf Shop** (808-742-8019) across from Po'ipu Beach.

BOOGIE BOARDING BEACHES

Below are some beaches worth considering. Also check the *Beaches* chapter for more.

Keiki shreddin 'em.

Camping Sites—County Sites in Black, State Sites in Purple.

Na Pali Coast State Wilderness Park
Hanakoa
Kalalau Beach
Miloli'i Beach
Koke'e State Park
Polihale State Park
Hanalei (Black Pot Beach)
'Anini Beach Park
Anahola Beach Park
Lydgate Beach Park
Lucy Wright Park
Salt Pond Beach Park

- **Kealia Beach** in Kapa'a is excellent, but the waves are powerful.
- **Kalapaki Beach** in Lihu'e is a smart choice for beginners and the timid.
- **Brennecke Beach** usually has good conditions but can be crowded.

CAMPING

The ultimate in low-price lodging is offered by Mother Nature herself. Kaua'i is a great place to camp with 13 different areas—six state camping areas and seven county campsites.

STATE CAMPING AREAS

To camp at a state-controlled site, you need to contact the **Hawai'i DLNR, State Parks** in Lihu'e at (808) 274-3444. You are *strongly* advised to get your permit before you arrive because the sites can fill up, especially during peak season (May–December). The state requires that you enter the driver's license or passport number of every adult who will be camping, as well as the names of any minors, along with your dates of travel. The permits are

$30 per group of up to 10 per night (except Na Pali, which is $35 *per person*) and should be acquired as far in advance as you can. They recommend at least six months in advance during the busy months. *More for Na Pali.*

The state enforces permits with uncommon zeal, so when officers swoop in to check your permits, stand at attention and wipe that smile off your face.

For more on beach campsites see the *Beaches* chapter.

Car camping from 4WDs at Koke'e State Park is lovely—especially Sugi Grove—and is convenient if you plan if you plan on doing a lot of hiking there.

COUNTY CAMPING AREAS

County campsites require a county permit. They will send you an application, or you can get it online. The cost is $3 per adult per night (except Lydgate, which starts at $25 for up to five campers). Call:

County of Kaua'i Parks & Recreation
4444 Rice St., Suite 105
Lihu'e, HI 96766
(808) 241-4463

CAMPING GEAR

If you need to rent camping or hiking gear, your best sources will be **Pedal 'n Paddle** (808-826-9069) in Hanalei or **Kayak Kaua'i** (808-826-9844) in Kapa'a. **Kaua'i Camper Rental** (808-346-0957) has VW camper vans as well as camping equipment for rent.

Propane can be found at **Walmart** (808-246-1599) in Lihu'e. For butane, call **Gaspro** (808-245-6766) in Lihu'e.

Good places to buy gear include: **Da Life** (808-246-6333) in Kalapaki Bay, **Pedal 'n Paddle** (808-826-9069) in Hanalei, **Aloha Xchng** (808-332-5900) in Kalaheo and **Discount Variety** (808-742-9393) in Koloa. Others are **Walmart** and **Costco** in Lihu'e for food.

Lastly, **TSA** can be fussy with camp stoves, even when checked. Just so you know… Readers have been enraged when stoves they bought here have been confiscated, even when they're clean.

Kaua'i's waters contain abundant fish. Of course, it's one thing to have 'em and another thing to catch 'em. Whether you want to go deep sea fishing, sit by a lake or cast off a cliff, you will be pleased to know that all are available on Kaua'i. Anyone can fish in the ocean—no permit needed (check size and season regulations, though). Freshwater fishing does, however, require a permit.

DEEP SEA FISHING

If deep sea fishing's your game, there are several charter companies around. They all provide the necessary gear. Tuna, wahoo (ono) and marlin, among others, are all caught in these waters. The seas around the islands can be rough if you're not used to them, and it's fairly common for someone on board (maybe you) to spend the trip feeding the fish. We advise that you take Dramamine or Bonine *before you leave*. Scopolamine patches work well but have side effects that can temporarily affect vision. (It can make close-up vision poor for a week.) Other alternatives may be available. See your doctor. (I've always wanted to say that.) Some people feel that greasy foods or citrus before or during your trip is a no-no; *many* swear by ginger tablets. Some seriously suggest putting a cherry seed in your bellybutton (and hope the fish don't laugh at you).

Most boats troll nonstop since the lure darting out of the water simulates a panicky bait fish—the favored meal for large game fish. On some boats, each person is assigned a certain reel. Experienced anglers usually vie for corner poles on the assumption that strikes coming from the sides are more likely to hit corners first.

You should know in advance that in Hawai'i, the fish belongs to the boat. What happens to the fish is entirely up to the captain, and he'll usually keep it. You may catch a 1,000-pound marlin and be told that you can't have as much as a steak from it. If this bothers you, you're out of luck. If the ono or another *relatively* small fish are striking a lot and there is a glut of them, you might be allowed to keep it—or half of it. You *may* be able to make arrangements in advance to the contrary.

Before deciding *who* to go with, decide if conditions warrant going at all. It might be calm on one side of the island and rough on another. Current ocean conditions can be obtained by calling the **National Weather Service** (808-245-6001) for weather.

Prices below do not include taxes, harbor fees, fuel surcharges or tip.

West Shore Charters

In the past, we've had astonishingly bad experiences with **Deep Sea Fishing Kaua'i** (808-634–8589) based out of Port Allen. They have improved considerably. Four-hour charter (shared with five others) is $179.

East Shore Charters

Hawaiian Style Fishing (808-635-7335) has a 25-foot boat that goes out of Kapa'a. Unlike most boats there's no deckhand, so it'll be a bit more hands-on (literally). If the trolling's not working, they'll bottom feed. A good, flexible outfit. $140 for a half-day shared charter, $600 for a private charter.

Leaving from Nawiliwili Harbor, **Lahela Sportfishing** (808-635-4020) uses a 34-foot Radon. They allow you to take the catch up to 30 pounds. *Shared* charters are expensive at $175 per angler (four minimum/six maximum) or a better deal at $700 for up to six anglers as a private charter.

Kai Bear (808-652-4556) has a 38-foot Bertram, making them the largest (and most comfortable) fishing boat on island. An ownership change has greatly improved the attitude and overall feel at Kai Bear. Half day is $160; 6-hours is $205. Half day private is $750. Prices include taxes, but not fees.

FRESHWATER FISHING

Tom Christy is the local tucunare guru, and you can book time with him from **Sportfish Hawai'i** at 877-388-1376. A pricey $265 for half-day trips, which includes gear, bait and beverages. Some readers haven't been impressed with this tour, but we haven't observed that.

Though **fly fishing** isn't very big in Hawai'i, die-hards now have an option on Kaua'i. **Fly Fish Kaua'i** (808-652-9038) offers both fresh and saltwater tours. The 4–5 hour tour is $360 for either type, and only one person is preferred so as not to spook the fish. Most gear *can* be provided, but you'll need to get your own tabis.

The **Pu'u Lua Reservoir** in Koke'e (see map on page 88), as well as several feeding streams, are stocked yearly with rainbow trout fingerlings. Lake waters are too warm for trout to spawn. Trout season in Koke'e is usually restricted to the first Saturday in July until the end of September (though some years it begins earlier). The rules are complicated. **Division of Aquatic Resources, Department of Land & Natural Resources** (808-274-3344) can fill in any additional blanks you may have.

Obtaining Freshwater Fishing Licences

Places to obtain licenses are: **Walmart** (808-246-1599) in Lihu'e and **Salt Pond Country Store** (808-335-5966) in 'Ele'ele/Hanapepe. Squid and shrimp can be obtained from most supermarkets.

With its bountiful nightly rainfall and warm, sunny days, Kaua'i is a perfect environment for golf. Its seven golf courses are diverse, ranging from a wealthy sugar magnate's private course donated to the island to a world-class resort course rated in the top five for the all the islands by Golf Digest in 2016. If golf is your game, Kaua'i is sure to please.

GOLF CLUB RENTALS

The prices described under Fees in the table reflect the highest category of fees. Check the specific course descriptions in our app for more information and possible discounts. Many have additional twilight specials. If you're planning on golfing

For those who venture off the fairway here at Po'ipu, we have some advice: Take the stroke.

multiple days at different courses, consider renting clubs from a third party.

Kauai Golf Club Rentals (808-346-0626) has Callaway clubs available for five days at $119, and they'll deliver and pick them up from your hotel or condo.

The **Kaua'i Bound Store** (808-320-3779) in Nawiliwili has Wilson clubs for $70 per week.

KAUA'I GOLF COURSES

Below we'll give you the skinny on the island's courses. We have detailed reviews of each course in our smartphone app, *Hawaii Revealed*, but didn't have space to fit it all in this book.

Golf courses are located all around the island. You'll notice that greens tend to break *toward the ocean* more than your eye will tell you. We'll start from the north shore and work our way down. If you only have time for one course, and money is no issue, we'd recommend **Po'ipu Bay**.

On the north shore, **Princeville Makai Golf Club** offers an impressive 18 holes with commanding and outstanding views and is one of the best on the island. The greens and fairways are in great shape and the layout fairly open.

On the east shore, **Wailua Municipal Golf Course** is pretty darned good for a muni and is reasonably priced (for Hawai'i). As it parallels the beach on Kaua'i's Coconut Coast, Wailua constantly reminds you that you are near the ocean.

In Lihu'e, **Ocean Course at Hokuala** embraces the ocean like no other, and the views and layout are *outstanding*. Their renovations in 2016 improved the infrastructure and brought golfboards (which are fun to ride).

In Puhi, **Puakea Golf Course** is a fun and moderately difficult course. It's not in the same league as some of the resort courses. Conditions—including the hazards—are poor, but the fees reflect this.

On the south shore, **Po'ipu Bay Golf Course** is a sprawling 210 acres of wide-open golfing. It has spectacular scenery, impeccable grooming and attention to

Course	Phone	Par	Yards	Rating	Fees
Kiahuna Golf Club	(808) 742-9595	.70	.6,214	.70.3	.$105*
Kukuiolono Golf Course (9 holes x 2)	(808) 332-9151	.72	.6,154	.70.0	.$15
Ocean Course at Hokuala	(808) 241-6000	.72	.6,626	.73.5	.$209*
Po'ipu Bay Golf Course	(808) 742-8711	.72	.6,610	.71.7	.$225*
Princeville Makai Golf Club	(808) 826-1912	.72	.6,596	.71.4	.$305*
Puakea Golf Course	(808) 245-8756	.72	.6,471	.71.0	.$105*
Wailua Municipal Golf Course	(808) 241-6666	.72	.6,991	.73.6	.$48–$60

Yards and ratings are from the blue tee.
* Indicates power cart included in fee.

detail. Greens are real consistent. They try to keep them as fast as they can, given the windiness.

At nearby **Kiahuna Golf Club** the fairways seem to be getting more love these days than we've seen in the past. Homes are all around the course, detracting from the natural beauty, and ocean views are scarce.

Heading west a bit, in Kalaheo **Kukuiolono Golf Course** is the personal ninehole golf course of a sugar magnate from the 20th century. It's simple, dirt cheap and has a certain charm. Cash only. $15 for as many rounds as you want. Rental equipment is charged per nine hole.

Of all the Hawaiian Islands, none offers more trails or better hiking than Kaua'i. You could spend an entire month on Kaua'i, hiking every day and not see half the trails that the island has to offer. And those are just the officially *maintained* trails.

We have *lots* of hikes in this book. We've also GPSed all the trails to assist on specific hikes. Additionally, there are several *excellent* hikes listed in the *Adventures* chapter since they're a bit...different.

If you plan to do a lot of hiking, contact the agencies below for information packets on their trails:

Hawai'i DLNR Division of State Parks
3060 Eiwa St., Suite 306
Lihu'e, HI 96766
(808) 274-3444

County of Kaua'i Parks & Recreation
4444 Rice St., Suite 105
Lihu'e, HI 96766
(808) 241-4463

If you need to **rent** camping or hiking gear, your best sources will be **Kayak Kaua'i** (808-826-9844) in Kapa'a or **Pedal 'n Paddle** (808-826-9069) in Hanalei. For walking in streams or anything slippery, nothing beats **tabis**. Like felt-covered mittens for your feet, they provide impressive traction on mossy rocks. (No ankle support, though—duct tape helps remedy that.) **Walmart** in Lihu'e or **Discount Variety** in Koloa are your best bets.

Good places to buy other gear include: **Discount Variety** (808-742-9393) in Koloa. In Lihu'e, **Da Life** (808-246-6333), has lots of outdoor clothing, shoes and camping gear. *Some* specialty gear (stuff the REI fans might like) can also be found at the **Aloha Xchng** (808-332-5900) in Kalaheo. Don't forget **Walmart** (808-246-1599) in Lihu'e.

A **hiking stick** can be helpful on some trails. We sometimes even use two on long hikes and find that they greatly ease climbing and descending and give better balance, in addition to their usefulness in probing mud puddles. It's also handy during the months when tiny **crab spiders** are active. Their minor bites aren't dangerous, just annoying, especially if you get one in the face. Just wave a stick in front of you if you notice any on the trail. In a flash of brilliance, they were brought to the islands *on purpose* to attack a farming pest. Didn't work—smooth move, guys! (Next, they'll probably want to bring in *tarantulas* to get rid of the mosquitoes.)

Lastly, it's nice to be able to visually see where you are on a trail and know you're going in the right direction. But many of the trails on the island do not show up on a typical GPS or Google maps. Well, it just so happens that we GPSed every trail on the island, and they are in our smartphone app, available online.

KOKE'E STATE PARK HIKES

In Koke'e State Park you'll find exceptional hiking, with the additional benefit of higher altitude and its accompanying cooler temperatures. The map on page 154 shows the layout of the trails and dirt roads. The dirt roads, even when graded well, become *very* slick when wet. As a result, you may have to walk to some of the trailheads, lest you find yourself stranded. It's a good idea to check in at the **Koke'e Museum** (808-335-9975, open 9 a.m. to 4 p.m.) before you hike to get up-to-date information. The state charges $5 parking fee per vehicle for out-of-state visitors.

These two people on the Alaka'i Swamp Trail's boardwalk are in for a treat: a spectacular sheer cliff overlooking the island's north shore 4,000 feet below the lookout.

By the way, some of the trails in Koke'e require a 4WD vehicle (or a *long* walk) to get to them. As an alternative to a 4WD, consider bringing a mountain bike up to the canyon in your car. Then ride it out and hide it in the forest near the trailhead (since you can't use it on Koke'e trails themselves), and you will find that your hiking options greatly increase.

Pihea Trail (2 Miles Round Trip)

If you only do one hike while visiting the canyon area, this is the one you want. This short trail is only about a mile, but it wraps around the upper rim of the Kalalau Valley, so give yourself plenty of time because you are going to be constantly stopping to take pictures. The view just keeps getting better and better.

The (often *muddy*) trail starts at the end of Waimea Canyon Drive at the **Pu'u o Kila Lookout**. (See map on page 155.) The beginning part skirts the edge of the valley, and then passes through native 'ohi'a and fern forests until reaching the backside, where the whole valley is laid out before you, with the ocean in the background 4,000 feet below. Near the end of the rim-hugging portion the footing gets chunkier and steeper due to erosion. Long legs help ascending the chunks. Soon you come to hog fence. To the right the trail continues another mile to connect with the Alaka'i Swamp Trail. To the left is very short but *steep* spur trail leading to Pihea Vista, your last chance to see Kalalau Valley. Turn around whenever you are ready, or continue on to the Alaka'i Swamp Trail.

Alaka'i Swamp Trail
(8 Miles Round Trip)

This trail starts in the canyon area on the island's west side and leads to a magnificent view of Hanalei Bay on the north shore, while taking you through the highest swamp in the world along the way. Thankfully, you're insulated from the mud most of the time by a boardwalk.

Start by taking the **Pihea Trail** (see map on page 155) until you hit the Pihea Vista junction. Just past here, the trail is covered in most spots by a boardwalk. (The part of the trail before the boardwalk is sometimes pretty muddy and slippery, so be forewarned.) After about a mile when the trail intersects the Alaka'i Swamp Trail, go left (east); it's 2 more miles to the end. (Many readers have said it's *way* more than that—hey, sorry, the GPS don't lie.) The Alaka'i Swamp Trail leads to the edge of a cliff where the **Kilohana Lookout** affords a majestic view of Ha'ena on the north shore, clouds permitting. Imagine hiking to this point before the boardwalk was installed. Then imagine that the hard part was *still to come*. That's because the ancient Hawaiians used this trail to get to the north shore when the surf precluded going by sea. Once at Kilohana, they went over and down the 3,400-foot cliff to the valley floor and along the sloping valley to the ocean. All this for westsiders to visit family on the north shore in the winter. (Remember this the next time you think you're too busy to drive across town to see Mom.) Along the trail you'll see old telephone poles. They were erected by the military after the attack on Pearl Harbor and stretched across the swamp, down the cliffs of Kilohana and into Hanalei. They served as a backup communications line in case the Japanese captured Lihu'e.

Even without the view at the end, it's probably the most unusual hike on the island. Full grown trees on the flats rarely exceed 5 feet tall. Submerged grasses, vines and moss-covered trees sheltering endemic birds (found nowhere else) make this a memorable hike. Fog rolls in and out con-

The Po'omau Canyon Ditch Trail sports some awesome views of the valley 1,500 feet below you.

stantly, adding to the mystery of the scenery. You've *never* seen wilderness like this. While you're on this boardwalk, you'll have the same thought as everyone else— "My *God*, this must have been a wretched hike before they installed this." Darned straight! It's about 8 miles round trip from your car, but you can just go as far as your desire takes you. The boardwalk system was created in the late '90s and was quite a task. Even with it, expect to get a little muddy from patches where the boardwalk was left out, and watch for areas where the metal mesh will want to snag your innocent, unsuspecting foot. If you want to avoid the sometimes sloppy stretch of the Pihea Trail, you can just do the Alaka'i Swamp Trail from its beginning off Mohihi-Camp 10 Road. (See map on page 155.) You'll probably need a 4WD or mountain bike to get to the Alaka'i Trailhead off Mohihi. Pihea's car access from the end of Waimea Canyon Drive makes it the better route.

Po'omau Canyon Ditch Loop
(Distance Varies)

This is an outstanding loop hike and one of our favorites in the park. It sports incredible views, lush and exotic surroundings, and a dizzying finger of land that sticks out into the canyon and overlooks two glorious waterfalls at one shot. This is a truly beautiful trail. Originally cut in 1926 to assist Koke'e Ditch workers, it's unofficially kept up by volunteers, such as the Sierra Club. Long pants can be useful if the blackberry bushes (and their evil thorns) are sticking out into the trail. The footing is occasionally obnoxious, and there are opportunities for the genetically clumsy or the vertiginous to take a long roll.

To get there, take Waineke Road (across from the Koke'e Museum) to Mohihi-Camp 10 Road. Park at the intersection of Mohihi and Kumuwela Road, then walk about a mile on Mohihi Road to the trailhead. The unmarked trailhead is *on your*

Koke'e Trails

The nature of the terrain at Koke'e makes it difficult to convey the type of hiking each trail provides. This accurate, computer-generated, shaded relief map is drawn from an angled perspective to give you a feel for the lay of the land. Since this is a perspective map, the mileage scale should be a little smaller at the top of the map (since it's "farther away" from your eyes) and a little bigger at the bottom of the map.

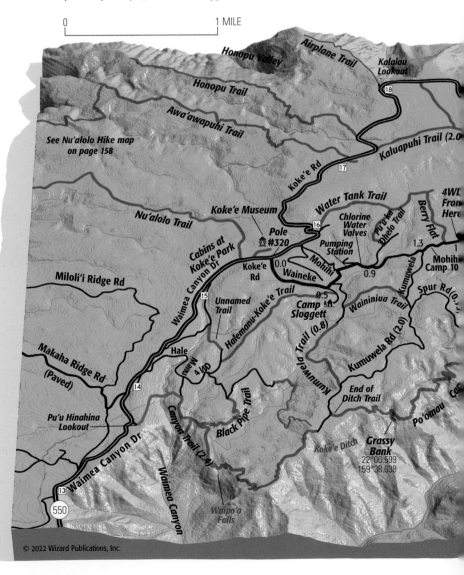

0 _____ 1 MILE

Honopu Valley

Airplane Trail

Kalalau Lookout

18

Honopu Trail

Awa'awapuhi Trail

Kaluapuhi Trail (2.0

See Nu'alolo Hike map
on page 158

Koke'e Rd   17

Water Tank Trail

Berry Flat

4WL
From
Here

Nu'alolo Trail

Koke'e Museum

Chlorine
Water
Valves

Pu'u ka
Ohelo Trail

1.3

Pole
☎ #320

16

Pumping
Station

Mohihi
Camp 10

Cabins at
Koke'e Park
Canyon Dr

Koke'e
Rd

0.0

Mohihi

0.9

Kumuwela

1

Miloli'i Ridge Rd

Waineke

Waininiua Trail

Spur Rd (0.

15

Unnamed
Trail

Halemanu-Koke'e Trail

0.5

Camp
Sloggett

Makaha Ridge Rd
(Paved)

Hale

Manu 4WD

Kumuwela Trail (0.8)

Kumuwela Rd (2.0)

14

End of
Ditch Trail

Po'omau

Pu'u Hinahina
Lookout

Canyon Trail (2.4)

Black Pipe Trail

Koke'e Ditch

Grassy
Bank
22°06.599
159°38.638

Waimea Canyon Dr

Waimea Canyon

13

550

Waipo'a
Falls

Note: Distances given for trails are one way. Distances listed along Mohihi-Camp 10 Road are from the intersection of Waineke Road and Kokee Road near telephone pole 320. Don't be fooled by a sign at that intersection saying Kumuwela.

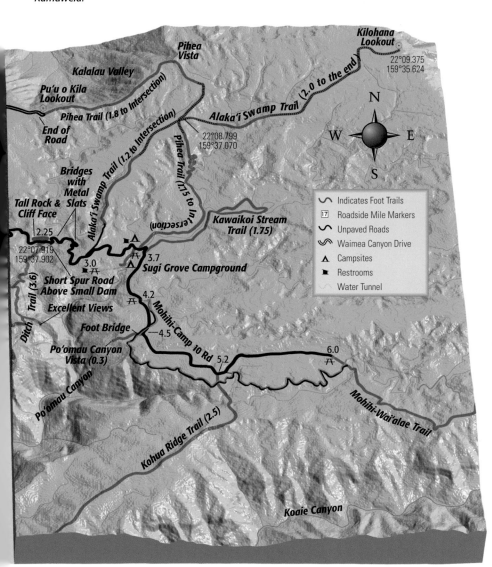

right, angling back toward the road. (If you come to a bridge with metal slats, you've gone 600 feet too far. The trailhead is *just before* a road turnout and might be marked with a near-invisible metal signpost (missing a sign). Look for it on your right when the road-cut wall of rock and dirt on your left is about to end. If you have to cross a concrete walkway at a small dam at the beginning of the trail, *you're on the wrong trail*. Using the map feature of our

You'll end up at the top of these two falls when you do the Waipo'o Falls hike. These falls can shrivel to a trickle during dry times and when they divert water to feed farm fields in Kekaha.

smartphone app is really helpful on this hike. The GPS works even when you don't have a cell signal, which is really useful in the remote canyon area where coverage is spotty.

Almost as soon as you start the trail, you will come to a small valley with a running stream. This is your canary in a coal mine. If the vegetation is too thick to walk through, it means you are unlucky enough to be here toward the end of this trail's volunteer-run maintenance cycle, and that the rest of the trail is overgrown as well. Might want to do a different hike.

The trail winds its way through primordial-looking jungle with ferns, birds and often the sound of running water to keep you company. Toward the end of the first half, there is a narrow finger of land jutting out into the canyon on your left; look for it. This is only for the intrepid The trail is plenty wide, but still choose your steps carefully, as the drop on either side is rather conclusive. At the end is a vista from a poet's dream. *This* is what you came for. On the far wall to your left a thunderous cascade of water pounds its way down. Next to it on the other side of a horseshoe-shaped canyon, a multi-step waterfall plunges into a deep pool. Expect it to take 1.5–2 hours of moderately strenuous hiking to get to this point.

After taking in the view, head back up the ridge to rejoin the main trail and then continue on it for a short distance until you encounter an easy-to-recognize spur road. Hikers used to have the option of continuing on the path to a second trail segment that eventually led to another scenic overlook, but that part of the trail is closed now, and for good reason: getting there requires traversing an unstable landslide area more than 200 feet wide and growing.

So instead of going that way, take the spur road to where it hits Kumuwela Road and then take a sharp right. Kumuwela will hit Mohihi, completing the loop and depositing you at your awaiting car. Now *there* is a hike to savor!

Canyon Trail to Waipo'o Falls
(4 Miles Round Trip)

Another favorite, this one is also moderately strenuous and will probably take you 2–3 hours, depending on how long you linger. Along the way you will get unparalleled views of the canyon from the other side, visit two waterfalls and find a cold pool to swim in, if you like.

Park your car at the **Pu'u Hinahina Lookout** between mile markers 13 and 14, walk to the back of the parking lot, through a clearing and to the trail to your left. If there's no parking, you can park at the top of Hale Manu Valley Road between mile markers 14 and 15 on Waimea Canyon Drive and walk 0.8 miles down the road (with a 240-foot loss in elevation) to another trailhead, unless you have a 4WD. (See map on page 154.)

About 0.5 miles into the trail from Pu'u Hinahina (which is steeper than the road option above) you have the option of going to the lookout off to your right. You might want to save that for the end, since other views will be better.

After you are exposed to the great canyon views, you will come to the top of a ridge. Keep an eye out for goats on the opposite walls. Look south for a provocative-looking rock arch, out where it's impossible for man to have created it. (You will see it closer from the larger waterfall ahead.) The light in this part of the canyon is usually best in the late afternoon.

Just past and below the ridge, you'll come to an intersection, with a small falls to your left and a bigger one to your right. The first one is tiny, but the pool is cool and refreshing. The bigger set of falls takes a two-step plunge down 800 feet. You come out at the top of the first step, so you won't get to look over the side at the largest drop. These falls sometimes have pretty low flow, especially in the summer or when they're diverting lots of the water for the fields below in Kekaha, so don't be disappointed. Just enjoy the delicious scenery, complete with wild ginger everywhere, before making your way back.

If you are feeling extra adventurous, it's possible to go beyond the stream and hike for about another mile to get even better canyon views.

Nu'alolo Awa-'awapuhi Grand Loop
(11.8 Mile Loop)

This is a great hike! It takes most of a day and is strenuous, but you're treated to views that will stay frozen in your mind for a lifetime. If you're up for a long day hike on Kaua'i, this is the one. And you may be surprised at how few people you see along the way.

First, the gory details. It's either 10 or 11.8 miles (the latter if you have to walk Waimea Canyon Drive back down to your car) and involves about 2,500 feet of climbing, 1,500 of which is climbing the last leg. But *oh*, the sights you will see. The vertiginous may object to a place or two, but they won't want to miss it.

There are three trails. Nu'alolo Trail starts near the Koke'e Lodge and heads toward the ocean, Awa-'awapuhi brings you back up, and Nu'alolo Cliffs links the two. When you finish at the Awa-'awapuhi trailhead, you're 1.8 miles up the road from your car. So either leave a car there, or you'll have to walk back down narrow Waimea Canyon Drive to your car. You can do the Nu'alolo or Awa-'awapuhi trails as out and back hikes, but this route is the very best.

This hike is downhill for the first third, mostly flat for the second and a somewhat gentle but constant incline for the last third.

Start at the **Nuʻalolo Trailhead** just south of Kokeʻe Lodge. (This is better than doing it from Awa-ʻawapuhi first.) *Coming from the lodge,* the 3.8-mile-long trail is on your right. After a short climb you'll descend through a landscape that will change from bird-filled koa forest to patches of wild flowers to dryland forest to exposed ridge. All are a tribute to the rain's infatuation with increasingly higher altitudes. The trail will split in a few places but quickly rejoins. By the way, part of this trail is open to hunting during some parts of the year. It's highly unlikely that you'll encounter a hunter, but it's probably best to avoid practicing those new pig calls you just learned.

About 3 miles into the hike is the intersection of Cliff Trail. Don't take Cliff Trail just yet; instead continue another .75 mile to Lolo Vista Point. Swallow hard.

You're on the upper edge of an Eden-like valley. The view will take your breath away—and then some. **Nuʻalolo Valley** is unimaginably beautiful, and the Na Pali Coast looks endless beneath you. This is the bluff where Harrison Ford had his tree-choking tantrum in *Six Days/Seven Nights.* (Though *he* got here by helicopter.) Surely, you think, it can't get better than this. Think again.

You gotta turn back and climb .75 mile to start the 2 mile-long **Nuʻalolo Cliffs Trail.** The old Cliffs trail was a bit too cliffy, and when a landslide rubbed out part of it, the state closed Cliffs Trail for about a decade while pondering what to do. They eventually rerouted the first part farther mauka and reopened it in 2017.

After a rest at the picnic shelter a third of a mile in, the trail turns into deeper forest. This stretch is one of the loveliest in the park, where birds abound and the scenery is delicious. There are a few false trails that lead to nowhere. Stay on the main trail. After playing in your own personal waterfall (yep, it's got one of those,

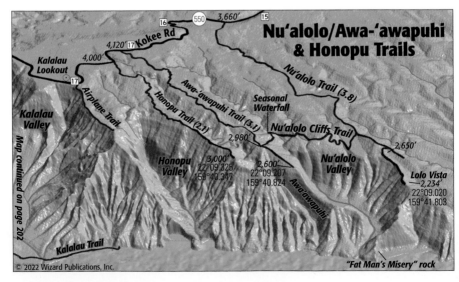

Map continued on page 202

© 2022 Wizard Publications, Inc.

Nu'alolo to the left of you, Awa-'awapuhi to the right. This is a great time to be a hiker.

too, though it's sometimes dry), you hit the **Awa-'awapuhi Trail**. The highway is to your right, but you head left for a third of a mile.

Nothing can prepare you for what you are about to see. Just when you thought it couldn't get any better, the Awa-'awapuhi Lookout steals your heart with cliffs so sheer and green they can't possibly be real. Can *this* be the same Nu'alolo Valley you saw before? High altitude-flying white-tailed tropic birds laugh and soar *beneath* you. Knife-edge ridges you didn't even know were there stand against the cliff. This is a side of God's handiwork that you never knew existed. Revel, savor, remember.

The view from past the guard-rail is even better, but you're unprotected. If you fall, the first step is a fairly jarring 2,000 feet. To the right is the almost vertical Awa-'awapuhi Valley. Check out the spires at the valley mouth.

Rested? Good. It's time to pay the piper. You're at 2,600 feet, and the road is 3.1 miles away at 4,120 feet. Fortunately, it's fairly gentle most of the way.

Some warnings: You should start this hike no later than 10 a.m. (earlier if possible). Hiking boots are a good idea. This is not a good trail to hike if it's been raining a lot in Koke'e. Avoid when muddy, or bring your bobsled. Hiking *up* Nu'alolo when it's muddy is awful—another reason we come back up via Awa-'awapuhi. As for water, bring at least twice as much as you think you'll need. After all, the first third of the hike is downhill or fairly flat, so lugging the water that far is relatively painless. Drink up before you start your ascent, and dump any water you don't want to carry. That's infinitely better than walking up Awa-'awapuhi dry (as we did the first time). There's a brochure at the Koke'e Natural History Museum that identifies marked plants on the Awa-'awapuhi Trail. It's great if you took the trail *down* (which we advise *against* since you're better off taking Nu'alolo down), but you're probably too pooped to care coming up. Besides, many of the markers have been removed.

In all Kaua'i it's unlikely you'll ever find a more pristine forest than along the Mohihi–Wai'alae Trail.

Kuku'i Trail (5 Miles Round Trip)

While gazing into Waimea Canyon, you may wonder if there's a trail down into it. Yup. And lucky for you, it's down the road at a lower elevation near mile marker 9, so you *only* have to descend (and, of course, *ascend*) 2,300 steep, unrelenting feet. Ah, but what views you'll see on your way down as the canyon changes in appearance. It's 2.5 miles to the river below. (Not much distance to lose almost half a mile in elevation, so the grade is steep.) At the bottom is Wiliwili Camp (which has a restroom). Make *sure* you bring enough water for the trek back up. Too many people underestimate the climb, and they're fantasizing about water on the way up. The climb back up is pretty grueling, and you'll be sore for a few days.

If you don't want to go all the way down, there's a good viewpoint 0.3 miles into the trail and a *spectacular* view-point 1 mile into (and 750 feet below) the trailhead. Past this, the trail goes through forest, which is sometimes pretty mosquito-infested. The state is sometimes slow to keep up with the annoying buffalo grass that adorns parts of the trail.

Mohihi-Wai'alae Trail
(7 Miles Round Trip)

First things first. If you don't have a 4WD vehicle, you probably won't be doing this trail unless it's *real* dry, you have *lots* of confidence it won't rain, and you're willing to beat your car like a rented mule. That's because it starts at the end of Mohihi-Camp 10 Road, 6 miles from Waimea Canyon Drive (Hwy 550). See the map on page 155 and the description of the road in the *Po'omau Canyon Ditch Loop* hike on page 153.

If you are blessed with a 4WD vehicle, you'll be treated to one of our favorite trails on the island. Not for any sweeping views—you only get one or two of those. This trail shines because it passes through one of the finest forests you'll ever see.

After parking at the end of Mohihi Road near picnic tables, you'll take the trail down a few minutes, across a footbridge, and walk toward and to the right of more picnic tables.

Down through a forest of sugi trees, you'll have to cross a stream that you can usually boulder-hop. A few dozen feet uphill after the stream there's an old metal sign with mohihi trail and an arrow. The trail angles back uphill to the right.

From here it's not so confusing. The trail gains 250 feet, levels out, undulates and climbs a bit more until you come to a broken bench. From here there's a grand view of **Koai'e Canyon**, part of Waimea Canyon.

For another 1.5 miles the trail undulates then emerges onto a plateau with a rain gauge. Until now the trail has been fairly wide. From here it's narrower, with passages through ferns, and there are a few areas that require care since they're on the side of a hill. Zip-on pant legs are nice to keep the ferns from clawing at your legs.

If you're game, the next mile is well worth it. It will drop to a luxuriant fern forest, then keeps getting better and better. When you're about 2.5 miles from your car, the trail completely levels out. The forest has gotten more and more exotic looking. Gone are the introduced plants of Koke'e. This is an old growth, native forest that looks utterly primeval. It's as if someone had a bucket of life and splashed it all over the ground. Be careful not to walk on the mosses themselves.

The ground is soft and gentle, like walking on a thickly padded carpet, and the area feels ancient and undisturbed. The 87 inches of rain this area gets per year are absorbed by the forest floor. Walk slowly and observe how life bursts from every nook and cranny. Native birds, though not numerous, show little or no fear of humans. We've been lucky enough to be here on a sunny day, but even rain won't obscure the healthiest, happiest and most prosperous forest you may ever walk through.

Although the trail keeps going for many, many miles, 3–3.5 miles is a good turning-around point since it'll get swampy and harder farther on. (There are mile markers.) Though this last portion is *reasonably* marked, keep track of where you've been for your return. Try to start early— by 9 a.m., if possible, so you can take your time on this trail. Camping at Sugi Grove can be handy for this.

NORTH SHORE HIKES
Hanalei 'Okolehao Trail
(4 Miles Round Trip)

So you've been especially gluttonous since you've been here, and the guilt is keeping you awake at night. Here's your chance to work off that lu'au you attended. This trail is a puffer. It gains 1,250 feet in less than 2 miles. That means the grade is steep, tiring and unrelenting. It will seem much longer than it is.

Most of the first 0.7 miles is on the dull remains of a steep old dirt road. By the time the road ends and the *real* trail starts (at a huge power pole whose lines swoop into the valley below), you'll probably hate the trail and hate us for mentioning it. Look to the left, and the trail continues through forest. It's prettier, as it quickly starts climbing the ridge, but just as strenuous. Climb, climb, climb, climb. Then climb some more. There are breaks in the vegetation affording grand views, but you couldn't care less because you're puffing so hard. After about 30 miles (really 1.8, but you'll swear we're lying) you are richly rewarded. A lovely plateau dotted with ti plants can offer impossibly sweeping views if it's not too overgrown. (Just before the trail ends at the plateau, a different spur trail to the right leads to a separate ridge. Nasty, scary, hard-core and death-defying make that a *must-miss* alternative.)

From the trail's end at the plateau you can see one-fifth of the entire island, weather cooperating, from Anahola all the way around to the end of the road at Ke'e. Behind you, you'll see Wai'ale'ale and the Hanalei River chiseling its way out of the mysterious center of the island, the Kilauea Lighthouse, Hanalei Bay…nowhere is there a more expansive view.

Was it worth it? Only you can say, but we think so. Is the hard part done? 'Fraid not. Coming down is also hard because the constant downhill is hard on the knees…and 'okole if it's wet and you slip.

To get to the trailhead, drive past Princeville and turn left just after you cross the Hanalei Bridge at the bottom. (See map on page 53.) At 0.7 miles from Hwy 560 is a parking lot on your left. The trailhead's on the opposite side at a small footbridge. After 500 feet you'll encounter a chain gate with an old road rising steeply to your left. Climb till the end or until you run out of sweat.

Incidentally, the word 'okolehao refers to liquor made from ti roots. In the old days, bootleggers planted ti up here to supply them with raw materials.

Hike Through Old Club Med
(1 Mile Round Trip)

This is a short, sweet hike that affords beautiful views of **Hanalei Bay** and gives an alternative way to **Pu'u Poa Beach**. The land is privately owned, but the owner has been generous enough to allow walking access. The grounds are dotted with the foundations and skeletons of old cottages and bungalows, with the jungle slowly trying to reclaim the them, giving it an abandoned *Jurassic Park* feel. (Don't climb on these structures, or the owner might take away access.) The trail is a gently sloping old road and the grounds are maintained (mowed), making for a very leisurely hike. At the end of the trail, the road splits. If you go left, you can go around the old clubhouse to reach the point that gives the best views of the bay. (The spot once was the site of the gazebo used in *South Pacific* as part of the Frenchmen's estate.) Go to the right and it leads downhill to the west end of Pu'u Poa Beach. To get here, drive to the end of Hanalei Plantation Road (the last right as you exit Princeville towards

Ti plants grace the end of the 'Okolehao Trail. Turn around and you'll see more of the island from up here than perhaps any other trail on the island.

The Pools of Mokolea top off a short but sweet shoreline hike.

Hanalei). The road becomes unpaved for the last 300 yards. Once you reach the gate at the end, find a place to park along the side of the road. (Make sure to face the correct direction, or they'll ticket you.) Parking may be limited. The trail access is on the left side of the gate.

Pools of Mokolea (1 Mile Round Trip)

For those looking for a beautiful, wild shoreline hike but who don't want something too long and strenuous, this may be the ticket. It only travels 0.5 miles from you car but has some tasty rewards.

From Kahili (Rock Quarry) Beach, cross Kilauea Stream and head to the right. (The stream is usually shallow—don't cross if it's raging.) You'll see a road, but earlier portions are on private land—hence your need to start the hike the way we're describing it. You'll eventually either go up and down next to a wire fence, or around—either way ending on the lava bench. You'll soon see tidepools. Fish and crabs scatter at your approach. Lots of ancient metal equipment and parts are scattered along the shore. For 100 years the sugar company

dumped worn-out gear here. What was once junk has been transformed by a century of melting rust into an intriguing part of the landscape.

More tidepools and more lava. It's slow going because you're mostly boulder-hopping on lava rocks, so take your time. Only 800 feet from the end of the road is a large, Jacuzzi-sized hole in the lava where the ocean surges in and out. It's great to watch, but beware of large sets of waves that can surprise you. (This goes for much of the walk along here. Monster surf needs to be evaluated.)

Soon you reach **Mokolea Point**. What a spectacular place! Waves often pummel the area, creating rivulets of water flowing across the lava bench. During low surf a wonderful lava pool graces the area. Several small pools behind the large rock make nice soaking pools if the surf isn't too high. Moderate waves sometimes wash over the bench, replenishing the pools. Overhead, white-tailed tropicbirds and shearwaters often soar on the thermals. Kilauea Lighthouse and Crater Hill are 1.3 miles across the water with Makapili

For those looking for an easy hike or if you have kids in tow, this is the payoff at the Stone Dam Hike.

Rock in front. During winter (October–April) the surf may overwhelm the area, and this hike should not even be considered. Low tide is best.

Just past the pools is the end of your hike. The ocean has cut a trench in the lava all the way to the cliff. When there's surf, the ocean comes roaring into the trench, which gets narrower and narrower, eventually undercutting the cliff in a small pocket. The result is a violent ricochet as the water and compressed air explode out of the trap that the lava has set for it. It's like a dragon breathing water instead of fire. Some waves even hiss as they are expelled. Sometimes rogue waves pound with such ferocity you think the ground will split beneath your feet. Some explosions of water may shower you, so be careful.

To get to the marginally defined trailhead, take Wailapa Road between mile markers 21 and 22 off Hwy 56 near Kilauea. Then take the smooth dirt road to Kilauea Bay. Park and find the best place to wade across the stream.

Historic Kilauea Stone Dam Hike
(4.25 Miles Round Trip)

This is one of the better hikes for those with kids. Serious hikers might not be as impressed. Though this trail can get muddy (it is the north shore, after all), it is one of the least strenuous hikes to be found—there's not much elevation gain, it is well maintained and has lots of shade. You can also use a mountain bike here. The payoff is a lovely garden and historic stone dam with plenty of spots to sit and enjoy the scenery. The dam was built in the 1880s to supply water to Kilauea Sugar Plantation and still supplies water to the Wai Koa farming community. The swimming hole isn't that great, but you might see local teens enjoying the rope swing.

The trail was once part of a larger loop trail called the **Wai Koa Loop Trail**, but these days it's a there-and-back hike. It passes through Wai Koa Plantation where a number of farmers utilize the idyllic conditions for a variety of crops, including banana, avocado, breadfruit and mahogany. In fact, you'll be walking through some of the 200 acres of the largest mahogany plantation in the U.S. The entire trail is a little more than 2.1 miles long from the dog park to the dam.

You can access the trail at the **Kaua'i North Shore Dog Park**. Find the park around half a mile down Kahiliholo Road, the first left past Kaua'i Mini Golf and mile marker 24, not far from Kilauea town. The entirety of the trail is well marked with yellow signs showing the way—as long as you stay on the trail there's no way you're going to get lost.

From the dog park, head to the left along the trail, following the signs to the stone dam. The road undulates through a wooded area (the most elevation gain you see is around 40 feet), and once you notice the trees lining up in perfect rows you'll know you're in the mahogany plantation. Around the .6 mile point you'll reach a spot where the trail splits. Here you can either continue straight along a small trail they call the "Enchanted Forest" which adds an extra half mile (but loops back to the main trail), or take the shorter, more direct route to the stone dam. We recommend taking the longer, more scenic route, saving the shortcut for the walk back. No matter which path you take, it's in this area that it becomes apparent this is a planted forest—long corridors of trees create a unique perspective, adding to the enchanted feeling. The trail can get muddy around here, especially in the wetter, winter months. Once you rejoin the main trail, it's another mile to the dam.

From here, the landscape will open up more and you'll get a view of some of the small farming operations. Keep an eye out for signage giving background and history on the area. Once you reach the trail down to the dam, before descending into the garden, take the time to first view it from the covered picnic area. If you're here in the late afternoon, the light shines directly onto the dam, making for great photos. Small bridges over the irrigation ditches and koi-filled ponds add to the ambiance here. This is a great place to meander and take in the

Surprises, such as this freshwater cave at the shoreline, await those who hike to Kalalau Beach.

scenery, with a few very visible paths leading toward the dam. Look for the path to the right that goes uphill to a bamboo thicket and Buddha statue—if you brought your bathing suit, it is also a back way to the swimming hole. You'll be swimming at your own risk here, but luckily there's a ladder (and sometimes a rope swing) to help you get in and out.

In all, the trail will probably take around two hours. You'll want to walk in shoes that can get a little muddy, and take some water and snacks—maybe even lunch—the last section through the garden to the dam is a great spot for a picnic.

Kalalau Trail (22 Miles Round Trip)

The ultimate hike is also the most famous hike in all Hawai'i. Eleven miles of

The Sleeping Giant's chin offers an incredible panoramic east shore view, for those with the nerve to go past the end of the official trail.

switchbacks, hills and beautiful scenery. This hike can be a real adventure. Because of this, we discuss it in detail in *Adventures* on page 203.

EAST SHORE HIKES
Sleeping Giant/Nounou Mountain (2, 4 or 5 Miles Round Trip)

This is a moderately difficult trail. Actually, it's three different trails. The vertical elevation you will gain from the East Trail is 1,000 feet. A thousand feet sounds like a big rise (OK, it *is* a big rise), but this is a hike worth experiencing. Nearly the entire hike is through forests with pretty views. This is a real trail, not an abandoned road like some hiking trails. Of the three trails, the East is the prettiest and the least steep, though it involves the most elevation gain. If you take the eastern route, at the third switchback after the 0.5 mile stake, the trail seems to split into two paths. *Do not take the left fork, which is on the side of the mountain!* This is probably a pig trail and

This jungle hike is fairly easy and rewards you with a nice place for a picnic.

not part of the main trail. You won't like it. In fact, other trails that deviate from the main trail are usually bad. Take the time to savor some of the luscious views of the entire east shore from spots. When you get to the main fork in the trail (diligently guarded by hala trees with their A-frame, cage-like roots), take the fork to the left for 3 or 4 minutes to the picnic table. From here you can see the entire **Wailua Valley** from Anahola to Lihu'e. The view is not to be missed and well worth the climbing effort expended. Anyone who becomes dizzy from heights should be aware that there are areas along the east side trail where the beautiful sweeping view off to one side is quite steep.

Up at the picnic table, there is a short trail dipping south across the giant's neck up to his forehead and nose. Or is it his chin? Hard to say. The view from up there is, literally, a once-in-a-lifetime experience. The vista is without rival. Think *real hard* before you take this part. It is steep, and the spine is almost vertical on both sides. A wrong step, or a slip anywhere near the nose, would almost certainly cost you your life. Just before the summit there is a short trail to your left leading to the hole in the giant's chin, seen from the bottom of Kuamo'o Road. This part of the Nounou Trail is what

they call a real 'okole squeezer. Stop at the picnic table unless you are very brave, very foolish and very well insured.

If you take the West Trail or the Kuamo'o-Nounou Trail, you'll find the climbing steeper. It's a good workout; we like to climb it every other day if we've enjoyed a few too many restaurant reviews lately. Kuamo'o-Nounou Trail and West Trail combine at a magnificent strand of Cook Island pines (a very tall and straight pine tree thought, during the Age of Discovery, to make good ships' masts).

Of the three trails to the top, we recommend either the East Trail or the Kuamo'o-Nounou Trail. (The latter has a stretch where mosquitoes might mug you. Use a repellent.) The map on page 63 makes it easy to find the three trailheads.

Kuilau Ridge Trail (3.5 Miles Round Trip or 4.3 Miles One Way)

This trail begins 1.75 miles past the Kaua'i Research and Extension Center. The trailhead marker is on the right side as you are driving west on Kuamo'o Road, and there are a few parking stalls. Otherwise, park at the nearby **Keahua Arboretum**.

This is a very nice hike. The first part is a gentle but constant incline that takes you past a myriad of birds. Watch and

Some call this Ho'opi'i Falls. Others use that name for the next falls down the river. These keiki couldn't care less. They're just enjoying the sound.

quaint wooden bridge. (Or continue onto **Moalepe Trail**, if you like, though Moalepe isn't in as good condition due to horses stomping the snot out of the trail base.) The entire hike should take you 2.5 to 3 hours if you hike at a semi-steady pace. Bring water. Hiking boots recommended, but tennis shoes OK. You can wash the mud off at the stream at the arboretum.

Jungle Hike
(1 Mile Round Trip + A Walk Up the Road)

If you want a *taste* of the steamy jungle and forest (but without the need for a machete and a gallon of insect repellent), this might be what you're looking for. It leads to a government stream gauging station and passes through some magnificent scenery. Your reward at the end is a small, picturesque stair-step little falls where two streams come together adjacent to a water diversion ditch. (The word ditch has ugly connotations, but often these small dams can make a nice place for a picnic.)

To get there, take Kuamo'o Road (580) all the way until it becomes dirt. (A sign at the **Keahua Arboretum** says 4WD ONLY.) The pavement stops, but you won't. You'll cross over a bridge and *through* a a stream and stay on the dirt road for over 2.5 miles. When you come to a Y, take the left fork and reset your odometer. Then at almost 1 mile is an-

listen for them. At the end of the incline (about 30 minutes), you will come to a small picnic area overlooking a lovely valley. If it's clear, you will get a stunning view of **Mount Wai'ale'ale**. This is a nice place to have lunch or just enjoy a long sip of water. *Make sure you go past the picnic tables.* The payoff is 5 minutes later. You will be rewarded with a wonderful razorback, winding, rolling, trek into paradise. *Gorgeous!* There are lush hillsides filled with ferns of every size and shape. Off in the distance you can see the ocean at Kapa'a and all the way to Lihu'e at another point. Very nice. Turn around where the Kuilau Trail ends and the Moalepe Trail begins (see map on page 62) at a other Y, then a gate; take the left fork. (If the gate's locked, you have to walk an extra 0.3 miles.) At 1.3 miles is the second gate probably in very poor condition. The map on page 213 shows all of this. (This part of the road fluctuates between pretty good and utterly wretched.) The gate is on state land and was erected years ago to prevent vehicles from going any farther, but it's perfectly legal to go through the gate and continue. Between that second gate and the trailhead coming up is where they filmed the Entrance Gate scenes in *Jurassic Park*. If you have our smartphone app we have the precise spot marked on the GPS-aware map. The views into **Wai'ale'ale Crater** from this dirt road can be exceptional, especially in the morning.

After walking 10–15 minutes (0.5 miles) from the second gate, you'll come upon an ascent. There will be an old turnout on the left side. The trail leading off to the left from this turnout immediately parallels for a short time a water ditch and passes through extremely lush territory. The ferns, birds and trees are abundant along this easy-to-follow but often slippery trail. A pleasant 10- to 20-minute trek up and over a 150-foot high ridge will bring you to a nice, freshwater pool, formed by the small dam. The area around the dam is covered with plant life and can be slippery. A wonderful, secluded spot to eat lunch.

If you don't want to walk *over* the hill to get to the falls, you can walk *through* it. Where the ditch becomes a tunnel (at a circular cement opening), you can access the tunnel that goes under the mountain. Most people will have to duck the entire 800-foot length and, of course, if the water were to start flowing while you're in there, you'd have a big problem to deal with. But last time we were here the ditch

feeding the tunnel was purposely blocked with rocks *and* the flume was closed so water wouldn't flow in the tunnel during normal times. Your call. Anyway, it's an adventurous option that we've done (when we had a flashlight), and it's a hoot.

The falls are actually formed by two streams. If you swim across the pool and climb the rocks, then take the right fork for only a few (slippery) minutes, you'll come to a small, hidden falls. At the base is something we call the **Jacuzzi**. During low to moderate stream flow the falling water creates bubbles and jets of air that feels remarkably similar to a spa (albeit a cold one). It's *wonderful* to soak in. Just stay out if the flow is too heavy, and read page 35 for precautions on swimming in streams. Use your own good judgment.

Ho'opi'i Falls Hike (1 Mile Round Trip)

Waterfalls have an amazing ability to bring peace of mind. Although Kaua'i is studded with many waterfalls, most of them are inaccessible for one reason or another—but not this one. There are two falls on the Kapa'a Stream—and one of them is named Ho'opi'i. Some locals call the first one Ho'opi'i, though government maps give that name to the second falls.

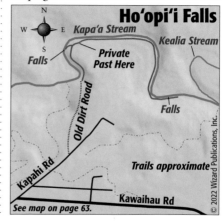

Ho'opi'i Falls

Kapa'a Stream
Kealia Stream
Private Past Here
Falls
Old Dirt Road
Falls
Kapahi Rd
Trails approximate
Kawaihau Rd
See map on page 63.

© 2022 Wizard Publications, Inc.

Look at the map on page 169. There are additional trails in this area, but the one shown is on state land. The top of the map on page 63 shows you where Kapahi Road is. An old *public* dirt road (now just a trail) is on your left as you come down Kapahi Road. Please be respectful of the neighborhood here. Residents don't want you driving faster than 15 mph on Kapahi Road. If there is no parking available on the trail side of the road next to the vegetation, your best option is at the nearby Kapahi Park, on the corner of Kawaihau and Kaapuni Roads. Then it's a short (.25 mile) walk to the trailhead.

Walk down the trail, and when you come to an intersection, go right. Head downstream, and eventually you'll see a side path leading down to the first falls. Wow, what a place! A flat lava bench offers a magnificent place to sit and breathe in the falls. The only way to get under those falls is either to go down-stream and wade back upstream, or jump into the pool as some daring locals do. (Do so at your own risk; check out the water first to make sure there's nothing dangerous submerged.) This is a great spot to cool off on hot days.

The second falls downstream are reached via a trail that veers away from the stream most of the time. There have been issues in the past regarding access, but at press time the trail was open, and there were no signs telling you not to proceed.

If you don't bring mosquito repellent, bring an extra pint of blood for the walk through the woods. Tennis shoes are OK. Bring water.

Hiking to the Top of Wai'ale'ale

A question we're often asked is *How can I hike to the summit of Wai'ale'ale?* Until fairly recently, you couldn't. In ancient times Hawaiians used to hike up a ridge on the northeast side of the crater (the ridge that's over the *Tunnel Hike* on page

Keep an eye out for some bizarre formations during the Po'ipu Shoreline Sandstone Hikes.

213). Near the summit they had rope ladders for the final portion. A landslide and lack of use in the 1800s shut off that route. In the 1970s a person tried, with a helicopter overhead to give radio guidance, and he failed. In 2006 another person tried and had to be rescued by helicopter. But the construction of a pig fence across the Alaka'i Swamp has created an opportunity. It's a *beast,* however, and listed in *Adventures* on page 209.

SOUTH SHORE HIKES
Po'ipu Shoreline Sandstone Hikes
(4 Miles Round Trip)

The lithified cliffs of **Makawehi** next to Shipwreck Beach, as well as the **Maha'ulepu** area, offer excellent shoreline hiking. The Makawehi cliffs are easily accessed by taking the trail from the parking lot between the Hyatt and the Po'ipu Bay Resort golf course (or simply walking to the east end of the beach). It's over half a mile long, formed from cemented sand dunes deposited here during the last ice age. The wind and salt have clawed and thrashed at these cliffs with impressive results. Part of the trail was destroyed by a landslide in 2006, so you'll get rerouted onto the golf course. Take your time, wander about and take a look at the remains of an old heiau. Look for (but don't remove) fossils in the sandstone, and enjoy the views.

Maha'ulepu is described in detail in *Beaches* on page 117. Another good hike is to start from the end of **Gillin's Beach** (see map on page 79). It's beyond the stream and past the last pocket of sand. It's wonderful to walk along here when the surf is raging. At one place there's a hole in the floor of the cliff, allowing you to see the ocean exploding beneath your feet on the lithified bench below. This area looks like an alien landscape. Weekends bring fishermen who tend to leave reminders of their hobby here.

You could walk all the way to the Hyatt, if you wanted. The wind, pounding surf and beautiful cliffs create an amazingly relaxing walk, even if the ground is a bit lumpy. About two-thirds of the way to the Hyatt, the cliff gives way to a sandy pocket affording a luscious view of the cliffs.

HORSEBACK RIDING

If you want to let someone else do the walking while you tour the island, try horseback riding.

Silver Falls Ranch (808-828-6718) inland (mauka) of Kilauea is hands-down our favorite. Their 300-acre ranch looks more like a palm arboretum, and the guides seem thrilled to see you and show you around their little piece of paradise. The horses are well-groomed and the trails well-kept. This is how rides should be done if you're looking to be pampered in a stunning location (although it's nose-to-tail). $104 for the 1.5-hour ride. For $144 it includes another half-hour and a trip to their small waterfall and large pool. Swim and lunch there. The only downside is that their location is rainier than some of the others, so you take your chances with the weather. Their weight limit is fairly high at 300 pounds but also based on your height. The minimum age is 7, but special accommodations can be made for those as young as 5. The menagerie of animals at their barn is also a plus for the little ones and animal lovers. Experienced riders may be champing at the bit (wow, I finally got to use that horse phrase in the proper context!) for some more spark.

CJM Country Stables (808-742-6096) in Po'ipu has two rides available. The afternoon picnic ride is 2 hours of riding, 1 hour for lunch. The ride is mostly along or near the coast to a "secret" beach (it's Ha'ula) but no swimming. $199 per person. Then there's a 9:30 a.m. and 2 p.m. Tuesday through Saturdays. Scenic Beach & Valley Ride—2 hours of riding on mountains and along the coast. If you're thirsty on the trail, your only choice is passion/orange/guava juice. (If you want water, bring your own or buy it at the office.) $169 per person. 230-pound weight limit. Minimum age of 8 and no riding with adults. (You're on your own, kid.) The amount of narration depends on your guide, but the nose-to-tail orientation for up to 24 people (in four groups) means only those near the guide will hear it. The leader may spend the entire trip on his cell phone, which has happened to us *repeatedly*. (They wrote to us saying, "our guide was discussing safety"—yeah, whatever. They have no way of knowing when we *anonymously* review them.) The fact that they are the only outfit offering rides along a beautiful beach with fantastic scenery offsets most of the shortcomings the company may have. They take lots of riders and feel a bit like a rider processing machine, but the rigid structure might make beginners feel pretty comfortable.

At check-in you may get a lesson in... paniolo wisdom, which some may find endearing while others will be put off. One caveat: They say no experience is necessary, but we have been on tours with horses that aren't as docile as those used by other companies. We were glad to have enough experience on horseback to keep in line with the tour.

Princeville Ranch Stables (808-826-7669) takes riders through a working cattle ranch without the nose-to-tail aspect of other outfits. You're encouraged to spread out. The terrain is mostly flat,

though you're not allowed to run—so hold your horses there, pardner. They have a 250-pound weight limit, but they also have *height-to-weight ratio* restrictions, so go onto their website if you're in doubt. You must be at least 8 years old to ride.

They have two lesson options, including a 1-hour arena lesson for $125 and a 2-hour trail riding lesson for $199. The trail lesson is the one you'll want if you're looking to get into nature. Bring your camera and a snack, and wear long pants and solid-toe shoes. Overall, you'll see some nice scenery on this ranch. Past mile marker 27 on Hwy 56.

Jet ski rentals are outlawed on Kaua'i. So if this is what you came to the island to do, you *sure* picked the wrong island.

A kayak can be a marvelous way to see Kaua'i. The quiet, peaceful nature of kayak travel appeals to many. There are four rivers on Kaua'i you can kayak and, of course, there is the open ocean.

RIVER KAYAK TRIPS

We've kayaked all the rivers in several kinds of craft. We prefer the rigid two-person, self-bailing kayaks for beginners, single person self-bailers for those who have kayaked before. Some use canoes, but we're not as fond of them since they can fill with water if tipped. (Inflatables are terrible since they are easily deflected by wind—called weathercocking, in case you're taking notes.)

Of the four rivers, the **Wailua** is by far the most popular. (See map on page 62.)

It's very scenic, and there's a waterfall called **Secret Falls** on the north fork you can hike to if you like. (Some brochures call it the most spectacular waterfall on the island. That's bunk, but it's a nice one just the same.) There's a more dubious trail just before the falls that goes to the top and exposes you to the more beautiful upper falls, but the trail is pretty sketchy and not recommended. It's 5 miles round trip and takes most people about 3 hours to paddle plus stopping or hiking time. Since large boats take passengers to the Fern Grotto, kayakers should always stay on the north side of the river. If you want to visit the Fern Grotto, consider pulling ashore *after* the docks at the so-called kayak landing area. To be honest, the grotto is not the same as it used to be and is barely worth the effort to get there. The best part about kayaking this river is the scenery and hiking to the waterfall.

Just enjoy the Wailua for its lushness, and watch out for the large boat tours.

Past the Fern Grotto, is a cliff-jumping area at a well-known swimming hole. (The state had an ongoing war with pesky rope swing builders there. State workers, with marching orders from their lawyers, relentlessly cut 'em down almost as fast as people put up new ones. Finally the state simply cut down the trees.) People line up to jump off the cliff into the water there, despite a state sign warning them not to. If you do, too, make *sure* there's nothing under the water first. The African village scene from *Outbreak* was filmed on a secluded plain here on your right; look for it. The wind will probably be in your face coming back, so hug the north bank tightly to minimize the wind. The earlier you leave, the less wind coming back, and you'll avoid crowds on the river and at the waterfall. (We start at 7 a.m.

When kayaking the Wailua River, the farthest reaches are the most serene.

and strongly suggest you do, even if you gotta rent the kayak the afternoon before.) To kayak this river *on your own,* which we prefer, there are special logistical considerations—see *Renting a Kayak for the River* on page 175. No kayak renting on Sundays except **Kamokila Hawaiian Village,** which makes for a super-short kayak trip.

On the Wailua River, first you kayak, then you hike…then you frolic!

The **Hanalei River** is the longest and goes mostly through plains. (Beautiful plains, but plains.) It takes about 3 hours (6.75 miles) round trip for most people to kayak this peaceful river. After a heavy rain, waterfalls etched in the distant valley walls can enhance the trip. The wind usually helps you a little coming back.

The **Hule'ia Stream** in Lihu'e is 5 miles round trip (2 hours or more). It starts from Nawiliwili Harbor (you can launch from **Niumalu Beach Park**), and the water flow is not great, so expect ickier water here. There are majestic mountains on your left as you go out, and you will pass the easy-to-miss Menehune Fishpond and an area where they filmed the swing-on-a-vine-to-the-waiting-airplane scene from *Raiders of the Lost Ark.* (Keep an eye out for the opening to the fishpond.) Lots of jumping fish in the shallow parts of the pond. The last navigable part is our favorite part of this river. This river goes through a wildlife refuge, but you'll see and hear more birds on the Hanalei River. The wind will probably be in your face coming back. If you're doing this on your own, you'll run into large guided groups at times.

The **Kalihiwai** is short but *very* sweet. You can kayak it in an hour (taking your time) if you decide not to do the additional 10-minute hike (more like a grope up the river, then through the jungle on the right side) to **Kalihiwai**

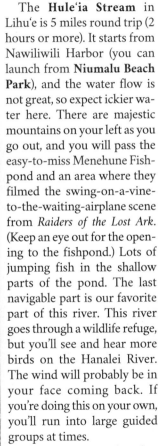

Falls. Put in at **Kalihiwai Beach**. You might not see the waterfall from where you stop kayaking. The scenery is the best of the four, and you might want to do it if you have any juice left after a Hanalei River trip. Expect to be hassled if you visit the beautifully manicured falls in any way that doesn't bring money to the horseback company that leases the land where the falls occupy.

Renting a Kayak for the River

You can rent a kayak and paddle any river you like, *except* the Wailua River. The state has rules making it harder to rent a kayak *on your own* to kayak the Wailua (which is the best one). They want you to go on a *guided* tour. (It's not a safety issue; it's a political one—long story.) So although we recommend doing river trips *on your own*, this may be harder to do on the Wailua. Companies that have permits can only rent six kayaks per day, and they might *pull* those from the rental pool if they can make more money putting a guided passenger in it. Of the companies mentioned below, **Kayak Kaua'i**, **Wailua Kayak Adventures** and **Wailua Kayak & Canoe** have them for rent for the Wailua River. (The last one is the most expensive, but they're right on the river and open at 7 a.m.) Call a week in advance to maximize your chances of getting one. An alternative is **Kamokila Hawaiian Village** (808-823-0559), which rents kayaks for $35 from a location so far up the Wailua River, that your paddle to Secret Falls is probably less than 10 minutes. They also rent them on Sunday. (Nobody else is allowed.)

All the other rivers on the island you can kayak on your own without a guide.

Prices change a lot in this competitive business, and prices for rentals on the Wailua cost more. For single-person kayaks (which are getting harder to find) consider **Pedal 'n Paddle** (808-826-9069) in Hanalei or **Wailua Kayak Adventures** (808-320-0680). Rentals run about for $20–$80 per day. Two-person kayaks are $40–$100 per day. Sometimes they are cheaper if you are willing to arm wrestle timeshare salesmen. Most cars will hold two or three kayaks on the roof, and staff will help you strap them on.

GUIDED RIVER TRIPS

For guided tours of the Wailua River, see a list of companies below.

Although the Wailua is our favorite *unguided* kayak trip, the best *guided* river trips are up the Hule'ia River in Lihu'e. **Outfitters Kaua'i** (808-742-9667) has a couple of tours of this river, but our favorite is the 7-hour Hule'ia River kayak/hike/zip trip called the Kipu Zipline Safari. About 2 miles of kayaking, then a half mile of hiking to a small falls with a rope swing. Then you're on a tractor-pulled wagon to two ziplines (the second one is 0.25-miles long) and lunch. Finally, you finish it off at a place they call "blue pool," which has a water zipline. Then back to an outrigger canoe that brings you to your car. The hiking and paddling are not overly tough, though you'll get wet and muddy, and some of the trail involves boulder-hopping. The guides do a good job, they're great with kids (who *love* the part where they feed some pigs and peacocks), and they don't rush you during the trip. However, they may have some accuracy issues in their narrations, and you need to know about the water you're swimming in. Though your group may repeatedly be told that the waterfall and "blue pool" (which is not blue) you're playing in is pure and clean, "straight from the top of Mt. Wai'ale'ale," analysis of topographic maps appear to us (we're not certified topographical surveyors) that the feeder stream water you're playing in comes from Haupu and through the Kipu *cattle ranch*. Meet in Lihu'e at Nawiliwili Small Boat Harbor for check-in. It's not cheap at $199 per person ($159 for kids), 20 people max, and you'll be tired and happy at the end. The only downsides are mediocre food, and the wait for the second zipline can be over half an hour. Bring shoes that can get wet.

Kayak Hanalei (808-826-1881) offers guided trips that start in the Hanalei River and go out into Hanalei Bay, eventually landing on a beach for some snorkeling. The 4.5-hour tour that starts at 8:30 a.m. is $109 for adults and $99 for kids (5–12). Deli lunch included.

OCEAN KAYAKING

Ocean kayaking can be an experience of a lifetime. The crown jewel is a summer Na Pali Coast trip. *National Geographic* named it the second best adventure in the United States. (Rafting the Colorado was No. 1, and dog sledding in Alaska was No. 3.) Na Pali can be an *incredible* trip for those who can do it, either guided or unguided. We try to do it every summer and camp along the way. Because paddling Na Pali is so involved, we have a complete description in *Adventures* on page 199.

Both **Kayak Hanalei** (406-8261881) and **Kayak Kaua'i** (808-826-9844) have guided tours of Hanalei Bay for $109 and $120, respectively. (Kids 5–12 are $99 for both companies). It's available year round, but winter swells can make exploring Hanelei Bay too dangerous. During those times the tour becomes an exploration of the upper reaches of the Hanalei River. The 4–5-hour tour is family-friendly, at least if your family is ready for a workout. (It's recommended for "hardier" families.) The bay is beautiful, and the guides are really good at pointing out the surrounding features—from mountain peaks and waterfalls to turtles and coral. Tours include snorkel gear plus deli-style lunch and beverages.

What if I want to rent a kayak and paddle the ocean on my own? Well, unlike all the other Hawaiian islands, Kaua'i is a very difficult place to rent a kayak *for the ocean*. Whether it's because companies want to make more money guiding you or because Kaua'i's ocean waters are not as calm (probably a little of both), most will turn you down cold if you tell them you're taking a kayak into the ocean. Of course, if you want the sit-on-top variety of kayak (which most here are) as opposed to canoe-types, that's what we use on the river or ocean anyway. If you have some experience and good judgment, there's no one to stop you from taking a rental kayak to the ocean.

KAYAK COMPANIES

The companies described below provide a variety of services.

Kayak Kaua'i (808-826-9844) in Wailua from April through September has one-day guided Na Pali tours starting from either Ha'ena or Polihale for $199–$280 per person. Lunch included at either Miloli'i or Nu'alolo Kai. They also have an overnight camping trip for the Na Pali coast starting at $380. For the Wailua River they have doubles to rent for $110. Guided Wailua trips with lunch for $110 *per person*. The more involved the trip, the better it is to call them in advance, *especially* for Na Pali.

Outfitters Kaua'i (808-742-9667) in Lihu'e has summer Na Pali trips (when available) for $249. Guided Wailua River kayak tours with lunch are available for $109 *per person*, as well as the awesome trip described under *Guided River Trips* on page 175. Outfitters is a big company with offerings beyond kayaking. They do things well, for the most part. Our biggest complaint is that their guides seem pretty fast and loose with their "facts" lately, and narrations might have some factual errors.

Kayak Hanalei (808-826-1881) rents kayaks right on the Hanalei River from their private dock. You don't need reservations, but they start renting them out at 8 a.m., so get there early. $35 per day for a single kayak, $60 for a double and $75 for a triple.

Pedal 'n Paddle (808-826-9069) in Hanalei specializes in one-stop shopping. They rent kayaks for the Hanalei, camping supplies, beach cruiser bikes and snorkel gear. They tend to have some of the better rental prices for the area, but prices fluctuate enough that calling them for the most recent prices is your best bet.

Wailua Kayak & Canoe (808-821-1188) operates near the Wailua River, and you'll probably be able to walk your kayak down to the boat launch on a kayak dolly. Their gear is similar to others, and customer service is scant. Doubles rent for a pricey $100 (it's $50 for a single), and you can only keep it 5 hours. The morning, guided Wailua trip is $90 per person and includes deli-style lunch, while the afternoon tour provides a cooler, but no food, for $75.

Wailua Kayak Adventures (808-320-0680) has river kayaks for rent—$40 for single kayaks, $80 for doubles. Guided Wailua trips are $100 per person ($50 for children under 12). Ask if they'll offer a discount for cash.

Kamokila Hawaiian Village (808-823-0559) is located far up the river, less than 10 minutes from the Fern Grotto and the trail to Secret Falls. Good for families with kids or anyone who wants a short paddle. They rent kayaks, canoes and

stand up paddleboards for $35, which also includes admission to the village.

Kayak Wailua (808-822-3388) is a no-frills family operation. They don't offer you lunch (they suggest you BYO—bring your own), and you'll pay an extra $5 for a seatback upgrade. Their price for guided trips, $75, includes tax and marina fee. That's still pretty cheap.

Ali'i Kayaks (808-241-7700) is a local outfit that does tours of the Wailua, including a hike to Secret Falls, for $75 per person. They meet at Wailua Visitor Center at Hwy 580 (Kuamoo Road) and Hwy 56.

In addition to standard bus tours, there are other land tours that may be worth considering.

MOVIE TOURS

Roberts Hawai'i (808-245-9558) offers an 8-hour **movie tour** in their smaller shuttles that will take you to several popular filming locations while showing you clips en route. Recommended for movie buffs but probably not a good choice for those with young children. Includes pickup, dropoff and lunch. Keep in mind that you won't be visiting any *exclusive* locations—you're only stopping at spots that anyone can get to, but you have a guide to give you the stories behind the movies that were filmed there. $121 for adults, $63 for kids age 4–11.

CHOCOLATE FARM TOURS

If you're interested in chocolate, there are two farms offering tours: **Lydgate Farms** (808-821-1857) and **Garden Island Chocolate** (808-634-6812). The tours are similar—each is 3 hours and includes extensive chocolate-tasting sessions. You'll also get to sample other fresh, tropical fruits found on the farms as well as learn how a football-shaped fruit pod becomes the magical delight we call chocolate. Lydgate Farms has tours daily, except weekends. Garden Island offer tours on Mondays, Wednesdays and Fridays. Lydgate Farm's tour is is $95 (kids 6–12 are $35), and Garden Island's is $89 ($29 for kids 4–12). Kids will enjoy the samples, but those younger than 7 may get antsy during the educational parts. Overall, we find Lydgate the better of the two for their professional approach.

HISTORIC SITE TOURS

Lawa'i International Center (808-639-5952) is the site of 88 Buddhist shrines from the early 20th century. This site has been the home of a Hawaiian heiau, a Taoist temple, a Shinto shrine and a Shingon Buddhist temple. Free 2-hour tours on the second and fourth Sunday of every month at 10 a.m., noon and 2 p.m. (Though you can call to make separate arrangements.) The shrines are on the side of a hillside, and the winding path is easy. They have a new, hand-carved temple that they are very proud of, and overall, it's a relaxing way to spend a couple of hours. History and culture buffs will get the most out of this. Off Hwy 50 near Lawai Road on Wawae Road.

GARDEN TOURS

Garden tours are numerous here on the Garden Island. You can either do them on your own (and set your own pace but learn less) or have a guide, many of whom stretch things longer than necessary.

The big daddy is the **National Tropical Botanical Garden** (808-742-2623) in Lawa'i. Rich and lush with remarkably varied plants and abundant birds, tours here are guided and last about three hours. The fee for the tour is $30 per person (self-guided) for **McBryde**, $60 for the guided, more exotic and photogenic **Allerton**. We've seen some shaky facts from some of the guides, but most are good. Reservations are required. Kids 2–12 years old are $15 at McBryde and $30 at Allerton. They won't take you as far as the beach or the old Allerton home. For that you have to take the sunset tour, but that one is $100 and will cost you some of the time in the garden. Personally, we'd skip the sunset in favor of the regular tour. The self-guided McBryde garden is more of a park atmosphere, and you've got room to roam for around 2.75 hours. A pretty nice garden. They also do a guided, moonlight tour that encompasses both gardens. The $70 tour is around 2.5 hours and is only for those 12 and older. Closed toe shoes are required. Closed Sundays and Mondays.

In Ha'ena on the north shore, **Limahuli Garden** (808-826-1053) has good guides and is the most educational regarding native plant life, but those looking for a multitude of colorful tropical plants might be disappointed. $40 for the 2.5-hour (no bathroom break) guided tour, which is better than the $25 self-guided tour. Tuesdays through Saturdays only.

Na 'Aina Kai Botanical Gardens (808-828-0525) near Kilauea (see also on page 52) is beautiful and the setting dreamy. Guided tours are the bulk of the offerings, and their pace is exceptionally slow. Lots of sculptures and very manicured. $20 for the self-guided walking tour all the way up to The Trek for $85. (Our least favorite is the Stroll & Ride.) The family tour is definitely recommended if you have little ones. You'll get to spend an hour at one of the best playgrounds in the state. Reservations are required.

Princeville Botanical Gardens (808-634-5505) near Princeville is small (8 acres) but packed with exotic tropical plants and fruits (which they are generous about letting you eat), including their own chocolate. They spend 3 hours covering the acreage (kids under 6 will probably stage a mutiny—not the best tour for them), and it's a bit overpriced at $85 (kids 3–13 are $35), but you can feel the family pride (and they have some of the best fruit we've ever tasted).

RIVER TRIPS

Kaua'i is the only Hawaiian island to offer river trips, and there are two ways to do it. You can take a riverboat ride up the Wailua River (often referred to as the only navigable river in all Hawai'i, but this is a relative term), or paddle your own kayak. **Smith's Motorboat Service** (808-821-6895) goes 3 miles up the Wailua River and stops at the Fern Grotto, a large natural amphitheater with ferns all about. This is a popular place to get married. It's 30 minutes each way with entertainment and interesting information provided throughout. They spend 30–45 minutes at the site. $30 per person ($15 for kids 2–12), and they leave four times each day in their 100-plus passenger boats.

The **Fern Grotto** is actually the result of an industrial accident. The cave was always there, but a leaky reservoir from the days of sugar accidentally watered the cave, creating an attractive environment for ferns. Then the sugar industry died, the reservoir was abandoned, and the grotto dried up. Efforts went into re-watering the ferns, and today it's pretty and reasonably cool. But you can't get very close to it, and some may find the destination a bit of a letdown given all the hype. Reservations required.

You can also rent a kayak at any of several places and paddle the Wailua, the Hanalei River, the Kalihiwai River or the

River trips up and down the Wailua River take you to the Fern Grotto, a fern-lined amphitheater.

Hule'ia Stream. The best thing about kayaking the Wailua River isn't the Fern Grotto. (In fact, they discourage landing kayaks there.) Instead, it's the overall scenery and a hike to a waterfall, if you like. See *Kayaking*.

Kaua'i is justly famous for many things: its incomparable lushness, gorgeous beaches and balmy nights. But Kaua'i is not famous for its diving. This is a shame because Kaua'i has some very good dive spots. Turtles are common, and many of them are downright gregarious. Lava tubes, ledges and walls are sprinkled around the island. Fish are abundant and varied. Coral growth is not as good as around the Big Island—at 22 degrees latitude, Kaua'i is on the fringe of the coral belt. Kaua'i's many rivers and streams cut visibility in some areas, but you can still see more than 100 feet on good days. The reefs on the north shore have been struck by a disease in recent

years that is killing some of the coral, but the rest of the island hasn't suffered.

Granted, you might find better conditions on the Kona coast of the Big Island or around Lana'i. It is dryer there and the lava's porous, so the ocean receives virtually no runoff. But this should not dissuade you from enjoying the wondrous underwater sights the Garden Island has to offer.

Kaua'i's ocean pattern is small summer surf on the north shore, larger summer surf on the south shore, and the opposite during winter months, so you should plan your diving activities accordingly. Summer is very popular, and the best companies book up early, so call them as soon as you know when you want to dive. The dive boat operators conduct their tours on the south shore year-round since the local government doesn't allow the boats to moor on the north shore. Some also have dives on the west side at Mana Crack and at Lehua Rock off the coast of Ni'ihau. Those dives are generally considered advanced due to the depths and currents involved, and prices are

Dive Operator	Services Available	Price of Dive	Rent Gear For Shore	Boat Size / Passengers	Dive Computer	Ni'ihau 3-Tank Dive	Dive Certification	Rx Masks
Bubbles Below (808)332-7333	Dive Shop & Boat Dives	$120–$160 (2 tank)	No	36' / 8 32' / 6	Included	$400	$540	No
Fathom Five Divers (808)742-6991	Dive Shop, Boat Dives & Shore Dives	$117–$170 (2 tank)	$71	25' / 6 35' / 6	Included	$400	$520	Yes
Garden Isle Divers (808)631-7447	Boat Dives & Shore Dives	$150–$190 (2 tank)	No	29' / 6	Included	None	No	No
Kaua'i Down Under (808)742-7422	Boat Dives & Shore Dives	$156–$196 (2 tank)	No	25' / 6	Included	None	$550	Yes
Seasport Divers (808)742-9303	Dive Shop, Boat Dives & Shore Dives	$135–$199 (2 tank)	$60	32' / 12 48' / 18	Included	$355	$499	Yes

higher than the spread we show in the table. The Niʻihau dive in particular involves at least 4 hours travel time (round trip), so those who get seasick (and those who aren't sure) should take Dramamine or Bonine *before* they depart.

Off Niʻihau, however, you're treated to ridiculously clear water, lots of big life (sharks, rays, dolphins and your best chance at a Hawaiian monk seal) and a close view of the "Forbidden Island." (The Robinsons, who own Niʻihau, *hate* it when you call it that.) See page 186 for more on this dive. Book in advance to ensure space.

So you'll know **our perspective** when we review companies, we should tell you what we do and don't like when we go on a dive. On a bad dive, the dive master takes the group on a non-stop excursion that keeps you kicking the whole time. No time to stop and explore the nooks and crannies. Good outfits will give you a briefing, tell you about some of the endemic species here, what to look for and will point out various things on the dives, keeping it moving but not too fast. Bad outfits kick a lot. Good outfits explain the unique qualities of Hawaiʻi's environment. Bad dive masters may tell you what *they* saw (but *you* missed). Good companies work around your needs, wishes and desires. Bad companies keep everyone on a short leash. Good dive masters know their stuff and share it with you. Bad dive masters don't know squat but imply they know it all in order to impress you. As divers, we tend to like companies that wander toward the boat for the latter part of the dive and allow you to go up when you are near the end of your tank, as opposed to everyone going up when the heaviest breather has burned up his/her bottle.

During times when we feel the diving conditions are bad (poor vis or big swells), we like to call around and ask about conditions. We appreciate the companies who admit it's bad, and we hold it against those who tell us how wonderful conditions are.

SCUBA TIPS

- Some of the dive boats on Kauaʻi feed you little or nothing between dives. We don't know about you, but we're tempted to gnaw on the side of the boat after a dive. Bring a package of cookies with you. You'll probably be able to sell them to other hungry divers at prices confiscatory enough to pay for your dive. *I have a bid of $8 for a chocolate chip cookie... Do I hear $9?*

- Shorty wetsuites are usually sufficient for most people *in the summer only*. Surface water temperatures range from a low of 73.4 °F in February to a high of 80 °F in October. Any company that will *only* provide you with shorties doesn't seem to care much about your comfort. Or maybe we've just lived here too long and have gotten wussy about the cold.

- Between morning and afternoon dives, morning is almost always best.

- Remember not to drive up to Waimea Canyon or the Kalalau Lookout after diving. As far as your nitrogen level is concerned, you're flying.

- Sometimes it's tempting to go with the cheapest dive operators. Remember that if you're herded in and out with a cheap company that doesn't know the underwater terrain, you may find that your "better deal" was no bargain at all. The spreads in our price table often reflect a short boat ride vs. a long trip to the north shore.

IF YOU'VE NEVER DIVED BEFORE

A lot of people mistakenly believe that you have to be a certified SCUBA diver to take a tour in the ocean. Most companies offer what is usually called an "Introduction to SCUBA" or "Try SCUBA" beginners' dives, which is how nearly all of us certified divers started. You'll get instruction on land to learn the basics, followed by a short session in the water to get comfortable with the gear and do a little exploring. Though many diving outfits around the country have you start in a pool, in Hawai'i most get you started with the real deal—the ocean. Most companies do intros as shore dives, which we feel is a much better option than intro dives from a boat. (Intro dives from boats can leave you feeling literally in over your head.) The two most popular sites for intro shore dives are Koloa Landing on the South Shore and Tunnels Beach on the North Shore. Though certified, we still do intros with companies to see how they perform. Note that you have to be in good health and at least 10 years old (for PADI certification; NAUI requires you to be 12, which we feel is a better age to start).

Fathom Five (808-742-6991) has historically been one of our favorites for intro dives. You get a one- or two-tank dive at Koloa Landing for $137 and $177. Tunnels is a two-tank only and will run you $210. You'll get all the required gear, an hour of instruction, the dive, and drinks and snacks for the price.

Seasport Divers (808-742-9303) does their intro dives exclusively on the South Shore at either Koloa Landing or Kukui'ula Small Boat Harbor. The harbor is protected, and though the scenery isn't all that great, the gently sloping, sandy bottom goes a long way to help timid divers feeling more comfortable. A one-tank dive runs $155, two-tank $175. Rental gear included.

Kaua'i Down Under (808-742-7422) which operates under multiple names, offers one of the cheapest options for an intro to SCUBA at $35, but it's in a pool. If you want an ocean experience, they go to Koloa Landing for a one-tank shore intro for $136 or $196 (two-tank), including all your gear. If conditions are poor, they'll do the shore dive from Kukuiula Harbor (they call it "Lawai Beach") for around $106. (You might see the cheaper intro on their website, but don't count on being able to book it—they default to $136 unless conditions are really nasty.)

Garden Isle Divers (808-631-7447) also goes to Koloa Landing for their intro dives. Most first-timers are ready for a second dive as soon as they come up from the first, so these guys only offer a two-tank intro for $190 (including gear, drinks and snacks). Though they do a good job with intros, it's a little hard to justify the price when other operators do two-tank dives for less.

If you're interested in getting **certified** or did your book work on the mainland and want an open water referral, **Fathom Five** or **Bubbles Below** are your best bets. The open water referral method allows you to do your class work at home, saving your Kaua'i vacation for the *fun stuff*.

RECOMMENDED FOR CERTIFIED DIVERS

One of our favorites is **Fathom Five** (808-742-6991). They use a 25-foot and 35-foot boat, only taking 6 divers at a time so they're able to keep the groups smaller. They tend to use one for more experienced divers and the other for rustier divers, so they don't mix the two unless you want them to. (Certifieds will love that.) As for their shore dives, they aren't as organized as we would like, but not

Though curious encounters from whales are rare, ya never know what the behemoths will do.

enough to not recommend. In addition to standard two-tank dives, they have twilight dives, night dives, premium three-tank dives and Ni'ihau dives. $102–$250 for shore and boat dives.

Bubbles Below (808-332-7333) has discovered many of the island's great dive spots. They focus on the west side more than the others, including Mana Crack off Na Pali, and they offer a nitrox intro for this dive to maximize bottom time. These guys are more willing to do Ni'ihau in the winter, but that usually entails a harder channel crossing. They'll take a maximum of eight on their 36-foot Radon (which has a hot shower). They also have a 32-foot power catamaran that takes six people. Na Pali and North Shore dives are pricier. $120–$300 for shore and boat dives.

Garden Isle Divers (808-631-7447) is a husband-wife team that does boat and shore dives. Their 29-foot boat (six divers max) leaves from Port Allen and focuses on south and west shore dive sites. They seem particularly adept at finding rare critters such as frogfish. If you are a couple and want the boat to yourselves, it's all yours for $540. Otherwise 2-tank boat dives are $180, shore dives are $150 during the day and $170 for twilight/night dives. And for intros they do 2-tanks for $190. They don't mix groups, provide dive computers for boat dives, and feed you pretty well, which we always appreciate.

DIVE SHOPS & RENTING SPECIALTY GEAR

There are only a few dive *shops* (as opposed to dive operators) on the island.

Seasport Divers (808-742-9303) in Po'ipu is the largest shop on the island with the best selection if you're looking to buy gear.

Fathom Five (808-742-6991) stands out because it has a few rental items the others guys don't carry. Their shop is on the small side, but they carry quality gear. They're on Po'ipu Road in Koloa.

Bubbles Below (808-332-7333) is somewhere between the above shops. Larger than Fathom Five, but not quite the same selection as Seasport.

Hawaiian Reefs—*Why is it that...?*

What is that crackling sound, like bacon frying, I always hear while snorkeling or diving?
For years this baffled people. In the early days of submarines, the sound interfered with
sonar operations. Finally we know the answer. It's hidden snapping shrimp defining
their territory. One variety is even responsible for all the dark cracks and channels you
see in smooth lobe coral. A pair creates the channels, then "farms" the algae inside.

Why are there so few shellfish in Hawai'i? It's too warm for some of the more familiar
shellfish (which tend to be filter-feeders, and Hawaiian waters don't have as much stuff
to filter). But Hawai'i has more shellfish than most people are aware of. They hide well
under rocks and in sand. Also, people tend to collect shells (which is illegal), and that
depletes the numbers.

Why do coral cuts take so long to heal? Coral contains a live animal. When you scrape
coral, it leaves proteinaceous matter in your body, which takes much longer for your
body to dispatch.

Why do some of the reefs appear dead? Much of the "coral" you see around Kaua'i isn't
the kind of coral you're used to. It's called coralline algae, which secretes calcium
carbonate. It's not dead; it's *supposed* to look like that. We do have a disease though,
that is killing some of the coral on the north shore, which is being investigated.

What do turtles eat? Dolphins. (Just teasing.) They primarily eat plants growing on rocks,
as well as jellyfish when they are lucky enough to encounter them. Unfortunately for
turtles and lucky for us, jellyfish aren't numerous here.

Is it harmful when people play with an octopus? Yes, if the octopus gets harmed when
someone tries to get it out of its hole. Best to leave them alone.

Why does the ocean rarely smell fishy here in Hawai'i? Two reasons. We have relatively
small tide changes, so the ocean doesn't strand large amounts of smelly seaweed at
low tide. Also, the water is fairly sterile compared to mainland water, which owes
much of its smell to algae and seaweed that thrives in the bacteria-rich runoff from
industrial sources.

Why is the water so clear here? Because relatively little junk is poured into our water compared to the mainland. Also, natural currents tend to flush the water with a
continuous supply of fresh, clean ocean water.

Why do my ears hurt when I dive deep, and how are scuba divers able to get over it?
Because the increasing weight of the ocean is pressing on your ears the farther down
you go. Divers alleviate this by equalizing their ears. Sounds high tech, but that simply
means holding your nose while trying to blow out of it. This forces air into the
Eustachian tubes, creating equal pressures with the outside ocean. (It doesn't work if
your sinuses are clogged.) Anything with air between it gets compressed. So if you
know people who get headaches whenever they go under water...well, they must
be airheads.

Getting up close and personal with our fishy friends.

Kaua'i Down Under's (808-742-7422) "shop" is really just a small outlet at the Sheraton Kaua'i in Po'ipu. Their boat dives are off a Zodiac, and they also offer scooter dives.

For renting gear, either of the first two shops above will do fine.

Renting Specialty Gear

For the heavy breathers among you, **Bubbles Below**, **Fathom Five** and **Seasport** have 100s available, so feel free to *suck 'em up.*

Dive computers are available for your own *independent* dives and can only be rented from **Fathom Five**.

Disposable underwater cameras in a watertight box for snorkeling are available at most grocery stores and sundry shops. If you have a GoPro, consider getting a red lens filter when shooting underwater—it will bring out the colors of fish and coral. **Fathom Five** rents even better still cameras for SCUBA, and **Seasport** carries lots of underwater GoPro gear.

Nitrox (or enriched air) is available at **Fathom Five**, **Bubbles Below** and **Seasport Divers**.

DIVE SPOTS ON KAUA'I
Boat Dive Locations

Kaua'i has many boat dive spots. Since the more resourceful operators are always finding new spots, and since you basically go where the boat operators go, we'll forgo a detailed description of all boat dive destinations. Suffice it to say that **Sheraton Caves**, **General Store**, **Brennecke's Ledge**, **Turtle Bluffs**, **Amber's Arches** and **Fishbowl** are all popular. Some sites, such as Sheraton Caves, are nice but a bit over-dived.

Shore Dive Locations

Below is a list of the best shore dives on the island:

Ke'e Beach, **north shore**—If the seas are flat on a calm summer day, this area offers interesting shallow relief. The area near the reef drop-off is good, again on calm days.

Tunnels, north shore—Easy access, lots of turtles, reef sharks, lava tubes, caves and nice underwater relief. Tunnels' allure is not its visibility, but the dramatic underwater topography. *If* you dive with someone who really knows the reef, this is unquestionably the best shore dive on the island and is often better than a boat dive. Low tide is best.

The Hole, north shore—Located just off the Pu'u Poa Beach. Like the name says, a hole in the reef. Acceptable underwater relief and easy access.

Kahala Point, east shore—Entry and exit is a bugger on the lava rocks with crashing surf. Underwater relief is good, and there are lots of fish. Near Anahola Beach Park.

Koloa Landing, south shore—Easy entry, usually calm conditions year-round and decent coral near the shore. After slightly murky water on entry, the sea is usually quite clear. High tide is best.

NI'IHAU DIVES

For SCUBA divers looking for clean, clear, virgin waters, several dive operators offer three-tank dives near the privately owned island of Ni'ihau, mostly off Lehua Rock north of the island. (For more information on Ni'ihau, see *Introduction* on page 17.) Since this island is in the rain shadow of Kaua'i, there are no permanent streams on the island (and consequently, no runoff), so visibility is often well over 100 feet. This is some of the most exciting diving in the state. The waters are rich in critters, arches, caves and pelagics. There's a good chance you will share the water with sharks, so be prepared. The dive requires a 70-mile round trip (if you leave from Port Allen) boat ride and involves drop-offs, currents and sometimes rough seas. This is not for the inexperi-

enced diver. Dives are usually deeper here and often drift dives. Summer is best. Coming back into the wind always makes for a rough trip.

Bubbles Below (808-332-7333) takes eight divers on their 36-foot boat, Kaimanu. There's not much shade, but there's space to stretch out. They require that you're fairly experienced to join the adventure. You'll need at least 20+ dives as well as nitrox, drift diving and buoyancy control experience. (If you don't have the chops, you'll have to learn the skills with a two-tank dive from Kaua'i.) Cost is $400 and includes two full tanks of 32% nitrox, a regular tank of air, weights, fruit-based breakfast, two lunches and drinks. It's a very good idea to book a month in advance to ensure space.

Seasport Divers (808-742-9303) uses the largest boat and takes up to 12 divers. There's a decent amount of shade compared to other boats, but if they're full, it can feel a little cramped if everyone's trying to take advantage of the shade. You'll need a similar amount of experience to go with these guys (more than 20 dives and nitrox). $355 for the trip, which includes two tanks of nitrox, a regular air tank, light breakfast, lunch, snacks and beverages. Gear is extra and costs $36 for the full set.

Fathom Five (808-742-6991) offers a three-tank dive for $370 and only takes 6 divers at a time. We like the smaller number of divers since fewer people means you're less likely to spook the sea critters. The experience requirements are similar to the other outfits, so if you're unsure if you're qualified, call them and ask. Price includes three dives, light breakfast and lunch, snacks, beverages, tanks, weights and a dive computer (we like that addition).

Shopping

When you think of Kaua'i, you think of rainbows, waterfalls and gorgeous beaches. But Kaua'i can also hold some special shopping adventures, and luckily many local businesses are happy to ship items home for you. So go ahead—allow yourself a break from the action to experience some of the island's great local shops.

NORTH SHORE SHOPPING

Across from mile marker 20 on your way north to Kilauea is **Hawaiian Hardwoods** (808-828-1504) for mostly large furniture pieces, following the natural forms found in the original wood. In Kilauea at Kong Lung Center you will find a variety of housewares, clothing and gift shops including **Aloha Xchng** (808-320-3900), one of the few places to find quality camping and outdoor equipment. Don't forget to walk across the street to the Kilauea Plantation Center where, tucked in the back, is **Hunter Gatherer** (808-828-1388). They have a treasure trove of home goods, jewelry and other locally made gift items. A must-stop.

In the Princeville Shopping Center, **Magic Dragon Toy & Art Supply** (808-826-9144) is one of our longtime favorite stops. There are a number of other shops worth a visit here. The second Sunday of every month the **Princeville Night Market** features live music and local artists from 4–8 p.m.

As you approach Hanalei, the north shore's shopping mecca, stop at **Hanalei Dolphin Center** on your way into town. There are so many shops and boutiques in the main section of Hanalei that we could spend an entire afternoon just browsing them all. You can pick up just about

anything in town from an 'ukulele to pearl earrings to camping gear.

Ching Young Village has a broad selection of shops and places to eat. Across the street in Hanalei Center a must-stop *behind* the building is **Havaiki Oceanic & Tribal Art** (808-826-7606). The name says it all, and you probably won't leave empty-handed.

EAST SHORE SHOPPING

Shopping on the East Shore stretches from Kapa'a all the way to Puhi. It's where most residents do their shopping. However, there are also many local boutiques and specialty stores sprinkled along the way.

In the northern part of Kapa'a, the **NoKa Fair** is making a slow comeback, open daily. Downtown Kapa'a offers the best local-style shopping. You can pick up everything from a gorgeous wedding dress from **a.ell atelier** (808-212-7550) to flip-flops from the **ABC Store** to handmade soap to a koa watch to a glass sculpture of a wave from **Kela's A Glass Gallery** (808-822-4527). You can even buy an orchid to send back to the mainland from **Orchid Alley** (808-822-0486).

Just south of town on the mauka side of the highway check out all the Kaua'i-made products at **The Kauai Store** (808-631-6706).

Coconut Marketplace is making a comeback from its years-long remodeling, and there are some shops you may find interesting as well as to pick up some souvenirs.

At **Kinipopo Shopping Village** you will find one of our favorite jewelers, **Goldsmiths Kauai** (808-822-4653).

In Lihu'e you will find **Walmart** (808-246-1599) on Hwy 56 before Ahukini and **Hilo Hattie's** (808-245-3404). Both are good stops for souvenirs close to the airport.

Every second Saturday of the month Lihu'e hosts a **Night Market** from 4 p.m. to 8 p.m. with pop-up vendors, live music, food and more lining Kress Street near Rice Street.

Kukui Grove Shopping Center is geared more toward locals. There is a **Macy's** and **Longs Drugs** (808-245-8871) there.

Across from Kalapaki Beach is **Harbor Mall**, where, if you want a kitschy Hawaiiana sign that will pack flat into your suitcase, try **Beachrail Hobby & Collectibles** (808-651-6165).

Back on Hwy 50, heading west, is **Kilohana Plantation**, a former plantation manager's private home. It nows houses about a dozen shops/galleries that are definitely worth your time.

If you'd like to arrange a shipment of tropical flowers or a plant grown on lava rock, try **Kaua'i Nursery & Landscape** (808-245-7747) in Puhi on the left side of the highway as you head toward Po'ipu.

SOUTH SHORE SHOPPING

Following Koloa Road will take you right into **Koloa Town**, where there are many shops and galleries to browse. Among the more interesting, starting from the east end of Koloa Road, is **The Wine Shop** (808-742-7305), which has a great selection of wines, spirits and gourmet foodstuffs. **Christian Riso Fine Art** (808-742-2555) is our favorite art gallery in town.

Continuing on Poipu Road toward Po'ipu, is **Poipu Shopping Village**. You will find many boutique fashions from $3 flip-flops to $30,000 pearl necklaces.

Farther along are **The Shops at Kukui'ula** with a nice mix of restaurants, high-end shops and galleries that are worth your time. **Malie Organics** (808-339-3055) has their main store here—they only use indigenous organic flora to create their beauty products. There's also a **Longs Drugs** (808-742-0350) here.

Just off Highway 50 in Lawa'i on Koloa Road is **Hawaiian Trading Post** (808-332-7404), which has the largest selection of Ni'ihau shell leis and Tahitian Black Pearls on the island, as well as other jewelry and gift items.

In Kalaheo, if you have decided to take up the 'ukulele, hit **Kalaheo Music & Strings** (808-332-8302) on the main highway.

WEST SHORE SHOPPING

Hanapepe has many galleries and shops. Stores you may want to check out during the day are **Talk Story Bookstore** (808-335-6469) specializing in used and rare books, as well as new works by local authors. On the main highway is **Salty Wahine** (808-378-4089), which makes gourmet salt blends using tasty local ingredients.

In Waimea, there a few gems to check out on the main highway. Don't miss **Aunty Lilikoi** (808-338-1296) near Big Save, for outstanding passionfruit products made on premises. They'll even share recipes.

Skydiving is available at Port Allen Airport on the west side.

We were not able—actually, more like *unwilling*—to re-review the company here, **Skydive Kaua'i** (808-335-5859), for this edition. We've reviewed them multiple times before and wrote that, "The plane didn't inspire confidence (their website referred to it as a 'state-of-the-art Cessna,' which was true—when *Lyndon Johnson* was president.)" We were also concerned with a general lack of instructions on what to do during a jump, and the fact that Port Allen is notorious for shifting

Stop bothering me! I'm trying to bond with the fish.

winds. I know the wind conditions well there since it's where I first learned to fly. But the final straw was in 2016 when they suffered a crash on takeoff that killed everyone aboard. Frankly, we're done reviewing them. We suggest O'ahu if you want to skydive in Hawai'i. But if you still want to try, it'll run you $239 plus $2 for every pound you weigh over 215 pounds, up to 250 pounds.

If you have ever looked into a saltwater aquarium and marveled at the diversity of the fish life, snorkeling is an experience you might want to try. Anyone who has ever hovered over hundreds of colorful fish can attest to the thrill they felt being in their environment.

WHERE TO SNORKEL

Where to snorkel depends on how good you are and what kind of experience you want. The best place for beginners is **Lydgate Beach Park** in Wailua. There you will find an area protected by a ring of boulders that shields you from the strong ocean. But visibility and fish count have not been good for awhile. See page 116 for more. The intermediate snorkeler will find **Ke'e** or **Tunnels** on the north shore to be fabulous during the calm, warmer months. **Hideaways** is also great during calm seas. **Po'ipu Beach Park** on the south shore usually offers good snorkeling and calm seas in cooler months on either side of the tombolo. The *Beaches* chapter has a description of all the beaches and the different characteristics they possess.

RENTING SNORKEL GEAR

As far as gear goes, there are numerous places to rent gear on the island. We always snorkel wearing water shoes and divers' fins (which fit over water shoes). This way we can enter and exit the water without worrying about stepping on anything. Cheap water shoes and snorkel gear can be found at many places, including **Walmart** in Lihu'e. Bootie socks or women's thin, ankle-length socks will keep you from rubbing the top of your tootsies raw. Divers' fins can be rented at most dive shops. If enough people ask snorkel companies about them, they will start to carry them, too.

Many people prefer to rent gear when they get here and leave it in the trunk, so they may snorkel when the opportunity arises. Your hotel or condo may have gear available. If they don't, try any of the following:

North Shore Rentals

Hanalei Surf Company (808-826-9000) has pretty good equipment for only $6 per day, $22 per week. *Rx* masks available for nothing extra.

Pedal 'n Paddle (808-826-9069) in Hanalei will rent you gear for $5 per day, $20 per week.

East Shore Rentals

Boss Frog (808-822-4334) on the highway in Kapa'a has decent gear for $2–$12 per day, $10–$84 for the week. *Rx* masks available for more.

Kapa'a Beach Shop (808-212-8615) next to Chicken in a Barrel in north Kapa'a has some great deals with full snorkel sets for $15 per day as well as wet suits for $15 per day. (Get either for $30 per week.)

Snorkel Bob's (808-823-9433 or 808-742-2206) has two locations: one on the highway in Kapa'a and the other located on Po'ipu Road past Koloa. You're likely to be tempted by the $30 or $68 per week gear. Although the equipment is pretty good, it's not *that* good. $10 gear is your best bet. Weekly rental is $10–$68. *Rx* masks available for more. You can also rent on Kaua'i and return equipment at Snorkel Bob's on another island.

South Shore Rentals

Nukumoi Beach & Surf Shop (808-742-8019) rents beach equipment, including snorkel gear, boogie boards and the like. A good selection. Convenient, since they are right near Po'ipu Beach Park. $8 per day, $24 per week.

See also **Snorkel Bob's** listed above.

SNORKEL LESSONS

If you've never snorkeled before and desire lessons and assistance, **SeaFun Snorkel Adventures** (808-742-2734) offers guided snorkel tours for $85 per person (children 5–12 cost $68). They're great with kids, but it's really the adults who have never snorkeled who benefit from their guidance. We once tried to teach a friend to snorkel and were unsuccessful at even getting her to put her face in the water (she was terrified). We were very impressed that in only a few minutes they had her snorkeling like an expert. Even *non-swimmers* go out with them. For $5 extra, they'll pick you up at *some* south shore hotels, take you to a place like Lawa'i Beach and provide you with gear, wetsuit (which helps you float), drinks, snacks and assistance. Prescription masks available.

SNORKEL TIPS

• Tropical gloves make snorkeling much more enjoyable. You can grab rocks to maneuver in shallow or surgy areas. (Please don't grab coral, however.)

• Use *Sea Drops* or another brand of anti-fog goop. Spread it *thinly* on the inside of a dry mask, then do a quick rinse. The old-fashioned method of spitting in the mask is not very effective. (It's particularly frightening to see tobacco chewers do this. Yuck!)

• Don't use your arms much, or you will spook the fish. Kick with gentle fin motion. Any rapid motion can cause the little critters to scatter.

• Fish are hungriest and most appreciative in the morning (before their coffee).

- If you have a mustache and have trouble with a leaking mask, try a little Vaseline. Don't get any on the glass—it can get *really* ugly.

If you've always wanted to see what it's like to SCUBA dive but are a bit worried or don't want to go through the hassle, try SNUBA. That's where you take an air tank and place it on a raft that floats above you. Anyone 8 or older can SNUBA. From the raft there's a 20-foot hose attached to a regulator. There you are, underwater up to 20 feet deep, no tank on your back, no hassle. You'll have some instruction before you (and up to seven other divers) go under, and the dive master stays with you the whole time. It can be an exciting way to see the underwater world for the first time.

SNUBA Tours of Kaua'i (808-823-8912) is the best (and only) stand-alone operator on island. They do their thing off Lawa'i Beach on the south shore. $97. Half hour underwater and an hour above for instruction. A video of your experience is available.

If you're looking to be pampered, there are several spas on the island worth mentioning, and the range is huge. You can go from a spoiled, opulent setting to someone's house where clothing throughout your experience is optional. Please note that massages in Hawai'i are *much* more expensive than what you're used to.

The grandest tropical experience by far is **Anara Spa** (808-742-1234) at The Grand Hyatt in Po'ipu, and their fabulous 45,000-

There's something undeniably cool about yelling the word, "Pull!"

sq.-ft. full-service spa is guaranteed to turn you to jelly. It's pricey, but their attention to detail and overall surroundings make it worth the splurge. (You'll love their lava rock showers and optional thatched huts for outside treatments.) You also get full use of all spa facilities, including lap pool, steam and saunas, gym, etc.

Spa by the Sea (808-823-1488) at the Waipouli Beach Resort in central Kapaʻa is your next best bet. The facilities are nice (though there are no day spa facilities), and with your ($165 or more) treatment, you and one other person can access their incredible meandering pool with its waterfalls. Good shower and locker room facilities and professional staff.

Spa at Koloa Landing (808-240-6622) in Poʻipu is relatively small but with large, nicely appointed rooms. If you have not had a Hawaiian lomi lomi massage—with long, gliding motions—they do it well here. Because they are small, if the gender of your practitioner matters to you, tell 'em on the phone or you might get a surprise. The two couples rooms have large Japanese soaking tubs. They have a cabana in front of the Sheraton that is oceanfront, but it's on the walking path and can be loud at times. Their pool is available before and after your treatment. A 20 percent tip is added to your bill.

Sport Shooting

If you came to Kauaʻi for our big game hunting…well, then you were misinformed. We don't have any of that here. But what we *do* have is a pretty well-run sporting clay business called **Kauaʻi Eco Sporting Clays** (808-651-6690). Whether you're into shooting or not, there's something oddly satisfying about hollering *"pull!"* and blasting a clay disk launched into the air

by one of eight different traps. My problem was I didn't really know how to shoot. That's why I was so impressed with these guys, because you can tell they *really* want you to bag some targets, and they do a great job teaching you. It's $118 for the intro course, which lasts 60–90 minutes. You'll get 25 shells and have to pay another $10 to have the 20-gauge shotgun cleaned. (They have 12-gauge as well, but it's really overkill.) When you're done, you'll have a smile on your face and never think of the phrase *cheek fat* the same way again. On Maalo Road heading toward Wailua Falls. Call in advance. This is a small outfit, and they sometimes don't run on time. But they're super friendly. Anyone 12 and up can participate.

SURFING

Ho, braddah, da shreddin's da kine! (Just trying to get you in the mood.) Surfing is synonymous with Hawaiʻi. And why not? Hawaiians invented *da bugga*. Learning isn't as hard as you may think. Depending on conditions, they may put you on a large, soft board the size of a garage door (well…almost), so it's fairly easy to master, at least at this level.

SURF SPOTS

Hanalei Bay is justly famous island-wide as one of the best and *most challenging* in Hawaiʻi. The chapter on *Beaches* can assist you in picking beaches with surfing possibilities. Cannons, Hanalei Bay, Kalihiwai, Kealia, Kalapaki and Infinities (Pakala Beach) are all well-known surf spots.

SURF LESSONS
North Shore Surf Schools

If you want lessons, the best teacher we've seen is **Learn to Surf** (808-826-

Local surfers combing the beach for the perfect morning wave.

7612). For $65 they'll spend 90 minutes with you at whichever beach has the right conditions. Good attitude and good place to rent a board.

Titus Kinimaka Hawaiian School of Surfing (808-652-1116) teaches out of Hanalei Bay, and you won't have the same crowd issue as on the south shore. With the sandier bottom at Hanalei (the south shore is reefier), it might be worth the higher price ($75 for 90 minutes).

Hawaiian Surfing Adventures (808-482-0749) has 90-minute group lessons for $75, $150 for private. We found them patient and eager to get you riding your first wave. They mostly go out of the north shore, too.

South Shore Surf Schools

Most of the companies on the south side teach at Kiahuna Beach. They might seem distracted and disinterested, but that's only because they're distracted and disinterested. But you'll probably eventually ride a wave here. Companies there include **Hoku Water Sports** (808-639-9333) and **Kaua'i Surf School** (808-651-6032).

SURFBOARD RENTALS

If you just want to rent a board (about $20–$40 per day), contact your hotel activity desk or any of the following: **Po'ipu Surf** (808-742-8797) and **Nukumoi** (808-742-8019), both in Po'ipu, **Hanalei Surf Company** (808-826-9000) in Hanalei. **Kaua'i Surf Rentals** (808-651-0541) has a nice variety of boards and will deliver free to north and east shore as long as you spend $80 or more. Contrary to what you see in the movies, beginners should look for crumbling waves, not the picturesque, breaking waves that slap the water.

By the way, a collection of surfboards is known in surfing lingo here as a *quiver*. A little kid surfer who doesn't have a job or car yet is called a *grommet*. Double *overhead* is when the waves are really big, and if you get good enough, you might get a chance to visit the *green room*. If someone says your girlfriend is *filthy*, it's a compliment. And a *landshark* is someone who says he surfs…but doesn't.

STAND UP PADDLEBOARD (SUP)

Stand Up Paddling, or SUP, is the latest craze in the surfing world. The

If pride comes before a fall, you're looking at one really proud dude here.

hardest part about learning to surf is standing up on the board while it's moving. This sport has made things easier by giving you a board big enough to dance on. SUP boards are wider, thicker and longer than the biggest longboards people commonly learn to surf on. SUP instruction focuses on keeping your balance while using a tall paddle to move you into the waves. (This provides an excellent central core workout, with your feet—of all things—hurting the most.) The sight of people standing and dipping long paddles in the water has earned SUP surfers the subversive title "janitors" or "moppers" from traditional surfers. The size of the board, as well as the fact that you are already standing up, gives you an advantage in catching waves early. You don't have to drop in exactly where the wave is breaking. Moppers can catch waves behind the lineup, but all surfing rules apply once you've caught the wave. Traditional surfers will be more inclined to drop in on your wave since they'll feel that you didn't work as hard to get it as they did.

SUP Lessons

Most of the surfing companies give lessons in SUP. Lessons start in the Hanalei River. If you're comfortable on the board, you'll want to ask for a Stand Up *Surfing* lesson. Because the last part of the road to the Hanalei River is closed to vehicles, your best bet is with **Kayak Hanalei** (808-826-1881). They are located right on the river and the 2-hour lessons are $85 as part of a group, $130 for private. Other companies meet up near the river mouth. **Hawaiian Surfing Adventures** (808-482-0749) has small groups up to four; $125 for a private 1-hour lesson, $75 each for two people, $65 per person if there are four. **Hanalei Surf School** (808-826-9283) charges quite a bit more and has an elaborate pricing structure of $160 for a private lesson to $300 for four people.

Tubing is where you sit in an inner tube and slowly drift along an old irrigation ditch. (We think their website makes things look *much* more exciting than the reality of the tour.) It's actually quite relaxing and calls for so little physical expenditure that you'll be tempted to look for your remote control and a can of beer while you're sitting there. Overall, however, we're kind of lukewarm on this. It's semi-lame, and there doesn't seem to be enough bang for your buck.

Kaua'i Backcountry Adventures (808-245-2506) does their tubing in an old sugar cane field between Lihu'e and Kapa'a. They'll pick you up in Hanama'ulu and drive you out to the area, narrating along the way. Then they'll put a helmet and gloves on you (wetsuits are extra), plunk you and 17 other people in inner tubes and off you go. This is *not* a whitewater adventure. Builders of these ditches didn't want to give up precious elevation quickly. So you'll putt-putt along at about 2 miles an hour. The best parts are the five tunnels, which represent about half your trip. They're dark, and the sounds of you and your fellow tubers bounce around in there.

Overall, the company does a pretty good job with what they have to work with, but they can be pretty disorganized at times. You won't see much in the way of views—the ditch banks block most of that. Deli lunch is included, but you'll be forgiven if you think the price—$126 per person—is pretty darned steep considering you're only in the water an hour. People with bad backs might not like the posture they're in for the ride.

Note that there's a 300-pound weight limit. They also have kid-size tubes, but they'll ride at the adult-sized price. They must be at least 5 years old and 43 inches tall.

At **Kaua'i Waterski & Surf Co.** (808-822-3574), you can waterski the Wailua River. They rent a ski boat for $225 per hour, $115 for half hour. This includes the boat, driver, ski equipment and lessons, if you wish. Since you pay for the boat and not for skiing, non-skiers come along for free, up to five customers in the boat. If you've never skied before, it's *much* more tiring than it looks, but it's gobs of fun. By reservation only.

Whale Watching

Although Maui sees more whales than Kaua'i, they are still very common here. Whales work in Alaska in the summer, building up fat, then vacation here from December or January to March or April, when the females give birth and the males sing the blues. Only the males sing, and they all sing the same song, usually with their heads pointed down. Humpbacks don't eat while they're here and may lose one-third of their body weight during their Hawaiian vacation. (I doubt that many *human* visitors can make that same claim.) These gentle giants are very social and have been known to come right up to boats to check out the sightseers. Regulations prohibit the boat companies from initiating this kind of intimacy, but they get close enough to enjoy the whales. If you want to go on a whale watching boat tour, see *Boat Tours* starting on page 138 for a description of the tour boat operators. Whale watching is mostly an opportunistic event here. Those boat companies that do a good job with their other tours (snorkeling, sunset cruises, etc.) are the ones that will give you similar treatment during whale season as well. If you hope to spot them from the land, elevation helps. Consider the Kilauea Lighthouse and the sandstone hikes along Po'ipu. Less wind on the water makes it easier to spot 'em.

Windsurfing

WINDSURFING

If you want to try windsurfing, you'll find that your options are limited on Kaua'i. Higher winds and more reefs mostly favor the experienced. A notable exception is 'Anini Beach. Celeste at **Windsurf Kaua'i** (808-828-6838) specializes in lessons for beginners on the north shore. Rates are $125 per person for 2 hours of lessons and practice.

KITESURFING/KITEBOARDING

We're hesitant to give this sport its own section because so many people still don't know what it is. It's an offshoot of windsurfing and over the years we've had a hard time finding anyone who *reliably* gives lessons. It's all the rage here in Hawai'i and is called **kitesurfing** or **kiteboarding**. Imagine a modified surfboard, shorter and boxier than a normal board, with fins at both ends and straps for your feet. Then let a special, controllable, two-line kite drag you along. Like windsurfing, you don't have to go the direction the wind takes ya—you have control (though not as much as on a windsurf board). It's harder to learn than windsurfing (usually lessons are multi-day), but *oh,* what fun it is! More fun than windsurfing, if you can get over the steeper learning curve.

Note that while there is a kite surfing community here, Kaua'i isn't the best place to *learn* to kitesurf. Maui has a better learning infrastructure as well as more consistently favorable conditions for kiting.

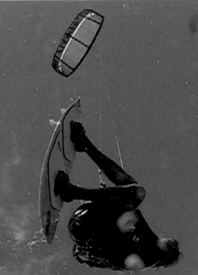

A kitesurfer soars overhead. Though Kaua'i waters are difficult for beginners, more advanced kiters can snag as much as 50 feet of air.

Here, you're going to have more success if you've already got some experience and come in the early fall when winds are more agreeable. That being said, if your heart set is set on trying this sport, we have a company that reliably offers lessons. **Kitesurf Kauai** (808-652-3227) offers a 3-hour beginner lesson for $350. All gear is provided, though you may want to bring your own rental wetsuit (trust us, you'll want one) and booties. Lessons usually take place on the North Shore at 'Anini Beach. All tours are one-on-one unless you bring your own group—they don't mix groups.

Ever seen movies where military commandos don a harness, hook a pulley onto a steel cable and zip down into the action? This is similar—without the hostile fire at the end.

There are lots of companies companies doing ziplines on Kaua'i. All have weight limits. Don't lie, or you might get turned away and still charged.

Probably our favorite is **Koloa Zipline** (808-742-2734). They may make a rotten first impression at the shop, but once on the course we've had good luck with the guides. The setting is around the Waita Reservoir, and the second half of the course has some knockout views. Three of the eight zips are over 1,000 feet with the final one—where I got up to 48 mph—an impressive 2,150 feet long, not 2,500 feet as mentioned on their website. (Most zipline companies seem to exaggerate their length of their cable—must be a guy thing.) They'll take up to 12 people, and they'll even let you hang upside-down if you're so inclined. There's about a mile of hiking during the tour, and you should bring water since

they are kind of skimpy with it. $149, includes snacks. Minimum age is 7 and maximum weight is 280 pounds.

Outfitters Kaua'i (808-742-9667) *used* to be our second favorite tour, but they removed three early zips around a pretty waterfall, so now it's just kind of *wham bam*—then you're done. It's a four-zip tour on Kipu Ranch near Lihu'e for $139. All in all, it will take up about 3 hours of your day. The longest zip is 3,600 feet, according to our GPS—not the 4,000 feet that they claim, but it's still the longest in the state. It doesn't have the best scenery, but you go head first, Superman-style, on that long zip, and you'll be grateful for sunglasses to help your watering eyes. The first few lines are much shorter (about 400–600 feet) and slower but pretty with expansive views of Kipu Ranch to gawk at. All zips are tandem, so couples can race each other or snap each other's picture during the zip (to a degree—because the bigger they are, the faster they fall). The guides do a good job, but you're kind of left with an *is that all there is?* feeling at the end. No hanging upside down on this tour. If you have never zipped before, there is no short warmup zipline. There are plenty of port-a-potties along the way, and water is provided along with cookies at the end. The hardest hike is climbing the last tower, which is tall. They have a different zip experience that also offers four lines (one you can flip upside down on), then a swimming hole and waterfall also for $139, but see our comments on page 175 before swimming there. You must weigh between 60–275 pounds and lived at least 7 years to zip. Expect muddy shoes.

Kaua'i Backcountry Adventures (808-245-2506) has seven lines, the longest of which is 950 feet. But they're all over the same valley, and they seem so preoccupied with "safety" that it takes some of the fun out of it. It's $125, which includes lunch and swimming in a stream. You'll need to weigh between 100 and 250 pounds. Tours are Monday through Friday only.

In the arms race to build faster, longer, and more thrilling ziplines, **Skyline Eco-Adventures** (808-201-2469) in Poʻipu lags behind the competition. The tour guides do their best to keep things fun on this eight-zip course with a distant ocean view, but you should hope that some of your group only paid for the five-zip option—fewer people means less waiting between rides. Speeds are tame, with most lines barely hitting 25 mph, if that. (We topped out at 30 mph on the seventh zip.) This is a no-frills experience; we were offered water from a jug at two drinking stations, and if you want to borrow a hip pack to store your stuff, you'll have to ask. Must be 10 years and up. Weight range is 80–260 pounds $140 for the eight-line zip course; $110 for the five line.

Not what you think about when you envision a zipline, the *concept* for this is cool with **Kauaʻi ATV's ZipBike** (808-742-2734) in Koloa. Ride a bike on a zip cable three stories above the water. The bike feels stable and you are also harnessed separately. The cable is pretty taut so the sag between each end is minor, creating a relatively straight ride. The problem is the length. You'll pedal 700 feet of cable, flip the bike and pedal back. Then…you're done, except for the fairly cool (but again very short) leap off the platform while someone on the ground is on belay to govern your short fall. The actual activity is only a few minutes long, but you'll spend an hour or two getting to and from in their van plus the set up and waiting time, not to mention their request that you show up 45 minutes early at their office in Koloa. In short—and *that's* a term that has relevance here—it's an activity that has potential but needs to be paired with something else to make it worth your time and money. $70, must be 7 years or older. Weight limit is 250 pounds.

Ziplining can bring a new perspective on how you view the world.

OK, so 16 miles along Na Pali Coast is a long way to paddle, whether over one day or several. But the wind, current and luscious scenery help propel you along.

The activities described below are for the serious adventurer. They can be experiences of a lifetime. We are assuming that if you consider any of them that you are a person of sound judgment, capable of assessing risks. All adventures carry risks of one kind or another. Our descriptions below do not attempt to convey all risks associated with an activity. These activities are not for everyone. Good preparation is essential. In the end, it comes down to your own good judgment.

NA PALI KAYAK TRIP

If you really want adventure, consider a kayak trip down the Na Pali Coast. June through August are normally the only months where ocean conditions permit kayak transit. Kayakers put in at Keʻe Beach on the north shore, exiting at Polihale Beach on the west shore, a total of 16 miles. Along the way you'll encounter incomparable beauty, innumerable waterfalls and sea caves, pristine aquamarine seas, turtles, flying fish and possibly dolphins. If you're doing this as a maverick trip (below), at night you can camp on beautiful beaches, sleeping to the sound of the surf. The experience will stay with you for a lifetime.

There are two ways to do this trip—either on a guided tour or on your own. Guided tours do the entire trip in one day, offering a more structured—though less leisurely—way to see the coast. These trips, usually led by experienced guides, offer the *relative* safety of an expert. The drawbacks to this method are a lack of independent movement, a more brisk paddling pace (it can be *tough* to do in one day) and the lack of an opportunity to camp. **Na Pali Kayak** (808-826-6900) and **Kayak Kaua'i** (808-826-9844). Of the two, we like Kayak Kaua'i for their deeper expertise. Expect to pay around $280. They bring the gear, food and know-how; you bring the muscles.

If you want twice as much cost and hassle but *10 times* the gratification, you can do a **maverick trip**. Na Pali Kayak and Kayak Kaua'i will give you a personal guide who will travel with you to Kalalau and then make a judgment call as to whether you're up to continuing on your own. You'll need a valid camping permit *with a kayak landing stamp* for Kalalau or Miloli'i before even applying for this service. See page 203 for info on permits, for info on permits, and expect to pay between $350 and $400 for the trip.

Doing it on your own allows *you* to set the pace and the schedule. You go when you like, how you like, where you like and at the speed you like. You can rent a two-person kayak, if you desire. Consideration of this method necessitates a dispassionate evaluation of your skills, abilities, strengths and weaknesses. Although you don't need to be an expert kayaker, it doesn't hurt to have experience. Though we try to do this trip every year, when we *first* did it on our own, our only kayaking experience had been a 3-hour trip up the Wailua River. On that first trip we experienced

Sunset from the caves of Kalalau is your rich reward for a morning's paddle.

ideal conditions, which don't always occur, even during the summer. Please bear in mind that this trip is not for everyone. The Na Pali Coast is wild and unpredictable, and you are exposing yourself to the ocean's capriciousness. The usually calm June through August seas can become difficult with surprising suddenness. Most of the Na Pali boat companies can tell you stories about kayakers who had to be rescued when they got in over their heads (so to speak).

If you decide to do it on your own, here are a few things to keep in mind:

- Learn as much as you can about kayaking. (*Paddling Hawai'i* by Audrey Sutherland was our main reference when we made the first trip.) Proper paddling and loading techniques are *vital*.
- Be sure to spring for *ruddered* kayaks for this trip. You'll have much more control while dealing with the varying ocean conditions. Na Pali Kayak most consistently offers this option.
- In addition to other essentials, make sure you bring water-resistant sunscreen, a hat, sunglasses, Chapstick and possibly Dramamine.
- Apply for camping permits for Na Pali *well in advance* (as much as 6–12 months). Only permits valid from May through September include kayak landings.
- Think through your food requirements. (You *won't* be living off the land.)
- Any water source you utilize along the way will require water treatment pills to avoid possible contraction of leptospirosis. Water filters that don't use chemicals are not considered reliable due to the corkscrew shape of the leptospirosis bacterium.

(We've used and trusted Sawyer filters and First Need XLE Elites, which purifies down to 0.1 micron, but you have to decide for yourself if it's good enough.) Fresh water is present at the following beaches along the route: Ke'e, Hanakapi'ai, Kalalau, Honopu, Miloli'i and Polihale, as well as some waterfalls that fall right into the ocean.

- Typical June through August conditions mean that the wind and currents are both pushing you in the direction you want to go, but *typical* doesn't mean *always*. Monitor ocean conditions by calling the **National Weather Service (808-245-6001)**.
- Paddling in the early morning usually offers the calmest seas (sometimes like glass, if you're lucky) and easier launchings.
- Unless you spring for pick-up service, you'll have to rent an extra car for a couple days and leave one on the North Shore and one at Polihale.

Here's some of what you can expect… From Ke'e, Hanakapi'ai Beach is slightly over a mile. With campgrounds and a freshwater stream, Hanakapi'ai is a favorite place for hikers to camp, but it's too soon for kayakers. Past Hanakapi'ai, you will start to see caves and waterfalls straight out of your dreams. Some of the caves are horseshoe-shaped, with separate entrances and exits. Explore 'em all if conditions are safe.

Keep an eye out for dolphins and turtles, which become more plentiful as you get farther down the coast. At Kalalau, you have paddled 6 miles. If you're on your own, this is a good place to camp with half a mile of sand, fresh water and portable toilets. We like to pitch our tents in the caves (hoping rocks won't fall on us) at the far end of the beach, and walk a few minutes to a waterfall to shower. Kalalau is as far as hikers can go, so from here on you are in exclusive company.

Less than a mile past Kalalau is Honopu Beach. Landing crafts of all types, including *surfboards*, are prohibited. The only legal way to visit Honopu Beach is to swim there from Kalalau Beach (which can be hazardous if there's surf), or you can anchor your craft offshore and swim in (which can also be hazardous).

In all the Hawaiian Islands, and perhaps in all the world, you'll never find a more glorious, moving and mystical beach. Unspoiled Honopu is only accessible by sea. It is actually two beaches, separated by a gigantic arch carved into Na Pali by Mother Nature's furious waves. During the summertime when the pounding Na Pali surf weakens, Honopu is reclaimed from the sea. As you approach by kayak, you're left speechless by the sheer majesty of what unfolds before you. *Vertical* walls 1,200 feet high are the first characteristics you see from the sea. If you're lucky enough to visit here, the giant arch draws

you toward it like a magnet. As you approach it, you can just make out the cascading waterfall around the bend. This is no mere trickle. This immense cataract can knock you down with its force. The stream continues through the arch and out to sea, providing a superb way to rinse off the saltwater. The southern beach of Honopu actually makes a better kayak landing than its northern counterpart, but the northern beach is the most dramatic, and its unfolding vista will surely stay with you forever.

Past Honopu, listen for goats. Although considered pests by island officials, it's charming to hear them from your position on the water. At 9 miles you come to a pair of reefs fringing a beach called Nu'alolo Kai. The waters inside the reef offer good snorkeling during calm seas (and you wouldn't be here if the seas weren't calm, right?). From your kayak, when the two signs onshore are aligned, you're heading toward the deeper channel and to shore.

In times past, the Hawaiians mostly lived in the hanging valley above the beach. Access required scaling the vertical

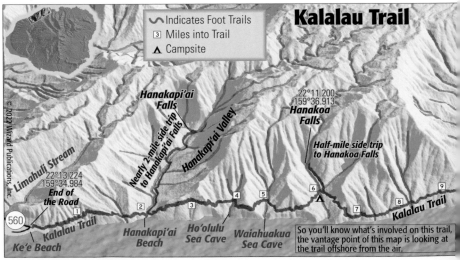

Kalalau Trail

Indicates Foot Trails
3 Miles into Trail
Λ Campsite

© 2022 Wizard Publications, Inc.

Hanakapi'ai Falls

22°11.200
159°36.913
Hanakoa Falls

Hanakapi'ai Valley

Nearly 2-mile side trip to Hanakapi'ai Falls

Half-mile side trip to Hanakoa Falls

Limahuli Stream
22°13.224
159°34.984
End of the Road

560

Kalalau Trail

Ke'e Beach

Hanakapi'ai Beach

Ho'olulu Sea Cave

Waiahuakua Sea Cave

Kalalau Trail

So you'll know what's involved on this trail, the vantage point of this map is looking at the trail offshore from the air.

wall (actually, it's worse than vertical; it leans outward!) up a ladder and along a "trail" in the cliff, which was often nothing more than cubby-holes for your feet. Worse yet was a large rock in the "trail" that was very difficult to get around. The Hawaiians even had a name for this dangerously placed, immovable rock. They called it "fat man's misery."

Next, Miloli'i is 11 miles into your journey. Camping and fresh water make Miloli'i an inviting respite. There is a reef all along the beach and the same system to mark the channel as at Nu'alolo. You need a permit to camp at Miloli'i.

After Miloli'i, you will see a radio transmitter on top of a mountain belonging to the Pacific Missile Range Facility. From the radar transmitter (helicopter pilots avoid getting too close to it, claiming they can feel their *da kines* cook), it's only 3 miles to Polihale. After your surf landing

An open-ceiling cave along Na Pali is one of the many places to poke your kayak into during your voyage.

there, you can look forward to dragging your kayak through 500 feet of sand in searing heat, a task that would make a Himalayan Sherpa weep. (Good thing you were smart enough to spring for pick-up service from your kayak company.)

Congratulations—you have now joined an elite club of adventurers who have braved the Na Pali Coast. A not-so-quick shower at Polihale Beach, and you are ready to dance all night. Or maybe not.

THE KALALAU TRAIL

So you don't like paddling or the surf is raging. You can still see Na Pali. Because the ultimate hike is also the most famous hike in all Hawai'i—11 miles of switchbacks, hills and beautiful scenery. Much of the trail is narrow and not without hazards—hiking boots or at least closed-toe trail shoes are recommended. The trail calls for several stream crossings (some extra water shoes are handy for this). Don't cross if the water is too high. Don't go if overnight hikes are a problem. To get the proper permits, contact: **Hawai'i DLNR, State Parks** in Lihu'e at

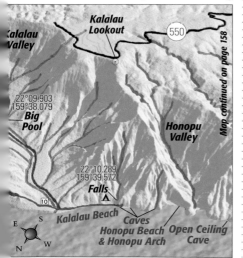

Map continued on page 158

Kalalau Lookout

550

Kalalau Valley

22°09.903
159°38.079
Big Pool

Honopu Valley

22°10.289
159°39.572
Falls

10

Kalalau Beach
Honopu Beach
& Honopu Arch

Caves
Open Ceiling Cave

N S E W

Wild, raw and unforgettable—the Kalalau Trail.

808-274-3444. (Our website, **revealed-travelguides.com**, has a link to a page where permit applications can be filled out online.) You won't be allowed to park your car at the trailhead but instead will need to catch the shuttle (**gohaena.com**). Your camping permit will also allow you access to Haʻena State Park at the end of the road.

Our map on page 202 is an accurate, computer-generated, shaded relief map drawn at a 45-degree angle to give you a perspective of when and how much climbing is involved—altogether about 5,000 feet round trip.

The first 2 miles of the trail leads to Hanakapiʻai Beach (sandy in the summer, bouldery in the winter). There are plenty of slippery and muddy sections, and the second mile is steep downhill (and tough coming back up). It's tricky in spots if you're a beginner hiker, but it's worth it. The views along the coast are exceptional.

Hanakapiʻai is a beautiful but treacherous beach to swim, and it takes most people 1.5–2 hours to hike each way. From here, there is a fairly tough 1.8-mile side trail upstream to Hanakapiʻai Falls, one of the more spectacular falls and pools on the north shore. There are lots of false trails, and it's easy to miss some of the river crossings, but you're in a valley, so you shouldn't stray more than a couple hundred feet from the stream. Many people like to reward themselves by swimming in the pool under the falls. Watch out for falling rocks.

This is as far as you can go *without* a permit. The authorities assume anyone going past Hanakapiʻai will be camping. If this is your plan, and you have your state camping permit, keep going. Four miles ahead at Hanakoa, you have the choice of either camping, continuing to Kalalau or taking the half-mile side trip to Hanakoa Falls, which is even lovelier than Hanakapiʻai. You'll cross the Hanakoa Stream and take a left at the trail near a shelter. After 50 yards take the left fork for 15 minutes. Watch for falling rocks at the falls. If you've come as far as Hanakoa, go see the falls. It's worth the walk.

Back on the trail, your toughest stretch is the last. From here to Kalalau Beach you'll find lots of switchbacks and a narrow trail at times. The stretch 7–8 miles into the trail has a couple of dicey spots, but they're not as bad as they used to be. The views are stunning. Persevere and you will be richly rewarded. Wow! This is the glorious valley you see from the top of Waimea Canyon Drive at the Kalalau Lookout. The beach, the valley and the isolation all make Kalalau a magical place. There is a 2-mile trail inland, which takes you to "Big Pool," a large natural pool in the stream.

Have you ever read *Koʻolau the Leper* by Jack London? It's based on the true story of Koʻolau, who fled to Kalalau in the 1880s after authorities refused to let his wife accompany him to the Kalaupapa leper settlement on Molokaʻi. On July 2, 1893, a ship carrying 12 police, 14 soldiers, the sheriff, many rifles and a howitzer came ashore to capture Koʻolau and the other lepers who had joined him. After Koʻolau shot two of the soldiers dead and a third accidentally shot himself in the head (oops), the authorities decided to leave Koʻolau alone. He died in Kalalau in 1896 from his affliction.

As you stand on the beach at Kalalau, it's amazing to think that the entire valley was once populated. It was only in 1919 that this isolated valley was finally abandoned as people sought the life available to them in Lihuʻe and other towns.

This is as far as you can go. A half mile farther down the coast is the most beautiful beach in all the islands, maybe in all the Pacific—Honopu Beach. There is none finer. Period. The only legal way to visit the beach is to swim there. If you do this, beware that the current is against you coming back. Only during calm seas, only with fins and only if you're a strong swimmer. In late summer Kalalau Beach snakes its way closer to Honopu, and people walk on the rocks and sand most of the way. Beware of unexpectedly large waves if you do this. For more information on Honopu, see **Na Pali Kayak Trip** on page 199.

Kalalau has composting toilets. The waterfall provides fresh water, which should be treated before drinking as should your en route sources at Hanakapiʻai and Hanakoa streams. In fact, *all* fresh water in nature should be treated to avoid possible bacteriological contamination from animals or people polluting the stream.

4WD MILOLIʻI RIDGE ROAD

The southern, dryer part of Na Pali is defined by a series of ridges. There are numerous roads such as Ka-uhao and Kaʻaweiki that wind their way along the ridges to the edge of Na Pali. (See map on page 88.) Unfortunately, these are hunter roads, always closed during the week, and you're supposed to get a hunting permit to drive on them on weekends. But Miloliʻi Ridge Road (see same map) is open all week long and, if you have a 4WD and it's not raining, you can probably drive to the end where you'll get a beautiful view of this part of Na Pali. Once at the road's end, look for a trail to the left that goes around and up a hill. Intrepid hikers might want to brave the ridge as far as their nerve takes them. (The ridge ends rather conclusively—right above Miloliʻi Beach, a dramatic 1,400 feet below you.)

Here's the deal: The road is maintained by State Parks, which means it may be rutted, nasty, impassible or even closed if they feel like it. Or it might be fine. Either way, when you get to some picnic tables (shown on the map on page 88), you've come to the last part you should consider driving if it's *been* raining or you *think* it will. Because after that the road gets steeper, and you might have problems returning if it's too slippery. All told it's just over 5 miles of 4WD each way. You access Miloli'i Ridge Road 0.3 miles into the paved Makaha Ridge Road between mile markers 13 and 14 on Hwy 550 (Waimea Canyon Drive).

MAKALEHA HIKE

This hike is in *Adventures* because it is only for the advanced hiker. The trail goes along a beautiful stream, through a bamboo grove and offers lush scenery. There are a number of places along the way to bathe in the stream, which can be deep in spots. Past the end of the trail are waterfalls just for you. The problem is that the trail is a trail-of-use and is not officially maintained. As a result, it is splendid in some parts, wretched in others. Some big steps up and down and mud spots keep it interesting. You will have to walk in the stream in some places, so we usually bring tabis (fuzzy mittens for your feet that work well on slippery rocks). Even without the waterfalls, you will get a real Indiana Jones feel for this part of God's country.

The trail starts at the end of Kahuna Road in northern Kapaʻa. (See top of map on page 62 to get there.) From here, you park and walk past the water tank to the

Hike through bamboo, cross the stream several times, step in mud, walk on wet rocks. All this just to marvel at Makaleha. It works for our hiker friend pictured here.

trail. At one point, the trail on the right (northern) bank veers away to a water tunnel. Don't go there, but instead cross the main stream at the remains of an old concrete dam. Follow the trail close to the stream as much as possible. From here, enter the bamboo grove. You'll see three large trees; behind the one on the far right is a trail that ascends into the bamboo, skirts the cliff edge and gives some opportunities (take the second one) to return to the river below. Remember that place for your return hike. From here, it can be muddy if it's been raining (and it probably has been). This is the real Kaua'i—lush, wet and beautiful.

When the bamboo ends, you have a choice of walking on the trail (which will be muddy and thorny and fern-filled), or walk in the stream on the rocks. (Many will find rock-hopping in the stream *the whole way* their best solution.) At one point the trail dumps into the stream, and you'll have to cross it onto an island in the river. Walk the length of the island, cross the stream to the left, and pick up the trail again. Follow it until you come to some large boulders that form a wall. Go over the wall and cross the stream. The trail gets difficult from here. Look for machete marks in the annoying hau trees that cross the trail, sometimes forming a jungle gym of limbs. You should always be able to hear the stream, but if you get into trouble, there probably won't be anyone coming along to help. Bring mosquito repellent or don't go. Footwear should include hiking sandals or boots and tabis (preferable) for stream walking. Bring water. You'll have to walk in the stream the last 50 yards before you come to a fork (where three streams converge at a stunning vista). A waterfall is up the left-most stream. *If you're feeling lucky,* a

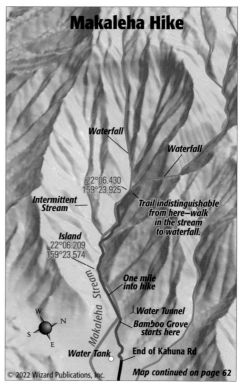

Makaleha Hike

Waterfall

Waterfall

22°06.430
159°23.925

Intermittent Stream

Trail indistinguishable from here—walk in the stream to waterfall.

Island
22°06.209
159°23.574

Makaleha Stream

One mile into hike

Water Tunnel

Bamboo Grove starts here

Water Tank

End of Kahuna Rd

© 2022 Wizard Publications, Inc.

Map continued on page 62

better waterfall is 20–30 minutes of rock-hopping to the right. It's an easier walk in a tall, narrow canyon, and the falls are two beautiful tiers with good swimming at the base. But that narrowness opens you up to the possibility of getting hammered by falling rocks, if one lets loose above you. Regardless, allow ample time to get back. In all, it's only 1.5 miles each way, but the going is pretty slow in many spots, and it *can* take much of the day.

HONOPU RIDGE TO A DROP-DEAD VIEW

Imagine a trail that cuts through forest, ventures down a ridge and culminates in one of the most inspirational views on the island. For two decades that's exactly what you had to do…*imagine* it. Back in 1982 one of Kaua'i's most delicious trails

Sometimes it's hard to capture the immensity of what you're seeing in a photo. The boat offshore and the helicopter (the light blip above our friend's hat) are testament to the grandness of what awaits you on the Honopu Ridge.

was damaged by a hurricane. State Parks folks, ever grumbling about budgets, decided not to put in the effort to reopen it. Over the course of more than two decades it became unrecognizable. But thanks to a few unsung volunteers, today Honopu Trail is available to ambitious hikers. Why ambitious? Because, although it's only just over 2 miles each way, much of the trail is still overgrown (largely due to disuse), making portions unpleasant, and there's opportunity to wander off the correct path if you're not careful. Most of the trail is obvious, but there are a few hunter trails (especially at the beginning) that might lead you astray. (See maps on page 158 and 154.)

Located on the west side, you take Hwy 50 to Waimea Canyon Drive (550). At 0.4 miles past mile marker 17 (not far from the end of the road at Kalalau Valley) there's a turnout on the curve about 100 feet past a telephone pole. Park there, and the unmarked trail a short way up the hill heads left toward the coast. After just 120 yards you come to your first confusing intersection. The trail to the left is the correct path. (Don't go straight.) At 0.2 miles the trail comes to a T intersection at a tree whose branches all point to the right. Turn right. (The incorrect faint left leads down to a stream bed.) From here you'll *really* be grateful for long pants, because the native Pacific false staghorn ferns tend to claw at your legs. (Jeans can feel heavy—we've become fond of lightweight pants with zip-off legs.)

It's mostly the first half mile that has the confusing intersections. Tips to staying on the correct trail include following the most beaten path, looking for logs or other barriers placed to block side trails and staying on the trail that has the most tags (ribbons) on trees. The easiest thing is to download our smartphone app, *Hawaii Revealed* and use the GPS map feature, rather than wasting time navigating a crisscrossing maze of trails.

Soon most of your 1,000 feet of elevation loss will occur. (You actually climbed a bit until now.) Always stay on the most worn path. About 1 mile into the trail (it will seem like more) you'll be on a wide ridge that will eventually get narrow enough to see Honopu on one side and Awa-'awapuhi on the other. Eventually the trail comes to a glorious lookout on a dirt bluff. The vista into Honopu Valley is so magnificent that it defies description. The entire heavenly valley is before you. Honopu Beach and the Pacific are to your left 3,000 feet below. The scene is so intense that it literally looks unreal. If clouds are in the valley, wait a while. They tend to come and go. The trail continues another 15 minutes, terminating at a point where the ridge takes a drop down to a razorback spine (which you *don't* want to visit). From the end you're treated to a tasty view of Na Pali Coast.

While on the trail, if you take a wrong turn, keep track of where you've been and backtrack. Nothing's worse than being lost in the forest. Our first time in (when the trail was more vague than it is now) we made two wrong turns, realized our mistakes, and returned to the intersection to find the right way. Also, make sure you're back at your car *at least* 1.5 hours before sunset. It will take most people 1.5–2.5 hours each way, and the trip back up is fairly strenuous. Bring gobs of water down, suck 'em up at the overlook, and bring only what you need back up. The trail has a few areas where there's opportunity to fall or twist an ankle. One short stretch is on the side of a dirt hill that may make some nervous. This hike is in *Adventures* because of the poor trail conditions in a few scattered areas and because of the potential to get off the trail. Coming

back, the quarter-mile closest to your car seems to present new opportunities to wander off the same trail you already took on the way down.

RAPPEL OFF A 60-FOOT WATERFALL

In Hawai'i, as elsewhere, ziplining has really taken off. But what if you want a *real* rush? That's where rappelling comes in. **Da Life Outdoors** (808-246-6333) has two waterfalls in Lihu'e that you'll get to rappel down. Think about it: You're at the top, you lean back and literally walk backward down a waterfall. First a 30-footer. Then the big dog—a 60-foot falls that involves walking as well as sliding down. I know what you're thinking: *What if I fall?* They have all the safety gear as well as a fireman's belay at the bottom. That means they will give you the freedom to do it by yourself (rather than completely mothering you), but all it takes is a gentle tug on your rope from the other guy *at the bottom* to increase the friction and stop you from falling. Which gives you the best of both worlds.

They'll lend you felt-bottomed shoes (tabis) to keep from slipping, give you lots of training and practice on a wall before heading out to the wilderness. The whole experience takes about 4 hours and involves a little hiking and swimming. Lunch is included. Book in advance. Weight between 70 and 250 pounds and and waist size between 22–48 inches. $224.

VISIT THE SUMMIT OF WAI'ALE'ALE

In every edition we've ever had of *Ultimate Kaua'i Guidebook*, we've always had to warn adventurous readers that it wasn't possible to hike to the summit of the highest point on the island, one of the wettest spots on earth. All of that changed with the construction of a conservation

He said, "Hey, babe. Take a walk on the wild side..."

fence. You see, until that fence was built, bagging the summit meant walking through miles of unnegotiable swamp in usually horrid conditions. Getting lost was almost assured, even with a GPS. But recent efforts to build a pig fence around the summit area also created an opportunity. Now, once you find the fence, getting lost is less of an option.

We need to stress, however, that this is still an *incredibly* taxing effort. We're talking a 20-mile round trip, nearly all of it above the 4,000-foot level, drilling your way into a wet, soggy, inhospitable world that will likely be ensconced in rain, wind and clouds. This could potentially take two days (though we know some über-hard core elites who can do it in one day), and odds are the only photos you get will be from a rain-spotted lens of a mostly treeless landscape. Rescues would be very difficult because you'll probably be in the clouds, and helicopters can't land in a cloud. Most

people should simply turn the page at this point. Hopeless idiots (of whom I include myself) should read on.

OK, we gotta start by saying you need to download our smartphone app, *Hawaii Revealed*. Not trying to pressure you into buying more Wizard products, but without the app, there's simply no easy way for us to describe where to find the arrow log. (More on that later.) And besides, you're gonna want to *know* if you're still on the trail to the fence, and the app is the only way.

You'll start by using your 4WD to get to the trailhead of the Mohihi-Wai'alae Trail in Koke'e. (See *Mohihi-Wai'alae Trail* on page 160 for directions and info on that trail.) The Sugi Grove campground near the trailhead is a good option for starting this hike as early as you should (before sunrise).

The mile markers end before you are 4 miles into the trail, at which point the

From the summit of Wai'ale'ale, the Wailua River is more than a half mile below your feet.

trail descends rapidly into a drainage. The footing getting down can be slippery if it's been raining (and it *has* been), and there are times you should face the mountain and actually climb down the trail. At the bottom you will find a river with a small waterfall and large boulders that make for a decent pit stop, especially before climbing back up on the way out. The trail is directly across on the east bank from where it ends on the west bank, and the boulders are aligned in such a way to make crossing easy.

Once on the other side of the stream, you head back uphill past a small cabin/shack used by hunters. It is from here that the trail gets harder to follow. The main trail *should be* flagged, and you should not go more than 5 minutes without seeing a flag marking the way. Again, we're assuming you have our smartphone app, because it's impossible to describe the entire trail, and parts are difficult and tricky.

At 5.5 miles, keep an eye out for an easy-to-miss arrow carved into a log on the ground, pointing the direction from which you came. That log will mark the spot where you will split from the main trail. Step over the log and slightly left. You'll see a faint trail and possibly some flagging tape. This is the trail you're looking for. It can be difficult to make out in places.

Once on the trail past the arrow log, you want to continue the same technique you have been perfecting over the last mile and half—look for the flagging tape, and always take the uphill path when applicable. Use the app to make sure you're on the trail. The terrain will be generally the same as what you have been seeing with some increased swampiness and the need to use whatever logs or roots you see to stay on solid ground.

About 0.75 miles along this path, trees begin to become more widely spaced, and you'll notice more shrub-like plants. You will suddenly burst out into open, Alaka'i Swamp land with the hog-wire fence right in front of you. The change in scenery is very dramatic and exciting, giving the promise of the extreme landscape ahead. This is a good place to clean your shoes and clothing of any alien hitchhikers to avoid tracking them any farther.

When you approach the fence, turn right and follow it to its end. It is approximately 3 miles of a circuitous fence line over varied terrain until you reach your ultimate goal. You won't find anything more difficult than you have already encountered, but there will be some steep climbs to keep you on the ridge tops and heading toward the summit. There is always the fence itself to help keep your balance in some areas. You're probably cold. You're *certainly* wet. A great, potential spot to wait through the night *might* be found within a quarter mile of your encounter with the fence. It is the old staging area for construction of the fence, and it offers a flat area with minimally squishy ground. This area allows you to have a better idea of whether you will have a clear day at the summit when the morning comes. Early mornings are your best chance of seeing the summit cloudless.

The summit of Wai'ale'ale is an otherworldly place. Other than a few clumps of sickly looking 6- to 10-foot trees, there is nothing over a foot tall for more than a mile in any direction. Not even the ubiquitous ferns are genetically programmed to deal with so much rain and cloud cover. So the dominant features carpeting the ground are moss, lichen and short grasses. The 3,000-foot cliffs plunging into the crater define the eastern portion, which is so sheer, you can literally walk up to it and look nearly straight down to the crater over a half mile beneath your feet.

Walking around is a bit awkward. The sponge-like ground is constantly threatening to steal your shoes. It takes about 2 hours just to go from one end of the summit to the other. No mosquitoes live up here, but huge dragonflies are everywhere. Only a handful of birds can be heard, some of them endemic—found nowhere else in the world except on this watery mountaintop.

Please be mindful of the cultural sacredness of this spot, and make sure you bring everything out that you take in. Be careful not to disturb the remains of the heiau in any way.

Return the way you came. (Those five words…Easy to type, a buggah to do.)

SECRET TUNNEL TO THE NORTH SHORE

Imagine that you're in an east shore valley. You come upon a tunnel that's a *mile* long. From the moment you enter, you can see the light at the other end. When you emerge, you're in the virtually inaccessible back of the north shore's Hanalei Valley, surrounded by nearly vertical mountains, a perfect river and no people. Aside from a few hunters, almost no one on Kaua'i had even *heard* of this tunnel until we revealed it. Those who had heard of it considered it one of those urban legends, a myth. Well, it's no myth.

In the 1920s a sugar company was seriously coveting the abundant water flowing out the Hanalei River. They needed the water for their east shore sugar. So for $300,000 they cut this

Tunnel & Jungle Hikes

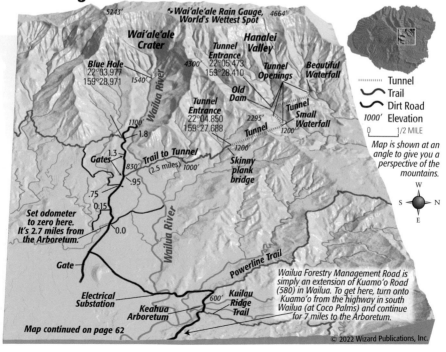

5243'

⚲ Wai'ale'ale Rain Gauge, 4664'
World's Wettest Spot

Wai'ale'ale Crater

Hanalei Valley

Tunnel Entrance 22°05.473
159°28.410 4300'

Tunnel Openings

Beautiful Waterfall

Blue Hole 22°03.977
159°28.971 1540'

Wailua River

Old Dam

Tunnel Entrance 22°04.850
159°27.688

2295'

Tunnel Small Waterfall
1200'

Tunnel

1100'
1.8

1200'

Skinny plank bridge

Trail to Tunnel
(2.5 miles) 1000'

Gates 830'

1.3

.95

.75

0.15

Set odometer to zero here. It's 2.7 miles from the Arboretum.

0.0

Wailua River

Gate

Powerline Trail

Kuilau Ridge Trail

600'

Electrical Substation

Keahua Arboretum

·········· Tunnel
〰 Trail
↝ Dirt Road
1000' Elevation
0 ___ 1/2 MILE

Map is shown at an angle to give you a perspective of the mountains.

W
S ✦ N
E

Wailua Forestry Management Road is simply an extension of Kuamo'o Road (580) in Wailua. To get here, turn onto Kuamo'o from the highway in south Wailua (at Coco Palms) and continue for 7 miles to the Arboretum.

Map continued on page 62

© 2022 Wizard Publications, Inc.

tunnel and diverted 28 million gallons of water a day under the mountain and into a series of ditches to quench their thirsty crops. But times change. As sugar production dwindled on the east shore, they found that they no longer needed the north shore's water. So, years ago, they stopped diverting the water and abandoned the dam. The flume to divert the water is no longer there. They couldn't divert water into this tunnel even if they wanted to without doing major reconstruction on the dam. But the tunnel, blasted out of solid rock, remains.

Getting there will be a sloppy affair. It involves walking 2.5 miles along a trail through muddy conditions. (It rains about 160 inches annually here, spread fairly evenly throughout the year.) The footing, terrain, overgrowth, washed-out trail sections and ferns hiding pockets of nothingness make it one of the harder 2.5 mile stretches you'll find in Hawai'i. Bring a low-profile pack to reduce snagging vegetation during the many incidences of ducking under brush.

A Few Basics

Driving to the trailhead means taking a dirt road. (See map on page 213.) A regular car can go part of the way, but it's hard to say how far. There's an old truism—*What's the difference between a 2WD rental car and a 4WD SUV? A 2WD rental car can go anywhere!* Meaning, it depends on how much you're willing to punish it. This road is sporadically improved, and it depends on your timing. But for our purposes, 4WD is the way to go here. See directions to the *Jungle Hike* on page 168, and stop *just before* the first gate. Accept from the get-go that there's *no* way to keep your feet dry. Spiked tabis (described on page 150) work best, and you might find them at **Discount**

Variety in Koloa or **Walmart**. The downside is that your feet will feel a bit tender when you're done. Long pants are also recommended. Ferns have a habit of sticking out in the trail, scratching at your legs. Jeans are OK, but they get heavy and stick to your legs, making it harder. Lightweight pants are preferred. Look for delicious red thimbleberries along the way. (The redder, the better.) Bring a flashlight/headlamp (or two) for the tunnel. Also bring water and snacks.

The trail to the tunnel is a hunters' trail, and it's *always* muddy. The first 100 yards are very sloppy with a permanent puddle near the place where you park. Several short stretches are on uneven terrain, and caution needs to be taken. In the first 5 minutes you'll have to cross the Wailua River twice. *Usually* it's done by hopping across a couple of rocks. If it's too deep and you aren't comfortable, don't go. If it's been raining a lot, don't go. During very heavy rains you may find that the river isn't crossable coming back, presenting you with a dilemma. Just after the first crossing, go diagonally upstream about 150 feet and look for a trail in the bamboo thicket. (It's not the trail going straight *ahead* from the river). Bamboo is the best natural material there is for walking sticks, and it's a good idea to have one on this hike. (It makes a good spider stick in case there are webs across the trail.) Cut it so that a knuckle is near the bottom, acting as a natural stopper, preventing dirt or mud from filling the hollow tube. Shortly after the bamboo thicket the trail becomes more vague—keep an eye out for where it bears right.

The trail is intermittently "paved" with 'ohi'a tree logs looking like railroad ties from long ago. Avoid false trails. Remember, you'll never go more than 15 minutes without seeing the 'ohi'a logs. (Hunters—

and their dogs—who use the trail mostly on weekends and Mondays often put their own tags on trees, and following them might help, or they might take you off the main trail.) You've gone almost a mile when you see your first old, abandoned wooden power pole. Just after this you come to a flat muddy area and a trail to the left. We've walked through the flat part and sunk 3 feet into a bog. You'll cross a couple of smaller streams (a foot wide) and a slightly larger stream.

After 1.5 hours or so, when the trail encounters a large stream again, it seems to end. This is where people get lost. It actually veers slightly left, away from the stream and over some rocks. Pick your way over the boulders, staying on the left side of the bank, and look for muddy stains on the rocks—they will lead you to the trail in the tall grass ahead. It crosses the stream where the stream makes a right turn. Once you cross, pick up the trail *directly* on the other side, and it's not far before you walk on a skinny plank bridge over a ditch. The trail goes to the left (and uphill) to the gauging station and tunnel. You'll notice a tunnel to the left and a little farther on, one to the right. You want the long one on the right (the left side is shorter and doesn't lead to anything). It takes us 2–3 hours *to* the first tunnel, and about 45 minutes *in* the tunnel. You'll gain about 600 feet with all the ups and downs.

Once in the tunnel, you'll notice that there's water standing in it. That's from the small amount of water that drips from the ceiling. It's just the right amount to keep about 4–8 inches of water fresh. The tunnel is about 6 feet wide and 7–10 feet high with an occasional need for a head duck on the straight portion. The bottom is flat and lined with small rocks, which makes for fairly straightforward walking. The tunnel reverberates with the ever-constant sound of the splashing of your feet in the ankle-high water.

A hiker marvels at the richness of Kaua'i, which is ever-present on this trek.

About 900 feet above you is the ridge that the ancient Hawaiians used to walk on to reach the summit of Wai'ale'ale where the remains of their altar, at one of the wettest spots on Earth, may still be found. As you approach what appears to be the end, you see an odd sight: railroad tracks in the shallow water, probably used to haul the debris out of the tunnel during construction. At the light at the not-quite-end of the tunnel, you can step outside momentarily to visit a small waterfall waiting for you. Then it's back in the tunnel for the remaining 0.25 miles. That latter portion is partially lined with cement and shorings, requiring anyone 6 feet tall or more to duck for a bit. At the real end you need to follow the now-exposed ditch for a hundred yards or so, keeping an eye out for a faint trail on the right that goes over a ditch. It goes down for about a minute

to the Hanalei River. During good weather the scenery is magnificent. The mountains tower all around you. Wai'ale'ale plateau is above and to your left, its side etched with waterfalls. The river, with some impossibly large boulders, makes a perfect place for lunch.

Most will be more than satisfied with this destination. But if you started early (hiking by 7 or 7:30 a.m.), there is one more challenge for the intrepid. You've been through a mile of tunnel already and are at the river. Directly across from the giant boulder and deep pool (you'll see it), there's a *very* faint trail on the other side of the river that leads 5–10 minutes upstream to *another* 0.7 mile-long tunnel. It's more dicey.

Follow the trail across from the boulder, past a bamboo grove where your route looks more like a game trail, until it meets an old diversion dam (that looks like a

Hikers entering the tunnel.

waterfall, which you'll hear). From the top of the dam look upstream, then turn to your right. You should see a vague trail going directly uphill. It will take you to a cement wall (part of the next ditch). The next tunnel entrance is over the wall to the right.

Once inside the tunnel (known to hunters as Ka'apoko Tunnel), there's lots of head ducking, and it has a more rickety feel. When the tunnel ends, there's an off-shoot to the left. Not far from there, you come to a low-ceiling incline with water gurgling down. Scoot up and you'll emerge in a Shangri-la that will make you giddy with joy. A cathedral of 200-foot sheer walls is so steep they actually lean *inward*. Water drips from above, creating an exotic backdrop. To the left is a pounding waterfall. The setting is unbelievable and worth all the effort you went through to get here.

Besides enjoying the sheer beauty of the scene, look for a third tunnel across the river. There is a small stream trickling down from the entrance. The tunnel takes another 10 minutes and gives different perspective on the valley.

The trail conditions seem to get worse every year, and at the risk of sounding self-promoting, you'd do well to purchase our smartphone app to keep from veering off the trail. It's geo-aware, and we GPSed this trail (and all Kaua'i trails) ourselves to make sure the track is spot on.

Needless to say, you'll have the opportunity to get big-time muddy, slip on your 'okole, bump your head, twist your ankle, etc., on this adventure. Use your best judgment. This trail and tunnel are not maintained for this purpose, so please don't complain to *anybody* if you have any problems. This is a strenuous, exciting and memorable adventure with absolutely *no* guarantees. *That's* why it's an adventure.

HIKE TO THE BLUE HOLE

The term *Blue Hole* is widely used on Kaua'i yet is oddly ambiguous. Some use it to refer to Wai'ale'ale Crater. Some use it for the dam at the end of the dirt road that marks the trailhead. And others say Blue Hole is the pool at the end of an arduous hike. Let's go with the latter.

Getting to the trailhead can be difficult if you don't have 4WD. Read the directions to the *Jungle Hike* on page 168. Instead of looking for that trailhead, keep going on the road 0.4 miles until it ends at a concrete diversion dam. If the water is turbid and nasty, it's an indication that heavy rains have occurred, and this ain't the day for you. (Of course, *any* river can flash flood at *any* time.)

Walk across the dam and take the trail *up* the river. You're on the right side and the trail stays close enough to the river to hear it, so veer to your left at early intersections. You'll think at several points that the trail peters out. Keep looking; it goes on. At 0.4 miles you come to an island, where the river splits. You'll work your way up the island and when it ends, cross to the left side and pick up the trail. In 0.25 miles (it's impossible to describe the spot, but if you have our app, *Hawaii Revealed*, the geo-aware map shows where) you cross to the right side and will stay on it to the end. Mud (occasionally over a foot deep) is common, and fallen trees and branches make it more challenging at times, but it's better than boulder-hopping your way up in the water. You'll be gaining 440 feet of elevation. Tabis or shoes with aggressive tread are recommended.

It takes 3 hours round trip for *good* hikers, twice that long or more for sketchier trekkers, or if you can't find the adjoining trail segments.

At last you arrive at your goal. Three streams come together with two of them

It takes time, a 4WD and wet feet to get to the so-called Blue Hole.

forming a glorious split waterfall. It's like a scene from heaven. You've been on the trail for less than 1.5 miles, but you'd *swear* it's more than that. (We're positive about that number, we promise.) Soak it all in (easy to do since you're already wet to the bone from your two stream crossings), and return the way you came.

For those who are tempted to continue into the crater, you should think *real* hard about that. If you've read our books to the islands, you know the tone of this warning is unusually strong for us. It's only 3 more miles (round trip) from the falls, but it is a *very* difficult and much less defined 3 miles that will exhaust even the toughest hiker. It has more po-tential for injury, more potential for bad weather (because it's much rainier in the crater) and more uncertainty of outcome. (All that in such a short distance? Yup.) It's muddy, undulating and filled with obstacles. Also, GPS signal degrades in parts of the crater due to the massive walls, so even our smartphone app might fail you. So if all this doesn't dissuade you, and because we *know* people will see this hike on the internet and try anyway, the photo of the crater shows the route. Don't say we didn't warn you. Don't do this unless you start at sunrise. And don't forget that when you come to a 3,000-foot wall in front of you at the back of the crater, you still gotta come back. See photo on page 10.

Looking down the 3,000-foot walls of Wai'ale'ale Crater, the line approximates the route to the back. It's difficult, and only for the hardiest of hikers who are on the trail at sunrise. The falls at Blue Hole are more than enough for most.

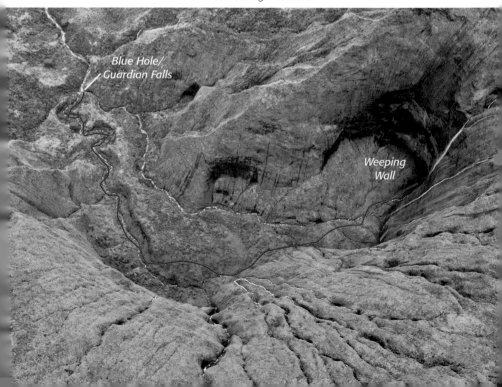

Blue Hole/
Guardian Falls

Weeping
Wall

First a day at the beach, then a romantic evening at the Sheraton Kaua'i.

By their very nature, restaurant reviews are the most subjective part of any guidebook. Nothing strains the credibility of a guidebook more. No matter what we say, if you eat at enough restaurants here, you will eventually have a dining experience directly in conflict with what this book leads you to believe. All it takes is one person to wreck what is usually a good meal. You've probably had an experience where a friend referred you to a restaurant using reverential terms, indicating that you were about to experience dining ecstasy. And, of course, when you go there, the food is awful and the waiter is a jerk. There are many variables involved in getting a good or bad meal. Is the chef new? Was the place sold last month? Was the waitress just released from prison for mauling a customer? We truly hope that our reviews

match your experience. If they don't (or even if they do), please drop us a line. Readers help us *tremendously* in keeping tabs on the restaurants, and we read and digest (so to speak) every email.

We often leave out restaurant hours of operation because they change so frequently that the information would be immediately out of date. (We do list them in our *Hawaii Revealed* app.) Most restaurants close around 9 p.m. If you're going to drive a long way to eat at an establishment, it's best to call first. Restaurants **ono** that stand out from the others in some way are highlighted with an *ono* symbol.

In some restaurants around the island you'll see guidebook recommendation plaques, guidebook door stickers and signed guidebooks, but you won't see ours.

The reason? We *never* tell them when we're there. We review everything on the island *anonymously*. We're more interested in being treated like everyone else than in copping a free meal. How could you trust our opinion if the restaurant *knew* who we were?

By their reviews, many guidebooks lead you to believe that every meal you eat in Hawai'i will be a feast, the best food in the free world. Frankly, that's not our style. Kaua'i, like anywhere else, has ample opportunity to have lousy food served in a rotten ambiance by uncaring waiters. In the interest of space, we've left out some of the dives. We did, however, leave in some of the turkeys just to demonstrate that we live in the real world.

For each restaurant, we list the price *per person* you can expect to pay. It ranges from the least expensive entrées to the most expensive, plus a beverage and usually an appetizer. You can spend more if you try, but this is a good guideline. *The price excludes alcoholic beverages since this component of a meal can be so variable.* Obviously, everyone's ordering pattern is different, but we thought that it would be easier to compare restaurants using actual prices than if we used symbols like different numbers of dollar signs or drawings of forks or whatever to differentiate prices between restaurants.

When we give **directions** to a restaurant, *mauka side* of highway means "toward the mountain" (or away from the ocean). The shopping centers we mention are on the maps to that area.

Very few restaurants care how you dress. A few discourage tank tops and bathing suits. Some of the fancy resorts like the St. Regis Princeville, Sheraton or Grand Hyatt have dress codes. Their dress codes require **resort wear**, meaning covered shoes and collared shirts for men

(nice shorts are *usually OK*), dressy sportswear or dresses for women.

It's legal to bring your own alcohol to restaurants in Hawai'i, and many restaurants, especially inexpensive ones, have no objections to letting you BYOB.

Local food can be difficult to classify. Basically, local food combines Hawaiian, American, Japanese, Chinese, Filipino and several other types and is (not surprisingly) eaten mainly by locals.

Pacific Rim is sort of a fusion of American and various countries around the Pacific, including Hawaiian and Asian. We used to categorize them separately, but it's a fine (and subjective) line between American and Pacific Rim, so we just lumped them in with American because even *we* were confused. We don't have a separate **Seafood** section because nearly every restaurant on Kaua'i serves some kind of fish.

Below are descriptions of various island foods. Not all are Hawaiian, but this might help if you encounter dishes unfamiliar to you.

ISLAND FISH & SEAFOOD

'Ahi–Tuna; raw in sashimi or poke, also seared, blackened, baked or grilled; good in fish sandwiches. Try painting 'ahi steaks with mayonnaise, which *completely* burns off when BBQ'd but seals in the moisture. You end up tasting only the moist ocean steak. Most plentiful April through September.

Lobster–Hawaiian spiny lobster is quite good; also called "bugs" by lobster hunters. Keahole Lobster is simply Maine lobster flown to the Big Island where it's revived in cold water.

Mahimahi–Deep ocean fish also known as a dolphinfish; served at a lu'au; very common in restaurants. Sometimes tastes fishy (especially if frozen), which can be offset in the preparation.

Marlin–Tasty when smoked, otherwise can be tough; the Pacific Blue Marlin is available almost year round.

Monchong–Excellent tasting deepwater fish, available year round. Usually served marinated and grilled.

Onaga–Also known as a ruby snapper; excellent eating in many preparations.

Ono–(Wahoo) *Awesome* eating fish and can be prepared many ways; most plentiful May through October. Ono is also the Hawaiian word for delicious.

Opah–(Moonfish) Excellent eating in many different preparations; generally available April through August.

'Opakapaka–(Crimson snapper) Great tasting fish generally cooked several ways. Common October through February.

'Opihi–Limpets found on ocean rocks. Eaten raw mixed with salt. Texture is similar to clams or mussels.

Poke–Fresh raw fish or octopus (tako) mixed with seaweed (limu), sesame seed and other seasonings and oil.

Shutome–Swordfish; dense meat that can be cooked several ways. Most plentiful March through July.

Walu–Also goes by other names such as butterfish and escolar. Be careful not to eat more than 6 ounces. The Hawaiian nickname for this oily fish is maku'u, which means—*ahem*, this is awkward—"uncontrollable bowel discharge." Eat too much, and you may pay more dearly than you intend.

LU'AU FOODS

Chicken lu'au–Chicken cooked in coconut milk and taro leaves.

Haupia–Coconut custard.

Kalua pig–Pig cooked in an underground oven called an imu (hot rocks go *inside* the beast), shredded and mixed with Hawaiian sea salt. Outstanding!

Laulau–Pork, beef or fish wrapped in taro and ti leaves and steamed. (You don't eat the ti leaf wrapping.)

Lomi salmon–Chilled salad consisting of raw salted salmon, tomatoes and two kinds of onions.

Poi–Steamed taro root pounded into a paste. It's a starch that will take on the taste of other foods mixed with it. Best eaten with kalua pig or fish. Visitors are encouraged to try it so they can badmouth it with authority.

OTHER ISLAND FOODS

Apple bananas–A smaller, denser, smoother texture than regular (Cavendish) bananas and a bit tangy.

Barbecue sticks–Teriyaki-marinated pork, chicken or beef pieces barbecued and served on bamboo sticks.

Bento–Japanese box lunch.

Breadfruit–Melon-sized starchy fruit; served baked, deep fried, steamed or boiled. Definitely an acquired taste.

Crackseed–Chinese-style spicy preserved fruits and seeds.

Guava–About the size of an apricot or plum. The inside is full of seeds and tart, so it is rarely eaten raw. Used primarily for juice, jelly or jam.

Hawaiian supersweet corn–The finest corn you ever had, even raw. We'll lie, cheat, steal or maim to get it fresh.

Huli huli chicken–Hawaiian BBQ style.

Ka'u oranges–Big Island oranges. Usually, the uglier the orange, the better it tastes.

Kim chee–A Korean relish consisting of pickled cabbage, onions, radishes, garlic and chilies.

Kona coffee–Grown on the Kona coast of the Big Island. Smooth, mild flavor. Better than Kaua'i coffee.

Kulolo–Steamed taro pudding. (Tasty.)

Laulau–Pork, beef or fish wrapped in taro and ti leaves, then steamed. (You don't eat the ti leaf wrapping.)

Liliko'i–Passionfruit.

Loco moco–Rice, meat patty, egg and gravy. A hit with cholesterol lovers.

Lychee–A reddish, woody peel that is discarded for the sweet, white fruit inside. Be careful of the pit. Good, small seed (or chicken-tongue) lychees are so delicious, they should be illegal.

Macadamia nut–A large, round nut.

Malasada–Portuguese donut dipped in sugar. Best when served hot.

Manapua–Steamed or baked bun filled with meat.

Mango–Bright orange fruit with yellow pink skin. Distinct, tasty flavor.

Manju–Cookie filled with a sweet center.

Methley plums–A wild fruit harvested with a permit at Koke'e State Park during the summer months.

Musubi–Cold steamed rice, often with sliced Spam rolled in black seaweed.

Papaya–Melon-like, pear-shaped fruit with yellow skin; best eaten chilled. Good at breakfast. Kaua'i has varieties called sunrise and strawberry papaya.

Plate lunch–An island favorite as an inexpensive, filling lunch. Consists of "two-scoop rice," a scoop of macaroni salad and some type of meat, either beef, chicken or fish. Sometimes called a box lunch. Great for picnics.

Portuguese sausage–Pork sausage, highly seasoned with red pepper. Tastes weird to some people.

Pupu–Appetizer, finger foods or snacks.

Saimin–Noodles cooked in either chicken, pork or fish broth. Word is peculiar to Hawai'i. Local Japanese say the dish comes from China. Local Chinese say it comes from Japan.

Sea salt–Excellent (and strong) salt distilled from seawater. Much of our sea salt comes from Salt Pond Beach Park.

Shave ice–A block of ice is "shaved" (never crushed) into a ball with flavored syrup poured over the top. Best served with ice cream on the bottom. Very delicious.

Smoothie–Usually papaya, mango, frozen passionfruit and frozen banana, but almost any fruit can be used to make this milkshake-like drink. Add milk for creaminess.

Taro–Found in everything from enchiladas to breads and rolls to taro chips and fritters. Tends to color foods purple. Has lots of fluoride for your teeth.

NORTH SHORE AMERICAN

Bar Acuda
5-5161 Kuhio Hwy, Hanalei • (808) 826-7081

ono This is the place for tapas, which is Spanish food served in small, communally shared portions. In this case, you order lots of small entrées and share them. The menu changes weekly and seasonally, so you'll have to explore it on your own. Expect to see items such as kale and blacked ahi, saffron arancini, roasted eggplant with a hazelnut Romesco sauce, etc. The food is pricey, but the flavors are unusual and very effective, and you'll sample a number of them. Limited but mostly deadly desserts. And the atmosphere, sort of a contemporary jazzy feel, works for us. Only disappointment is the drinks, which are overpriced, small and not up to the level of the food. Stick with the wine. $35–$75 for dinner. In Hanalei Center. Reservations *required*. Open Wednesday through Saturday.

Bistro Kilauea

2484 Keneke St, Kilauea • (808) 828-0480

A small, open-air restaurant in Kilauea's Kong Lung Center that is a favorite with our readers for lunch thanks to the cool trade winds blowing through the restaurant. The lunch menu features a handful of pupus (consider the fish rockets), good salads, burgers and some seafood. Dinner brings steaks, seafood, chicken and some pasta but feels overpriced. Love the prosciutto and goat appetizer. Tiny serving but delicious. Service is normally quick, and the atmosphere is comfortable. Drinks are disappointingly weak tasting. The desserts are tasty but on the pricey side. $10–$20 for lunch, $15–$40 for dinner. Lunch starts at noon, which is a bit late. Limited menu from 2 p.m. to 5:30 p.m. Saturday they open at 3 p.m. Live music Thursday and Saturday evenings. Closed Sundays.

Chicken in a Barrel

5-5190 Kuhio Hwy, Hanalei • (808) 826-1999

The name refers to their method of smoking beef, pork, ribs and chicken in a barrel. As you might guess, chicken is your best bet here, and though it has *historically* been super moist and flavorful, it has been pretty dry the last few times we've tried it at multiple locations, and we had to pull the *ono* for this edition. Pulled pork and shredded beef also available. Their sampler is so massive you may have trouble lifting it. Otherwise, the ribs, brisket and chili round out your choices. Oh, and hamburgers are also available but only if you like onions, be-

cause they sneak raw onion chunks into the meat before they grill them. $14–$23 for lunch and dinner. Near the entrance to Ching Young Village in Hanalei. There is also a location in Kapa'a .

Foodland Deli

5-4280 Kuhio Hwy, Princeville • (808) 826-9880

Though the Foodland grocery store in Princeville Center will never be considered a bargain (their grocery prices are confiscatory), the deli is a good deal. For $7–$10 you can pick up a fairly decent sandwich (either packaged or custom made) and be on your merry way to the beach. They also have some very inexpensive sushi.

Hanalei Bread Co.

5-5161 Kuhio Hwy, Hanalei • (808) 826-6717

ono Despite its understated name, consider this *the* coffee shop of Hanalei. Owned by the same folks as Bar Acuda, Hanalei Bread Co. bills itself as an organic bakery and coffee shop. The small, pricey menu of café-style breakfast items features frittatas, breakfast burritos, grilled cheese panini, lunch sandwiches and baked goods (the pound cake is excellent) along with a multitude of topped toasts. They offer high-end, gourmet coffee from around the islands as well as smoothies and juices made from fresh, local ingredients. (Good O.J., but the last time you paid $8 a glass it probably included vodka.) The space is small but open, and it's good for taking in the Hanalei scene. $10–$20 for breakfast and lunch. Service will be either friendly or disinterested. In Hanalei Center. Closed Wednesday.

Hanalei Dolphin Restaurant

5-5016 Kuhio Hwy, Hanalei • (808) 826-6113

ono This is a north shore tradition that is much more consistent these days than we've seen in the past. They have some outdoor tables on a lawn next to the Hanalei River—very nice at lunch or while waiting for your indoor table at dinner. They are often busy and don't take reservations—so if waiting bothers you, arrive early or you're out of luck. Their seafood selection is excellent. Pick a fish and a side item. The teriyaki 'ahi is awesome and best ordered med-rare, even if you're a medium kind of diner. *Love* it with the asparagus wraps. They have a seafood market, a good place to pick up fish for cooking back at the condo. And the western-style sushi is high quality. Bartending skills tend to be lacking—avoid the Blue Dolphin. This place (also called Dolphin Hanalei) pleases most of the time. But, perhaps because of the price, when they tank, they *really* tank. $15–$20 for lunch (Saturdays and Sundays only), $30–$60 for dinner. Pupus and cocktails are served between 3 p.m.–5:30 p.m. On the highway in Hanalei; can't miss it. Their other location at The Shops at Kukui'ula is called **Dolphin Po'ipu**. Same menu, smaller space and no view.

Hanalei Street Eats

5-5088 Kuhio Hwy, Hanalei

ono Hanalei's food truck location on the right as you enter town. A half-dozen or more trucks to choose from most of the time, but the players come and go, so just wander from truck to truck till you see something you like. Once you have your food, choose from multiple tables strewn about, or take it to go. No alcohol, but there's a liquor store just a tad farther up the road. $10–$20 for lunch and dinner. Hours will be hard to predict, but most trucks are open for lunch and dinner daily.

Kalypso Island Bar & Grill

5-5156 Kuhio Hwy, Hanalei • (808) 826-9700

Items are hit or miss. A lot of readers have told us how much they love the drinks and the food, and we can't help but wonder if the former influenced their opinion of the latter. (We've done more than our fair share of restaurant reviews where the food was *great*... after a couple of potent drinks... but less stellar with a clearer head.) The menu runs the gamut from American to Mexican to Italian to Pacific Rim. Burgers and the steak sandwich are your best bets, though they come with no sides. We've had good fish and junk fish at dinner. *Love* the taro burger, though. Consider it with mozzarella on top. Breakfast is the one area where they bring up their batting average—good mahimahi eggs Benedict, mac nut bananas foster pancakes and French toast. $10–$25 for breakfast and lunch (Weekends only), $18–$35 for dinner. On the highway in Hanalei; can't miss it. The place is almost always packed, so what do we know? Closed Monday.

Kilauea Bakery & Pizza

2484 Keneke St, Kilauea • (808) 828-2020

ono Delicious baked goods and breads. (Try the macaroons or macadamia shortbread cookies.) The pizza is pricey, but the unusual fresh ingredients and the flavor combinations of the whole pizza specials work well. An example: Their island-stylin' pizza is ham, pineapple, roasted garlic and chipotle peppers—much more interesting than traditional Hawaiian-style. More typical pizzas by the slice, which are too pricey given the less-glamorous toppings and tendency to get soggy later in the day. (At least the crust is very good.) Service can be friendly, but more often you'll be put off by their attitude—they sometimes seem to pride themselves on their surliness. And it's been this way for years and years. We probably should have pulled the *ono* for this reason; consider it marginal. They have indoor and outdoor tables. $5–$10 for limited breakfast menu, $12–$24 for meals. Bakery is reasonably priced. In Kong Lung Center off Kilauea Road. Open at 6 a.m.

Kilauea Market & Café
2555 Ala Namahana Pkwy, Kilauea
(808) 828-2837

A local market store with a café inside that serves burgers, pizzas and sandwiches. Quality is good, and the hefty burgers weigh in at a half pound. Consider the hapa fries—half regular and half sweet potato fries with garlic aioli. Salads are super fresh. They also serve pizzas—slightly larger than normal personal sized—and local plate lunches. Breakfast offers a small selection with a couple of egg dishes, a couple of sandwiches, waffles and loco moco for $7–$18. Lunch and dinner is pizza, plate lunches, burgers (including a taro one) and sandwiches for around $15–$20. There is a small seating area, or you can take it to go. Beer and wine only. In general, not a place to be avoided, but neither will we steer you here with unbridled passion. In Kilauea on Kilauea Road, left side before you get to Kong Lung Center.

Nanea at the Westin
3838 Wyllie Rd, Princeville • (808) 827-8808

There might be only a half dozen entrées on the menu, but they will be steak, seafood, chicken, short ribs and maybe an entrée salad. Lots of potential, but nothing is executed well enough to justify the prices. Good recipes but overcooked or under seasoned entrées. Staff is friendly, but you won't see them enough. Ambiance by the pool is nice, but they might ruin the outdoor tables with tacky roll-down walls to protect you from the elements even on the nicest of nights. Drinks are hit or miss. It takes more than a nice atmosphere to make a good restaurant. If you're paying this much, they gotta go the extra mile—and they don't here. $18–$22 for lunch, $30–$50 for dinner. At the Westin in Princeville on Wyllie Road. Take-out only for now.

North Shore General Store
5-4280 Kuhio Hwy, Princeville • (808) 826-1122

It's pretty rare that we'd be reasonably happy with food at a *gas* station. (Especially one with *their* prices.) Using quality lean Princeville Ranch beef, (which you can also purchase for grilling), these guys make one of the better burgers around. If you're into BBQ sauce, onion rings and bacon, try the Braddah's BBQ burger. Burgers range from $7–$9, a pretty reasonable price *in these here parts*. They also have fish and chips as well as pizza, which *tastes* like gas station pizza and is ridiculously priced at $7–$8 per slice. Hot dogs come split and on a hamburger bun. Their breakfast sandwiches are tasty at $8. Add a hash brown patty, which works best when you put it in the sandwich. A few tables outside or to take it to go. Service can be *slooooow*. In the 76 gas station at the Princeville Center. Breakfast is $7–$10, lunch and dinner are $8–$15. Full pizzas go up to about $27 and are only available after 3 p.m. They close at 1 p.m. on Sunday.

NorthSide Grill & Sushi
5-5190 Kuhio Hwy, Hanalei • (808) 826-9701

ono A nice ambiance in this second-story, open-air setting that overlooks the town and towering mountains, making window seats a treat. Food is usually top notch. Dinner is more steak, seafood and sushi. (If sushi is your main goal, we recommend sitting at the sushi bar—the chef tends to give extra effort to those who sit and engage rather than order from afar.) The food and ambiance make this an enjoyable, albeit pricey indulgence. Good mai tais. **$20–$40** for dinner. In the Ching Young Village. Closed Monday and Tuesday.

Postcards

5-5075 Kuhio Hwy, Hanalei • (808) 826-1191

Formerly a seafood and vegetarian restaurant that bragged that no four-legged creatures were served, but I never met a lamb with less than four legs, so things have changed. The food is distinctive and can be fairly well prepared. They use organic ingredients and have creative selections. The fresh fish is recommended. They also have vegan choices. Ambiance is homey. The service can be slow. **$25–$45** for dinner. On mauka side of the highway. Reservations required for parties of six or more. Closed Sunday and Monday.

Tahiti Nui

5-5134 Kuhio Hwy, Hanalei • (808) 826-6277

ONO Tahiti Nui is a longtime Hanalei institution that has seen great highs and huge lows. Currently they have an energy along with a comfortable, if slightly seedy, feel. (And we actually mean that in a good way.) It has a genuine Tahiti bar feel (and an owner who's from Tahiti as well). Food is usually pretty good (try the fish burger), their mai tai can be good, but it's variable, and they have live music some nights. Tahiti Nui is like a living entity, and it's hard to say what you'll find. That's part of the charm. It might be a place with great food and colorful characters, or a place with over-the-top characters bordering on *too* seedy. Either way,

this is the center of north shore nightlife, both for visitors and locals. It's because of this we give them an *ono*. If you don't like uncertainty of outcome when you go to a restaurant, this may not be your place. Dinner stresses seafood and only a few pupus, and at **$25–$35** is overpriced. Lunch is burgers, pizzas (hence the sign outside saying Tikiman Pizza) and sandwiches for **$15–$25**. Brunch is weekends only and they open at 9 a.m. for **$15–$32**. They also hold a lu'au on Wednesday nights. It's different from any other lu'au found on Kaua'i (in a good way). On the ocean side of the highway.

The Spot

5-4280 Kuhio Hwy, Princeville • (808) 320-7605

ONO It's all about the breakfast bowls. Choose your size, then decide whether you want a vegan coconut cream soft base or soft banana, then pick your fruits and their "superfoods," and finally select your toppings. They have lots of pre-chosen blends or devise your own. The ingredients are quality, and service is usually friendly. Take your bowl (or smoothie) to a covered table and go at it. The have a decent selection of coffees and teas. Overall, the place works. **$10–$15** for breakfast (served until 1 p.m.) or early lunch. In the Princeville Shopping Center. Closed Monday.

Tiki Iniki

5-4280 Kuhio Hwy, Princeville • (808) 431-4242

ONO This is what happens when a classic rocker (Todd Rundgren) and his wife open the tiki bar of their dreams. Food is American bar food with Pacific Rim offerings, and service is usually quick. A casual, fun atmosphere with creative cocktails that pack a big punch. The Iniki burger has ground Spam incorporated into it. (You can't even taste it, in our opinion.) Open later than other restaurants, and after 11 p.m. they *may* still be serving drinks for a couple hours. (That's hard to find on Kaua'i.) Plus they have live music most weekends. Happy hour is 3–5 p.m. Overall, a good place to get a burger and a drink if you're nearby. $11–$20 for lunch, up to $30 for dinner. In the back of the Princeville Center, behind Ace Hardware. Reservations recommended for dinner. Closed Sunday and Monday.

NORTH SHORE ITALIAN

Hanalei Pizza Shop
5-5190 Kuhio Hwy, Hanalei • (808) 827-8000
A small shop in Hanalei's Ching Young Village. Wish we could steer you to it for a tasty slice. The only thing missing is the tasty part. Unimpressive pizza, though the prosciutto with garlic butter sauce is probably their best offering. Overall, if you're jonesin' for pizza, and you're in the neighborhood, they're here. They have vegan and gluten-free pizza options, too. $5–$15 for lunch and dinner. No lunch on Tuesday for now.

NORTH SHORE JAPANESE

Ama
5-5161 Kuhio Hwy, Hanalei • (808) 826-9452
ono A Japanese ramen noodle house that has a fairly small selection, but what they do offer is outstanding. Though their signature dish is the Ama Ramen, our favorite is the Don-Don Mazemen, which has a touch of spice. For pupus they have several kushiyaki skewers, but we usually order their Nuoc Cham fried Brussels sprouts. (We ate here with a fervent Brussel sprouts *hater* who was stunned that he couldn't get enough of them.) Service is friendly but can be inattentive, and their mixed drinks are downright horrible. Stick with the wine, beer or sake. Overall, an *ono* for their tried-and-true ramen and great outdoor setting with awesome mountain views if you eat dinner early enough. $20–$30 for dinner, no reservations. In Hanalei Center, mauka side, behind Bar Acuda. Open Thursday through Sunday.

NORTH SHORE LOCAL

Hanalei Gourmet
5-5161 Kuhio Hwy, Hanalei • (808) 826-2524
Quality comes and goes with this place. Good fish and chips, burgers, sandwiches and salads for lunch; steak, seafood, pastas and burgers for dinner. The place has a pretty good vibe, and much of the atmosphere gravitates toward the bar. $13–$17 for lunch, $20–$36 for dinner (less if you want a burger). If you stick with the burgers or fish and chips and maybe the salads, you'll probably be happy. Other items, *no guarantee, brah*. In the Old Hanalei School across from Ching Young Village. Happy hour is 3:30–5:30 p.m. They close after happy hour on Friday and Saturday for now. Live music some nights.

Hanalei Wake-up Coffee Bar
5-5144 Kuhio Hwy, Hanalei • (808) 826-5551
Restaurants around here tend to open late for breakfast, if they open at all. This place opens at 7 a.m. Very small menu and less-than-pristine surroundings—think *greasy spoon*. They're usually packed. Service is fast, but the food is hastily assembled, and they *hate* substitutions. Omelets are avoidable and you'll probably find the coffee weak, but other items will fill the need. Décor is an homage to all things surfing. $10–$20 for breakfast and lunch. On ocean side of the road. Can't miss it. A local food

truck moved into the space, so things may be changing.

Kilauea Fish Market
4270 Kilauea Rd, Kilauea • (808) 828-6244
Besides the usual fresh seafood, they carry some pricey free-range beef. If you don't want to cook at home, we suggest their Andy Irons burrito or the fish tacos. They also have salads, plate lunches and unique specials. The outdoor seating is covered, so if you want some sun, take it to the beach. It's pricier because you're in Kilauea. Behind the Kilauea Plantation Center, kitty-corner from Kong Lung Center. $12–$21 for lunch and dinner. Closed Sunday.

Village Snack & Bakery Shop
5-5190 Kuhio Hwy, Hanalei • (808) 826-6841

ono Their baked goods are excellent and very reasonably priced. Ambiance is…well, they don't have any. But if you want a restaurant that has looked the same since the island rose from the sea, this is the place for you. Hearty, cheap food. Try the apple crisp—very ono and only $3. Or consider the chili pepper chicken or a tuna sandwich. $6–$13 for breakfast and lunch. Not bad food for the price. Simple, homey and cluttered. In Ching Young Village. Open at 7:30 a.m. Closed Wednesday.

NORTH SHORE MEXICAN

Federico's Fresh Mex
5-5161 Kuhio Hwy, Hanalei • (808) 320-8394
Slightly different from standard Mexican offerings plus burgers. Because of the height of the posted menu, you'll have a hard time choosing your items until you're right at the no-nonsense counter. So there you are, head aimed high, trying to figure it out. And you *need* to read the menu because preparations are a bit different. The taco salad has ranch dressing, burritos can come "mojado style," which means red and green sauce on top with cheese. And if you don't know that Kauai Pescado Del Dia Burrito means a seafood wrap with chipotle ranch sauce and other stuff, you gotta read it. Items are hit or miss. Pretty good chicken enchiladas, unimpressive salads. We won't warn you to stay away, but we won't recommend it either. Across from Ching Young Village, Hanalei. $11–$17 for lunch (served weekends only) and dinner. Closed Monday through Wednesday.

Paco's Tacos
4460 Hookui Road, Kilauea • (808) 828-2999
Traditional Mexican fare, such as tacos, burritos and quesadillas, with an authentic taste and feel. They use fresh fish, and the burritos are dense and tasty. Avoid the enchilada unless it comes with their mole sauce. There might be a language barrier, so speak clearly when you order your food. $10–$15 for a meal and a drink. In Kilauea on Hookui Road just before (east of) the main road into Kilauea. Just a stand with some tables.

Tropical Taco
5-5088 Kuhio Hwy, Hanalei • (808) 827-8226
If you're wondering why there's a likeness of a green truck inside this location, it's because the owner operated Tropical Taco out of one for over 20 years. The food is comfortable but not a good deal. (It's too expensive, the portions could be bigger, they tend to overuse refried beans as filler and service is slow.) You're better off hitting up one of the food trucks next door. Lunch and (early) dinner are $17–$20. Located in the green Halele'a building on the ocean side of the highway in Hanalei. They may close earlier or later than 5 p.m. Closed Monday.

NORTH SHORE THAI

Lotus Garden Chinese & Thai Cuisine
5-4280 Kuhio Hwy, Princeville • (808) 826-9999

Literally a hole in the wall in the back of Princeville Shopping Center. Service is less than chummy, so order your food at the counter and sit at one of the outdoor covered tables and wait. The tables don't always get cleaned between customers. Food is not particularly good, but you ain't paying a lot. Most items are around $10, so we shouldn't whine—but we will anyway. $10–$20 for lunch and dinner.

NORTH SHORE TREATS

Chocolat Hanalei
5-5190 Kuhio Hwy, Hanalei • (808) 826-4470

Microscopic chocolate shop that sells Hawaiian-grown chocolate. The raw materials might come their farm in Wainiha or perhaps from O'ahu, but this mom and pop operation is worth a stop to get your sweet tooth soothed. Across the street from Old Hanalei School next to Na Pali Properties. $5–$10. Don't blink, or you'll miss it. Hours may be unpredictable. Closed Monday.

JoJo's Shave Ice
5-5190 Kuhio Hwy, Hanalei • (808) 378-4612

Crazy high prices considering the cheap ingredients. Other shave ice companies get away with high prices by offering organic syrups, often made by hand. Not here—they use good, old-fashioned artificial colors and flavors. The closest to natural flavor they have is coffee (which JoJo's does better than other companies—it's not too sweet). $7–$10. In Hanalei at Ching Young Village. Add in long lines (which are common), and all we can say is you can do better.

Kalalea Juice Hale
4390 Puuhale Rd, Anahola • (808) 346-0074

ono The orange colored shack across the road from Whalers General Store has some tasty treats. This family-run operation has local, organic juices, smoothies, açai bowls and shave ice. In case you didn't get the health food memo, an açai bowl is like a big fruit parfait with more fruit and a base of the superfood açai berry. The attitude is right and the flavors are fresh—we haven't had a bad experience here, though the smoothies are only as good as the combo you choose. Try the fresh-pressed sugar cane juice. It has a sweet yet earthy taste that tickles the taste buds. $6–$15. Closed Monday and Tuesday.

Lappert's Ice Cream
5-4280 Kuhio Hwy, Princeville • (808) 826-7393

ono Compelling flavors and some stupid-rich gelatos, including a nearly radioactive chocolate. (Better than their chocolate *ice cream*.) In Princeville Center. $4–$8.

Pink's Creamery
4489 Aku Rd, Hanalei • (808) 212-9749

A cute little ice cream shop in Hanalei that serves a variety of treats as well as Hawaiian Grilled Cheese. They take Hawaiian sweet bread, muenster cheese, shaved kalua pork, grilled pineapple and voilà—a delicious mix of great ingredients. Add to this an ample selection of Hawai'i-made ice cream (awesome haupia-coconut), frozen yogurt, dairy-free ice cream/sorbet, comfort food with a Hawaiian twist, and you have Pink's. The ice cream is pretty good, milkshakes pretty ordinary. The Hanalei Sunrise is worth a try. $5–$10. Take the first right when you enter Hanalei onto Aku Road.

Wishing Well Shave Ice
5-5080 Kuhio Hwy, Hanalei • (808) 639-7828

ono A long-time north shore landmark. While the traditional flavors are available, their local, organic syrups (which are chilled) bring the experience to a new level. Definitely get ice cream in the bottom, or consider a snow cap (sweetened-condensed milk) and a fresh fruit topping. You'll have a treat that is so picturesque and delicious that it may break your social media page posting a photo of it. The traditional flavored shave ice starts at $5, while the organic starts at a pricey $8. The price is worth it, though. Organic flavors rotate depending on what's in season. We've even been impressed with their non-sweet flavors like coffee. Find them in a truck on the ocean side of the highway in Hanalei.

EAST SHORE AMERICAN

Avalon Gastropub
4-356 Kuhio Hwy, Kapaa • (808) 822-9368

ono Tucked away and easy to miss in the Kinipopo Shopping Village, this dinner-only eatery has a small but well-chosen menu. The BBQ brisket sandwich with garlic aioli is pretty good. And they added a fresh catch which changes daily. The burgers have some unusual toppings, such as the Avalon burger, which includes drunk onions, pickled jalapeño, Havarti cheese, bacon and chipotle aioli. Start things off with Scotch egg or the fried mac and cheese with tomato jam. We were a bit leery of some of the cocktail descriptions (a Smoking Jacket—*really?*) but have to admit the ones we've tried have been pretty tasty, and the variety is might impressive. An easy place to like, though not cheap. $18–$35 for dinner. Consider the sticky toffee pudding for dessert—delicious. Closed Sunday and Monday.

Bubba's Burgers
4-1421 Kuhio Hwy, Kapaa • (808) 823-0069

ono Funky place to get decent, but *small* burgers (might want to opt for a double), chili rice, etc., with a limited choice of burger toppings. Love the chocolate banana shake. If it wasn't for their sassy attitude, we probably wouldn't give them an *ono*. Their motto is, "We cheat tourists, drunks and attorneys." So if you are a drunk attorney visiting the island, you're on your own, counselor. $8–$16. On highway in north Kapaʻa; can't miss 'em. Also in Poʻipuʻs The Shops at Kukuiʻula near the roundabout. Nothing stands out individually, but overall the place works fairly well. We should point out that our reader e-mail seems to be pretty split for Bubba's (about two-thirds love it and the other third *hates* it), so maybe we're being too generous with the *ono*.

Bull Shed
4-796 Kuhio Hwy, Kapaa • (808) 822-3791

Formerly a solid place for fairly good grub and nice ocean views, they disappoint too often to retain their *ono*. Dinner only, known for hearty beef and seafood and moderate portions. An unabashed meat and potatoes place (the bone-in prime rib looks like something out of the Flintstones) with lamb and a few seafood items, but you may find the meat not cooked to the temperature you ask for. They also lag on the sides. The window seats are particularly close to the water (we've been there when the waves actually splashed against the glass), but arrive 10–15 minutes before they open (they start serving dinner at 5 p.m.) to get one and hope that they clean the salt spray off because windows can get pretty filmy. Their outdoor tables are better if it's not rainy. Because the shoreline faces southeast, the building blocks the trade winds most of the time, especially tables closest to the building. All items come with a choice of salad for $2 or... salad. Sorry, no soup. You only get rice with entrées and have to pay $3 to upgrade to a baked potato. **$30–$55.** Limited desserts such as coconut cream pie and a pretty good and reasonably priced wine list (which they pair well) along with a nice martini selection. In all, you're paying for the ocean proximity, not consistency of food. On the ocean side of highway across from Kaua'i Village. Reservations only for six or more.

Chicken in a Barrel
4-1586 Kuhio Hwy, Kapaa • (808) 823-0780
The original, roadside stand in north Kapa'a and the only location where you can easily see the barrels used for smoking the chicken. As you might guess, chicken is your best bet here, and though it has *historically* been super moist and flavorful, it has been pretty dry the last few times we've tried it. Pulled pork and shredded beef also available. Their sampler is so massive you may have trouble lifting it. Otherwise, the ribs, brisket and chili round out your choices. Oh, and ham-burgers are also available but only if you like onions, because they sneak raw onion chunks into the meat before they grill them. For a better overall meal go to their location in the Coconut Market-place, which has covered community seating and a large number of self-service beer taps at around $.50 per ounce and is open seven days a week. **$15–$23** for lunch and dinner. The original location is across the street from the East Kaua'i Professional Building on the ocean side of the highway and is closed Sunday.

Coconut's Fish Café
4-831 Kuhio Hwy, Kapaa • (808) 320-3138
ono You're in Hawai'i, and you want fish without paying a fortune. These are the cats to hit. (The place is named after the owner's kitty, Coconut.) Simply great seafood tacos, fishburgers, fish and chips (which are not at all greasy), etc., as well as pasta, salads and soups. Presentation is better than you'd expect for these prices, and if you order a sand-wich, your sides will come stacked on top. They make everything on the spot, and they have nice buns, if we do say so ourselves. **$15–$20** for lunch and dinner. Easy to recommend, though they *occa-sionally* disappoint. In Kaua'i Village Shopping Center (drive past the Ross in the parking lot). Beer and wine available. Closed Wednesday.

Daddy O's
4303 Rice St, Lihue • (808) 245-6778
A small breakfast and lunch place (a dozen or so tables) popular with local residents. The Kanaka breakfast delivers an enormous amount of food that could easily feed two. We prefer the Local or one of their breakfast sandwiches. The breakfast selection is impressive. Lunch focuses on plate lunches and $10 bento boxes (to go). Local dishes include kalbi (short ribs marinated in Korean sauce), loco moco and burgers. Residents are their main market, so you'll eat like a local. In Rice Shopping Center on Rice Street in Lihu'e. **$10–$17** for breakfast and lunch. Closed Monday.

Duke's Kaua'i
3610 Rice St, Lihue • (808) 246-9599
ono So before we talk about the food, we should mention that this is one of the better places on the island to have a tropical cocktail, down-

stairs outdoors on the **Barefoot Bar** over-looking Kalapaki Bay. We also like the indoor table by the small indoor waterfall. The menu downstairs includes flatbread pizzas, burgers, seafood and other items that are not as overpriced as most resort foods. Service there is only fair, and prices are $15–$20. Now as for the restaurant *upstairs*, the beef and seafood are very good. Consider the fresh catch prepared Duke-style. If the special is the fish sautéed in a miso bur blanc with mac nut and crab encrusted—*jump* on that. The prime rib is huge and delicious, and their salad bar is probably the best on the island. (Add it on for only $5.) The only ding on Duke's is that portions seem to get smaller every year. Lanai tables at the railing are best, offering a nice view of the bay. $25–$50 (more if you spring for lobster), which ain't bad for the quality of the surroundings. Located at the Royal Sonesta Kaua'i Resort. (You can park in their lot or next to Anchor Cove at the beach parking lot.) They also have free valet parking from the road next to Anchor Cove Shopping Center, but it often fills up. Reservations recommended.

Deli & Bread Connection
3-2600 Kaumualii Hwy, Lihue • (808) 245-7115

ono An absolutely dandy place to get sandwiches (although you'll often have to wait a while at lunch time). Large selection of traditional meats and veggies, plus some extras. Try the TOPSS sandwich. Chowders are variable. $7–$12. In Kukui Grove next to Macy's. Some effective baked goods (though sometimes stale). But overall, a very steady place. Closed Sunday.

Greenery Café
3146 Akahi St, Lihue • (808) 246-4567

Unique, easy to love and hard to find—just how we like it. Greenery Café serves soul food with an island twist. Ingredients are mostly local and organic. The blending of flavors works very well, and you can get a plate with BBQ chicken, collard greens, black-eyed peas, sweet potato and cornbread—as soul food as you can ask for—or get an ahi or mahimahi salad—more local. Their signature meat is the rosemary chicken (seasoned with rosemary from their herb garden), which is very good and downright addicting as rosemary chicken salad. Wraps, sandwiches, salads and lots of vegetarian and vegan items round out the menu. $10–$17 for lunch. Across the street from the Tip Top Café between Hardy and Ahukini Road. Needed sprucing up on our most recent visit. Closed weekends.

Hukilau Lanai
520 Aleka Loop, Kapaa • (808) 822-0600

ono Fish is their specialty, and they do it very well, though their non-fish items also hold up. The complex flavor combinations here are skillfully conceived. The sweet potato ravioli or the lobster and goat cheese wontons make killer appetizers. And don't overlook their bartending skills, which are unusually well crafted. The Hukilau Mixed Grill is a tasty selection of seafood items. And their mushroom meat loaf is deadly. The atmosphere and views of the courtyard are peaceful and romantic, and if you have kids, you could turn 'em loose on the large lawn adjacent to the dining room. Easy to recommend and always booked; get reservations well in advance. Biggest issue is sometimes total indifference and incompetence at the bar. At Kaua'i Coast Resort, next to Coconut Marketplace. $25–$45 for dinner. Closed Monday.

Island Country Markets
4-484 Kuhio Hwy, Kapaa • (808) 821-6800

A local grocery market that also serves a variety of food. The deli makes great sandwiches with Boar's Head meats. They also have pizzas (which cook in only a couple minutes), burgers, salads, chicken, hot dogs, local items such as Spam musubi, poke bowls and loco moco, some steak and salmon and a gelato and coffee bar. A pretty large selection for a market. Take your choice to one of the outdoor tables after grabbing a beverage from the market. The pizza is downright terrible. The "crust" seems more like a thick flour tortilla, and the sauce is fairly ketchupy. But most of the other items hit the mark. $8–$17 for lunch and dinner. In the Coconut Marketplace, ocean side of Hwy 56 in central Kapa'a.

Java Kai
4-1384 Kuhio Hwy, Kapaa • (808) 823-6887

ono A small coffee place loved by residents and visitors alike. They roast their coffee in-house daily with good results. If you're a true caffeine fiend, consider a Chemex Hand Pour—it takes a while to make, but you'll be vibrating by the time you finish it. Smoothies, juices and granola bowls are also popular if you're more health conscious. Breakfast items include mostly egg sandwiches and breakfast burritos goods and breakfast bagels are pretty tasty, too. Lunch is about sandwiches and wraps. Indoor and outdoor seating is available, but the small space gets crowded quickly (which also slows the service down). If you're in a rush, take advantage of their to-go counter in the back. $13–$18 for breakfast and lunch. On highway in north Kapa'a. Open at 6 a.m.

Jo2
4-971 Kuhio Hwy, Kapaa • (808) 212-1627

They call themselves *natural cuisine*, but we don't know what that means. This is the most recent dining expression of a well-known Kaua'i chef with a longtime knowledge of local flavors augmented by high-end chef skills. That's a fancy way of saying the menu is impossible to define. Seafood plus some "from the land" options. Their poached scallop ravioli is an amazing appetizer, and both the lemongrass sesame crusted mahimahi and seared Hunan style rack of lamb are good choices. Top it off with Valrhona chocolate crème brûlée. So why no *ono*? Great presentation, good, sometimes epic food, (sometimes not) and a surprisingly bad bar are what you will find. When you pay this kind of money, you need consistency. We haven't observed that here. The variability is possibly related to the times the boss is in. $35–$55 for dinner. Reservations recommended. In Waipouli Complex. Closed Tuesday and Wednesday.

Kaua'i Beer Company
4265 Rice St, Lihue • (808) 245-2337

ono Kaua'i is certainly not known as a haven for craft brew beer. These guys might change that. Not only do they make the best beer on Kaua'i, but they also brew some of the best in the state. They have eight or so regularly available libations plus a rotating nitro tap (brewery regulars know what this is—try it, if you don't), but the Bavarian-style Shwarzbier Black Limousine is a real crowd pleaser. They also have a *very* reasonable price to refill 32-ounce growlers. The menu is kind of small, mostly burgers, a couple sandwiches and maybe a seared ahi, but the food's good. Most items are made in house with locally sourced ingredients, and the quality is top notch. If you have kids or a DD, they make home-brewed root beer. Thursday nights *might* feature a rotating roster of food trucks that come at dinner to serve you in the restaurant—super popular with residents. The main dining room gets really loud. We prefer the "wave room" or the outdoor tables by the road. Some nights they have selected food trucks come in to provide food. $17–$25 for lunch and dinner. On Rice Street between Kress and Hardy. Closed Sunday.

Kenji Burger
4-788 Kuhio Hwy, Kapaa • (808) 320-3558
This ain't your typical burger joint. Kenji is a James Beard-winning chef, and his burgers and sandwiches are pretty exotic. Sure, you can get what they call an "old school burger" made from beef and the usual toppings. But they also have burgers with teriyaki and ponzu aioli, Japanese BBQ sauce and sriracha pineapple slaw, a chicken katsu burger, and a fish burger made from black cod that has marinated in miso for three days. They also have sushi burritos and poke bowls. Uncommon flavors are the norm. Most work pretty well. Order at the counter and take it to the indoor tables or outdoor counter. $10–$17 (but more for the lobster burrito). Ocean side of the highway in the middle of Kapa'a. Closed Tuesday. There is a second location in Lihu'e.

Kountry Kitchen
4-1485 Kuhio Hwy, Kapaa • (808) 822-3511
A reliable breakfast standby (served all day) with a huge menu that includes lots of ways to deliver eggs, and the ambiance matches the name. Lunch also available, but their DNA is breakfast-based. Omelets here are hit or miss—consider the lu'au omelet. The pancakes, however, are very

fluffy. Though the price ain't cheap, you're paying for a great selection and mostly good results (with exceptions, such as the tasteless cornbread or the biscuits and gravy). They also have extensive coffee drinks and waffles—like the Salty Monkey with banana, mac nuts, salted caramel and whip cream. The reason we don't give them an *ono* (and maybe it's not fair) is that there is usually a long wait, and the food's not good enough to wait 30 minutes for it. $12–$20 for breakfast and lunch. On the mauka side of the highway in northern Kapa'a. Closed Wednesday.

Lava Lava Beach Club
420 Papaloa Rd, Kapaa • (808) 241-5282
ono How do you put a restaurant on a beach when that's not allowed? These guys accomplished it by bringing sand onto their property *adjacent* to the beach, and the setting works. (Being on the east shore also means that wind and rain can send people to the inside tables.) In the past we felt that they relied too much on their location, but they've picked it up and now deserve an *ono*. Their selection is mostly American fare with a definite Pacific-Rim bent. Breakfast is probably their strongest showing with options like benedicts and omelets plus good breakfast cocktails. Lunch brings fish and chips, ribs, burgers, sandwiches and fish tacos. Dinner expands the meat and seafood offerings. $15–$20 for breakfast, $17–$23 for lunch and $20–$40 for dinner. (Don't forget to retrieve your credit card from the Spam can.) We only wish they'd put something on the bottom of the chairs so they don't sink so far into the sand. After they work their way down, we feel like kids at the grown-up table. Behind the Coconut Marketplace at the Kauai Shores Hotel. Live music some nights.

Mamahune's Tiki Bar

3-5920 Kuhio Hwy, Kapaa • (808) 823-1625

This place has *so* much potential. A tiki bar by the sea that also serves burgers, vegetable and meat bowls. Little else as far as entrées are concerned. The location is awesome—on a lawn overlooking the ocean. They have a particularly great vantage point over the mouth of the Wailua River, but the way they situated the seating, unless you go strolling a bit with a beverage in hand, you won't see much of the view. Execution is a bit spotty and service can be lacking, but it has become a place we like to go for pupus and a drink, rather than a full meal. The edamame potstickers and the charred shishito peppers make great appetizers. Live music some nights. Drinks started out spectacular but have morphed into merely average. Figure about $12–$21 for dinner, or stick with the drinks and pupus. Located on the south side of the Wailua River at the Hilton Garden Inn. But don't use their parking lot. Instead drive to Lydgate Beach Park, then park at the end of the road, and walk the lawn to their location—it's shorter. If the weather is poor, the umbrella-covered tables will not be much fun. Hours are kind of squirrely, even on their website. Food is served from 4–8 p.m.

Mermaids Café

4-1384 Kuhio Hwy, Kapaa • (808) 821-2026

A brightly painted hole in the wall that serves healthy wraps, 'ahi tacos, a noodle plate or two and bountiful salads from their tiny menu. Portions are ample and flavors can be great if they don't overdo it on sauces. (Ask them to go light on any fish.) Really like the tropical fish tacos and the 'ahi cilantro wrap. Seating is cramped and limited. Bountiful salads. They have a number of tasty and unusual drinks, such as hibiscus lemonade. They have historically been very good, but the last few visits not so much, and we had to pull their *ono*. On Kuhio Highway near 581. $13–$20 for lunch. Closed Saturdays or when they don't have enough staff, which causes hours to be variable.

Noka Food Trucks

Kuhio Hwy, Kapaa

ono In the north end of Kapa'a (north Kapa'a—NoKa, get it?) is the biggest food truck area in town. It's kind of split in two with a large former furniture store between them. The farthest north section has a nice dining area right next to the ocean, and they sometimes have live music there, but only if you buy from Jimmy's. Food truck players come and go, but the anchor tenant there is **Jimmy's Grill**, and that one probably won't go away since Jimmy, who owns the land, is the guy they all pay rent to. (Jimmy's also serves alcohol—uncommon for food truck locations.)

You also might find a Mexican truck, some Thai, a great Indian place, and across the street **Carabella's Wood Fire Pizza**, which has some slightly unusual flavor combinations. The 12-inch pizzas are filling but a bit on the bland side. Your best bet in the southern area is **Al Pastor Tacos**, which does fish tacos fairly well.

We give this an *ono* because if you pick the right truck, you'll have a great meal. If you pick a bad truck, well, today was not your lucky day. $10–$20 for lunch and dinner. Hours and days may vary.

Oasis on the Beach

4-820 Kuhio Hwy, Kapaa • (808) 822-9332

ono They have an awesome, breezy location next to the beach in front of the Waipouli Beach Resort with a thatched, woody atmosphere. Small but well-chosen menus using fresh local ingredients with clever preparations. Dinner brings a small menu of steak and seafood plus many pupus. Their drink called okolehao is tasty and potent, and we like their beer selection. Prices ain't cheap, but most of the entrées can come as a half portion for less money, and the results work for us. Service is usually (but not always) good. They have a pretty cool catamaran bar in back. You'll have to park on either side of the resort and stroll along a beachside path to the restaurant. They open at 3 p.m. for happy hour until 5 p.m.—drinks only during that time. **$18–$40** for dinner. Closed Sunday and Monday.

Olympic Café
4-1354 Kuhio Hwy, Kapaa • (808) 822-5825

ono A funky, local standby that has stayed consistent through the years. The menu here is vast, and most portions are bulky. Breakfast scrambles are tasty, and the burritos and burgers work well at lunch. Dinner adds some more expensive items like steak, pasta and fajitas. For dessert, the tasty Kaua'i Pie has nearly a half-gallon of ice cream and can easily satisfy a table of four. Drinks, while not stellar, tend to be fairly well-crafted. If you order fries or onion rings, it's a buck and a half if you want something to dip them into. **$8–$18** for breakfast, **$14–$20** for lunch (available at night as well) up to **$30** for dinner entrées. Service can be spotty. Window seats overlook the highway. Across from ABC Store in downtown Kapa'a.

Paniolo Santa Maria Style BBQ
4-1345 Kuhio Hwy, Kapaa • (808) 431-1668

ono In case you're not familiar, Santa Maria-style BBQ centers around beef tri-tip, usually seasoned with black pepper, salt and garlic before grilling. They have more than that—ribs, chicken and hot sandwiches—but it's the tri-tip that's at their core. Once you order, you mosey out to their rustic wood table area and wait. These folks are actually from California's Santa Maria Valley, so they are not posers. Portions are ample, flavors are tasty, and overall it's a good experience. They do have some vegetarian dishes and even make a nod to seafood, but this place really is for red meat lovers. **$5–$15** for breakfast, **$10–$20** for lunch and dinner. Live music most nights. No alcohol, but you can grab some from the store next door and BYOB. In north Kapa'a, mauka side of the highway before the prominent ABC store and across from the Olympic Café. No lunch or dinner on Sunday.

Papaya's Natural Foods & Café
4-901 Kuhio Hwy, Kapaa • (808) 823-0190

ono A good health food store that also serves mostly veggie items and fish, plus a nice salad bar (which costs around $10 per pound). Their portabella mushroom burger is huge and a worthy meat substitute. They also have a good taro burger, wraps, a likable Reuben and blackened fresh catch. Good smoothies and fish tacos, too. **$10–$20** all day. Very limited seating out front, making it best to grab and go to a nearby beach park. In Waipouli Plaza. Parking is tight and full most of the time, but there is more parking around back.

Passion Bakery & Café
4-356 Kuhio Hwy. Kapaa • (808) 821-0660

ono A pretty good place for breakfast (consider the chorizo potato eggwich, the loco moco or the fried rice omelet). They also bake their own pastries, though the selection might be scant. Having said that, what pastries they *do* have are usually really tasty, especially the hand pies. Fresh malasadas every Tue., Thur. and Sat. Lunch is less compelling with sandwiches, a burger and pizzas, which have fairly ordinary sauce, but the medium-thick crust has a really nice flavor and chewiness to it. They don't always serve the pizza, and it takes 30 minutes, so call and perhaps order in advance. With a few indoor and outdoor tables, the only negatives are that the service is slow (unless you get a pastry), and expect lots of traffic sound from Kuhio Highway. In Kinipopo Shopping Village, South Kapaʻa, **$10–$15** for breakfast and lunch. Closed Sundays.

Rob's Good Times Grill
4303 Rice St, Lihue • (808) 246-0311

ono Rob's is a local sports bar/watering hole that has a pretty broad menu. Some things they do pretty well, such as their beef burgers. (The bison burgers, however, are a bit underwhelming and not worth the upgrade price.) A nice poke selection—you'll want to read what's in it before you order, oysters on the half shell, flatbreads, lots of sandwiches, steaks, seafood, salads and bowls. All this makes the food pretty hard to classify other than *this ain't bar food*. Rob's does lots of different things to keep local repeats coming back—their main clientele—such as live music in the afternoon, trivia nights, some dancing, some karaoke, etc. In all not a bad place to tip a pint and enjoy the local scene. **$15–$25** for lunch and dinner. During NFL football season, they have brunch on Sundays from 7–11 a.m. In the Rice Shopping Center. They charge extra to use credit cards but have an ATM nearby.

Sam's Ocean View
4-1546 Kuhio Hwy, Kapaa • (808) 822-7887

ono Just a disclaimer. Your humble author happens to own the building, not the restaurant. He has no stake in the business, but he has had others review this place to keep it simple. One of the better views in Kapaʻa that also captures the evening breezes, making for a cool and relaxed atmosphere. The food is pretty good, too. Like many restaurants around the island, Sam's has embraced local ingredients and serves them well. They feature steak, seafood and some pasta dishes plus more appetizers (such as boards of cheeses to be shared among a group and the crispy cauliflower—excellent when they use small pieces). The chocolate mousse cake truffle is deadly. Their bartending skills are high, and we recommend both their mai tai and the painkiller. It's a bit pricey, but you're paying for the killer view. (And I guess the landlord's rent…) **$16–$35** for dinner. Across the street from Hanai and Tamba Surf in north Kapaʻa. Closed Tuesdays and Wednesdays. They also have a Sunday brunch from 9 a.m. to 3 p.m.

Street Burger
4-369 Kuhio Hwy, Wailua • (808) 212-1555

ono We like this place, but if you're expecting grass skirts and coconuts, then you'll want to head somewhere else. The stark industrial design is more befitting the downtown of a major urban area on the mainland than it is Hawaiʻi. (The change of pace is probably why those of us who live here enjoy it.) The gourmet burgers are good, but they do drop the ball on occasion. And they won't let you upgrade to specialty fries, meaning if you want to try one of their more interesting flavor combinations, you have to get a separate side order that can run as much as $13 extra. The bar is beer and wine plus a few specialty cocktails, and they stay open a little later than most other places here.

$15–$23 for dinner. On the highway near Haleilio, just north of the river. Closed Sunday and Monday.

The Plantation House by Gaylords
3-2087 Kaumualii Hwy, Lihue • (808) 245-9593

ono This place has a lot of ambiance and history. Located in the courtyard of a former sugar baron's 1930s home, the old world feel and cozy outdoor setting really work. We've seen them go up and down over the years, and our *ono* has come and gone. This time it was pretty easy. The menu at lunch is fish tacos and a fresh catch, burgers and a few sandwiches as well as numerous salads. Dinner brings a bit of fresh fish, cioppino, sake short ribs and a good filet mignon. Only dings are that sounds from the nearby lu'au sometimes intrude, and their bartending skills change with every visit. They make up for it with an extensive (and expensive) wine list and usually a very good mai tai. Live music some nights. **$15–$20** for lunch, dinner is **$25–$40**. Happy Hour is 3–5 p.m. Mauka side between mile markers 1 and 2 on Hwy 50 between Lihu'e and Puhi in Kilohana. Closed Sundays.

EAST SHORE CHINESE

Garden Island Barbecue
4252 Rice St, Lihue • (808) 245-8868

Despite the name, it's a Chinese restaurant with a local twist, not a BBQ. The selection is dizzying—over 150 items! (And no, we haven't tried every one.) Portions are good, and the price is reasonable. There will almost certainly be something that interests you. Service is lightning fast. Although the food's not the greatest, you ain't paying for the greatest. You're paying for a large selection, large portions, and you want to get in and out fast. So you're getting what you pay for. **$10–$15** for lunch and dinner, plus a cheaper special and a few pricier items. At Rice and Hardy. If there are no parking spaces along the street, there should be some behind the building.

Ho's Chinese Kitchen
3-2600 Kaumualii Hwy, Lihue • (808) 245-5255

We don't want to sound mean, but since our very first edition this has been the most consistently hideous food on the island. Plus, the service is only slightly better than the food. We've taken "friends" here just to punish them. But Ho's is still here, so they must be doing something right. We just don't know what it is. **$10–$12**. In Kukui Grove Center.

Super No. 1 BBQ & Chinese Food
4-361 Kuhio Hwy, Wailua • (808) 823-1268

Because we have a responsibility when giving a review of a company, we make *multiple* visits before giving a review as strong as this one. (It ain't all fun and games and mai tais, folks.) They would seem to bring the use of MSG to new heights (or lows, depending on your perspective). Anything that we didn't immediately spit out, should have been—it sits like a rock in your stomach. At least the portions are large. Their name is *No. 1*, but after eating here and sampling their flavors, what comes to mind is more like *No. 2*... **$5–$12**. In Wailua Shopping Plaza.

EAST SHORE GREEK

Greek Gyro Stand
4-733 Kuhio Hwy, Kapaa • (808) 212-5704

ono A small menu of fantastic Greek food, including lamb or chicken gyro, a vegan falafel pita and some spanakopita. Flavors are incredibly good, especially the thinly sliced lamb. Baklava to die for. Hefty portions, and the price is right, but you'll have to take it to go or eat on a small bench outside the nearby laundromat. **$12–$17** for lunch or very early dinner. Midtown Kapa'a behind the Saimin Dojo restaurant. We get the feeling this guy is going somewhere, so this location might change. Closed Saturdays during the summer.

EAST SHORE INDIAN

Shivalik Indian Cuisine
4-771 Kuhio Hwy, Kapaa • (808) 821-2333
Most of your Indian standards are here such as chicken and lamb vindaloo, curry, tandoori, tikka, etc. Their bread selection expands beyond just naan. They also do a dinner buffet on Friday nights for $22. It's a decent deal, but the food is not as tasty as other nights off the menu. Overall flavors are good, and it's a refreshing change of pace from other island offerings. Vegetarians and vegans will have lots of selections. **$20–$30** for lunch and dinner. Beer and wine only (and it's *bad* beer and wine). In Waipouli Town Center near Foodland. Closed Tuesdays.

EAST SHORE ITALIAN

Bobby V's
4-484 Kuhio Hwy, Kapaa • (808) 821-8080
Three different seating areas to choose from. Indoor tables, outdoors or in their separate, air-conditioned bar area. Food is underwhelming. Pizzas are on the greasy side and not particularly flavorful. They also have lots of pastas and hot sandwiches. Flavors aren't terrible, nor are they compelling. But if you're washing them down with cheap beer, it's not so bad. They also have wine nights and family nights where you get a giant bowl of pasta to share. **$10–$20** for lunch and dinner. In Coconut Marketplace.

Café Portofino
3481 Hoolaulea Way, Lihue • (808) 245-2121
Their view alone creates a very tasty atmosphere for those fortunate enough to get a railing table. Kalapaki Bay waves create a background hum that can enhance any food. The owner is Italian, and some of the flavors smack of the real Italy, for good and bad. (After spending a month in Italy, we came to expect good wine and bad bread—just like this restaurant.) Overall, the food and service are not commensurate with the price. **$25–$50** for dinner. The 12-inch pizzas come from their adjacent sister restaurant, Pizzeria Portofino and are more subtle than American-style pizzas and come with thin, limp crusts. Located at the Royal Sonesta Kaua'i Resort. (You can park in their lot or next to Anchor Cove at the beach parking lot.) They also have free valet parking from the road next to Anchor Cove Shopping Center, but it often fills up. Reservations recommended.

KP Lihue Italian Grill & Bar
3-3142 Kuhio Hwy, Lihue • (808) 245-2227

ono A pretty easy place to like for the most part. Expect a few pastas and four sauces, plus panini and Parmesan for lunch, add a few pricier items at dinner. Seafood options are almost nonexistent here, so look elsewhere if you're in a fishy mood. The quality is good for the price and portions ample, except for the tasty bread that they are so stingy with. Their lunch salads are very large, so consider ordering only one per couple. Entrées have a $3 split charge. Well-chosen wine and beer list, while their cocktails are simple but well conceived. (The Irie Italian goes well with pasta dishes.) A trendy urban-style atmosphere. Lunch is **$15–$25**, dinner is mostly between **$20–$30**. On the highway in the middle of Lihu'e with parking on the street or in a small lot on the side.

Pizzeria Portofino
3481 Hoolaulea, Lihue • (808) 212-1100

ono At most pizza places we think of Americanized pizzas served from a pizza oven. This is more authentic Italian with ingredients—and techniques— imported from Italy. Combos like prosciutto and greens finished with Parmesan cheese or the diavola (spicy salami and spicy olive oil with mozzarella and Parmesan cheese) are straight out of Italy. Other combos are equally uncommon here. As a dinner-only place they take their pizzas seriously, and it's all they serve along with antipasto. The 12-inch pizzas are thin crust Napoli-style cooked in 90 seconds in a 700-degree oven. Full bar, which delivers mixed results. You have to know this place is here because it's hard to find, despite its location at a resort. Park past the Nawiliwili Tavern at the bottom of Rice Street, cross the foot-bridge, and look for it under (which owns it). Or find your way to Kalapaki Beach, and go around the right side of the beach. We give them an *ono* because it *really is* like pizza in Italy. But many may disapprove because of the more subtle flavors and limp crusts—just like in Italy. This isn't the pizza you grew up with. But we are saving you an airline ticket to Italy to find out for yourself. The service also reminds us of Italy—friendly, but you might be forgotten, even if they aren't busy. Desserts consist of a good tiramisu, and the mezzaluna with Nutella is delicious and big enough for… everyone you know. $20–$25 for dinner.

Scorpaciatta
4-1306 Kuhio Hwy, Kapaa • (808) 634-3061

ono A food truck serving Neapoli-tan-style pizza from a 600-degree oven. It's served very quickly, and the ingredients are locally sourced. What's not to like? One pizza is enough to share with two people, making it one of the better deals on the island. Classic flavors like pepperoni and margarita, but consider the Hawaiian with caramelized pineapple and smoked pork tenderloin with a balsamic glaze. Scorpaciatta is probably the second best pizza on the island at *half* the cost of the best. $12–$17 per pizza. Next to Wailua Shave Ice in downtown Kapa'a, ocean side south of the prominent ABC store. They may close early if they sell out. Closed Sunday.

EAST SHORE JAPANESE

Sushi Bushido
4-484 Kuhio Hwy, Kapaa • (808) 822-0664

ono Their motto is "Not your aver-age sushi bar," and they defi-nitely live up to it. The space is open with a modern feel, though it can get a little noisy (more of a place to laugh and be loud than a spot for a romantic dinner for two—unless yelling at your date is something you're into). The sushi bar is reserved for patrons who want to eat, with a small alcove set aside for those who just want a drink and a roll.

Owned by a self-made sushi chef, Sushi Bushido offers an interesting take on traditional dishes (though the traditional stuff can be found here as well). The Golden Roll (a deep-fried rice roll with ahi, imitation crab and salmon) is their most popular dish, while the Lollipop Roll (a cucumber hollowed out with yellow tail, yellowfin and salmon inserted in the middle and served on bamboo sticks, like a lollipop) gets extra points for presenta-tion. Another diner commented, "I would have preferred it with rice." Just goes to show that looks aren't everything. If sushi's not your thing, they have tempura and teriyaki dishes as well.

Everything is well made and delicious, including cocktails such as The Geisha—a mixture of lychee sake, Tito's Vodka and pomegranate liqueur. (It's definitely a "sneaker"—you'll feel it when you stand up.) Our only complaint is that the chairs in the main dining room are a little uncomfortable, but not so much to take away from the meal. Overall, a great place for sushi. $9–$26 for dinner, though it's easy to spend more when it comes to sushi. In an unassuming front at the south end of **Coconut Marketplace** in Kapaʻa. Closed Sunday.

EAST SHORE KOREAN

Korean BBQ
4-356 Kuhio Hwy, Kapaa • (808) 823-6744

ono A good place to try some Korean food plus a lot of local items. The combo plates are the best deal. One or more meats—Korean-style BBQ beef, kalbi (short ribs), etc.—plus plenty of side dishes—rice, mac salad, kimchee, etc. The Korean seaweed soup is excellent but it tastes terrible if you eat it with the meats. Overall, consistently good, except for the disappointing chicken katsu. $10–$20 for lunch and dinner, except for a couple of much pricier items. In the Kinipopo Shopping Village in the south part of Wailua on Hwy 56. Closed Monday and Tuesday.

EAST SHORE LOCAL

Fish Express
3-3343 Kuhio Hwy, Lihue • (808) 245-9918

ono A long-time local favorite, this is the place to get your seafood fix to go, either raw or cooked. Along with luʻau foods and salads (both very good), they make some wicked fish specials.

Seven different preparations are paired with a fresh fish that changes daily. You can't go wrong with macadamia nut-crusted fish with lilikoʻi, or have it sautéed with garlic and herbs. Get brave and try some of the unusual but tasty seafood creations at the deli counter. The ʻahi poke is a good place to start. $10–$14. Across from Walmart on Hwy 56. Open 10 a.m. to 4 p.m. (Grill closes at 2 p.m.) Sometimes no grilled items on Sundays.

Hamura Saimin Stand
2956 Kress St, Lihue • (808) 245-3271

ono Universally loved by locals and forewarned visitors alike, they've been here since 1950 and have some of the *best* saimin on Kauaʻi. (See page 224 for a definition of saimin.) It is wildly popular, and people come from other parts of the island to eat here. Their selection is scant, but the food is good and cheap. Consider the "special" saimin, which has more ingredients and is tastier. Their only dessert— lilikoʻi pie—is light and fairly good but sells out early. Food is served lunch-counter style—so seat yourself and smile at your neighbor on the bench. Though dumpy, it'll be here forever unless the sodium police raid the place. Makes for good takeout, but it's so hot that transporting it almost necessitates a hazardous materials permit. (Spill any on you, and you may burst into flames.) $7–$11 for lunch and dinner. Kress is off Rice Street. See map on page 69. Cash only.

Kalena Fish Market
2985 Kalena St, Lihue • (808) 246-6629

Sort of out of the way and hard to find, which in this case is OK. 'Cause the food is not worth searching for. Plate lunches, chicken katsu and some Korean BBQ items served with avoidable results. Oh, and by the way, despite the name, it's not a fish market. **$14–$21**. On Kalena (south of Kress Street.) near Rice Street. Cash only. Closed Saturday and Sunday.

Mark's Place
1610 Haleukana St, Lihue • (808) 245-2522

ono One of those places that you'd never know was here if someone didn't tell you about it. And if you want to eat what many locals eat and don't want to spend much, this is the spot for you. They often serve the best local food on the island. The prices are reasonable and the portions ample. Consider the mixed plate with chicken katsu, teriyaki beef and beef stew for around $17. The loco moco is really good as is their burger. Be sure to check their daily specials, which often feature fresh fish. This is local-style food, so don't expect low calorie or low cholesterol. Eat it out on the picnic tables or grab it to go. **$7–$17** for lunch. From Hwy 50, take Puhi Road, right on Hanalima. Closed weekends.

Pono Market
4-1300 Kuhio Hwy, Kapaa • (808) 822-4581

ono One of our readers' favorites, the friendly folks here serve a great plate lunch with lots of aloha. If you don't know what an item is, they take the time to explain. It's the perfect place to try some local dishes like lau lau or kalua pork. Their 'ahi poke is arguably the best on island. It can get busy around lunch, but they run the place like a well-oiled machine. **$8–$18** with some cheaper sandwiches. They also have a small coffee bar on the side with espressos and so-so ice cream. On the ocean side of Hwy 56 in downtown Kapa'a. Closed Sunday.

R & J Bakery
4303 Rice St, Lihue • (808) 245-7520

ono This small Filipino bakery and lunch counter is one of those places that's easy to overlook. It really feels like stepping into a small lunch shop in a foreign country. The family that owns and operates the restaurant has a great passion for their food and are sometimes helpful in explaining dishes and giving recommendations. (Other times they just smile at you and don't say a thing.) They specialize in Filipino comfort food, and everything we tried, we liked. Plates are priced by size with the smallest only about $4 and the largest about $7. The baked goods selection is mostly sweets, such as danishes, muffins and mochi. Good, cheap, local grub. **$5–$10** for breakfast and lunch. In the Rice Shopping Center. Open 5 a.m. to 3:30 p.m. *in theory*. Sundays they *only* sell Filipino bread until 9 a.m.

Saimin Dojo
4-733 Kuhio Highway, Kapaa • (808) 320-3248
Their saimin (think gourmet ramen noodles) comes from a longtime noodle maker on O'ahu where everything is made from scratch. They also have local-style plate lunches and a dojo fried chicken. Seating consists mostly of a community-style counter with a few tables. *However*, the food looks and sounds better than it tastes. Flavors are underwhelming. Local food is usually a bit saltier than this, and the flavor combos all seem to be missing something. Even the fried rice is pretty blah. But we've also had times when the saimin is very good and properly seasoned. The standout is their chicken katsu curry, which is awesome and the reason we keep coming back. (Teriyaki chicken is pretty good, too, but sometimes dry.) **$10–$15** for lunch and dinner. Just south of Foodland Shopping Center in central Kapa'a.

Sleeping Giant Grill
440 Aleka Pl, Kapaa • (808) 822-3474
Besides the usual fresh seafood, they

carry some pricey free-range beef. If you don't want to cook at home, we suggest their Andy Irons burrito or the fish tacos. They also have salads, plate lunches and unique specials. The outdoor are under umbrella. In the Coconut Marketplace in on the ocean side of the highway in Kapaʻa. $12–$19 for lunch and dinner. BYOB. Closed Saturday and Sunday.

Tip Top Café
3173 Akahi St, Lihue • (808) 245-2333
Eating here is something of a cultural experience. It is recognized by locals as an outstanding bargain for breakfast and lunch. The menu includes some non-traditional breakfast items, such as beef stew and oxtail soup served first thing in the morning. Try the pineapple pancakes—very tasty. Diner-style weak coffee. Great cream puffs and pastries in the morning (pass on the cookies, though.) Eggs are their weak spot, and the hash browns are hard and greasy—stick with pancakes which are reliably good. Clean, unpretentious heartiness, less-than-bubbly service. Readers are split—some *love* the place, others (including us) are less happy. Let us know if you think we were wrong. They've been here over a century, so odds are they don't really care what we think. $8–$20 for breakfast and lunch. Closed Mondays.

EAST SHORE MEXICAN

El Taco Feliz
4-1395 Kuhio Hwy, Kapaa • (808) 634-4736
This food truck next to Mariachi's at the north end of town has all the right parts—homemade tortillas, fresh ingredients and good prices. Unfortunately, the food isn't much better than their poorly conceived, brick-and-mortar neighbor. They serve the usual lineup of Mexican food, but you really need to use their homemade hot

sauce to bring out the dull flavors in any of the dishes. They have a few tables, umbrellas and potted plants to up the ambiance, though it's still the side of the road. They're friendly folks here, and we wanted to like 'em, but the food doesn't rate. $7–$15 for lunch and dinner.

Mariachi's
3501 Rice St, Lihue • (808) 246-1570
4-1387 Kuhio Hwy, Kapaa • (808) 822-1612
Consistently mediocre. The menu is a broad selection of standard Mexican items plus some Mexican seafood dishes. Quality is slightly above average, but flavors are muted and prices are too high for what you get. The combination plates are a good deal if you get them as is—but they'll nickel and dime you for extras. We like to get the burritos enchilada-style. And the taco salad is pretty good. Festive atmosphere with brightly colored décor on the inside, including sombreros hanging on the wall. The outside seating has a nice view of the ocean, if you can mentally block the huge powerlines and roar of traffic from the street below. (It's not often you have to say *that* on Kauaʻi.) Service can be slow. $12–$14 for breakfast, $14–$24 for lunch and dinner. Upstairs in the Harbor Mall.

The Kapaʻa location is also on the main highway, at the north end of town near Hwy 581. That location has more of a sports bar feel and slightly better food.

Monico's Taqueria
4-733 Kuhio Hwy, Kapaa • (808) 822-4300
A Mexican restaurant that leans a bit more heavily on seafood than most. Let's start with their margaritas, because they speak for everything else. Their top shelf Super Silver Sierra Margarita is a bit bland and small for the price. And so goes the rest. In fact, *everything* here feels about 25 percent overpriced. Their seafood items are

certainly fresh, though. Get the enchiladas with mole sauce and the fresh catch inside. While it *tastes* fresh, it's also dull. (And mole is rarely described as dull.) If you're hungry, go for the burrito, which is more generously sized.

Indoor and outdoor tables. The ones overlooking the coconut grove are kind of peaceful if you can ignore the traffic noise from Kuhio Highway. Parking lot is small for the center, and you may have trouble finding a spot. Service is friendly, but overall... *meh*. **$18–$28** for lunch and dinner. Prominent on the mauka side of the highway, mid Kapaʻa. Closed Sunday and Monday.

Paco's Tacos

4-1292 Kuhio Hwy, Kapaa • (808) 822-9944

Traditional Mexican fare such as tacos, burritos and quesadillas. They use fresh fish, and the authenticity is there. The burritos are dense and tasty. Avoid the enchilada unless it comes with their mole sauce. The taco salad with steak comes with an enormous amount of meat. There might be a language barrier, so speak clearly when you order your food. You can get a couple tacos for around $10, otherwise expect **$17–$22** for lunch and dinner. On the ocean side of Hwy 56 in Kapaʻa south of 581.

Tiki Tacos

4-971 Kuhio Hwy, Kapaa • (808) 823-8226

ONO "No rice, no beans, no chips and salsa." Just an appetizing selection of tacos and quesadillas at the small shop in Waipoili Complex. Lots of different innards from spicy steak to fish and shrimp to pork to lamb, all on handmade tortillas. Tacos are stuffed and tasty. (Make *sure* you make use of their sauces.) Snag one of the few indoor or outdoor tables, or take it to go. Their

motto is "Mexican food with a Hawaiian heart," and sure enough the service here is usually warm and friendly. **$8–$17** for lunch and dinner.

Verdé

4454 Nuhou St, Lihue • (808) 320-7088

ONO A nice Mexican joint that features less typical items. They call it New Mexican, and the results are probably the best Mexican food on the island. Familiar Mexican flavors with refreshing ways to deliver them. Love the stuffed sopaipillas, and the stacked enchiladas really work, especially with chunks of pork. Flavors are bold, and they're proud of their chilies. Add fish burritos and tacos and a full bar, and you have the kind of place that is easy to return to. To go items don't travel well, however. **$15–$20** for lunch and dinner. In Lihuʻe at the Hokulei Village Shopping Center.

EAST SHORE THAI

Anatta's Thai Street Food

4100 Rice St, Lihue • (808) 651-0640

ONO A Thai food truck in the Ace Hardware parking lot that dishes out fairly good Thai food. The menu is small—hey, it's a *food truck*—but they have a few more exotic dishes like green papaya salad in addition to your typical pad Thai or green curry with rice. Meat portions can be a little stingy—especially the shrimp—but you probably won't leave hungry.

A lot of Thai places here tend to underestimate how much spice their customers want. If you like it hot, look them in the eye and tell 'em to lay it on you—they'll do their best. Then either grab a spot at their picnic table or take it to go. Wait times are longer than we'd like, but the quality and price earn them an *ono*.

$10–$15 for lunch and dinner. At the corner of Rice and Hoolako. They also have a truck in the **Noka Food Trucks** area in north Kapa'a.

Coconut Thai Chinese
4-484 Kuhio Hwy, Kapaa • (808) 823-8988
A small shack with some outdoor tables in the Coconut Marketplace that has a fairly small selection of Thai dishes such as curries, drunken noodles and fresh Kaua'i shrimp with several Thai preparations, and a much larger selection of Chinese dishes such as Peking duck stir fry, lots of stir fries and noodles, egg foo young and Szechuan string beans. The Thai flavors are pretty bad—avoid the curries especially. You're marginally better off with the Chinese dishes. In all, not a compelling reason to drill your way into the shopping center. $12–$20 for lunch and dinner.

Lemongrass Grill
4-871 Kuhio Hwy, Kapaa • (808) 821-2888
Despite being right next to the road, ambiance here is really nice—something of a throwback to Hawaiian Tiki bars. The eclectic menu is a bit hard to classify, but we stuck them in Thai. (Think of it as Pacific Rim with Thai tendencies.) Lots of fresh seafood dishes, curries and prime rib that all hit their marks pretty well. (Even their duck dish is well executed.) Cocktails are strong but tasty—consider the mango mai tai, which uses real fruit pureé. Live music some nights adds to the atmosphere and almost keeps the road noise from being noticeable. Biggest dings are that service can be slow, and the portions are a bit small for the prices. $20–$30 for dinner. On the mauka side of the highway, just north of Kaua'i Village Shopping Center and the whale mural. Last seating at 8:30 p.m. Closed Thursday.

South East Asia Cuisine
3501 Rice St, Lihue • (808) 359-7896

ono Currently the best Thai food on Kaua'i. The curries are rich and flavorful, there's good Pad Thai, and since they also serve sushi, they have items such as the tasty avocado roll available as appetizers. Consider also the drunken noodles or the crying tiger. They offer good lunch specials (with reasonable prices) daily. $15–$25 for lunch and dinner. Full bar available. In the back of Harbor Mall in Nawiliwili. Great ocean views of Kalapaki Bay across the street from the lanai tables.

Sukhothai Café
4-1330 Kuhio Hwy, Kapaa • (808) 821-1224
Let's start with the positive. It's fairly nice inside, and they have a full bar. Oh, and the folks there are friendly. Having said that, the food is wretched and doesn't resemble any Thai, Chinese or Vietnamese food we've ever had. Recipes are weird; flavors and preparation are hideous. Sorry, gotta call it like we see it. $15–$30 for lunch and dinner. North end of town on the ocean side of the highway south of 581.

EAST SHORE TREATS

Aloha Aina Juice Café
4454 Nuhou St, Lihue • (808) 378-4256
Don't confuse these guys with Kaua'i Juice Co., which truly specializes in local, cold-pressed juices. Aloha 'Aina focuses more on fruit bowls and smoothies with different combinations of banana, mango, kale, cucumber, peanut butter, blueberry, live spirulina, etc. The results are pretty good, and they also serve coffee drinks. In the Hokulei Shopping Village next to Panda Express in Puhi just off Highway 50. It'll be about $8–$12 during breakfast and lunch. Closed Sunday.

Daylight Donuts

4100 Rice St, Lihue • (808) 245-7414

Small donut shop in strip mall behind Ace Hardware on Rice Street. Horrid coffee and dull, overly processed donuts are something you can find in a gas station back home. Even though the prices are reasonable (get a dozen for $11), you'd do better to get the day old, discounted baked goods from the grocery store. A definite pass. Closed Saturday through Monday.

Ha Coffee Bar

4265 Rice St, Lihue • (808) 631-9241

Ha is the Hawaiian word for breath. (No they don't mean *coffee breath*; it's deeper than that.) The setting is comfortable, spacious and conducive to both relaxing and working. The coffee is pretty good, and the limited baked goods, though not made on site, are tasty when fresh. The staff is friendly and attentive. WiFi is free but only good for 30 minutes (hopefully, it was just a few emails you needed to send). Not an *ono* and not exactly on the way to many things, but we wouldn't steer you away. $3–$6. On Rice Street across from the Garden Island BBQ. Closed Sundays. They also have a location in Wailua next to **Russell's**.

Hee Fat General Store

4-1354 Kuhio Hwy, Kapaa • (808) 823-6169

ono This is currently one of our favorite shave ices on the island. In addition to lots of artificially flavored syrups, they also carry a limited number of natural syrups, and they hit those flavors out of the park—guava is particularly good. Their lava flow is an interesting combination with a snow cap of melted vanilla ice cream on top. Only wish they'd chill the syrups because their ultra-fluffy ice melts fast. We admire that they sweat the ice before shaving. While we highly recommend the shave ice, everything else in the store is *waaay* overpriced. $5–$9. North Kapa'a on highway across from the ABC Store.

Kaua'i Bakery & Café

3-2600 Kaumualii Hwy, Lihue • (808) 320-3434

ono From 6 a.m. to 2 p.m. every day but Sunday this is the best place on the island to get fresh malasadas, a filled Portuguese donut. They have other items such as empanadas and cinnamon rolls, but really it's the malasadas that keep us coming back over and over. They have chocolate filled, dark malasadas with purple Okinawan sweet potato filling (which is delicious) and just plain doughnuts. The earlier you get there, the fresher they are. In the Kukui Grove Shopping Center next to the Times Supermarket on the Kalepa Street side of the center. $2–$8 depending on how gluttonous you're feeling.

Kaua'i Fruit & Flower

3-4684 Kuhio Hwy, Lihue • (808) 320-8870

On Hwy 56 near the airport. *$7 for a pineapple!* Minimum purchase is two. They also have papayas you can carry-on your flight at the premium price of $58 for about 10 pounds. Need we say any more? Closed Sunday.

Kaua'i Juice Company

4-1384 Kuhio Hwy, Kapaa • (808) 631-3893

ono Local, cold pressed juices, and we ain't talking just pineapple and OJ. They go from celery, kale and clover sprouts to ginger, beet, carrot and many more. Flavors are not watered down (though neither are the prices). Their "elixirs" are 2-ounce bottles of over-the-top concentrations for $4. For instance, one called The Healer has a couple *pounds* of turmeric reduced to juice—*very* intense. Same for their gingersnap. This company is beloved by locals, who grudgingly pay $11 for a glass of juice because it's darned good juice. In north Kapaʻa behind Mermaids on the mauka side of the highway near Hwy 581. This location tries to open at 7:30 a.m. but officially they open at 8 a.m. Also in Kilauea at Kilauea Road and Keneke near the fish market and in the Poʻipu Shopping Village.

Ko Bakery + Coffee
1611 Haleukana St, Lihue • (808) 212-9437

ONO First of all it's not Ko, it's Kō Bakery. (Kō is the Hawaiian word for stale…Just kidding, it means sugarcane.) Located in a hard-to-find industrial area in Puhi, they do wedding cakes and desserts for restaurants. But if you're in the area, perhaps eating at the nearby local favorite called Mark's Place, try some of their excellent banana bread or cookies as well as coffees and teas. $2–$5. From the highway in Puhi turn onto Puhi Road, right on Hanalima. Stop when you smell the baked goods. They close around noon. Closed Sunday and Monday.

Matcha-Ya Café
4-1400 Kuhio Hwy, Kapaa • (808) 652-4063

ONO If you have been trying to "go green," this the place to do it, because it's all about matcha—the green tea made from stone-ground powder from tea leaves. Their tea comes from Kyoto, Japan, and the owner is not only an expert but a certified instructor of the Urasenke Tea School. Matcha is an antioxidant, and a very tasty one. The menu combinations are unique, such as Strawberry Matcha Lemonade, Boba Matcha Latte and Matcha Frappe Mango, to name a few. There are so many choices you may have a hard time making up your mind. We loved the Matcha Green, which contains matcha, spinach, avocado, banana, ginger, almond milk, kiwi and soy yogurt with chia seeds. Purists can choose a matcha shot served in a specially made ceramic bowl. Most drinks come with a side sample of matcha dorayaki (a small pancake treat). All drinks contain no dairy, only a choice of soy or almond milk. Other items include soft-serve matcha ice cream, açai bowls, mochi matcha cakes, dorayaki pancakes stuffed with fresh fruit, cold-brewed coffee and shave ice with real fruit syrups. $7–$11.

A great spot to hit after doing the bike path in Kapaʻa. Across from Kapaʻa Beach Park on the mauka side of the highway tucked behind Kela's Glass Gallery. The address is Kuhio Highway, but it's on Niu Street. Closed Tuesday and Wednesday.

Pono Coffee & Bakery
4-1298 Kuhio Hwy, Kapaa • (808) 431-4707

ONO A bakery and coffee joint next to Pono Market that has pretty good baked goods, malasadas and some more savory items such as sausage or ham and cheese rolls and a few local style breakfasts, including loco moco. Decent coffee, too. Also, if you look in the chilled case, they often have pumpkin crunch, which is kind of like a square of pumpkin pie but with a thicker, crunchy bottom—pretty tasty. In all, not a bad place to grab a simple breakfast on the go and easy on the wallet. $5–$10 for lunch and dinner. North Kapaʻa, ocean side of the highway just before a small cemetery on the mauka side. Closed Tuesday.

Skinny Mike's Hawaiian Ice Cream
3501 Rice St, Lihue • (808) 245-9386

ONO There really is a skinny Mike, and we don't know how he stays that way operating this place. Ice cream (Tropical Dreams made on Big

Island), sorbet, vegan-style ice cream, smoothies, shave ice and coffee drinks round out the offerings here. The ice cream is rich and dense, and the interior has A/C and tables—preferred over racing to eat before melting outside. $4–$10. On the ground floor of the Harbor Mall.

Small Town Coffee
4-1543 Kuhio Hwy, Kapaa • (808) 638-4799

ono An artsy, hodge-podge red bus with personality. Their coffee is consistently good and organically grown. Powerful espressos, homemade hot chocolates and lattes. Some tasty baked goods and vegan items. Diehard regulars usually occupy the tables where they solve the world's problems among themselves. Open 6 a.m. (food starts at 7 a.m.). $8–$12. On mauka side of Hwy 56 in north Kapaʻa in the parking lot across from the Kauaʻi Beach Hostel. Closed Sunday.

Tropical Dreams
4-831 Kuhio Hwy, Kapaa • (808) 822-1010

ono This is simply the best ice cream we know of, and we're thrilled to get it on Kauaʻi. Made on the Big Island, flavors and texture are superb. It ain't cheap, but if you're really looking to indulge yourself, you won't find a better place. In the Kauaʻi Village Shopping Center. $5–$9.

Wailua Shave Ice
4-831 Kuhio Hwy, Kapaa • (808) 634-7183

ono A shave ice joint with a great creative bent with fresh, local flavors and unique toppings. We've liked everything we've tried, especially the coconut x coconut x coconut, which features coconut milk, haupia foam and roasted coconut flakes—subdued flavors that work. Also consider the lava flow—pineapple juice, strawberry purée and coconut foam.

About $7. Next to Starbuck's in the Kauaʻi Village Shopping Center.

EAST SHORE VEGAN

Russell's by Eat Healthy Kauaʻi
4-369 Kuhio Hwy, Wailua • (808) 822-7990

ono Trying desperately to find vegan and gluten-free options on a menu? This is your place. A cute café set in a garden-like atmosphere with tables perched on tiny ground glass stones with canopies above (because of possible showers). This place is kid-friendly with entertaining resident cats and chickens. (Those chickens *will* jump on your table for a chance to get at your food.) Breakfast starting at 8 a.m., available until noon, is mostly tofu scrambles with your choice of fillings, toppings and sauces and various fresh fruit bowls. Smoothies are great here. We love the Protein Dream. Lunch brings salads, sandwiches and appetizers, such as the tasty summer rolls. Dinner is pastas, a tofu dish, salads and pasta. Pupus here are the bomb—especially the Okinawan purple potato samosa with banana chutney. Be sure and ask if they are out of anything (we've had our heart set on the popular chickpea curry wrap only to be told they ran out earlier). Friendly, helpful staff. We always leave happy and healthy—hence our *ono*. $8–$15 for breakfast and lunch, $10–$26 for dinner (Thursday–Saturday). Behind some shops at the south end of Wailua on the main highway across the street from Kinipopo Shopping Village. Closed Sundays and Mondays.

EAST SHORE VIETNAMESE

Pho Kapaʻa
4-831 Kuhio Hwy, Kapaa • (808) 823-6868

ono Good, authentic Vietnamese food that is priced right (though not as cheap as in Lihu'e). The folks here are friendly, attentive and especially helpful in showing you how to get the most out of your meal with all those mysterious sauces on the table. Their namesake phở soup is very good as are the vermicelli noodle dishes such as lemongrass beef. However, it is their $7 bahn mi sandwich that keeps us coming back. **$8–$16** for lunch and dinner. In the Kaua'i Village Shopping Center. Closed Mondays.

Pho Kaua'i
4303 Rice St, Lihue • (808) 245-9858

ono If you're a fan of phở, that Vietnamese beef noodle soup (which is really hard to type because of that squiggly thing above the o), this is the best place on the island to get it. It's not exactly fancy inside, but prices are really reasonable, and you can get your fix for around $10. They also have lots of vermicelli bowls, rice plates and vegetarian items. Buried in the back of the Rice Shopping Center, Rice Street. **$9–$13** for lunch and dinner. Closed Sunday.

SOUTH SHORE AMERICAN

Beach House Restaurant
5022 Lawai Rd, Poipu • (808) 742-1424

ono A longtime south shore landmark, they have the best oceanfront location on the island—and they *know* it. Consequently, we've seen them rest on their laurels and charge high prices for mediocre food and so-so service. An ownership change with a proven restaurateur brought them back to their glory years. Nice sunsets from here. Tables are reasonably spaced. Vast wine list. Steak and seafood dinner will run you **$35–$60** for dinner. They have a happy hour from 3:30–4:30 p.m. On Lawai Road in Po'ipu on the way to Spouting Horn. Reservations *strongly* recommended days in advance.

Brennecke's Beach Broiler
2100 Hoone Rd, Poipu • (808) 742-7588
Their motto says, "right on the beach," though they're actually *across the street* from Po'ipu Beach Park. Brennecke's is one of those places that has made a great living off their view. Then for years their view was blocked by trees across the street at Po'ipu Beach Park. These days the view has returned as the gardeners at the park have kept the vegetation low. (No sunsets, though, since they face south.) As for the food, it's burgers and sandwiches at lunch; add steak and seafood and some pastas at dinner. Quality is good, but it's a bit overpriced at dinner. Their mai tai is good, and they claim to have sold over a million of them. The large selection of nonalcoholic drinks makes it a pretty good choice if you've got kids. **$17–$30** for lunch, **$17–$89** at dinner. Thursday through Sunday they offer brunch from 9 a.m. to 2 p.m. Brennecke's is not a *bad* choice, but it *is* an overpriced one. It's on the second floor, but there is an elevator, if needed.

Downstairs and next door, **Brennecke's Beach Deli** has breakfast items before 10:30 a.m., as well as sandwiches, hot dogs (tasty) and bad shave ice. Though the food's certainly not gourmet, it's amazing how much better it'll taste if you take it across the street to one of the beach park tables and gaze at the delicious scenery. **$10–$20**.

Bubba's Burgers
2829 Ala Kalanikaumaka St, Poipu
(808) 742-6900
Funky place to get decent, but *small* burgers (might want to opt for a double), chili rice, etc., with a limited choice of burger toppings. Love the chocolate banana shake. If it wasn't for their sassy attitude, we

probably wouldn't give their Kapa'a location an *ono*. Their motto is, "We cheat tourists, drunks and attorneys." So if you are a drunk attorney visiting the island, you're on your own, counselor. $6–$14. In Po'ipu's The Shops at Kukui'ula near the roundabout. We should point out that our reader email seems to be pretty split for Bubba's (about two-thirds love it and the other third *hates* it). This location doesn't work quite as well as Kapa'a. No dinner on Monday or Tuesday.

Dolphin Po'ipu

2829 Ala Kalanikaumaka St, Poipu
(808) 742-1414

ono ┌ A peaceful plantation-like setting on the outdoor lanai, this place specializes in seafood, and they usually deliver it well. (No dolphins on the menu, but they do have dolphin*fish*—the other name for mahimahi.) They keep things simple here. Fish is either charbroiled with their special seasonings or blackened with cajun seasonings, both with drawn butter. The exception is the teriyaki 'ahi, which is awesome and best ordered med-rare, even if you're a medium kind of diner. *Love* it with the asparagus wraps. Good sushi selection here. They have a seafood market, a nice place to pick up fish for cooking back at the condo. The Dolphin is a bit set in its way: no substitutions, no split checks, no cell phones in the fish market area, no nonsense. $25–$45 for dinner. At The Shops at Kukui'ula. Reservations suggested. They also have a location in Hanalei called the **Hanalei Dolphin Restaurant**. Same menu.

Eating House 1849

2829 Ala Kalanikaumaka St, Poipu
(808) 742-5000

ono ┌ A rustic chic atmosphere that is open and loud with good food and mostly good service. First of all, the tables near the bar must be for decoration only, because the servers and bartenders will almost certainly ignore you. And once you're inside, the service is good but often forgetful. But the food makes up for it. Menu is seafood and steak with some Asian. In fact, the kamameshi (hot pot rice bowl) with butterfish is incredible, and the crispy cauliflower and Brussels sprouts—which I dreaded as a kid—are awesome. Flavors are bold. Ask your server about more popular dishes, which taps you into what nearby local residents find most pleasing. Nice selection of wines (including 50 under $50), good signature cocktail (love the Hawaiian martini, which is better with Hangar One than Skye) and beer choices. Consider the warm apple volcano dessert. We have had disappointments here, but overall great food, mostly good service and an interesting environment with distant ocean views makes it *ono* worthy. $25–$60 for dinner. At the Shops at Kukui'ula. Reservations recommended.

Ilima Terrace

1571 Poipu Rd, Poipu • (808) 742-1234
All right, enough is enough. We love this location at the Grand Hyatt but had to pull the *ono*. They offer good food in a beautiful, open-air setting near a resort waterfall. But the breakfast is crazy overpriced. How else can you describe $11 for half a papaya or $19 pancakes? And at lunch you have $23 burgers or pricier dinner-style entrées for more. Their once-mighty breakfast buffet does not have a selection that deserves $39. Admittedly, the setting is fantastic but not enough to justify the price. $11–$39 for breakfast, $21–$32 for lunch. Dinners are buffets that run from $59–$175 (the latter includes the lu'au). Reservations recommended. And if you're wondering

about that chicken wire between you and your view, it's to keep the birds from flying onto your table and plate while you're not looking.

Kalaheo Café & Coffee Co.
2-2560 Kaumualii Hwy, Kalaheo
(808) 332-5858

ono Comfortable coffee house ambiance with lots of room, quality breakfast choices and a large list of coffee drinks make this a good spot to stop on your way to a boat tour on the west side. (One of the best Bloody Marys on the island, too.) Order at the counter and grab a seat. Great omelets. We like the bonzo burrito and the bagel benny. Their cinnamon knuckles are deadly and best eaten hot. Sandwiches and salads at lunch. Dinner offers an eclectic menu from Thai veggie curry to fresh fish tacos to turkey meat loaf. The coconut shrimp appetizer will keep us coming back. $8–$17 for breakfast and lunch, $18–$35 for dinner (Wed.–Sat.). Open at 7 a.m. On highway in Kalaheo. Across from Brick Oven Pizza.

Kalapaki Joe's
1941 Poipu Rd, Poipu • (808) 742-6366

A local watering hole with a sports bar atmosphere. Huge selection of burgers, sandwiches, tacos, gobs of salads, hearty dishes and seafood. Results are mixed, especially with appetizers, as some ingredients taste cheap. Burgers tend to be your best bet, and the variety of toppings keeps things interesting. Breakfast has plenty of eggs and meats with local twists, but it's pricey for what you get. Service manages to be friendly yet uncaring at the same time. They seem perpetually understaffed. Good beer selection, though. In all, not quite an *ono*, but it's above average bar food for a decent lunch and dinner price. Good happy hour from 3–6 p.m. We won't steer you away. $12–$18 for breakfast (Saturdays and Sundays only), $15–$25 for lunch and dinner. Nowhere near Kalapaki Bay (but it used to be). On Poipu Road between Hoowili and the Koloa–Po'ipu Bypass. The Kuku'i Grove Mall location in Lihu'e is very popular during football (or any sports) season.

Keoki's Paradise
2360 Kiahuna Plantation Dr, Poipu
(808) 742-7534

ono This is a special sort of place that people either love or hate (we love it). The ambiance is the story here with plants everywhere, a large fish lagoon, waterfalls and thatched roof booths (try to say *that* three times fast). It's the South Pacific that never really existed except in movies. (Their website implies it's on Po'ipu Beach—uh, no it's not. It's in a shopping center on the mauka side with no views of anything.) The tables in the main area are arranged on several levels. Purists will sniff that the ambiance is not real—so what?! It's still exotic inside. If you are in the right mood, this is the sort of place you will remember for a long time. As for the food, it's a steak and seafood restaurant with above average food and (usually) good service. Many styles of fish and steak plus their signature prime rib. The hula pie is huge and tasty. The place can get pretty busy. This can have an effect on the service, which can be their weak point. The exotic bar area serves burgers, sandwiches, ribs and *very* cold beer at lunch for $15–$25. (Brunch is served on weekends from 10 a.m. to 2 p.m.) $18–$52 for dinner. Reservations recommended. They haven't changed over the years, but if it ain't broke, don't fix it. In the Po'ipu Shopping Village.

Koloa Food Trucks
Just Outside Koloa Town, Koloa

Koloa has two main food truck areas. One is on your right just as you're pulling into town from the upper highway. The smaller one is not far away. Turn left when you hit town, then take a right on Weliweli. Food trucks come and go in these areas. You'll probably have a variety to choose from, but it's kind of a crapshoot as to the quality. The larger area has some tables scattered under the large banyan tree next to the remains of the old sugar mill. Expect to spend **$8–$20** for lunch or an early dinner. Hours and days vary depending on vendor.

Merriman's
2829 Ala Kalanikaumaka St, Poipu
(808) 742-8385

ONO A gourmet fish house that has picked it up in recent years. Only a few lanai tables (requestable) have views of the distant ocean. Crazy good chocolate purse dessert goes well with their entrées, most of which are very good, but some are underwhelming. (Stick with the fish—hence the *ono*.) Awesome mojitos. Service has historically been snotty but has improved of late. **$20–$50** for dinner. Live music some nights. In The Shops at Kukui'ula.

Puka Dog
2100 Hoone Rd, Poipu • (808) 742-6044

ONO Hard to believe we'd give an *ono* for a $9 hot dog. Granted, it's overpriced. But these are very good hot dogs served in an unusual way and right across the street from the beach. The dogs are roasted (giving them the slightly crunchy skin), then embedded in a wraparound bun served with a choice of sauces inside, from mild to habañero. Get the fresh fruit relish—more like chutney—to smear on the tip each time you bite. (Love the mango.) Only two dogs—a Polish sausage and a veggie dog. But with their sauces and fixin's you'll be pleased. Inside **Brennecke's Beach Deli** (across from Po'ipu Beach) whose offerings are less compelling except for the shave ice. **$10–$17** for lunch and dinner. Take 'em to a table at Po'ipu Beach Park.

Red Salt
2251 Poipu Rd, Poipu • (877) 276-0768

ONO The name derives from the strong red Hawaiian sea salt that accompanies many items (and the bread with the unsalted butter). Ambiance is modern with splashes of Asian. Very good and very expensive. Entrées range from steak and lamb to their vanilla bean mahimahi to lobster gnocchi. They have uncommonly good mixed drinks. Sushi also available. **$30–$60** for dinner. In the Koa Kea Hotel. Reservations are strongly recommended.

RumFire
2440 Hoonani Rd, Poipu • (808) 742-4786

ONO This one has been surprisingly variable for a restaurant at a large resort. They started off great, sank to mediocrity for several years and now *seem* to be back. They serve an American/Pacific Rim fusion. Their crab-crusted fresh catch is very good. They also have a local filet, which might not be as tender as you're used to. Expect a pasta or two in addition to the steak and seafood. Ambiance is modern, and the layout of the restaurant is spacious but doesn't embrace the island's surroundings—some may find it cold rather than modern and hip. **$30–$55** for dinner. In the Sheraton Kaua'i Resort.

Savage Shrimp

2829 Ala Kalanikaumaka St, Poipu

(808) 320-3021

This one-time food truck grew up to be a brick and mortar restaurant. The name is in reference to the locally sourced *unpeeled* shrimp, while the savage part…just get one of the spicy items and you'll find out. (If you don't like peeling shrimp they will do it for you for an extra $2.) Ordering is pretty straightforward. You either get a plate of 10 shrimp (which includes rice and coleslaw) or shrimp tacos (baja style with five shrimp in each taco). If you get a plate, then you choose the sauce, and the shrimp are cooked in it. They have eight different styles that run the gamut of garlic scampi to tangy, Thai-like sauces (we like the Aloha and Savage styles best). They also have a few fried versions such as coconut shrimp. Not as pricey as most of the other eateries in the Shops at Kukui'ula. $12–$17 for lunch and dinner.

Tidepools

1571 Poipu Rd, Poipu • (808) 240-6456

ono Located at the Grand Hyatt Po'ipu, their best feature is a very romantic atmosphere. A thatched roof, a stocked freshwater lagoon next to your table and flickering tiki torches outside provide a calm, quiet dinner environment. The limited menu highlights fresh fish (their specialty), with some beef and at least one vegetarian item. Their desserts are usually deadly. $35–$55 for dinner. (They open at 4:30 p.m. for cocktails.) Service can be on the slow side. Reservations recommended and resort wear requested.

SOUTH SHORE ITALIAN

Brick Oven Pizza

2-2555 Kaumualii Hwy, Kalaheo • (808) 332-8561

We have a lot of affection for this place and we eat here often, but we have to admit that it's overpriced. Though not baked in a real brick oven, they pride themselves on making their own sauce, sausage and other ingredients. The crust is thin with scalloped edges and brushed with garlic butter with tasty results. You can get gluten-free crust only on small pizzas. The sauce is simply perfect. Simple Italian atmosphere, attentive, friendly service and excellent pizza. But the prices—it's just shy of $40 for a large four-topping pizza. It's still a great place for pizza and sandwiches, but the price is so high that when they started charging an extra 3.5 percent for credit cards the same day we watched them pour wine into a measuring cup to make *sure* they didn't accidentally give you extra, enough was enough, and we pulled their *ono*. Nickel-and-diming might be expected if prices are cheap, but they ain't cheap here. $10–$40 for lunch and dinner. No reservations. Kids are given a wad of pizza dough to play with—nice touch. (And fitting, since adults will *spend* a wad of dough.) Located on mauka side of highway as you enter Kalaheo. Closed Tuesday.

La Spezia

5492 Koloa Rd, Koloa • (808) 742-8824

ono A hip, contemporary Italian wine bar atmosphere, the two-person tables are pretty small. Appetizers are good. The antipasti is an awesome collection of items, and the flatbread pizza appetizer is tasty if a bit filling. Dinner has offerings such as their home-made tortellini and short rib ravioli, both winners. Nonna's lasagna can best be described as divisive—you'll either love it or hate it. Spaghetti with arancini (crispy mozzarella risotto balls) on zucchini noodles is bold and unusual. $17–$30 for dinner (except Sunday). Brunch is $12–$20 Friday through Sunday from 8 a.m. to 1 p.m.

Across from the Post Office in Old Koloa Town. Closed Monday.

SOUTH SHORE LOCAL

Koloa Fish Market
3390 Poipu Rd, Koloa • (808) 742-6199

Previously located in Koloa town, their current digs just south of town are clean and open with more selections than at the old spot. You order on the right side where you'll find menus posted on the wall. We recommend figuring out what you want before you step up to the counter, so you're not feeling pressured by the line that is sure to form behind you if you dally too much. Daily specials and poke bowls are their specialties with three sizes of bowls to choose from. (If you're hungry, get the large.) Plate lunches are a close second and are the same great quality we've come to expect from these guys. Other items are called *island specialties* and include fried chicken, Korean chicken and teriyaki beef. A large sides gives you more than enough opportunity to create the meal you want.

Seating is limited to benches in the front, and they can fill up fast, but with the beach 5 minutes away, grabbing your food to go might be the best choice. They also have cookies and brownies that they told us were "freshly baked," but we didn't find that to be the case. (We had three people try our cookie, and *no one* wanted a second bite.) They also have a very well-stocked (although expensive) fish market with a decent selection if you decide you'd like to BBQ fish that evening. Lunch is $10–$15. On Poipu Road just south of Koloa Town. Closed Sundays.

Sueoka's Snack Shop
5392 Koloa Rd, Koloa • (808) 742-1112

ono Beloved by local residents for decades for serving the cheapest food on the south shore, everything is under $10, and most are under $5. Burgers, lau lau, fish burgers, plate lunches, etc. We're not giving 'em an *ono* because it's the *finest* food on the island, but because their price/calorie ratio is *impossible* to beat. And sometimes you just want to get your fill without emptying your wallet. Some items may be different than you'd expect. For instance, the teriyaki burger is not flavored ground beef—it's strips of teri beef on a bun. In Koloa on Koloa Road near Poipu Road beside the market. $5–$10 for breakfast, lunch and dinner. Cash only.

SOUTH SHORE MEXICAN

Chalupas
3477 Weliweli Rd, Koloa • (808) 634-4016

These guys are an example of how a captive audience can ruin good food. This is a taco truck next to Koloa Zipline, which is where a lot their customers come from. What was once one of the best tacos in town has become inferior with joyless service. Some items still hold their flavor, like the carnitas, but the fish tacos are disappointingly bland. $8–$15 for lunch. A few covered tables here, but watch out for the aggressive chickens looking for a handout. Closed Sundays.

Da Crack
2827 Poipu Rd, Poipu • (808) 742-9505

ono Great *crack in da wall* for Mexican grinds, brah. Order your food through their small take-out window next to Outfitters Kaua'i. They offer massive burritos, tacos, nachos and quesadillas, big enough to feed two. (Consider the keiki menu if you want a single portion.) The burritos are stuffed with your choice of beef, chicken, pork or local vegetables, and they proudly claim that they use no MSG, hydrogenated oils or lard. Best Mexican food for the money on the south shore. Grab it to go. $11–$15 for lunch and dinner. Sunday they close at 3 p.m.

SOUTH SHORE THAI

Bangkok Happy Bowl Thai Bistro & Sushi Bar

2360 Kiahuna Plantation Dr, Poipu
(808) 742-9888

Good idea, badly executed. A Thai restaurant that also has a sushi bar. First time we've seen that done. But we have yet to try an item that tasted good. Which is a shame, because we really wanted to like the place. Instead of exciting food, it is fairly tame—Americanized in its flavor and presentation. (They don't crank up the spice no matter how much you assure them you want it to set off fire alarms.) Avoid any of the fried appetizers as they are way too greasy. Portions are small for the price. $14–$20 for lunch, up to $30 for dinner. In the Po'ipu Shopping Village.

Craving Thai

3477 Weliweli Rd, Koloa • (808) 634-9959
A small food truck behind main Koloa Town off Weliweli Road, they have your typical selection of curries, larb (Thai chicken salad), spring and summer rolls and pad Thai. The food is pretty good for a food truck and the prices acceptable, though not cheap. Overall, we wouldn't steer you away if you're (ahem) craving Thai… (Oh, we fell into their trap, didn't we?) They may close early and perhaps restrict your selection if they have a catering job that night. $10–$15 for lunch and early dinner. They take their last order at 6:45 p.m. Closed Saturday and Sunday.

SOUTH SHORE TREATS

Koloa Mill Ice Cream & Coffee

5424 Koloa Rd, Koloa • (808) 742-6544
Mostly good ice cream, and they make a mean blueberry cheesepie (like a cheesecake) as well as some other baked goods. Smoothies aren't bad. In Koloa Town. $4–$7. Be warned that none of the neighboring shops want you to bring ice cream in with you.

Lappert's Ice Cream

2829 Ala Kalanikaumaka St, Poipu
(808) 742-1272

ONO A beautiful ice cream shop in The Shops at Kukui'ula. Lappert's went from great locally made ice cream to mediocre to good quality again. Compelling flavors and some stupid-rich gelatos, including a nearly radioactive chocolate. (Better than their chocolate *ice cream*.) Coffee and baked goods for a morning bite. $4–$8.

Papalani Gelato

2360 Kiahuna Plantation Dr, Poipu
(808) 742-2663

ONO Outrageous gelato made on the premises as well as dairy- and sugar-free frozen concoctions. It ain't cheap, but it's utterly delicious. $4–$9. In Po'ipu Shopping Village as well as various restaurants all around the island, but it doesn't seem *quite* as good as getting it from the source. (We can only attribute that to perhaps the way it's stored.)

The Right Slice

2-2459 Kaumualii Hwy, Kalaheo
(808) 212-5798

ONO Think pie. Did you visualize sweet, like apple or pumpkin? Or savory like chicken pot pies? They have both here, and they do 'em right. They have over 50 flavors of sweet pies (plus gluten free), many of which are made with fresh, local ingredients (love the mango liliko'i). Only a handful of flavors are available fresh at any given time, but call ahead and your options increase. Buy them whole, by the slice or as one of their smaller variations. We think their savory pies are the real treat, though. For around $10 you can take one home and bake, or call an hour ahead and get one baked to go. (They also have family-sized pies that serve six to eight but require 24-hour notice.) They always have chicken pot pie and shepherd's pie available as well as specials for that week. Their value packs are a good way to get a picnic lunch to go and require calling ahead as well. **$5–$15** for most single items, up to $66 for family-sized. In Kalaheo on the mauka side of the road just before the streetlight.

Uncle's Shave Ice
2829 Ala Kalanikaumaka St, Poipu
(808) 742-2364

ono So here's the deal. Their signature shave ice is their poorest offering. They're not keeping the blades sharp enough, and we keep getting ice that's too coarse. But the real reason to come here (and the reason for the *ono*) is the shave *snow*. They mix the water with dairy and syrup, then freeze it. Must not be as hard as pure ice because the result is ultra light and fluffy with a nice consistency, especially if you have 'em put a cap on top. **$5–$10.** In The Shops at Kukui'ula. Also in Hokulei Village Shopping Center, Lihu'e.

Waikomo Shave Ice
2827 Poipu Rd, Koloa • (808) 651-5169
They won't win any awards for selection—really just a handful of flavors. But what we really liked is the fineness of the ice (they must really keep the blade sharp)

and the extra touch of putting fresh fruit, coconut cream and honey on top. Really adds to the experience and gives it a gourmet feel. If they had more selection, we'd probably give 'em an *ono*. On Poipu Road just mauka of the traffic circle between Koloa and Po'ipu in a small trailer next to Da Crack. **$7–$10.** Closed Friday.

WEST SHORE AMERICAN

Da Booze Shop
9883 Waimea Rd, Waimea • (808) 338-9953

ono If you're looking for tasty booze preparations made with skill and care… well, you came to the wrong place. They don't have any. Instead, they have a sign saying, "We serve God Instead of Alcohol." So let's move on to the food. It's a local joint that serves burgers, salads, lunch plates with barbecue ribs and/or chicken, plus some surprisingly good wraps. This is local comfort food that's popular with hunters, those who have just hiked around Waimea Canyon, and anyone else looking for good food with large portions at reasonable prices. Our only complaint is that the inside is a bit cramped and can get *very* hot and stuffy midday. Best to take your food across the street to Cook Park and enjoy some shade. Look at their Underground menu for specials and out-of-the-ordinary offerings such as furikake fries. (You'll either love em or hate 'em, but you *won't* be indifferent.) Lunch and dinner are **$6–$15.** In the middle of town next to Big Save. The *ono* is for the value. Closed Sunday.

Kaua'i Island Brewery & Grill
4350 Waialo Rd, Port Allen • (808) 335-0006
A brewpub with a large vaulted ceiling, warehouse-style dining room that is nicely done in soft wood. There is upstairs table seating or on the rail if you want a great

vantage point for people watching. The main dining room is alive with hustle and bustle with hit-or-miss service. As for the beer offerings, the "hoppiest" of their brews are fairly homogenized with one being mostly indistinguishable from the next. However, their Ele'ele Brown and especially their Cane Fire Red are both standouts. All the brewing is done on site, and you can glimpse some of the process through the viewing window to the production floor. Sandwiches, tacos, fish and chips plus burgers. The food's not stellar (with appetizers being the weakest attempt), but it's not bad, and you came for the brew and atmosphere, especially after a long day on a snorkel boat tour. $16–$20 for lunch and dinner. On your left before the Port Allen Harbor.

Koke'e Lodge
3600 Kokee Rd, Kokee • (808) 335-6061

ono The best (and only) place to grab a bite to eat around Waimea Canyon. Though you might not expect a park concessionaire to shine, the food's actually pretty good. If the cool weather is getting to you (well, cool to us wimpy Hawai'i residents), consider the cornbread and chili or the Portuguese bean soup. They also serve breakfast all day, plus burgers, sandwiches and a couple of salads. Their coconut pie is excellent. Don't expect to be treated like old friends, 'cause you ain't one. $10–$15. Located *waaaay* up the road in Koke'e on Waimea Canyon Road past mile marker 15. They have a cool-looking bar and fireplace adjacent to the dining room, and they make a good Bloody Mary. That may be most folks' drink of choice since they're only open 9:30 a.m. to 4 p.m. (Get there by 3:30 p.m.) They have live music on weekend afternoons starting about 12:30 p.m. If they weren't the only game in town they would probably not get an *ono*.

Porky's
9899 Waimea Rd, Waimea • (808) 631-3071

ono The menu, which reflects their food truck roots, is super simple, pretty much pulled pork on a pork pineapple sausage—their best offering— or on a beef frank, in a grilled cheese sandwich or on a plate with rice. They also have shave ice. The dining room is small and can get a little warm in the summer. We also appreciate how they press and grill the French rolls. The food is hearty, tasty and ample. $10–$14 for lunch. Near Big Save on Waimea Road. Closed Sunday and Monday.

Shrimp Station
9652 Kaumualii Hwy, Waimea • (808) 338-1242

Most items are pretty mediocre. Some items, like the sweet chili garlic shrimp, are tasty, and you'll have to peel them. Their best item is the shrimp taco. Others, like the coconut shrimp, taste very cheap (as do the fries). Most items are $13, though some are less. On the ocean side of Hwy 50 in Waimea just before Waimea Canyon Road. Just some outdoor picnic tables (flies can be a problem). Though close to Kaua'i's shrimp farm, they use imported frozen shrimp.

Wrangler's Steakhouse
9852 Kaumualii Hwy, Waimea • (808) 338-1218

Well, with a name like Wrangler's, you ain't a'lookin' for no Mongolian food, and you ain't a'gonna find it here. (Cowboy twangs are hard to do in print.) The dinner menu is steak, which they do reasonably well (the pulehu steak is our favorite, but sauté anything in butter and garlic, and you'll make us happy) and seafood. All entrées come with soup and a salad, which features some unfamiliar items, such as pickled daikon radish and boiled peanuts. Some outdoor tables in sunny Waimea can make for a pleasant meal. Their biggest issue is service—you have a better chance of signaling a passing helicopter than your server. $20–$40 for dinner. Sushi also offered Thursday through Saturday. Reservations strongly suggested for those nights. On the ocean side of the highway in Waimea. The adjoining bar, **The Saddle Room**, is consistently better than the steakhouse in terms of food, service and overall experience. Overall, not quite an *ono*, but we won't turn you away either. Closed Sunday and Monday.

WEST SHORE JAPANESE

Japanese Grandma's Café
3871 Hanapepe Rd, Hanapepe • (808) 855-5016

ono A (very) small restaurant in a newly restored building in the heart of Hanapepe with some outdoor seating. Light, healthy options of noodles, salads and poke as well as some heartier tempura offerings and teriyaki meats. Dinner brings more meat options, including very good sushi. At lunch time consider the futomaki-rito, a Japanese-style rice burrito wrapped in seaweed and filled with a choice of seafood. A must-try at dinner is the soft shelled crab served on a bed of greens. $12–$20 for lunch, $13–$30 for dinner (up to $48 if you get the sushi). Last seating is one half hour before closing for lunch and dinner. They take reservations for groups of six or more; otherwise, you may have to wait a while (the only ding). On the right as you enter Hanapepe Town. Closed Tuesday.

WEST SHORE LOCAL

MCS Grill
1-3529 Kaumualii Hwy, Hanapepe
(808) 431-4645
A popular spot with locals that has decent food for a reasonable price. Even when food isn't stellar, they really shine when it comes to seasoning. Steak, chicken, some fish, burgers, fries, even the mac salad is tastier thanks to their salt and pepper mastery. The onion strings appetizer is pretty good and is more than two people can comfortably eat. Dinner brings a few pasta dishes, but it's steak they do the best. It looks like a warehouse from the outside (because it's part of one), but the interior has diner written all over it. $10–$18 for lunch, couple more bucks for dinner. In Hanapepe next to Kaua'i Kookie. Closed weekends.

WEST SHORE MEXICAN

Island Taco
9643 Kaumualii Hwy, Waimea • (808) 338-9895
A cursory glance might give the impression of a hole-in-the-wall gem—and it *can* be. The quality lies in the ingredients. They make tasty, homemade tortillas and use a good grade of fish and pork, but the end result can be bland. Perhaps you can improve that with sauce, but not everyone likes things spicy. Taco plates are a bit pricey. Choose from options such as the Cajun or seared wasabi 'ahi (say *that* one out loud) in your tacos or burritos. We recommend getting your burrito wet for the extra dollar. The atmosphere is bare bones (indoor counter and outdoor tables). The staff can be hot or cold toward their customers. On the mauka side of the highway toward the west end of town. (They close at 3 p.m., so keep that in mind if you're hiking). $11–$25 for lunch. Closed Friday and Saturday.

WEST SHORE TREATS

G's Juicebar
9679 Kaumualii Hwy, Waimea • (808) 634-4112
ono Smoothies, açai bowls and juice. Gotta say, the açai bowls are

really good and give you a surprising amount of energy. We've tried açai bowls at numerous places but have yet to find one as good as G's, though it helps if you like bananas. No dairy products are used. Give the Gandhi a try. **$6–$8**. This small, cosmically themed juice bar is across from the West Inn in Waimea. Portions are on the small side. Their hours/days may be flexible, so go with the flow. Closed Saturday.

JoJo's Shave Ice

9734 Kaumualii Hwy, Waimea • (808) 378-4712

ono The most prominent shave ice shop in Waimea, they've gone through periods of very good and very bad. They are currently in their good phase. Around 30 flavors of syrups, some of their combinations are delicious, such as the banana split and the Jojo's Special. Their small (called da kine) is big enough for most people. **$8–$10**. On the main highway in Waimea almost across from mile marker 0. There is outdoor seating under a shade cloth (much appreciated in the blazing Waimea heat). They have two other locations in Hanalei at Ching Young Village that has fewer flavors and in Kapa'a at Coconut Marketplace.

Kaua'i Chocolate Company

4341 Waialo Rd, Port Allen • (808) 335-0448

Homemade chocolates, fudge and ice cream. None are great; none are bad. It's solidly mid-level quality. In the Port Allen Marina Center. **$3–$6**.

NIGHTLIFE

I know what you're thinking. "Gee, this section sure is small." True. Let's face it—Kaua'i won't be confused with Las Vegas when it comes to nightlife. That's part of our charm. But hey, it's not like we spend *all* of our nights rearranging our sock drawers. (Usually just Fridays, and *oh,* what a crazy time *that* is!) Besides, if you did most of the things in the previous two chapters, you're too pooped to party.

That said, there is probably enough nightlife on Kaua'i to satisfy *most* people's needs. Many of the restaurants feature entertainment at night, but the schedules are always changing. You can select a restaurant from the listings above and inquire about their entertainment.

People have different desires when it comes to nightlife. Here we simply try to describe what's available and let you pick what you want.

Po'ipu—Stevenson's Sushi & Spirits (808-240-6456) at the Grand Hyatt is designed to appeal to anyone who ever wanted to visit the private library of one of the Rockefellers. Richly decorated, bookcases filled with the classics, pool tables (not billiards), large aquarium, chess tables and a terrace with great ocean views. The bar is the center attraction and is beautifully crafted out of strips of koa and monkeypod. Pupus are available, as is sushi. Good but pricey cocktails.

Lihu'e—Rob's Good Times Grill (808-246-0311) on Rice Street offers entertainment most nights. It can also be a good option if there's a sporting event you're hoping to watch. Mostly a local spot, though sometimes it's a bit rough.

Kapa'a—The Crooked Surf at the Sheraton Kauai Coconut Beach Resort (808-320-3651) is a decent place for a beverage near the pool. Some like to grab a drink here and stroll along the beach.

Princeville—Happy Talk Lounge (808-431-4084) in Princeville has a good variety of live music nightly, offers beautiful views of Hanalei Bay plus tasty (but pricey) pupus and drinks.

LU'AU

If you've ever seen a movie that takes place in Hawai'i, odds are there was a lu'au scene. This is where everyone stands around with a mai tai in one hand and a plate of kalua pig in the other. There's always a show where someone is twirling a torch lit at both ends, and, of course, the obligatory hula dancers. And the truth is that's not far from reality. The pig is baked in the ground (called an imu) all day and is absolutely delicious. Shows are usually exciting and fast moving. Although lu'au on O'ahu can make you feel like cattle being led to slaughter, *most* of Kaua'i's lu'au are somewhat smaller and more pleasant.

All in all, a lu'au can be a real blast. If your time allows for one, it is highly recommended. On Kaua'i, the lu'au are all different, so your choice might be easier than on the other islands. **Kilohana** is high-production, story-line oriented; **Grand Hyatt** is more traditional; and **Smith's** is a blend of the two.

Lu'au Kalamaku at Kilohana

3-2087 Kaumualii Hwy, Lihue • (877) 622-1780
Lu'au Kalamaku at Kilohana is one of the largest lu'au in the state. Their 20,000-square-foot pavilion can hold nearly 1,000 people. You may not see it at maximum capacity, as some nights are cruise ship-only performances. Instead of waiting in line at the entrance, you're encouraged to roam their manicured grounds, visit the vendor booths, and grab a drink while the line diminishes. They also offer a 30-minute train ride for $20 (leaves the station at 5:30 p.m.), which can be a good add-on for those with kids.

Seating is assigned, and there's hardly a bad table in the house. Considering the cost of this lu'au, we expected the food to be better. The main dishes are simple, and there's little variety in the side items. Dessert is very weak, and waiting in line for 20 minutes to get it (which has happened to us) makes it worse. At least the bar is accommodating, but it closes at 7:30 p.m., just as the show begins. There are only eight women's restroom stalls, meaning on a full night it comes to 62.5 women per stall. So get it done quickly, gals. Someone is waiting and giving you stink eye.

The show is energetic, captivating and highly entertaining. Instead of the traditional Polynesian revue, they offer a theatrical production of the Polynesian migration to Hawai'i. There is a plot to the show, and each element is presented with quality sound, inventive lighting and a level of intensity that remains constant throughout the show (also good for keeping the attention of keiki). The fire knife dance is especially exciting but is marred somewhat by a protective net. **$127** for adults, $85 for teens, $49 for kids 3–12.

Smith's Tropical Paradise

3-5971 Kuhio Hwy, Kapaa • (808) 821-6895
We also like Smith's Tropical Paradise. The food is not the star; it's the marvelous setting. (And they need more desserts.) Smith's is surrounded by a huge garden area. Though the garden could use a little polishing, the site works perfectly for a lu'au. After dinner, you move to a separate show area where a small pond separates the audience from the stage. (This is also last call—consider grabbing two libations to bring to the show.) While not authentic by any means, it's dazzling, well-choreographed and quite entertaining, complete with an erupting volcano. **$125**, $35 for teens and $25 for children. Free open bar, but it closes at 7:30. Allow 30 minutes for a garden tour before the

imu ceremony. You can also attend the show alone, without the food, for $20.

Tahiti Nui Lu'au

5-5134 Kuhio Hwy, Hanalei • (808) 652-9995

If you'd rather have a more intimate experience, Tahiti Nui Lu'au gives you the feeling of being invited into a (very talented) family's home. Instead of an audience of several hundred people, you're in a dining hall next door to the Tahiti Nui bar with 60 (usually fewer). The seating is shared (and can be pretty tight), the entertainment is decidedly low-tech, and the food selection only takes up two tables. The food isn't as varied as others but seems higher quality (even the poi tastes better here). Having the restaurant's well-conceived mai tai rather than the watered-down alternative found at most lu'au might affect our judgment, but we still appreciate their different approach. Though there are fewer dancers than at other lu'au, they cover traditional hula all the way through Samoan fire dance. The biggest ding is that they start charging for drinks at 6 p.m., so suck 'em up early. All in all, an interesting and one of the more affordable lu'au on Kaua'i. Wednesday nights in Hanalei for **$125**, children are $85 and children 4 and under are free.

Grand Hyatt Kaua'i Lu'au

1571 Poipu Rd, Poipu • (808) 240-6320

Next on our list is the Grand Hyatt Kaua'i Lu'au. The line to get in can be long, and they serve only fruit punch until you're inside. The food is well-prepared. When they have the lu'au in their Ilima Garden, it's a nice setting. But when it's in the courtyard or ballroom, it suffers. And there's no way to know which one they'll use in advance, so it's lu'au roulette. It has a more comfortable dining experience

than Smith's and a more traditional MC-dominated show. The performances aren't as polished as other lu'au, but everyone seems to actually *enjoy* being there. Seating can be confusing; grab a table in the front center. Free, open bar all night, plus table service for drinks. They do a good job with desserts here—try the guava mousse cake. **$175** for adults, teens are $117 and $80 for children.

'Auli'i Lu'au

2440 Hoonani Rd, Poipu • (808) 634-1499

'Auli'i Lu'au at the Sheraton in Po'ipu sits solidly in the mid-range of Kaua'i's lu'au. The food selection is wide and of pretty good quality. We like that they have appetizers out before the full buffet (no imu ceremony, though). The show is the more traditional, MC-driven type. What really shines here is the setting—this is the only lu'au that is next to the ocean. This makes for some beautiful ambiance, especially as the sun sets. They start feeding you mai tais while you're in line, which are free through the show. There are a few craft vendors around but not much in the way of cultural demonstrations—mostly they encourage you to get comfortable and talk with your neighbors. **$179** for adults, $140 for teens, $115 for kids 4–12.

Lu'au Maka'iwa

650 Aleka Loop, Kapaa • (808) 672-2520

Lu'au Maka'iwa is held under big tents next to the Sheraton Kaua'i Coconut Beach Resort in Kapa'a. They say it's oceanfront, but you won't be able to see the ocean from where you sit. The seating is open unless you sprung for VIP, which is not worth it here because everyone has a good view of the stage. Things feel a bit disorganized before the food is served. There are some craft vendors and even quasi-cultural demonstrations that seem more like the dancers getting warmed up rather than an interactive experience for guests. The food is good (though no imu ceremony here), but be sure to get it while it's out— they start clearing it away by 7:30, and if you're one of the last tables to eat, you won't be able to get seconds. Also, make sure you load up your drinks as the bar closes at 8 p.m. The show itself is heartfelt, featuring several generations of practitioners representing Tahiti and Hawai'i. The MC-driven show feels a bit stiffer than most. Overall, adequate. **$99–$129** for adults, $65–$79 for kids 4–12.

LUNCH & DINNER CRUISES

Maui and O'ahu have multiple choices when it comes to dinner cruises. On Kaua'i the pickins are more slim. Fortunately, there's a winner here. One of **Captain Andy's** (808-335-6833) boats is a beautiful 65-foot catamaran called Southern Star adorned with nice touches such as wooden decking and lots of high-end furnishings. Food is excellent (though you should eat that steak fast because the breeze will chill it). Open bar. Though the boat cuts through the water well, this is still Kaua'i, so some passengers will get seasick. You'll probably power upwind toward Po'ipu, then sail downwind, but they *may* go up to Na Pali. Don't get too comfortable in the back; suck up some of the breezes on the bow. Some of the narration is classic Captain Andy bad, but the staff is warm and helpful, and the experience is easy to recommend. $205 for 4 hours. They also have a 4-hour tour on a smaller boat that goes to Na Pali (though most of the trip is along the bland Mana Plain). The boat's not as nice, and the food's not as good, but it's cheaper at $185.

Kaua'i Sea Tours (808-826-7254) offers sunset dinner cruises on either a sailing catamaran (the Lucky Lady Deluxe) or a power cat (the 'Imiloa Express). The food is more modest than Captain Andy's (think teriyaki chicken rather than steak), the boat's not as cushy, and the bar serves only beer, wine and mai tais (but they're included in the price). Depending on the time of year, you can add the option to snorkel as well. Whether or not you snorkel, the length of the trip depends on the boat—'Imiloa Express trips are 4.5 hours at $185 with the snorkel option and $145 without, while Lucky Lady Deluxe trips are 5.5 hours at $195 with snorkeling and $155 without. Overall, we prefer the Lucky Lady to the 'Imiloa, but that's mainly because dinner on a sailboat just seems to better capture the mood.

Blue Dolphin (808-335-5553) has a very similar product and boat (though dinner is a buffet) for $165 as well as one that includes snorkeling or SCUBA for $180 (June through September).

DINNER ON A BEACH

The Grand Hyatt Kaua'i Resort (808-742-1234 ext. 54) features the *Share the Stars with Someone You Love* dinner for $700 per couple (though not *technically* on the beach). It's in a gazebo overlooking their pool. What a perfect way to make up for forgetting your anniversary. Requires 48-hour advance reservations.

Sheraton Kaua'i (808-742-8200) offers a more affordable option. Their Halelani Romantic Dinner is $365 per couple for a three-course meal or $410 for the five-course. You are closer to the beach than at the Hyatt, but the table doesn't feel quite as private. Not available on Sundays or Mondays.

ABOUT THE AUTHOR

More than two decades ago, I bought a one-way ticket to the island of Kaua'i after another venture failed spectacularly. (That's a *really* good story… for another time.) I was devastated, broke, and working in the construction industry as an unskilled laborer just to survive, thinking that I had peaked at such a young age, and it was all downhill from there. But at least I was living in Hawai'i. I spent my free time exploring, but I got frustrated when weekend after weekend I couldn't find a particular beach I'd heard about that I wanted to go to. I looked at a couple of guidebooks, but they all referred to a road that hadn't existed in a long time. And I dreamed that maybe I could find a way to do it better.

Within days of of entertaining that dream, however, I had to return to the mainland due to the declining health of my mother, who passed away shortly thereafter.

It was while I was away that a plan emerged—I would return to Kaua'i and start writing guidebooks. There were just a few problems with this plan: I had no writing skills, I didn't know how a book was published, I wasn't good at photography, I didn't know how to use a computer, *and I had no money.*

So I spent a year on the mainland and applied for every credit card I could and tried to acquire the skills I would need to make my dream come true. Just when I was ready to return to the islands in 1992, I watched in horror as a category 4 hurricane smashed into Kaua'i, causing widespread devastation. I couldn't pick another island because Kaua'i was the one I knew, the island I had fallen in love with. Knowing that hurricanes clear out old growth, giving sunlight (and a chance) to encourage younger foliage, I figured that the same might be true in business. So with a huge stack of credit cards and two suitcases, I moved back to a ravaged island and got to work.

I completely covered one of the walls of my 290-square-foot rented room with highly detailed topographic maps of the island, so I could study them while drinking my morning coffee (gotta have coffee). This was before Google Earth, after all.

Over the next year, I spent my mornings exploring the island and checking out various visitor activities like helicopter rides and snorkel tours (which I did anonymously and paid for with my credit cards—*at 22 percent interest*). I'd review a restaurant at lunch, and then I'd spend my afternoons doing a hike or swimming a beach in multiple conditions to assess its safety, before returning to my room to have a simple dinner of canned chicken and rice (because it was so cheap), then worked into the evening making my own maps of the island. Before going to bed each night, I would read every book about Hawaiian history I could get my hands on.

The first edition of "the blue book" came out in March 1994. I paid to print the first 10,000 books (with cash advances from that stack of credit cards) and mailed free copies to newspapers for review. The first order was for only one case, but a year later a nationwide bookstore chain agreed to stock the book. It took off from there. Next came Big Island, then Maui and O'ahu. I packed up my equipment and lived for two years on each island researching, mapping, writing and photographing.

Today the *Revealed Series* is no longer a one-man show. I have an awesome team that has expanded over the years, but ultimately the books and the apps are an expression of what I think about Hawai'i and comes from the experience of actually *doing* all the things you'll read about. And our ability to keep current and find new things is greatly helped by feedback from our incredibly enthusiastic readers. Please keep it coming.

Once in a while, if you are *really* lucky in this life, you find the place and circumstance to which you belong. I hope you will fall in love with Hawai'i the way I did, and return often. But wherever you travel in life, take chances, embrace the uncertainty of outcome, go with an explorer's heart, and most importantly, share what you find with others.

—One lucky buggah, *Andrew Doughty*

INDEX

Island Dining Index on page 220.